Schriftenreihe des
EUROPA-KOLLEGS HAMBURG
zur Integrationsforschung

Band 76

Markus Kotzur | David Moya
Ülkü Sezgi Sözen | Andrea Romano (eds.)

The External Dimension of EU Migration and Asylum Policies

Border Management, Human Rights and Development Policies in the Mediterranean Area

Nomos

The Deutsche Nationalbibliothek lists this publication in the Deutsche Nationalbibliografie; detailed bibliographic data are available on the Internet at http://dnb.d-nb.de

ISBN 978-3-8487-5629-2 (Print)
978-3-8452-9837-5 (ePDF)

British Library Cataloguing-in-Publication Data
A catalogue record for this book is available from the British Library.

ISBN 978-3-8487-5629-2 (Print)
978-3-8452-9837-5 (ePDF)

Library of Congress Cataloging-in-Publication Data
Kotzur, Markus / Moya, David / Sözen, Ülkü Sezgi / Romano, Andrea
The External Dimension of EU Migration and Asylum Policies
Border Management, Human Rights and Development Policies in the Mediterranean Area
Markus Kotzur / David Moya / Ülkü Sezgi Sözen / Andrea Romano (eds.)
353 pp.
Includes bibliographic references.

ISBN 978-3-8487-5629-2 (Print)
978-3-8452-9837-5 (ePDF)

1st Edition 2020

Acknowledgements

This edited volume is the final output of a project started in 2018 and funded by the *Deutscher Akademischer Austauschdienst* (DAAD) within the framework of the research programme *Hochschuldialog mit Südeuropa* carried out by virtue of the cooperation between the Universität Hamburg and the University of Barcelona. The first part of the project was realised through a summer school held at the University of Barcelona from 17 to 21 September 2018 and organised by the editors of this volume. The summer school gathered a number of asylum and migration law and policy scholars from the countries targeted in the DAAD research programme – namely Spain, Germany and Italy – and was attended by PhD and Master's students from a number of EU and third countries (Belgium, Bulgaria, Germany, Italy, Spain, Turkey and the UK). At the end of the summer school, students had the chance to present their papers in a final workshop and to receive feedback for further research from the editors of this book. The summer school was a laboratory for sharing the ideas, problems and challenges around EU external migration and asylum policies and their impact on the human rights of migrants and refugees. In collecting the chapters for this book we gathered multiple opinions dealing with several aspect of EU asylum law, not necessarily endorsed by other authors and the editors. Namely, the views expressed in this book are personal to the authors and are not binding to the institutions to which they and the editors belong. The usual disclaimer applies.

Having reached the final step of this project which started in 2018, we would like to express our deepest gratitude to the *Deutscher Akademischer Austauschdienst* (DAAD) for the financial support provided and in particular for publishing this volume. We are also grateful to the authors who contributed to the realisation of this project for having accepted our invitation as well as for their cooperation and understanding throughout the publication process. Last but not least, we owe special thanks to Amelie Bruhn and Bastian Richter, whose editing work has been extremely helpful.

Table of Contents

Preface

Prof. Dr Markus Kotzur, Prof. Dr David Moya, Dr Andrea Romano and Ülkü Sezgi Sözen

At a time when humanitarian crises and warfare scenarios are enduring or emerging in a number of areas bordering Europe, the internal migratory policies of the EU and its Member States are increasingly unfit to provide for long-term answers to multiple challenges posed by international mobility in present times. Establishing a network of partnerships, agreements and soft-law instruments between the EU and third countries has long been recognised as crucial in order to guarantee the effectiveness of a common migration and asylum policy. Yet it has taken on a new momentum following the crisis of 2015, exacerbating the relevance of EU external action in this area and the need to ensure coherence between the latter and internal migration and asylum policies. This volume aims at tackling the implications for the EU's external action in the area of migration and asylum posed by such a crisis in perspective, reflecting on existing features of this subject and elaborating on challenges ahead. In particular, it aims to reap the harvest of the reflections and discussions generated over the 2018 summer school and to channel them into one introductory chapter and three parts covering the most salient and urgent aspects as far as EU external migration policies are concerned. The introductory chapter of *Markus Kotzur and Leonard Amaru Feil* lays the theoretical background of the volume, offering a reflection on the conflictive nature of migration law and the institutional and normative framework of international migration law. Hence, the first part draws on the structural elements of the external dimension in the field of migration and asylum, by looking upon its main features and evolution. To this end, *Claudia Candelmo* provides a detailed analysis of both primary and secondary legislation in this area and elaborates on the multiple instruments of cooperation between the EU and third countries, with a particular focus on visa, readmission agreements and non-binding measures. Ultimately, the chapter highlights their relevance in the reduction of the push factors of international mobility and in the management of migration flows. Two further chapters enlarge upon the architecture of the external dimension. On the one hand, *Annalisa Morticelli* focuses on the relationship between the external dimension and irregular migration by addressing the number of measures that prevents migrants from accessing the territory of the EU and their implications on human rights. From this perspective, after having discussed the relevant international legal framework on human rights, the chapter provides for an attentive analysis of the origin of the concept of irregular migration and the tools adopted under the EU legislation. On the other hand, *Andrea Romano* engages in the controversial issue of the legal pathways for accessing international protection, tackling one of the main pitfalls of the EU asylum regime, which is represented by the fact that it applies only insofar as asylum seekers are on the borders of the State that will grant protection. Hence, the chapter focuses the analysis on resettlement and humanitarian visas considering the relevance that both instruments have gained at the EU level. Finally, *Claudia Pretto*'s contribution closes the second part by providing a diachronic analysis of development and cooperation in the area of migration, tackling a further central piece of the EU external dimension. In particular, the contribution puts in perspective the policies and instruments adopted in this area – with especial attention paid to the Global Approach on Migration and Asylum – and discusses their effectiveness from the perspective of human rights protection.

One of the most important roles in the context of the EU external dimension belongs to the neighbouring countries which the EU use as a shield for its external migration and asylum policies. Therefore, it is fundamental to understand the essential function of some third countries with regard to migration law and policies in the Mediterranean area. For this reason, the second part shines a spotlight on the gatekeepers of the European Union. One of the crucial players and an EU partner in the Mediterranean area is Turkey. In this section's first chapter, *Ülkü Sezgi Sözen* and *Chad Heimrich* examine relations between the EU and Turkey in migration matters, which have never been straightforward, as the past 50 years have clearly demonstrated. In light of this, they place special attention on the EU–Turkey readmission agreement as the official starting point of Turkey's gatekeeper role in this relationship as well as the EU–Turkey deal, in order to offer some perspectives on this highly disputed issue. In the second chapter, *Francesco Luigi Gatta* analyses the European and international response to the human rights situation of migrants in Libya. In this context, he concentrates on Libyan detention centres as well as giving an overview of several European and international cooperation programmes in Libya in order to show some shortcomings regarding the EU's external migration policies towards Libya. In the third chapter, *Arolda Elbasani* and *Senada Selo Sabic* change compass direction towards the Balkans in terms of the EU external dimension. They embed the manifold migratory trends in the

Balkans' case because of their simultaneous role as countries of origin and countries of transit, which, in the authors' words, define the Balkans as a chaotic exterior guardian of the Schengen area. In the last chapter of the third part, *Francisco Javier Donaire Villa* discusses external migration and asylum policies from a Member State perspective and examines, in this regard, the bilateral legal relationship between Spain and Morocco. After sketching a historical background, he focuses on the factual and legal problems of pushbacks at the borders between the two countries and the European exceptional legal status of the Spanish–Moroccan borders at Ceuta and Melilla according to the Schengen acquis. He also pays special attention to the bilateral legal framework on migration and asylum between the two countries, such as the agreements on labour migration, readmission and unaccompanied minors.

The third part entails a forward-looking perspective, focusing on the multiple problems, strategies and challenges that analysis of the external dimension policy opens up for the coming years. *Catharina Ziebritzki* tackles a new problematic aspect of EU policies that places itself at the crossroads between the internal and the external dimension, such as the legal framework of hotspots in Greece and, in particular, the responsibility for potential human rights violations carried out therein. The analysis elaborates on the administrative legal framework of such asylum processing centres, explores the applicability of EU public liability law to that context and engages with the jurisprudence of the Court of Justice of the European Union. *David Fernández Rojo*'s contribution addresses a further current challenge that interrogates the external dimension: integrated management of the EU's external borders. From this perspective, the chapter provides a detailed explanation of the reform that transformed Frontex into the European Border and Coast Guard Agency and critically examines whether the new legal framework is capable of achieving complete supranational administration of the external borders. Finally, in their chapter, *Carmine Conte* and *Valentina Savazzi* look at the budgetary aspects of the external dimension of migration and asylum. In particular, the authors perform a comprehensive analysis of the conditionality approach in the management of EU external funding policies and examine in detail how resources are allocated under the main EU instruments adopted so far, namely the EU–Turkey statement, the EU Emergency Trust Fund for Africa and the new Multiannual Financial Framework. This chapter thus closes the volume on a crucial yet underestimated subject, putting the instruments and policies examined throughout the previous chapters in perspective with the decisions over their funding.

The editors.

Migration Management by the Means of Human Rights in Times of Crisis

*Markus Kotzur[*] and Leonard Amaru Feil[**Y]*

I. Migration and its conflicts

Migration law is often described as a law of conflict. And indeed, migration, and especially international migration[1], is a potentially conflictual phenomenon. Conflicts almost inevitably arise when persons, groups, or even masses start to move in search of bare chances for survival or better conditions for life. When this happens, movements can become encounters and encounters can become confrontations. In such situations, migration law is likely to be interpreted in a preventive way and to be used as an instrument of defence against unwanted migration in order to prevent – alleged or existing – conflicts. This is illustrated by the European Union's reaction to the crisis of the European asylum system in 2015/2016. An agreement with Turkey was concluded which obliged Turkey to prevent irregular migration from Turkey into the EU,[2] thereby following this preventive logic just described. However, the humanitarian situation on the Greek islands in March 2020 and at the Greek–Turkish border after Turkey stopped complying with the agreement, as well as the aggravation of the situation due to the COVID-19 pandemic which resulted in the fire destroying Greece's largest refugee camp Moria on the island of Lesbos in

---

* Professor of Public Law, European and International Public Law, vice-dean for International Relations at the University of Hamburg and director of Europa-Kolleg Hamburg.

** Research assistant at the Chair of Public Law, Public International and European Law (Prof. Dr. Jörn Axel Kämmerer) at Bucerius Law School, Hamburg.

Y Another version of this article will be published in the Handbook of Culture and Migration, edited by *J. H. Cohen* and *I. Sirkeci*, forthcoming in 2020.

1 The term migration encompasses all kinds of migration: voluntary and forced migration (on these aspects see *P. Boeles/M. den Heijer/G. Lodder/K. Wouters*, European Migration Law, 2nd edition, 2014, 49 ff. and 243 ff.), internal and external/international migration. Human rights certainly always play a role for migration, but for the purpose of this essay, migration shall be understood as international migration.

2 EU-Turkey statement, 18 March 2016, https://www.consilium.europa.eu/en/press/press-releases/2016/03/18/eu-turkey-statement/.

September 2020, show that a purely preventive strategy does not avoid conflicts permanently and cannot be upheld in the long term.

But the area of conflict encompasses more than that. While, from the perspective of world history, migration represents a continuum of human socialisation,[3] migration always takes place in the light of ever-changing social, political and economic conditions: in the real-world context. Rooted in their own time and context, migratory movements thus can very well challenge fundamental assumptions about the establishment of political communities. Furthermore, it is in particular the lesser-developed regions of the world, for example on the African continent, which have to deal with a disproportionally large share of the global migratory movements[4] – an issue likely to be missed in Eurocentric discourses,[5] which is unfortunate considering Europe's colonial past.[6]

Dealing with conflicts arising from migration becomes more complex when realising that, despite all approaches to categorise migratory movements by type, migration can often not be explained in a monocausal way. It is difficult, or sometimes impossible, to draw a clear line between different forms of migration, such as forced migration, labour migration, and lifestyle migration.[7] Who can say where exactly the extrinsically forced pursuit of survival ends, and where the intrinsically motivated pursuit of happiness starts?

---

3 *M. H. Fisher*, Migration: A World History, 2014.

4 In 2018, Bangladesh, Chad, Tanzania, Uganda and Yemen were hosting 33 per cent of all refugees worldwide, while accounting for only 13 per cent of the global population and 1.25 per cent of the global gross domestic product, see UNHCR, Global Trends – Forced Displacement in 2018, 20 June 2019, pp. 17f., https://www.unhcr.org/statistics/unhcrstats/5d08d7ee7/unhcr-global-trends-2018.html.

5 *T. Straubhaar*, Towards a European Refugee Policy, Intereconomics 50 (2015), 238, 238.

6 On colonialism and migration see *E. Gutiérrez Rodríguez*, Conceptualizing the Coloniality of Migration: On European Settler Colonialism-Migration, Racism, and Migration Policies, in: D. Bachmann-Medick/J. Kugele (eds.), Migration. Changing Concepts, Critical Approaches, 2018, pp. 193 ff.; *M. Harper/S. Constantine*, Migration and Empire, 2010; *P. M. Amakasu Raposo de Medeiros Carvalho*, Migration and Global Politics in Africa and Asia, in: P. M. Amakasu Raposo de Medeiros Carvalho/D. Arase/S. Cornelissen (eds.), Routledge Handbook of Africa-Asia Relations, 2018, 424 ff.; A. L. Smith (ed.), Europe's Invisible Migrants. Consequences of the Colonists' Return, 2002.

7 On these forms of migration from a sociological perspective see *K. O'Reilly*, International migration and Social Theory, 2012. *P. Boeles/M. den Heijer/G. Lodder/K. Wouters*, European Migration Law, 2nd edition, 2014, 5 argue for a wide understanding of migration.

The whole complexity of migratory phenomena is illustrated by the inner conflicts of the individual. On the one side, there is the cosmopolitan desire of the individual, articulated in *Seneca's* well-known phrase, "*patria mea totus hic mundus est*" (Epistulae morales – Epistula 28). In an interconnected and globalised world, this cosmopolitan ideal seems ever more seizable. At the same time, the insecurities of the age of globalisation provoke a desire for protection provided by the nation state as a space of security. This apparent paradox of the individual's desires is reflected in human rights law: The *universalism of human rights*[8] strives for a concept of global citizenship, and thereby opens up the nation state. In contrast, the right of peoples to *self-determination*, understood as the democratic sovereignty of the people and based in human rights,[9] allows for the formation of consciously distinct political communities on the basis of exclusion and inclusion.

II. Migration management by the means of human rights?

Acknowledging that human rights do not only function as a limitation for measures aiming at the prevention of migratory movements leads to the assumption that human rights can also serve as a means of managing migration. Due to the conflictual nature of migration, the question of how to deal with the movement of persons should not be subjected to the free play of political forces. There is a need for *normative* management to prevent conflicts before they occur, and to deal with conflicts once they arise. It is needless to say that human rights law is by far not the only possible management resource for the conflicts arising in the context of migration. Yet, as the apparent contradiction between the universalism of human rights and the right to self-determination is inherent in human rights law,

---

8 *R. Arnold*, Reflections on the Universality of Human Rights, in: R. Arnold (ed.), The Universalism of Human Rights, 2013, 1 ff. *M. Mutua*, The Complexity of Universalism in Human Rights, in: A. Sajó (ed.), Human Rights with Modesty: The Problem of Universalism, 2004, 51 ff. suggests a cautious approach to universality. On the struggle between universalism and cultural relativism see *A. Dundes Renteln*, International Human Rights. Universalism versus Relativism, 1990.

9 *J. Fisch*, The Right of Self-Determination of Peoples. The Domestication of an Illusion, 2015, 61 f.: "Popular sovereignty thereby becomes a preliminary stage of the right of self-determination in the sense of being a necessary but not sufficient condition. Where there is no popular sovereignty, there can, but need not, be a right of self-determination." On provisions on self-determination in human rights conventions see *C. Griffioen*, Self-Determination as a Human Right, 2010, 50 ff.

it is worth critically examining the potential of human rights guarantees for the management of migration.

1. Legal management and international human rights law

While the need for migration management is evident, the idea of human rights as a means of management implies that migration can actually be managed, and that international human rights law offers adequate and effective courses of action. This might seem questionable, as international law has often been criticised for lacking effective enforcement mechanisms.[10] This might be true for many other areas of international law, but especially in the field of human rights law, with its differentiated mechanisms of monitoring and control, it has proven useful. The jurisdiction of regional human rights courts[11] serves as an example, as well as the impacts of the discussion about a human rights-based "responsibility to protect".[12] And, as already mentioned, human rights do not only serve as a limit for states' attempts to impede migration, which is their *status negativus.* More than functioning as a limit to and defence of state power, human rights also oblige states to act, which is their *status positivus*, *status activus* or *status processualis*. They serve as an orientation point, allowing migration and limiting migration at the same time, but always from the perspective of human freedoms. In this way, human rights activate courses of action, as they oblige the responsible actors both within and beyond the state to take creative action.

Law can be used as a means of management in two ways: reactively and proactively. Reactive legal management can be used to design a framework that is necessary to process social and political changes. Law can also serve as an instrument to bring about, to proactively shape processes of change. In the first case, law follows reality, while in the second case, reality fol-

---

10 For example by *J. L. Goldsmith/E. A. Posner*, The Limits of International Law, 2005; critically *A. van Aaken*, To Do Away with International Law? Some Limits to "The Limits of International Law", EJIL 17 (2006), 289 ff. On the effectiveness of international law, American Society of International Law (ed.), Proceedings of the 108th Annual Meeting, 2015.

11 For instance the European Court of Human Rights, *Y. Shani*, Assessing the Effectiveness of International Courts, 2014, 253 ff.

12 Report of the International Commission on Intervention and State Sovereignty (ICISS), The Responsibility to Protect, 2001; UN Doc. GA/Res. 60/1 (2005 World Summit and Outcome); *C. Stahn*, Responsibility to Protect. Political Rhetoric or Emerging Legal Norm?, AJIL 101 (2007), 99 ff.

lows law. In any case, law cannot (and should not) dictate social developments. Regarding migration, this means that law can build a framework and, serve as an orientation point in response to migration. This is of course only possible if the *rule of law* is comprehensively secured in all matters of migration. Hasty retreats into states of emergency which are beyond the law make the required normative management of migratory conflicts impossible.

Legal management by the means of international law is management in a broader sense than in national law. But unlike national parliamentary legislation, norms of international law can *horizontally* bind state and non-state actors alike, and *vertically* use the mechanisms of multilevel governance[13]. These mechanisms include the establishment of "international benchmark norms"[14] that serve as orientation for national lawmaking and national law enforcement. Even if international law lacks the high degree of effectiveness and precision of management through national law, it has the advantage of being able to address transnational phenomena like migration much better than national law and can have an integrating effect. Due to these dynamics, national sovereignty does not constitute an impermeable shield against international legal management impulses anymore. This applies particularly to the international human rights system with its differentiated possibilities of individual complaints. The individual's right to directly make a claim under various human rights regimes helps to activate international human rights law as a resource for the management of migration. Lastly, human rights are suitable for migration management as they do not take the simple perspective of protection against dangers emanating from migration, but the perspective of migration as an issue of individual freedoms and liberties. In this way, they can capture the problems and conflicts in the context of migration much better than solely defensive approaches. Such a human rights-based approach to migration management may be structured into the three conceptual dimensions of the "re-

---

13 H. Enderlein/S. Wälti/M. Zürn (eds.), Handbook on Multi-level Governance, 2010; *I. Pernice*, Multilevel Constitutionalism and the Treaty of Amsterdam: European Constitution-Making Revisited?, Common Market Law Review 36 (1999), 703 ff.; on the multilevel governance structures in the context of European migration law *P. Boeles/M. den Heijer/G. Lodder/K. Wouters*, European Migration Law, 2nd edition, 2014, 21 ff. For the Australian context see K. A. Daniell/A. Kay (eds.), Multi-Level Governance. Conceptual Challenges and Case Studies from Australia, 2017.

14 *C. Calliess*, Auswärtige Gewalt, in: J. Isensee/P. Kirchhof (eds.), Handbuch des Staatsrechts, vol. IV, 3rd edition, 2006, § 83 MN 6: „Maßstabsnormen".

sponsibility to protect": the responsibility to prevent, the responsibility to react and the responsibility to rebuild.[15]

2. *Migration management and human rights-based belonging*

Sovereignty and individual freedoms mark the starting points of migration management based on human rights. The classical sovereign nation state has the authority to freely decide at its own discretion who may enter its territory, be it for temporary or for permanent stay.[16] This leaves only a little room for migration management through human rights, as long as the state has not bound itself to relevant human rights treaties. But once this happens, the protective armour of sovereignty starts to open, and a humanisation of sovereignty can be witnessed. There are good reasons to believe that the principle of sovereignty (Art. 2 para. 1 UN Charter) can no longer be understood as a value solely serving itself, but that the modern, human rights-rooted nation state is at the service of *humanity*.[17]

It would therefore be wrong to assume that sovereignty and humanity must be antagonisms. It might be true that the construct of sovereignty rather implies the territoriality of the state and the sedentariness of its people, so that international migratory movements conceptually challenge it more than they do challenge universal human rights guarantees. But this does not necessarily lead to the conclusion that sovereignty automatically closes borders, and that human rights automatically open them. Both are social constructs, and as such they are susceptible to absolutist argumentations. Still, painting an irreconcilable contrast between self-determined territorial sovereignty on the one hand – as the only guarantor of freedom in security – and self-determined individual freedom on the other hand – which must not be completely subordinated to security and break at the borders of territorial sovereignty – does not do justice to the complex relation between the two. Sovereignty has been losing its claim to exclusivity.

---

15 *A. Hurwitz*, The Collective Responsibility to Protect Refugees, 2009; *S. Martin*, Forced Migration, the Refugee Regime and the Responsibility to Protect, Global Responsibility to Protect 2 (2010), 38 ff.

16 *R. Jennings/A. Watts*, Oppenheim's International Law, vol. I, 9th edition, 2008, § 400.

17 *A. Peters*, Humanity as the A and Ω of Sovereignty, EJIL 20 (2009), 513 ff.

Discussions about a humanitarian intervention[18], the "responsibility to protect", the concept of "human security"[19], or about human rights-based relativisations of state immunity[20] illustrate this development, even if the legalisation of these approaches may in part be doubtful. Then again, human rights can also establish state obligations towards its own nationals, which can be invoked against non-nationals, together with the human rights-based right to self-determination. As an example, Art. 32 para. 2 of the 1951 Refugee Convention[21] can be read as acknowledging this ambiguous nature of human rights when it stipulates that refugee protection does not always prevail over fundamental security interests of the community.[22] But to formulate such fundamental interests of the community on a human rights basis helps to reveal where the real conflicts lie, and where, in contrast, the reference to sovereignty is only a pretext for arbitrary exclusion. In this way, more concrete standards for the balancing of the different interests involved can be obtained.

However, the awareness that human rights do not exclusively convey free movement of persons should not lead to the reinterpretation of the individual right to asylum as a solely objective guarantee. With an individualised understanding of asylum as a subjective and actionable right, the individual is empowered to step on the scene as an actor in the migration game, and – with the help of courts – to enforce the rule of law, which is a prerequisite for normative migration management. Here, the development

18 See *J.-P. L. Fonteyne*, The Customary International Law Doctrine of Humanitarian Intervention, California Western International Law Journal 4 (1974), 203 ff.; *W. D. Verwey*, Humanitarian Intervention, in: A. Cassese (ed.), The Current Legal Regulation of the Use of Force, 1986, 57 ff.; *F. R. Tesón*, Humanitarian Intervention: An Inquiry into Law and Morality, 3rd edition, 2005; recently *A. J. Bellamy/S. McLoughlin*, Rethinking Humanitarian Intervention, 2018.

19 *C. Tomuschat*, Human Rights. Between Idealism and Realism, 3rd edition, 2014, 159 ff.

20 *K. Parlett*, Immunity in Civil Proceedings for Torture: The Emerging Exception, European Human Rights Law Review 2006, 49 ff.; *H. Fox*, State Immunity and the International Crime of Torture, European Human Rights Law Review 2006, 142 ff.; *P. De Sena/F. De Vittor*, State Immunity and Human Rights: The Italian Supreme Court Decision on the Ferrini Case, EJIL 16 (2005), 89 ff.

21 Convention relating to the Status of Refugees, signed at Geneva on 28 July 1951, UNTS 189 (1954), 150 ff.

22 *E. Lauterpacht/D. Bethlehem*, The Scope and Content of the Principle of Non-Refoulement: Opinion, in: E. Feller/V. Türk/F. Nicholson (eds.), Refugee Protection in International Law, 2003, 87, 128 ff.; *J. C. Hathaway*, The Rights of Refugees under International Law, 2006, 342 ff.; *G. S. Goodwin-Gill/J. McAdam*, The Refugee in International Law, 3rd edition, 2007, 234 ff.

of the EU Dublin system can serve as an example: while initially the Dublin regulation was interpreted as a purely objective interstate law for the organisation of the EU asylum system between the member states,[23] the reform of the Dublin III regulation in 2013 created individual rights of asylum seekers to challenge states' transfer decisions based on the regulation,[24] and thus, enabled them to insist on the observation of the rule of law in times of crisis.

But when a binary codification of international migration law between sovereignty on the one side and human rights and freedom of movement on the other is too simplistic, what other categories are there to approach migration legally? In the end, sovereignty and human rights imply an idea of different forms and levels of *belonging*[25] to political communities. The idea of belonging is the core question of migration management: It is about balancing wishes to belong with abilities and possibilities of belonging. Human rights offer a differentiated system of belonging, which starts with the basic right to survival, emanating from the mere fact of belonging to the human family. Human rights-based belonging is organised in statuses, from the defensive *status negativus*, to rights of participation (*status positivus, status activus*) and procedural rights (*status processualis*). This interpretation of human rights as a system of belonging is where their potential for migration management lies.

But belonging on the grounds of human rights does not end with the basic right to survival. A "bare life" alone would be nothing more than an empty shell, if there was not at least a *right to have rights*,[26] to secure the right to life and to allow for a development of the personality in dignity. It

---

23 See the opinion of the Advocate General *N. Jääskinen*, delivered on 18 April 2013, C-4/11, ECLI:EU:C:2013:244, para. 58 – Bundesrepublik Deutschland v. Kaveh Puid, which was confirmed by the European Court of Justice, C-4/11, ECLI:EU:C:2013:740, judgement, 14 November 2013, paras. 24 ff. – Bundesrepublik Deutschland v. Kaveh Puid; also European Court of Justice, C-394/12, ECLI:EU:C:2013:813, judgement, 10 December 2013, paras. 47 ff – Shamso Abdullahi v. Bundesasylamt.

24 European Court of Justice, C-63/15, ECLI:EU:C:2016:409, judgement, 7 June 2016, paras. 34, 51 – Mehrdad Ghezelbash v. Staatssecretaris van Veiligheid en Justitie; European Court of Justice, C-670/16, ECLI:EU:C:2017:587, judgement, 26 July 2017, paras. 55 ff. – Tsegezab Mengesteab v. Bundesrepublik Deutschland.

25 This can also be named "allegiance" or "identity". On these categories F. Jenkins/M. Nolan/K. Rubenstein (eds.), Allegiance and Identity in a Globalised World, 2014.

26 *P. Owens*, Beyond 'Bare Life': Refugees and the 'Right to Have Rights', in: A. Betts/G. Loescher (eds.), Refugees in International Relations, 2010, 133 ff.

is the minimum condition for seeking opportunities in life, be they related to education, work or personal freedoms. The right to survival applies long before the formation of political communities, and therefore it must be fundamental for all attempts to manage migration. Once political communities constitute, and the more specific they become, the more specific become the rights of the individuals, as the addressee of the corresponding obligation – the community – assumes a more specific form. The spectrum of rights and players ranges from the most fundamental human rights to the right to self-determination, from the elusive international community to the nation state, also encompassing other intermediate, regional entities such as the European Union. Faced with migratory movements, international law has the task of designing a normative framework based on human rights, in which political communities can form their own regimes of belonging, according to the principle of subsidiarity and – most importantly – under the observance of the fundamental belonging of the human to the human family.[27]

III. International migration law as the tool for the management of migration

1. International migration law: some terminological remarks

International law addresses migration phenomena in a number of legal fields, classically in the international law of aliens[28], furthermore in inter-

---

27 For different constructions of belonging in mobile societies, see *D. Kostakopoulou*, Thick, Thin and Thinner Patriotism: Is This All There Is?, Oxford Journal of Legal Studies 26 (2006), 73, 84. On the idea of "global citizenship", UNESCO, Global Citizenship Education Topics and Learning Objectives, 2015.

28 On the international minimum standard concerning the treatment of aliens, *A. Verdross*, Les règles internationales concernant le traitement des étrangers, Recueil des Cours 37 (1931-III), 323 ff.; *A. H. Roth*, The Minimum Standard of International Law Applied to Aliens, 1949; *K. Hailbronner/J. Gogolin*, "Aliens", in: MPEPIL (2013); *J. Crawford*, Brownlie's Principles of Public International Law, 9th edition, 2019, 591 ff. On the roots of universal human rights protection in the international law concerning the treatment of aliens, *M. Kotzur*, "Fremd bin ich eingezogen" – Überlegungen zu den Wurzeln universellen Menschenrechtsschutzes im völkerrechtlichen Fremdenrecht, in: G. Jochum/W. Fritzemeyer/M. Kau (eds.), Grenzüberschreitendes Recht – Crossing Frontiers. Festschrift für Kay Hailbronner, 2013, 585 ff.

national refugee law, in the law of migrant workers,[29] or in universal human rights catalogues. Still, the term of migration is not a clearly defined legal term in international law. When talking about migration, this should thus be done with semantic sensitivity. The term migration, as used in everyday language, is connoted with problems, linked to all the potential conflicts that have already been described. This is why it has been suggested to speak preferably of "mobility"[30] or "movement of persons"[31] rather than of "migration". This notional differentiation makes sense not least because "migration" implies sedentariness as the norm and mobility as the exception, while "movement" is the rule and the reality of the globalised 21st century with its mobile societies.[32] Furthermore, "movement" and "mobility" are better able to express that the concepts of belonging and the respective attributions of identity have become more variable and have started to move themselves.

Nevertheless, migration is the well-established term in jurisprudence and literature, which is why we want to stick to this nomenclature – however, always having in mind the semantic nuances and the normality of mobility. Therefore, we want to suggest a wide understanding of migration, leaving out domestic migration, and defining migrants as "persons who leave their country of origin or the country of habitual residence, to remain either permanently or temporarily in another country with the possible consequence of establishment".[33] International migration law can therefore be understood as the entirety of all norms of international law dealing with migration in the aforementioned sense.

---

29 According to Art. 2 para. 1 of the International Convention on the Protection of the Rights of All Migrant Workers and Members of Their Families, "the term 'migrant worker' refers to a person who is to be engaged, is engaged or has been engaged in a remunerated activity in a State of which he or she is not a national", UNTS 2220, 3 ff. On the law of migrant workers see *R. Cholewinski*, Migrant Workers in International Human Rights Law, 1997.

30 *J. H. Cohen/I. Sirkeci*, Cultures of Migration. The Global Nature of Contemporary Mobility, 2011, 7.

31 *P. Boeles/M. den Heijer/G. Lodder/K. Wouters*, European Migration Law, 2nd edition, 2014, 5.

32 *S. Sassen*, Globalization and its Discontents, 1998, XXI; *A. McGrew*, A Global Society, 1992. Globalisation changes realities in a way "that state, civil society and market are inextricably intertwined", as *P. Boeles/M. Den Heijer/G. Lodder/K. Wouters*, European Migration Law, 2014, 6 state, referring to J. A. Camilleri/A. P. Jarvis/A. J. Paolini (eds.), The State in Transition. Remaining Political Space, 1995, 223.

33 *D. Kugelmann*, "Migration", in: MPEPIL (2009), MN 4.

2. *The fragmented nature of international migration law: institutions, substantive law and cooperative responsibility*

Certainly, this definition of international migration law does not establish an independent field of public international law, nor does it lay claim to intradisciplinary status. International migration law is in fact highly fragmented. This is true for the substantive law as well as for the institutional framework. For some specific parts of international migration law, there is a certain level of institutionalisation. The United Nations High Commissioner for Refugees (UNHCR) in the area of refugee protection, or the EU and its institutions, such as the European Court of Justice, with regard to the EU regime of free movement of persons, serve as examples. Beside these two actors, also the UN Security Council can step on the scene as a player in international migration law, when it activates its powers according to Chapter VII of the UN Charter by defining migratory pressure due to armed conflicts as a threat to international peace and security.[34] The pluralism of institutions and the diversity of their respective areas and subareas of international migration law reveal the lack of a coherent governance structure.[35] This becomes evident in the light of mass migration scenarios, when cooperative structures between the players would be most needed. Even the 1951 Refugee Convention does not entail an international obligation of states to cooperate, and includes only a vague appeal for international cooperation in its preamble.[36] The absolute absence of a specific legal framework for people fleeing from natural disasters and other consequences of climate change[37] completes the fragmented picture of international migration law.

At the same time, cooperation is of fundamental importance for the effectiveness of all attempts to manage international migration. Internation-

---

34 For examples see *N. Krisch*, in: B. Simma/D.-E. Khan/G. Nolte/A. Paulus (eds.), The Charter of the United Nations. A Commentary, vol. II, 3rd edition, 2012, Art. 39 MN 23.

35 *S. Benz/A. Hasenclever*, "Global" Governance of Forced Migration, in: A. Betts/G. Loescher (eds.), Refugees in International Relations, 2010, 185 ff. In general K. Blome/H. Franzki/N. Markard/A. Fischer-Lescano/S. Oeter (eds.), Contested Regime Collisions: Norm Fragmentation in World Society, 2016.

36 Convention relating to the Status of Refugees, signed at Geneva on 28 July 1951, UNTS 189 (1954), 150, 150.

37 *J. McAdam*, Climate Change, Forced Migration, and International Law, 2012, 187 ff.; *E. Ferris*, Governance and Climate Change-Induced Mobility: International and Regional Frameworks, in: D. Manou/A. Baldwin/D. Cubie/A. Mihr/T. Thorp (eds.), Climate Change, Migration and Human Rights, 2017, 11 ff.

al migration law is indeed international law of cooperation par excellence. The fact that the legal framework is in practice often dominated by the strategic considerations of power politics,[38] thus retaining a certain anarchic character,[39] does not change the necessity of cooperation. Regardless of whether duties of cooperation can arise from an international law principle of solidarity,[40] the question here shall be what potential human rights have for the governance of cooperation. In the first place, human rights create subjective rights for individuals. What might prima facie seem as a factor limiting their potential for cooperation management, can become a genuine duty to cooperate, when the least protection of the individual becomes impossible without a certain degree of cooperation, as for example in cases of mass migration.[41] In the globalised world with transnational migratory movements, the *status processualis* expands to a cooperative *status infrastructuralis.* Those bound by human rights guarantees are obliged to provide at least the minimum of procedural infrastructures, without which the individual rights would in their substance be empty. In this context, it is important to note that "procedure" should not be understood in a narrow and formal sense, only meaning judicial remedies. This logic is illustrated by the idea of the "responsibility to protect", where a single state is unwilling or unable to guarantee the most fundamental human rights of its population, so that the responsibility to protect shifts to the international community as a whole. The realisation of this shared subsidiary responsibility goes along with a responsibility to cooperate. The

---

38 *A. Betts*, International Cooperation in the Refugee Regime, in: A. Betts/G. Loescher (eds.), Refugees in International Relations, 2010, 53 ff.

39 *A. Hurrell*, Refugees, International Society, and Global Order, in: A. Betts/G. Loescher (eds.), Refugees in International Relations, 2010, 85, 86.

40 See *M. Kotzur/K. Schmalenbach*, Solidarity among Nations, AVR 52 (2014), 68 ff.

41 The preamble of the 1951 Refugee Convention stresses the necessity of burden-sharing: "considering that the grant of asylum may place unduly heavy burdens on certain countries, and that a satisfactory solution of a problem of which the United Nations has recognized the international scope and nature cannot therefore be achieved without international co-operation". On burden-sharing *P. Hilpold*, Quotas as an Instrument of Burden-Sharing in International Refugee Law – The Many Facets of an Instrument Still in the Making, ICON 15 (2017), 1188 ff.; *J.-P. L. Fonteyn*, Burden-Sharing: An Analysis of the Nature and Function of the International Solidarity in Cases of Mass Influx of Refugees, Australian Year Book of International Law 8 (1978–1980), 162 ff. Whether fixed refugee quotas are helpful for such burden-sharing is however a different question, see *P. Hilpold*, Unilateralism in Refugee Law – Austria's Quota Approach Under Scrutiny, Human Rights Review 18 (2017), 305 ff.

UN Security Council with its extensive Chapter VII policy[42] could in terms of competences well take this responsibility, also in the context of migration.

3. Human rights law as the normative resource beyond all fragmentations

Migratory movements have, from a human rights perspective, two dimensions concerning the freedom of movement. Firstly, there is the freedom to leave a country. This dimension of freedom is normatively recognised and protected in a number of human rights texts. Art. 13 para. 2 of the Universal Declaration of Human Rights[43] stipulates the right to leave any country, including one's own, and so do Art. 12 para. 2 of the International Covenant on Civil and Political Rights (ICCPR)[44] as well as Art. 2 para. 2 of Protocol No. 4 to the European Convention on Human Rights. In contrast, the counterpart, the freedom to enter a country, is hardly accepted in international law. It is generally in the discretion of all nation states to decide, whom to let into their territory and whom not. Already in 1892, the U.S. Supreme Court stated:

"It is an accepted maxim of international law that every sovereign nation has the power, as inherent in sovereignty and essential to self-preservation, to forbid the entrance of foreigners within its dominions or to admit them only in such cases and upon such conditions as it may see fit to prescribe."[45]

Even Art. 14 para. 1 of the Universal Declaration of Human Rights, which grants everyone the right to seek and enjoy asylum from persecution, was in its genesis not intended to establish a right of the individual to be granted asylum, and is thus commonly read in a sovereignty-centred way: It is "the right of every state to offer refuge and to resist all demands for extradition", as the British delegate phrased it during the drafting of

---

42 For an overview see *N. Krisch*, in: B. Simma/D.-E. Khan/G. Nolte/A. Paulus (eds.), The Charter of the United Nations. A Commentary, vol. II, 3rd edition, 2012, Art. 39 MN 23 ff.

43 General Assembly resolution 271 (III) A.

44 UNTS 999 (1976), 171 ff.

45 U.S. Supreme Court, *Nishimura Ekiu v. United States et al.*, 142 U.S. 651, 142. See also ECtHR, *Abdulaziz, Cabales and Balkandali*, Appl. Nos. 9214/80, 9473/81, 9474/81, 28 May 1985, para. 67; on this see *P. Boeles/M. Den Heijer/G. Lodder/K. Wouters*, European Migration Law, 2014, 15.

the declaration.[46] The declaration does not accord the individual a "right to be granted asylum", only a "right to enjoy asylum", establishing no obligation for the state.[47]

However, state practice has evolved since 1948. In 1951, the Convention relating to the Status of Refugees was signed in Geneva and has, together with its 1967 Protocol, become the core document or "Magna Carta"[48], for international refugee law.[49] The Convention, which in its preamble classifies itself as a human rights treaty, provides for a limited individual right to asylum in its Art. 33. The prohibition of expulsion or return (so-called *refoulement*) of a refugee to territories where his or her life or freedom would be in danger, contained in this provision, is generally interpreted as applying at the frontiers,[50] and in this way establishing a right to enter the territory of the state in which he or she seeks protection.

In universal human rights treaties, no express right to asylum can be found. Neither the international Covenant on Civil and Political Rights (ICCPR), nor the International Covenant on Economic, Social and Cultural Rights (ICESCR) contain a parallel provision to Art. 14 of the Universal Declaration of Human Rights. Nevertheless, general human rights provisions have a reinforcing effect on the principle of *non-refoulement*. While Art. 3 para. 1 of the Convention against Torture[51] expressly prohibits *refoulement*, similar obligations not to expel a person can originate from certain rights of the Convention on the Rights of the Child[52] (for example Art. 9 and 10), or from general human rights obligations, such as the right

---

46 *H. Lauterpacht*, The Universal Declaration of Human Rights, British Yearbook of International Law 25 (1948), 354, 373.

47 For more on this aspect of the drafting history *R. Boed*, The State of the Right of Asylum in International Law, Duke Journal of Comparative & International Law 5 (1994), 1, 9 f.

48 *J. M. Read*, Magna Carta for Refugees, 1953.

49 On the historical development see *C. Skran*, Historical Development of International Refugee Law, in: A. Zimmermann (ed.), The 1951 Convention Relating to the Status of Refugees and its 1967 Protocol. A Commentary, 2011, 3 ff.; *T. Einarsen*, Drafting History of the 1951 Convention and the 1967 Protocol, in: A. Zimmermann (ed.), The 1951 Convention Relating to the Status of Refugees and its 1967 Protocol. A Commentary, 2011, 37 ff.

50 *G. S. Goodwin-Gill/J. McAdam*, The Refugee in International Law, 3rd edition, 2007, 306 ff.

51 Convention against Torture and Other Cruel, Inhuman or Degrading Treatment or Punishment, adopted on 10 December 1984, UNTS 1465 (1987), 85 ff.

52 Convention on the Rights of the Child, adopted on 20 November 1989, UNTS 1577 (1990), 3 ff.

to life[53] and the prohibition of torture[54]. In the case of general human rights treaties, the establishment of a right to enter a country faces the problem of the very limited extraterritorial applicability[55] of the respective treaties. As a consequence, human rights convey "complementary protection"[56] to the prohibition of *refoulement*, reinforcing it once the person has reached the territory of a state bound by the human rights treaty. Some regional human rights treaties such as the European Convention on Human Rights (ECHR) go even further[57] and contain additional protection, for example from collective expulsion in Art. 4 of Protocol No. 4,[58] or residence rights (Art. 8 ECHR).

And yet, genuine freedom of movement, complementing the freedom to leave a country with a corresponding freedom of entry, only seems to have a chance when, on the basis of international treaty law, more comprehensive processes of integration take place, as for example in the case of

53 Contained for example in Art. 6 para. 1 ICCPR, Art. 2 para. 1 ECHR.

54 Art. 7 ICCPR, Art. 3 ECHR. See ECtHR, *Soering*, Appl. No. 14038/88, 7 July 1989, para. 91; ECtHR, *Chahal*, Appl. No. 22414/93, 15 November 1996, para. 74; ECtHR, *Saadi*, Appl. No. 37201/06, 28 February 2008, para. 125 ff. The ECtHR has also considered that "an issue might exceptionally arise under Article 6 [ECHR] by an extradition decision in circumstances where the individual would risk suffering a flagrant denial of a fair trial in the requesting country", ECtHR, *Ahorugeze*, Appl. No. 37075/09, 27 October 2011, para. 113.

55 The ECtHR has assumed a relatively wide extraterritorial responsibility of the parties to the ECHR, see ECtHR, *Medvedjev*, Appl. No. 3394/04, 29 March 2010; ECtHR, *Al-Skeini*, Appl. No. 55721/07, 7 July 2011; ECtHR, *Hirsi Jamaa*, Appl. No. 27765/09, 23 December 2012; see also ECtHR, *Khlaifia*, Appl. No. 16483/12, 1 September 2015. With regard to maritime borders *A. Fischer-Lescano/T. Loehr/T. Tohodipur*, Border Controls at Sea: Requirements under International Human Rights and Refugee Law, International Journal of Refugee Law 21 (2009), 256 ff.

56 *G. S. Goodwin-Gill/J. McAdam*, The Refugee in International Law, 3rd edition, 2007, 285.

57 On Europe *A. Klug*, Regional Developments: Europe, in: A. Zimmermann (ed.) (fn. 49), 117 ff.; on Asia *S. Blay*, Regional Developments: Asia, in: A. Zimmermann (ed.) (fn. 49), 145 ff.; in Africa, the relevant treaty is the 1969 Refugee Convention of the OAU, see *J. van Garderen/J. Ebstein*, Regional Developments: Africa, in: A. Zimmermann (ed.) (fn. 49), 185 ff.; for the Americas it is the 1984 Cartagena Declaration, see *F. Piovesan/L. L. Jubilut*, Regional Developments: Americas, in: A. Zimmermann (ed.) (fn. 49), 205 ff.

58 But see the recent decision of the ECtHR, *N.D. and N.T.*, Appl. Nos. 8675/15 and 8697/15, 13 February 2020, establishing an exception from the prohibition of collective expulsion which has been strongly criticised, see *M. Pichl/D. Schmalz*, "Unlawful" may not mean rightless. The shocking ECtHR Grand Chamber judgement in case N.D. and N.T., Verfassungsblog, 14 February 2020, https://verfassungsblog.de/unlawful-may-not-mean-rightless/.

the EU. The EU has established a legal space with an advanced regime of free movement of persons for the citizens of the Union.[59] This shows that it is often more effective to seek regional or even bilateral answers to global challenges, using regional instruments and institutions of international law and unfolding the potential of the close relations of the respective players. It might by all means be fruitful to think global, but to act and re-act local.

IV. Conclusions for migration management based on human rights

1. Management in advance of migratory movements

To act locally when faced with the global issue of migration starts before migration occurs. In this stage, migration management – from the perspective of human rights – is preventive. In a narrow sense of the word, it is about the prevention of unwanted causes of migration. Preventive migration management in a wider sense also encompasses the dismantling of existing infrastructural barriers to freedom of movement. What can be framed as a "responsibility to prevent", can address migration in all its facets: from precarious economic situations to the lack of opportunities for young people,[60] from environmental disasters as a reason for displacement[61] to human rights violations in civil wars and other armed conflicts. Of course, deep-rooted ethical, religious, political or cultural conflicts cannot be solved by legal management alone. But conflict resolution, being first and foremost a political process, can and should be normatively accompanied and safeguarded by law. This implies the usage of the common instruments of good governance, protection against forced displacement as part of the freedom of movement,[62] as well as the usage of international criminal law instruments against gross violations of human rights. Other

---

59 See for example Art. 20, 21 and 45 TFEU and Art. 45 of the EU Charter of Fundamental Rights.

60 On factors for migration, see *E. Lee*, A Theory of Migration, in: J. A. Jackson (ed.), Migration, 1969, 282, 285 ff.

61 *R. Cohen/M. Bradley*, Disasters and Displacement: Gaps in Protection, Journal of International Humanitarian Legal Studies 1 (2010), 95 ff.; *D. Farber*, International Law and the Disaster Cycle, in: D. Caron/M. Kelly/A. Telesetsky (eds.), The International Law of Disaster Relief, 2014, 7 ff.

62 Art. 12 para. 1 ICCPR stipulates, "Everyone lawfully within the territory of a State shall, within that territory, have the […] freedom to choose his residence".

issues to be envisaged are the strengthening of international institutions such as the United Nations High Commissioner for Refugees,[63] and a focus on international environmental law and development policies. The EU Agenda on Migration, for example, defines "the development of the countries of origin" as one goal of the EU's legal migration policy.[64] Human rights-based migration management is thus a cross-sectional task of international cooperation, involving various fields of international law.

2. *Management of migratory movements*

Once migration occurs, there is a need for reactive management. Compliance with this "responsibility to react" is difficult, due to the many deficiencies of international migration law. It starts with the assumption of the 1951 Refugee Convention that refugees will only stay temporarily in the host countries. In reality, permanent resettlement is the rule. This can challenge societies and their ability to integrate migrants whom they might consider a threat to their wish for a self-determined decision about questions of permanent belonging. On the other side, permanent emigration can potentially cause problems for the countries of origin, when they experience "brain drain" and thus might even lose their capacity to rebuild after conflict resolution. Furthermore, the problem of mass exodus scenarios remains inadequately solved in international refugee law. While the 1951 Refugee Convention remains silent with regard to mass influxes of refugees, Art. 3 of the UN General Assembly resolution of 1967 establishes an exemption for mass influx scenarios:

> "1. No person referred to in article 1, paragraph 1, shall be subjected to measures such as rejection at the frontier or, if he has already entered the territory in which he seeks asylum, expulsion or compulsory return to any State where he may be subjected to persecution.
> 2. Exception may be made to the foregoing principle only for overriding reasons of national security or in order to safeguard the population, as in the case of a mass influx of persons."[65]

---

63 *R. Cohen/M. Bradley*, Disasters and Displacement: Gaps in Protection, Journal of International Humanitarian Legal Studies 1 (2010), 95, 138.

64 COM (2015) 240 final, 16.

65 UN General Assembly, Declaration on Territorial Asylum, 14 December 1967, Res. 2312 (XXII).

This is, however, not a satisfying solution because particularly in such occasions of mass displacement, when the protection of human rights is at stake on a massive scale, refugees are vulnerable. At the same time, a single state cannot handle the need for protection alone.[66]

Migration management by the means of the Refugee Convention becomes even harder with its restrictive refugee definition in Art. 1, limiting the Convention's applicability to individual persecution for reasons of race, religion, nationality, membership of a particular social group or political opinion, and excluding other important factors for forced migration, such as armed conflicts or environmental disasters. But the crucial point from a human rights perspective is that the Convention requires successful flight. The core principle of refugee protection, the prohibition of *refoulement* in Art. 33, only applies once the refugee has – be it legally or illegally – entered the territory of the state, or at least reached the border.[67] Yet some of the greatest threats for life and physical integrity of refugees lie on the route to the countries of destination. The lack of legal entry possibilities in the countries of destination results in illegality becoming the only way to make use of guaranteed human rights, and it incentivises the taking up of dangerous journeys in the hands of criminal traffickers. The issue of humanitarian visa, as proposed by the Advocate General *P. Mengozzi* in a case before the European Court of Justice with regard to situations where there is a genuine risk of infringement of certain human rights,[68] would be difficult to put into practice, considering the potential run on the diplo-

66 In 2001, the Council of the EU adopted the Council Directive 2001/55/EC of 20 July 2001 on "minimum standards for giving temporary protection in the event of a mass influx of displaced persons and on measures promoting a balance of efforts between Member States in receiving such persons and bearing the consequences thereof". The directive has, however, never been activated, see *J. Koo*, Mass Influxes and Protection in Europe: A Reflection on a Temporary Episode of an Enduring Problem, European Journal of Migration and Law 20 (2018), 157 ff., who argues that the concept of temporary protection has failed; but also *M. Ineli-Ciger*, Time to Activate the Temporary Protection Directive. Why the Directive can Play a Key Role in Solving the Migration Crisis in Europe, European Journal of Migration and Law, 18 (2016), 1 ff.

67 *E. Lauterpacht/D. Bethlehem*, The Scope and Content of the Principle of Non-Refoulement: Opinion, in: E. Feller/V. Türk/F. Nicholson (eds.), Refugee Protection in International Law, 2003, 87, 113 ff.; *Hathaway*, The Rights of Refugees under International Law, 2006, 315 ff.; *G. S. Goodwin-Gill/J. McAdam*, The Refugee in International Law, 3rd edition, 2007, 246; *W. Kälin/M. Caroni/L. Heim*, in: A. Zimmermann (ed.) (fn. 49), Art. 33 para. 1 MN 105 ff.

68 Opinion of the Advocate General *P. Mengozzi*, delivered on 7 February 2017, C-638/16 PPU, ECLI:EU:C:2017:93, para. 109-175 – X and X v. État Belge.

matic and consular missions in the countries of origin, and does therefore not serve as a practicable solution. Still, it does shine a light on the imminent need for legal pathways to security.

Coping with the shortcomings of the existing international legal framework is only possible by complying with the already mentioned duty to cooperate, deduced from human rights obligations. The challenges posed by (mass) migration require international solidarity, burden-sharing and cooperation.[69] Given the impossibility of enforcing these principles legally, the key would be a creative mix of established instruments of international law, such as self-commitments. It might also be worth thinking about transferring governance mechanisms from other contexts to the area of migration. A system, inspired by emission trading rules, that defines certain refugee quotas, and at the same time establishes financial compensation obligations in the case of falling short of the quota, might *prima facie* seem unusual in the context of human rights. But it can serve as a pragmatic approach to "flexible solidarity".[70] Such quotas must not be misinterpreted as rigid maximum limits for the admittance of refugees, though, which would be incompatible with human rights. In any case, as long as there is no realistic chance for a comprehensive multilateral reform of the universal legal framework for migration, regional and bilateral solutions – in the form of refugee resettlement agreements or even bilateral migration regimes – should be sought. This should certainly always encompass the necessary institutional and procedural instruments for migrants to be able to enforce their individual rights.

3. *Management in the aftermath of migratory movements*

In the aftermath of migratory movements, the "responsibility to rebuild" demands, on the one side, efforts to rebuild the political system in the countries of origin, (re-)establishing the necessary institutions and precautionary measures for the guarantee of fundamental human rights and secu-

69 See UNHCR Executive Committee, Conclusion No. 22 (XXXII), Protection of Asylum-Seekers in Situations of Large-Scale Influx (1981).

70 *R. Drachenberg*, Outcome of the Informal Meeting of 27 Heads of State or Government on 16 September 2016 in Bratislava, 3 October 2016, https://epthinktank.eu/2016/10/03/outcome-of-the-informal-meeting-of-27-heads-of-state-or-government-on-16-september-2016-in-bratislava/ (accessed 30 October 2019); see also *M. Kotzur*, Flexible Solidarity – Effective Solidarity?, Völkerrechtsblog, 16 November 2016, doi: 10.17176/20180522-202034.

rity. Here, coping with the consequences of migration has at the same time a preventive function of the kind described above, serving the future "responsibility to prevent". On the other side, in the light of the realities of migration in the countries of destination, the task for human rights-based post-migration management is to provide constructive perspectives for the integration of those who will most likely stay permanently. It aims to provide the framework for the nation states to fulfil their responsibility for the integration of these people, autonomously and in a self-determined way, but with respect for the fundamental requirements of human rights law. The "responsibility to rebuild" turns into a responsibility "to build".[71] That applies to the law of residence, the access to the labour market, family reunification, and all other areas of public life. For example, limited diplomatic protection for non-citizens has to be provided.[72] In all of this, the management potential of the human rights-based approach proposed here lies in the dismantling of the dichotomy between exclusion on the grounds of self-determination and inclusion on the grounds of human rights freedoms, opening up a perspective of a differentiated status of belonging.

4. The overall perspective: a differentiated status of belonging

The initial thesis of human rights creating a system of differentiated statuses of belonging is based on the acknowledgement that, in principle, it is the right of political communities to decide who may participate. This cannot be neglected without giving up a fundamental principle of international law. However, with the principle of self-determination being itself rooted in human rights, human rights convey rights to belong, to participate in the community, differentiated by the degree of threat for the individual. In concrete terms this means: The more existential the threat for the individual, the greater the individual's right to belong to the political community, weakening the exclusionary force of the community's will to self-determination.

The 1951 Refugee Convention provides for the very minimum in terms of belonging to a political community, limiting the status to the fear of

---

71 On this idea, *U. Werner-Pietsch*, The Impact of SDGs on International Law – A Nucleus of a Right to Peace?, OZP – Austrian Journal of Political Science 47 (2018), 18, 21.

72 *A. M. H. Vermeer-Künzli*, The Protection of Individuals by Means of Diplomatic Protection. Diplomatic Protection as a Human Rights Instrument, 2007.

persecution for reasons of race, religion, nationality, membership of a particular social group or political opinion.[73] Persons fleeing from armed conflicts thus do not fall under the Convention protection.[74] However, the Convention itself follows a logic of differentiated statuses of belonging. The stronger the attachment between a refugee and the receiving state becomes, the more rights the refugee is attributed by the Convention.[75] With its status of subsidiary protection, EU law has created an additional, wider status of belonging, in order to cope with the deficiencies of classical refugee protection vis-à-vis the – often no less existential – threats from armed conflicts, when there is no individual persecution on the aforementioned grounds. The range of imaginable reasons for other, further rights of belonging extends from a colonial past[76] to such – rather utopian – concepts like a responsibility based on participation on the global market. It is up to regional communities of responsibility to create and further develop new models of belonging. The path the EU has taken, with the market citizen having emancipated to a genuine *citoyen*,[77] is only one possible way. In all this, thinking in human rights-based categories of belonging is certainly much more effective than a desirable, but elusive concept of global citizenship.

73 On the reasons for persecution, *G. S. Goodwin-Gill/J. McAdam*, The Refugee in International Law, 3rd edition, 2007, 70 ff. Comprehensively on the refugee status, *J. C. Hathaway/M. Foster*, The Law of Refugee Status, 2nd edition, 2014.

74 *P. Boeles/M. Den Heijer/G. Lodder/K. Wouters*, European Migration Law, 2014, 307 f.

75 *J. C. Hathaway*, The Rights of Refugees under International Law, 2006, 154 ff.: The Convention differentiates between rights of refugees physically present, rights of refugees lawfully present and rights of those lawfully staying.

76 *E. Tendayi Achiume*, Reimagining International Law for Global Migration: Migration as Decolonization?, AJIL Unbound 111 (2017–2018), 142 ff.

77 While in the beginning free movement of persons in the European Communities was only possible for economic purposes, EU citizens nowadays enjoy general freedom of movement under Art. 21 para. 1 TFEU. *P. Boeles/M. Den Heijer/G. Lodder/K. Wouters*, European Migration Law, 2014, speak of "free movement of the market citizen" (p. 30) and "free movement of EU citizens and members of their family" (p. 49). On citizenship see also *R. Dahrendorf*, Citizenship and Beyond: The Social Dynamics of an Idea (1974), in: B. S. Turner/P. Hamilton (eds.), Citizenship. Critical Concepts, vol. II, 1994, 292 ff.

V. Outlook

Faced with the partly substantial deficiencies of the institutional and normative framework of international migration law and contemporary migration phenomena, comprehensive reforms – a reform of the international legal instruments, the creation of a new international organisation for migration with wider competences, the inclusion of an explicit right to asylum in human rights treaties, the taking up of civil war and climate "refugees" into the 1951 Refugee Convention, or the development of adequate normative responses mass refugee movements – might appear more desirable than ever. But with today's renaissance of sovereignty-oriented politics and restrictive migration regimes, it might be more promising to pursue a consequent "piecemeal engineering"[78] on the basis of the existing human rights instruments. The belonging to the human family and the "freedom from fear" as a new global common, together with a protective responsibility of the international community, could serve as the leitmotif in this process, as the leading utopia for international cooperation in the service of humanity.

78 *K. R. Popper*, The Open Society and its Enemies. Volume 1: The Spell of Plato, 1945, 138 ff.

PART ONE

THE EXTERNAL DIMENSION OF EU MIGRATION AND ASYLUM POLICIES: EVOLUTION AND FEATURES

A General Overview of the Legal Framework of the EU External Action on Migration and Asylum

*Claudia Candelmo**

I. Introduction

The EU stands as a living actor of the international community in different ways. It can conclude treaties and agreements, have delegations[1] in third countries, and, thanks to the recent creation of the European External Action Service (EEAS), promote cooperation and development of local communities and provide humanitarian aid in case of emergencies or disasters.[2]

One of the fields in which the external action of the European Union is particularly relevant is the area of migration and asylum. It is so, both in light of the sensitiveness of the migration phenomenon for Member States and in connection with the evident need to cooperate with third countries, in order to build a safe Area of Freedom, Security and Justice (AFSJ),[3] of which migration is part.[4] In fact, the efficient handling of migratory flows cannot be implemented successfully by the EU without looking outside the EU itself,[5] where such flows originate or where they transit before approaching the European borders. This has been widely acknowledged since

* PhD in International Order and Human Rights (Sapienza University, 2017) and currently post-doctoral research fellow in European Union Law at the Department of Political Science, LUISS University.

1 On the nature and characteristics of EU Delegations, see *Kerres/Wessel*, Apples and Oranges? Comparing the European Union Delegations to National Embassies, CLEER Papers, The Hague 2015.

2 *Pusterla*, The European Union and Humanitarian Crises. Patterns of Intervention, London 2015.

3 *De Bruycker/Weyembergh*, The External Dimension of the European Area of Freedom, Security and Justice in: Telò (ed.), *The European Union and Global Governance*, Abingdon 2009, 210.

4 On this point, see Art. 3 para. 2 TEU as well as Articles 77 and ff. TFEU, on Policies on border checks, asylum and immigration, under Title V on the Area of Freedom, Security and Justice.

5 *De Bruycker/Weyembergh*, in: Telò (ed.) (fn. 3), 212.

the nineties,[6] and seems to have been confirmed by the recent situation of migration towards the European Union: protection of borders and strict control of frontiers proved insufficient in the face of massive influxes, such as those that hit European shores in 2015 and 2016,[7] while solidarity[8] among Member States also proved to be lacking, as relocation schemes elaborated by European Institutions did not prove as effective as expected.[9]

It should be made clear at the outset that it is not possible to refer indiscriminately to migration and asylum. In the first, general concept, all those who travel from one State to another for work, family, personal or study reasons are included. The second notion identifies a well-defined[10] category of migrants, to which particular protection is afforded. Therefore, as is well known, when asylum seekers become officially recognised as refugees, they have a very specific status that allows them to stay in the territory of the State that has welcomed them. And, first of all, this entails protection from being sent back to where the threat of persecution originated.[11] This protection is not afforded to people who do not face any threat in their home country or in another State that may be ready to welcome them: in this case, if they are not entitled to international protection or to stay in the Member State for other reasons, they can be readmitted in their home country.

This means that, first of all, applications must be examined and migrants have to be welcomed in reception centres: this can create a heavy burden on States whose infrastructure is not ready to receive and accommodate thousands of people with urgent basic needs, who lodge applications for international protection. So, if Member States' reception systems are under deep stress, and the fundamental principle of non-refoulement

---

6 See Tampere European Council 15–16 October 1999 – Presidency Conclusions.

7 Data on arrivals on European territory are available here: https://migration.iom.int/europe?type=arrivals.

8 For an overview of the role and potential of solidarity in EU asylum policy, see *Moreno-Lax*, Solidarity's reach: Meaning, dimensions and implications for EU (external) asylum policy, Maastricht Journal of European and Comparative Law 24 (2017), 740.

9 *Tsourdi*, The Emerging Architecture of EU Asylum Policy: Insights into the Administrative Governance of the Common European Asylum System, in: Bignami (ed.), EU Law in Populist Times. Crises and Prospects, Cambridge 2020, 209.

10 See Art. 1, Geneva Convention 1951 and Art. 2 para. d, Directive 2011/95/EU, on the definition of refugee.

11 See Art. 32, Geneva Convention 1951. On the more general protection from return ('refoulement') to the territories where the life of a refugee is in danger, see Art. 33 of the Geneva Convention.

must be preserved, cooperation with third States on readmission and legal avenues for migration reveals its full relevance.

Such partnerships can take various legal forms, from informal deals to proper international agreements, even if most recent practice shows a tendency towards unconventional and legally blurred forms of cooperation, whose consequences[12] have raised concerns in terms of human rights protection. The subject of these partnerships varies extensively and deals with the most disparate aspects of migration, ranging from development aids and visa agreements to readmission deals.

European cooperation with third countries, in fact, can, on the one hand, enhance the avenues for legal migration (for instance, through visa facilitation agreements), while also helping the countries of departure create safer environments and reducing the reasons that push people to leave their homes; on the other, it can decrease the number of third-country nationals present in EU territory through readmission agreements with transit countries.

Notwithstanding the difficulties they may raise, migratory flows cannot (and should not) be stopped. Concerted work between the EU and third countries is still crucial in mitigating crises and reducing the factors that push people to leave their homes, as well as in making the efficient handling of migration flows a reality: but the realisation of so-called "Fortress Europe" is little more than utopia.

II. External action on migration and asylum: recent evolution and main features

EU external action is a multifaceted issue.[13] On the one hand, it involves the external dimension of those subjects on which the EU has explicit internal competence.[14] On the other hand, it is the way in which the EU, as a

---

12 On the consequences of external policy measures on migration, see *Reslow*, Horizontal and vertical diversity: unintended consequences of EU external migration policy, The International Spectator 54 (2019), 31–44.

13 On the external action of the European Union, see *Engbrink*, The European Union's External Action: Coherence in European Union Foreign Policy Despite Separate Legal Orders?, Legal Issues of Economic Integration 44 (2017), 5.

14 See Art. 216 TFEU. See also *García Andrade*, EU external competences in the field of migration: how to act externally when thinking internally, Common Market Law Review 55 (2018), 157, 161 and *Martenczuk*, Migration Policy and EU External Relations, in Azoulai/de Vries (eds.), EU Migration Law. Legal Complexities and Political Rationales, Oxford 2014, 69, 80.

global actor,[15] interacts with third countries and the international community.

With the adoption of the Amsterdam Treaty,[16] entered into force in May 1999, the fields of immigration and asylum were "communitarised"[17] and the EU acquired competence on them.[18]

From the internal perspective, involving the reception and custody of migrants, needless to say, the whole policy, now and then, has been affected by events. And, when instruments like the Dublin Agreement were first shaped in 1990, massive flows such as those that the EU has experienced in recent years, could not be envisaged.

Migration and asylum matters became a compelling issue in the nineties, when the first extensive influxes of migrants and asylum seekers flowing, first, from former Yugoslavia and, shortly after, from Albania and Kosovo, started arriving on European coasts.[19] Furthermore, when the integration put forward by the Schengen scheme was coming to completion, Member States pushed for stronger border controls and stricter regulation of migration flows, if free circulation on the European territory should be granted without a detriment to security.[20]

However, the flows experienced in those years were hardly comparable to those that occurred in recent times. The solution elaborated by the Dublin Convention aimed to ensure safety, certainty and, at the same time, orderly procedures, imposing on asylum seekers to request refuge only in one country. On the one hand, such architecture built on the general belief that conditions of reception, as well as procedures,[21] would be roughly similar in the various countries of arrival. On the other hand,

---

15 *Telò*, Introduction: the EU as a model, a global actor and an unprecedented power, in: Telò (ed.), The European Union and Global Governance, London, New York 2009, 1.

16 Art. 73 and ff.

17 *Bendel/Ripoll Servent*, Asylum and Refugee protection. EU policies in crisis, in: Ripoll Servent/Trauner (eds.), The Routledge Handbook of Justice and Home Affairs Research, London 2017, 60.

18 Until the Maastricht Treaty, in fact, migration fell within the intergovernmental pillar, in order to leave more space to States' action.

19 *Bendel/Ripoll Servent*, in: Ripoll Servent/Trauner (eds.) (fn. 17), 60.

20 *Carrera/Allsopp*, The irregular immigration policy conundrum. Problematizing 'effectiveness' as a frame for EU criminalization and expulsion policies, in: Ripoll Servent/Trauner (eds.) (fn. 17), 71.

21 Legislative texts have been adopted to establish similar standards on asylum in Member States. These include the Asylum Procedures Directive (2013/32/EU), the Qualification Directive (2011/95/EU) and the Reception Conditions Directive (2013/33/EU).

however, this structure posed a heavy burden on "border" countries such as Italy, Greece and Spain.

Looking at the external action that the EU could put in place, it was soon clear that dealing with migration, like other transboundary phenomena, entailed cooperation with third countries. Migration fluxes, indeed, originate outside the European Union, in closer or farther States: cooperation with origin or transit countries, therefore, was revealed as crucial in order to reach the objectives of EU migration policy.[22] Furthermore, the growing connection between irregular migration and security instances, rendered international cooperation with third countries a compelling issue in order to establish the AFSJ,[23] as demonstrated also by the inclusion of migration, together with terrorism and organised crime, under the pillar of Justice and Home Affairs (JHA) of the Maastricht Treaty[24] and, even before, in the TREVI Working Group themes.[25]

In order to strengthen cooperation on migration and asylum, on the one hand, the then European Community pushed for the involvement of third States in limiting access to the EU[26] and in enhancing returns through readmission agreements.[27] On the other hand, it tried to tackle the root causes of migration, adopting a "preventive" approach[28] which aimed at reducing migrants' will to leave their homes by addressing key problems such as poverty or low economic and job opportunities in their own countries.

Such an approach emerged in policy instruments adopted throughout the years, which outlined the general direction of EU action on migration. From the outset, in many meetings and documents it was reiterated that policies in this area should follow a comprehensive approach.[29] But what exactly does a "comprehensive approach" mean? Such a term was employed in the Tampere Conclusions to explain the need to adopt measures

---

22 *Boswell*, The 'external dimension' of EU immigration and asylum policy, International Affairs 79 (2003), 619.

23 *Hein*, L'azione esterna dell'Unione europea in materia di migrazioni alla luce dei valori comuni, in Sciso/Baratta/Morviducci (eds.), I valori dell'Unione europea e l'azione esterna, Torino 2016, 170, 172.

24 *Yıldız*, The European Union's immigration policy. Managing migration in Turkey and Morocco, London 2016, 44.

25 *Düvell*, Irregular Migration, in Betts (ed.), Global Migration Governance, Oxford 2011, 78, 82.

26 *Boswell*, International Affairs 79 (2003) (fn. 22), 622.

27 Tampere Programme, paras. 26–27.

28 *Boswell*, International Affairs 79 (2003) (fn. 22), 624.

29 See Tampere (para. 11) and The Hague Programme (para. 1.2).

which address the early causes of migration up to the eventual readmission policies, with the aim of handling migration flows in a more efficient way. In particular, "comprehensive" seemed to include both the necessity of tackling conditions of origin and transit countries as well as factors to take into consideration once migrants reached EU territory. Building on the results of the Tampere Programme, the Hague Programme, which adopted the same "comprehensive" approach,[30] dealt with all the different dimensions of the AFSJ, including migration and asylum, both from its internal and its external perspective. Anticipated in the Tampere Programme,[31] but reaffirmed in the Hague Programme,[32] the birth of the Common European Asylum System (CEAS) was envisaged as a way to ensure common procedures and analogous conditions for reception. The "external" importance of having a uniform set of procedures on asylum for all Member States cannot be underestimated: it implies that the Union stands as a single actor in this context and that nationals from third countries can rely, with a reasonable degree of certainty, on equal procedures, irrespective of the country in which the application is lodged. Furthermore, effective management of asylum seekers can arguably be put in place if the burden is left exclusively to one single State. Cooperation among Member States is thus vital, albeit solidarity has been seriously tested in the most recent migration events.[33]

Not surprisingly, the Stockholm programme, adopted in 2009, pushed for the same approach, with a specific focus on burden-sharing, solidarity and partnership in migration and asylum matters.[34]

The external policy on migration and asylum was also coupled with the European Neighbourhood Policy (ENP), where the EU put particular effort into partnerships with neighbouring countries on migration issues.[35] Given their proximity to the EU, these States can have a crucial role in stopping migrants before they even approach the European territory, acting almost as "filters".[36] Externalisation then was already starting to be con-

30 Para. 1.2. and 1.5 of The Hague Programme.

31 Para. 13 of the Tampere Programme.

32 Para. 1.3 (18) of The Hague Programme.

33 *Knodt/Tews*, European solidarity and its limits: insights from current political challenges, in Grimmel/My Giang (eds.), Solidarity in the European Union. A fundamental value in crisis, Cham 2017, 47, 59.

34 See para. 6 (59) of the Stockholm Programme.

35 *Delcour*, The EU: shaping migration patterns in its neighbourhood and beyond, in Kochenov/Amtenbrink (eds.), The European Union's shaping of the international legal order, Cambridge 2013, 262.

36 *Delcour*, in Kochenov/Amtenbrink (eds.) (fn. 35), 266.

sidered as an efficient way to reduce the problem of migration, albeit this strategy received a boost in recent years, when it became one of the main avenues through which the EU has tried to control arrivals on its territory.[37] In this regard, the ENP envisages partnerships with the States closest to European borders, offering them preferential treatment, as will be shown further, as far as visas or the access to the internal market are concerned, in exchange for the possibility of influencing their response to migration flows.[38]

The massive 2015 flows pushed for the adoption of a renewed document: this urgency was partly fulfilled by the European Agenda on Migration,[39] this time adopted by the Commission for the period 2015–2019. The Agenda identifies four main pillars that can serve as a basis to solve the "structural limitations of EU migration policy",[40] thereby also recognising the inherent flaws of the approach taken until that moment. The Agenda sums up the objectives and the various steps of an efficient management of flows, from the prevention of irregular migration, to the handling of influxes once people arrive in Europe and to the promotion of safe and legal avenues to migrate. It is in this framework that the Blue Card scheme is included, in order to attract highly qualified and specialised workers to European States.

III. The legal framework of the EU external action: constitutional foundations of migration policies

The legal framework of the EU external action is provided in both the TEU and the TFEU. The inclusion of the relevant provisions in both Treaties provides a "constitutional" basis for the external action of the EU in the fields of migration and asylum.

While the TEU gives the general provisions on the Union's external action[41] and specific provisions on the Common Foreign and Security Policy (CFSP),[42] the TFEU, in Part Five, describes the peculiar aspects of the ex-

---

37 *Reslow*, "Not everything that counts can be counted": Assessing 'success' of EU external migration policy, International Migration 6 (2017), 156.
38 *Delcour*, in Kochenov/Amtenbrink (eds.) (fn. 35), 263.
39 European Commission, A European Agenda on Migration, COM (2015) 240, 13 May 2015.
40 European Commission, 2015 (fn. 39), 6.
41 Art. 21 TFEU.
42 Art. 22 TFEU.

ternal action of the Union, the fields in which it can take place as well as its means,[43] for example the conclusion of international agreements with third countries.[44] This is true both in general terms and with specific reference to the issues of migration and asylum: one of the ways in which the EU has been cooperating with third countries in this field, is precisely the conclusion of international agreements (for example, readmission accords).

The necessity to legally ensure autonomy to the EU in its external action arose already in the seventies and, as it often happened inside the European legal order, the action of the CJEU was fundamental in this respect. Through the now famous ERTA doctrine and the recognition of implied powers of the European Union,[45] the Court affirmed that the EU authority to conclude an international agreement arises not only when the Treaty expressly provides so, but may "equally flow from other provisions of the treaty and from measures adopted, within the framework of those provisions, by the Community Institutions".[46]

Further specifications followed in Opinion 1/76, where the Court also recalled that "whenever Community law has created for the Institutions [...] powers within its internal system for the purpose of attaining a specific objective, the Community has authority to enter into the international commitments necessary for the attainment of that objective even in the absence of an express provision in that connexion".[47] In this way, the judges of the Luxembourg Court promoted a systemic interpretation of the rules concerning the external action, one that would allow the EU to operate fully through its conferred powers, without being hampered in the possibility to conclude international treaties.

But this legal reasoning, which flows from the necessity to ensure that the EU can act outside as it does within its institutions and towards its Member States, is also followed by a more political consideration, which is the need to foster coherence between the internal and external action of

---

43 See Art. 205 TFEU and ff.

44 As provided by Art. 218 TFEU.

45 European Court of Justice, 1/76, EU:C:1977:63, opinion, 26 April 1977, para. 3 – Draft Agreement establishing a European laying-up fund for inland waterway vessels.

46 European Court of Justice, 22/70, ECLI:EU:C:1971:32, judgment, 31 March 1971, para. 16 – Commission/Council (ERTA). See also joined cases 3, 4 and 6/76, EU:C:1976:114, judgment, 14 July 1976, paras. 19–20 – Cornelis Kramer and others.

47 Opinion 1/76, para. 3. See *García Andrade*, Common Market Law Review 55 (2018) (fn. 14).

the Union. Such "political" concern, however, is also displayed in the Treaties: in general terms, coherence in the action of the EU is safeguarded by the Commission, pursuant to Art. 11 TEU[48] and, with specific reference to the external action of the EU, Art. 21 TEU recalls that presence on the international scene must be guided by the same founding principles of the EU, among which, of course democracy, human rights and fundamental freedoms are included.[49] The same provision goes on to affirm that the EU must ensure coherence between the various sectors of the external action and between these and other policies.[50] Such external coherence appears necessary not only with specific reference to the external action on migration and asylum, but also to prove reliability with commercial and political partners of the EU and to strengthen its standing as a decisive actor of the international community.

Art. 21 TEU further reinforces such an assumption by highlighting that partnerships with third countries or international organisations are possible when these States share the *principles* of the EU.[51] Therefore, if the Union has internal competence on a subject, it is necessary to ensure that the external action in that domain coherently follows the principles that guide its internal action.

This might seem like a self-evident assumption, but the need for coherence between internal and external policies of the EU is restated in so many documents[52] that its blatancy may be questioned. Sensitive areas like migration and asylum, where internal reception rules go hand in hand with external action and cooperation with third countries, are no exception. If European values and principles ensured inside the EU are not also promoted outside, when it comes to taking care of migrants and potential refugees, the reliability of the EU could be called into question.

Art. 21 TEU further identifies the main principles of external action and especially the objectives that such activity must pursue. Indeed, the objec-

---

48 Art. 11 TEU recalls that "The European Commission shall carry out broad consultations with parties concerned in order to ensure that the Union's actions are coherent and transparent".

49 Art. 21 para. 1 TEU.

50 Art. 21 para. 3 TEU.

51 See Art. 21 para. 2 TEU. On the specific shade that differentiates values and principles of the EU in the framework of External Action, see also, *Latino*, Valori, principî e obiettivi della dimensione esterna della politica migratoria dell'Unione europea, in Sciso/Baratta/Morviducci (eds.), I valori dell'Unione europea e l'azione esterna, Torino 2016, 186, 189.

52 Among others, Tampere Programme, para. 11; The Hague Programme, para. 1, 11; Stockholm Programme, para. 1.2.4, 7.

tives are linked to issues of a global nature, such as the protection of the environment or development of third countries. More general objectives such as the prevention of conflicts and the strengthening of international security[53] are mentioned, as well.

Details on the areas where the Union has competence to take external actions are included in Part Five of the TFEU,[54] which encourages cooperation with third countries as well as international (also, regional) organisations and identifies the instruments devoted to doing so.[55]

It is interesting to note that the so-called solidarity clause, which operates among Member States when one of them is under a particular threat,[56] is included in this section devoted to EU external action, as if solidarity operated as a "glue" among Member States in the face of external threats[57].

The inclusion of different provisions in the two treaties has raised questions about the relationship existing between them. Although they might seem to operate separately, for instance looking at Art. 40 TEU, they are also necessarily coordinated and both sections are subject to the general provisions laid down in Art. 21 TEU, as Art. 205 reiterates.[58] This also confirms that both treaties' provisions ask that the external action be inspired by the principles of the European Union, a *fil rouge* to be respected and promoted in all sectors of EU action.[59]

A notable example of the relevance "constitutionally" attributed to external action is the role specifically envisaged for the EU in the fields of asylum law and policy in the treaties. Especially after the entry into force of the Lisbon Treaty, which abolished the old pillars established under the

53 Art. 21 para. 2 TEU.

54 With particular reference to the EU Common Commercial Policy (Title II), cooperation with third countries and humanitarian aid (Title III), restrictive measures (Title IV), international agreements (Title V), the Union's relations with international organisations, third countries and Union delegations (Title VI) and the solidarity clause (Title VII).

55 See, in particular, Art. 208–211 TFEU.

56 See, Art. 222 TFEU.

57 Among the threats listed are terrorism and/or natural disasters. See Art. 222 para. 1.

58 *Schütze*, European Union Law, 2nd edition, Cambridge 2018, 269.

59 On this point, see *Sciso/Baratta/Morviducci* (a cura di), I valori dell'Unione europea e l'azione esterna, Torino 2016 and *Eeckhout/López-Escudero* (eds.), The European Union's External Action in times of crisis, Bloomsbury 2016.

Maastricht Treaty and “definitively communitarised the field of asylum”,[60] the EU has enhanced its role in managing flows at the community level.

In particular, Art. 78 TFEU, which deals with the competences of the EU on the creation of the CEAS, focuses on the capability of the EU to work in partnership and to cooperate with third countries for the management of asylum seekers.[61] This provision is included in Title V of the TFEU, which deals with the creation and establishment of the AFSJ. Such an inclusion creates a clear link between migration matters and internal security: from a constitutional point of view, internal freedom and security are guaranteed only if external borders are checked and migration is managed efficiently.

Art. 79 TFEU allows the EU to legislate on the conditions of entry and residence for long-term visas and residence permits. Indeed, since the adoption of the Dublin Convention in 1990, Member States have resorted to instruments belonging to the European legal order to enhance unity in their approach to migration, either through internal legal instruments or through international agreements.

The internal law of the EU is of course directed primarily at its Member States. This means that EU law on migration issues tackles first of all the ways in which European States deal with influxes once they reach EU territory, from the perspective of creating an AFSJ, where procedures, conditions of reception and even the rules regulating the examination of asylum seekers’ applications are homogeneous.[62] However, practice has shown that this is not the case, as percentages of acceptance of asylum applications[63] as well as conditions of reception[64] broadly vary from one Member State to another.

Moreover, it should be noted that, despite being purely internal laws, the rules on asylum have an impact on the external dimension of EU asylum and migration policies. As the Dublin Regulation imposed on refugees the requirement to apply in the country of first arrival, asylum seekers tried to find ways to reach (legally or illegally) the country in

---

60 *Cherubini*, Asylum Law in the European Union, Oxon 2015, 159.

61 Art. 78 para. 2 (g) TFEU.

62 European Court of Justice, C-394/12, ECLI:EU:C:2013:813, judgment, 10 December 2013, para. 55 – Shamso Abdullahi/Bundesasylamt.

63 See *Cherubini* (fn. 60), 254. Also, for the latest data on application outcomes, see first instance decisions by outcome and recognition rates of 1st quarter 2019, available here: https://ec.europa.eu/eurostat/statistics-explained.

64 *Slingenberg*, The Reception of Asylum Seekers under International Law. Between Sovereignty and Equality, Oxford 2014, 72.

which they wanted to apply for asylum, either for expectations of results or because it was in that State that they wished to reside for the following years.[65] This in turn and paradoxically also prompted irregular movements, as it influenced individuals who arrive first in a country where they do not wish to apply for asylum due to, for example, personal links with another Member State. Therefore, the impact of the Dublin Regulation, as well as the other directives adopted in this field, potentially started before the arrival of the asylum seekers on the territory of the EU.

As mentioned above, the EU has been using extensively international agreements to cooperate with third countries. On the one hand, agreements have been employed to prevent the arrival of migrants and asylum seekers on the territory of the Union, somehow externalising the examination of their requests for international protection, or to help third countries to secure their borders and reduce irregular transit.[66] On the other hand, agreements have been concluded to favour the readmission of migrants who are not entitled to stay on the EU territory[67] either because their request has been rejected or because they are not asylum seekers and do not have the right to stay on the territory of the Member State where they are residing, often in exchange for visa facilitation or liberalisation agreements.

The overall policy of the EU in the field of migration seems to be that of removing the "problem" of migrants from its eyes. The focus is often on avoiding arrivals to Europe or on the readmission of third-country nationals to their home States. Less focus has been put on having a more efficient mechanism of reception among Member States. Proposals of reform of the Dublin Regulation have been put forward on several occasions[68] but this hypothesis still seems far from future implementation.

---

65 *Maiani*, The Dublin III Regulation: A New Legal Framework for a More Humane System?, in Chetail/De Bruycker/Maiani (eds.), Reforming the Common European Asylum System. The New European Refugee Law, Leiden 2016, 101, 108.

66 *Papagianni*, Forging an external EU migration policy: from externalization of border management to a comprehensive policy?, European Journal of Migration and Law, 15 (2013), 283, 284.

67 Art. 79 para. 3 TFEU.

68 Among others, see the Proposal for a Regulation of the European Parliament and of the Council establishing the criteria and mechanisms for determining the Member State responsible for examining an application for international protection lodged in one of the Member States by a third-country national or a stateless person (recast), COM(2016) 270.

1. Visa agreements

Visa procedures within the EU are regulated by the Schengen Agreement and, in particular, by the Schengen Visa Code,[69] which establishes common rules to issue visas for stays not exceeding 90 days in any 180-day period. Furthermore, Regulation 2018/1806[70] identifies common positions of Member States in relation to determining third countries whose nationals need visas when crossing external borders of the EU and those which, in turn, do not. These are respectively identified as "black" or "white" lists of countries.[71]

Visas are a powerful tool of foreign policy, which allow Member States[72] to handle legal migration flows and regulate entrance of third-country nationals on the European territory. Therefore, the EU has extensively employed visa agreements to manage migration flows in the territory of the Union, especially with neighbouring countries. In this regard, visa facilitation agreements had the additional purpose of lowering the perception that the EU was somehow an exclusive possibility[73] of few people, finding new avenues for regular migration.

Such agreements can either be characterised by facilitated procedures[74] or by complete liberalisation.[75] The difference between the two is fairly straightforward: in the first case, the EU and the third country agree on fa-

69 Regulation (EC) 810/2009 establishing a Community Code on Visas.

70 Regulation EU 2018/1806 listing the third countries whose nationals must be in possession of visas when crossing the external borders and those whose nationals are exempted from that requirement, adopted on 14 November 2018.

71 See, respectively, Annex I and II of Regulation 2018/1806.

72 As *Meloni* explains in EU visa policy: What kind of solidarity?, Maastricht Journal of European and Comparative Law 24 (2017), at 660, responsibility for evaluation of visa applications still lies with Member States.

73 *Zhyznomirska*, At a distance. The European Union's management of irregular migration in Eastern Europe, in Zaiotti (ed.), Externalizing Migration Management: Europe, North America and the spread of 'remote control' practices, Abingdon 2016, 148.

74 Visa facilitation agreements have been signed with (listed in chronological order of entry into force): Russia (1 June 2007); Albania, Bosnia and Herzegovina, FYROM, Montenegro and Serbia (1 January 2008); Georgia (1 March 2011); Moldova and Ukraine (1 July 2013); Armenia (1 January 2014); Azerbaijan (1 September 2014) and Cape Verde (1 December 2014). The agreement signed with Belarus on 8 January 2020 is not yet in force.

75 Many of the visa facilitation agreements were followed afterwards by visa liberalisation. See https://www.consilium.europa.eu/en/infographics/visa-facilitation-liberalisation/.

cilitated procedures to issue visas for short stays; in the second case, short-stay travels are visa-free and countries benefitting from a visa waiver are included in the "white" list of Regulation 2018/1806.

Indeed, these agreements touch a very sensitive area of national policy, therefore Member States have not always been keen on accepting them. In fact, most of the agreements are a follow-up to readmission agreements with the same countries, an offset that Member States generally require before accepting facilitations or liberalisations on visas.

Also, Regulation 2018/1806 lists the factors that the EU may take into account when evaluating visa exemptions, including human rights and fundamental freedoms in the country concerned,[76] therefore limiting the application of visa liberalisations to those countries where fundamental rights are respected. This criterion is also stated in the preamble to the Regulation, which suggests the continuous monitoring of human rights protection in the country concerned, when considering eventual suspensions of the exemption.[77]

However, the persistence of such a "safeguard" clause also highlights the political relevance of visa agreements: requirements can be reintroduced, for instance, in case of risks to the internal security or if rejected readmissions requests surge.[78] Member States clearly want to leave open the possibility of reintroducing visa requirements, albeit also envisaging a role for the European Commission that, in the interest of the EU, can trigger the suspension mechanism if the conditions listed in Regulation 2018/1806 materialise.

The objective of this requirement from the EU side should also be to influence third countries' policies, in exchange for the preferential treatment that is accorded to them, within the general EU rule to deal externally with actors that accept and respect the principles of the EU. However, potential side-effects on human rights may also exist, and these should not be underestimated. In fact, while the conditions imposed by the EU may put pressure on non-democratic governments to change their attitudes towards human rights and fundamental freedoms, they might also substantially act as a limitation against those who want to leave oppressive countries and see a possible legal avenue for freedom in Europe suddenly blocked.[79] Therefore, due consideration before suspending the exemption

---

76 Regulation 2018/1806, Art. 1.

77 Paras. 26 and 28 of the Preamble.

78 Para. 22 of the Preamble of Regulation 2018/1806.

79 See *Meloni* (fn. 72), 655.

mechanism should be adopted, in order to strike a fair balance between EU (and Member States) interests and human rights concerns.

2. *Readmission agreements*

Often in combination with visa deals, readmission agreements[80] have also been extensively employed as a tool to facilitate the repatriation of people illegally staying on EU territory. The Lisbon Treaty has explicitly codified the competence of the EU to conclude agreements to facilitate the readmission of third-country nationals to their States of origin, through the introduction of Art. 79, para. 3 TFEU. A significant number of such agreements is today signed with countries located at the external frontiers of the EU, neighbours of the EU itself, with whom the cooperation to reduce irregular migration is particularly important. The partnership with these countries, often candidates to accede to the EU, is also a significant effort to enhance pre-accession policies while effectively combating irregular migration.[81]

As mentioned above, one of the main objectives of readmission agreements is that of ensuring that those who are not entitled to be on the EU territory have a legal and secure path to return to their home countries. However, the conclusion of readmission agreements is significantly more difficult,[82] as compared with visa facilitation agreements. Third countries might not be interested in being parties to such agreements: the main interest, in this case, is for the EU, to enhance security and to implement expulsion decisions adopted by Member States that are often left unapplied; the main burden, on the other hand, is on the country that commits

80 Currently, Readmission Agreements are in force with (listed in chronological order of entry into force): Hong Kong (1 March 2004); Macao (1 June 2004); Sri Lanka (1 May 2005); Albania (1 May 2006); Russia (1 June 2007); Ukraine, fYROM, Bosnia and Herzegovina, Montenegro, Serbia and Moldova (1 January 2008); Pakistan (1 December 2010); Georgia (1 March 2011); Armenia (1 January 2014); Azerbaijan (1 September 2014); Turkey (1 October 2014) and Cape Verde (1 December 2014). The agreement signed with Belarus on 8 January 2020 is not yet in force.

81 *Ottaviano*, Gli accordi di riammissione dell'UE, in: Cherubini (ed.), Le migrazioni in Europa. UE, Stati terzi e migration outsourcing, Rome 2015, 109.

82 See, for the cases of Tunisia and Morocco, *Abderrahim*, A Tale of Two Agreements: EU Migration Cooperation with Morocco and Tunisia, PapersIEMed 41 (2019), 16–17.

to welcoming back its citizens. Therefore, incentives[83] need to be provided to States that accept the conclusion of a readmission agreement: and it was when this necessity appeared on the negotiation scene, that visa facilitation and readmission agreements became so closely interlinked. As a consequence, today, negotiations are usually carried out in parallel, as the most recent visa facilitation and readmission agreements, concluded with Belarus in January 2020,[84] also shows.

These deals usually regulate both the readmission of third-country citizens in their State of origin and the readmission of third-country nationals if a link with the receiving State is proven or if it is thought that the person has transited through the territory of the receiving State to unlawfully enter the territory of a Member State.[85] This last aspect is particularly sensitive, as often the countries involved are not very happy to welcome, and handle, citizens that are not their own. Therefore, sometimes the scope of the agreement can be explicitly limited, or the receiving State does not always commit itself to fully admitting third-country nationals and negotiates some exceptions.[86]

The efficacy of readmission agreements appears significant, albeit limited in its geographical scope. As the number and distribution of agreements signed by the EU shows, the countries involved are often those on which the EU is capable of exercising a real leverage, while countries that are not immediate neighbours of the EU are less willing to commit themselves to such agreements. In other words, the EU must be able to give effective incentives to the relevant country in order to enhance the attractiveness of such agreements.

Furthermore, like visa agreements, readmission agreements also raise important issues in terms of human rights protection.[87] Some countries in which human rights are not entirely respected are indeed partners in the

---

83 *Cassarino*, Informalising Readmission Agreements in the EU Neighbourhood, The International Spectator 42 (2007), 183.

84 The European Commission and Belarus started negotiations of both agreements on 30 January 2014, following a Council decision of authorisation, adopted on 28 January 2011.

85 *Lagrand*, European Union's Readmission Policy in the Post-Stockholm Programme Era, in: Goudappel/Hirsch Ballin (eds.), Democracy and the Rule of Law in the European Union, Heidelberg 2016, 178.

86 *Carli*, EU Readmission Agreements as Tools for Fighting Irregular Migration: An Appraisal Twenty Years on from the Tampere European Council, Freedom, Security & Justice: European Legal Studies 1 (2019), 19.

87 *Ottaviano* in: Cherubini (ed.) (fn. 81), 113.

readmission policy of the EU[88] and their definition as "safe" is not sufficient to ensure the protection of people readmitted on their territory. The EU should keep the definition of "safe third country" as rigorous as possible, to avoid its becoming a shield for the expulsions of third-country nationals to States where fundamental freedoms are at risk. Also, once readmission agreements are signed, pressure and constant scrutiny should be exercised by the Union, to be sure that human rights in the countries at risk are respected as much as possible.

3. *Informal instruments of cooperation*

As shown above, external action of the EU on migration issues has often taken the form of international agreements, especially to advance visa facilitations and simplify readmissions. However, the EU has also been extensively using non-binding instruments[89] which can take various formal denominations (for instance "declarations" or "plans of action"), but whose legal nature is not always crystal-clear. The employment of such instruments has been growing over time and has recently taken the worrying form of informal and atypical deals,[90] which in many cases endow the third country involved with the authority to do a "pre-screening" of the applications before asylum seekers even arrive in Europe. Therefore, these external tools quickly raised concerns,[91] both in light of their unclear legal

88 See, for instance, Azerbaijan and, more recently, Turkey or Belarus.

89 *Vara*, Soft international agreements on migration cooperation with third countries: a challenge to democratic and judicial controls in the EU, in: Carrera/Vara/Strik (eds.), Constitutionalising the external dimensions of EU migration policies in times of crisis, Cheltenham 2019, 21.

90 *De Vittor*, Responsabilità degli Stati e dell'Unione europea nella conclusione e nell'esecuzione di "accordi" per il controllo extraterritoriale della migrazione, in Nesi (ed.), Migrazioni e diritto internazionale: verso il superamento dell'emergenza?, Napoli 2018, 205, 207.

91 *Frelick/Kysel/Podkul*, The Impact of Externalization of Migration Controls on the Rights of Asylum Seekers and Other Migrants, Journal on Migration and Human Security 4 (2016), 190, 196.

nature[92] and of the potential consequences that they could create in terms of human rights violations.[93]

In particular, preoccupations were advanced in connection with the so-called EU–Turkey Statement[94] reached on 18 March 2016. The "deal", which entailed the return of illegal asylum seekers to Turkey in "exchange" for legal asylum seekers crossing the borders to be relocated to Europe, sparred concerns on the legal safeguards that such returns to Turkey would cause in terms of human rights guarantees. It did not take long before asylum seekers who had been returned to Turkey after illegally crossing the border with Greece challenged[95] the legality and compatibility of said Statement with EU law and principles before the Luxembourg Court. However, the applications never reached the merits stage as the judgments recognised a lack of competence by the ECJ. In fact, the Court quite interestingly rejected the thesis that the deal is an EU law instrument,[96] affirming that it is attributable only to the Member States and not to the EU as a whole. This, irrespective of the fact that when the Statement was endorsed, the Heads of State and Government were sitting together with the President of the Commission and the High Representative for Foreign Affairs, which is the "typical" European Council formation. Also, the Court did not take into consideration that such a deal *de facto* imposed burdens on the EU and not on the single States, in particular to mobilise further funding for the Facility for Refugees in Turkey.[97] The Court in fact considered that the meeting of 18 March, when the deal was reached, was a gathering of Heads of State or Government, acting in their capacity and not as mem-

---

92 *Carrera/Vara/Strik*, The external dimensions of EU migration and asylum policies in times of crisis, in Carrera/Vara/Strik (eds.) (fn. 89), 1, 11.

93 *Di Stasio*, Le recenti misure dell'Unione europea per uscire dalla crisi migratoria: criticità irrisolte e prospettive future, in Nesi (ed.), Migrazioni e diritto internazionale: verso il superamento dell'emergenza?, Napoli 2018, 299, 304.

94 Council of the EU, Press Release 144/16, 18 March 2016, on EU–Turkey Statement, available here: https://www.consilium.europa.eu/en/press/press-releases/2016/03/18/eu-turkey-statement/

95 European Court of Justice, T-192/16, ECLI:EU:T:2017:128, judgment, 28 February 2017 – NF/European Council; European Court of Justice, T-193/16, ECLI:EU:T:2017:129, judgment, 28 February 2017 – NG/European Council; European Court of Justice, T-257/16, ECLI:EU:T:2017:130, judgment, 28 February 2017 – NM/European Council.

96 European Court of Justice, T-192/16, ECLI:EU:T:2017:128, judgment, 28 February 2017, para. 70 – NF/European Council.

97 Council of the EU, Press Release 144/16 (fn. 94).

bers of the European Council.[98] This approach was in substance confirmed in the appeals, albeit the Court, again, did not examine the application on its merits. In fact, the judges stated that no new elements had been brought by the appellants at the appeals stage and, therefore, no revision of the judgment challenged was possible.[99]

But the so called EU–Turkey Statement is only the most blatant example of the way in which potential violations of human rights can take place without having a clear legal basis to ascertain responsibility. Other instruments have been employed that, despite being referable to the EU, still do not take the form of international agreements but of informal, non-binding, deals such as the *Joint Way Forward on migration issues*, signed between the EU and Afghanistan in 2016,[100] which also demonstrates the increasingly extensive use of non-formal agreements to enhance the response against irregular migration especially in times of crisis.[101]

Human rights concerns remain. And, if doubts in terms of human rights protection have been raised in connection with the cooperation with Turkey, which has ratified the 1951 Geneva Convention and adopted its 1967 Protocol but still applies a geographical limitation to asylum seekers, even stronger concerns come up in connection with other partners, such as Libya, which has never ratified the 1951 Geneva Convention, let alone its 1967 Protocol,[102] but is still an important partner in regulating and handling migratory fluxes coming from the African continent.[103]

In this regard, again, the doubt on true coherence between external and internal action of the EU emerges. How can the EU be considered a reliable partner, if it is ready to give up inalienable protection and rights of

98 European Court of Justice, T-192/16, ECLI:EU:T:2017:128, judgment, 28 February 2017, paras. 68–69 – NF/European Council.

99 European Court of Justice, C-208/17 P, C-209/17 P, C-210/17 P, ECLI:EU:C:2018:705, Order of the Court, 12 September 2018, paras. 28–30 – NF, NG, NM/European Council.

100 Signed in Kabul on 2 October 2016 as a ten-page document dealing with joint commitments of the EU and Afghanistan on migration.

101 *Warin/Zhekova/Zheni*, The Joint Way forward on migration issued between Afghanistan and the EU: EU external policy and the recourse to non-binding law, Cambridge International Law Journal 6 (2017), 144.

102 Libya is a Party to the OAU Convention governing the specific aspects of refugee problems in Africa, adopted on 10 September 1969 and entered into force on 20 June 1974, which incorporates many principles of the 1951 Geneva Convention in its text.

103 A proof of this assumption is the deal reached by Italy and Libya and signed on 2 February 2017, available online.

individuals in a third country in exchange for help in protecting its interests?

IV. Concluding remarks

In dealing with migration and asylum, the EU has long searched for that "comprehensive" approach, often recalled in policy and legal instruments. Strenuous efforts have been made over the years and contribute to the creation of a long-term approach, one that cannot only try to find solutions in the immediate aftermath of a migration crisis, but also elaborate ways of dealing with migration in the long run. Such a comprehensive approach should serve as a basis for erasing the view that migration fluxes are to be dealt with as an emergency phenomenon and to understand migration as a long-lasting reality which not only is not going to end soon (human beings have always moved in search of better living conditions[104]), but is most likely to increase in the coming years. Climate change, desertification, floods and conflicts, as well as poverty are phenomena that can barely be limited, let alone erased in a few months. And, although flows may have lows and highs, migration is not destined to stop.

In the face of this situation, the EU has made considerable progress over the years, but still seems a long way from standing in unity, as the recent migration crisis has shown. Contemporary efforts (such as the temporary agreement reached among a few European countries on the relocation of migrants and asylum seekers[105]), seem to revive attempts of stronger cooperation among EU countries, but solidarity still has to "fight" against national interests which often prevail over shared responsibility for migration.[106]

However, if the agreement over reception and shared responsibilities for the management of migrants still sees division within the EU, a more shared terrain for agreement is external action and cooperation with third countries.

As we have seen, the treaties' provisions in this respect are clear: they provide an articulate legal basis that, coupled with secondary law instru-

104 *Cherubini*, Una valutazione complessiva dell'azione esterna dell'Unione europea per la lotta alla immigrazione irregolare, in: Cherubini (ed.) (fn. 81), 296.

105 See details on the proposal and the temporary agreement https://www.france24.com/en/20190924-malta-italy-migrants-ocean-viking-deal-distribution-dublin-regulation

106 Art. 80 TFEU.

ments and international agreements, creates the framework upon which external action on migration and asylum is built. Such a framework allows the burden of migration to be shared with other States, including neighbouring third States.

The treaties also make clear that cooperation with third countries must be carried out when the same principles (and values) are shared. However, many of the initiatives that the EU takes in the international scene raise human rights concerns and compatibility doubts with EU principles, especially when informal deals are adopted with countries whose human rights record is poor. While cooperation with third countries cannot be given up, it will be a responsibility of the EU and its Member States to really uphold the treaty provisions and to promote externally the same values whose implementation is a cornerstone inside the EU.

The External Dimension and the Management of Irregular Migration in the EU: A Human Rights Approach

Annalisa Morticelli[*]

I. Introduction

This chapter aims to illustrate and analyse with attention to the external dimension, the phenomenon of irregular migration within the European Union (EU) with reference to the protection of the human rights of this category of migrants.

The external dimension policy of European Union can be defined as the set of economic, legal, military, cultural, mainly extraterritorial actions carried out by state and supra-state entities, with the indispensable support of further public and private actors, aimed at preventing or to hinder, in the specific case, entrance to irregular migrants into the territory of a State in order to take advantage of the guarantees, also jurisdictional, provided for in that State.[1]

The external dimension is, therefore, a complex mechanism that sees the intervention of different actors who, while playing different roles, contribute to the achievement of the objectives set: the EU institutions, the individual Member States, some States not belonging to the European Union, the United Nations High Commissioner for Refugees (UNHCR) and the International Organisation for Migration (IOM).

The EU migration policies include an external dimension as migration flows come also from third countries and therefore a regulation and a management of this dimension is necessary to better afford this phenomenon. In relation to irregular migration, the EU adopted several legal

---

* PhD in EU Refugee Law (Universität Hamburg, 2020) and external researcher at LUMSA University.

1 *Frelick/Kysel/Podkul*, The Impact of Externalization of Migration Controls on the Rights of Asylum Seekers and Other Migrants, Journal on Migration and Human Security 4 (2016), Ed. Center for Migration Studies of New York, at the link http://jmhs.cmsny.org/index.php/jmhs/article/view/68. The definition given in the text takes into account the recent discussions and proposals for reform of the Common European Asylum System.

measures: agreement policies with third countries and a specific legislation that clearly regulates the external dimension are, therefore, needed.

In this context it is fundamental to maintain the centrality of the protection of human rights that must be guaranteed through a delicate and continuous balance with the security-oriented policy of the EU, an aspect that has played an important role until now in European policies. The EU should avoid the risk, in the context of its external dimension, of reducing its legal responsibility in the matter of protection of fundamental rights, in relation to the violations that take place in third countries of transit or origin.

Therefore, respect for international conventions and the adoption and correct application of the legislation of the European institutions in this sector are very important in order to guarantee the responsibility of the EU also in the case of its external dimension.

In the light of what is mentioned above, it is interesting to analyse which are the measures adopted by the EU on the topic of irregular migration in the context of external dimension and in particular how the protection of fundamental rights of these migrants fits into this framework.

In order to be able to analyse the aforementioned issue, after an analysis of the origin of the concept of irregular migration, a look at the tools adopted by the EU to regulate and protect the fundamental rights of irregular aliens within the EU, is necessary. The first part of this chapter analyses these measures such as the European Convention on Human Rights, The European Union Charter of Fundamental Rights, etc. Subsequently, an analysis will be conducted of the roots and definition of the category of irregular migrants within the European Union. Therefore, the Chapter will analyse the legal tools adopted by European Union institutions, in the framework of its external dimension, to manage the phenomenon in respect of these migrants' human rights, for instance the EU naval operations, the Return Directives, and so on. Lastly, some reflections on the analysis conducted in the Chapter will be carried out.

II. Irregularity and human rights: origins of the concept and main legal instruments of protection for migrants in an irregular position.

Human rights are universal, inalienable, egalitarian and indivisible. The Universal Declaration of Human Rights (UDHR) defines human rights as "basic rights and freedoms that all human beings are entitled to, without distinction of any kind, such as race, colour, sex, language, religion, political or other opinion, national or social origin, property birth or other status".[2] Nevertheless, migrants in an irregular situation are more likely to face discrimination, exclusion, exploitation and abuse at all stages of the migration process.

In 1948, the UDHR was adopted by the UN General Assembly. It was drafted in the aftermath of World War II as the first international human rights treaty for the benefit of mankind composed of a catalogue of rights. One of the most important principles set out is the principle of non-discrimination which is central to all important international human rights treaties and an exception to non-discrimination is only permissible if the differential treatment at stake pursues a legitimate aim, can objectively be justified and is proportionate to the aims sought to be achieved.[3]

In 1999, the Commission on Human Rights created the post of the UN Special Rapporteur on the Human Rights of Migrants. This post has the task of examining ways and means to overcome the obstacles to the full and effective protection of the human rights of this vulnerable group, including obstacles and difficulties for the return of migrants who are undocumented or in an irregular situation.[4] The conclusion of this Special Rapporteur has been "all persons should by virtue of their essential humanity enjoy all human rights unless exceptional distinctions, for example, between citizens and non-citizens, serve a legitimate State objective and are proportional to the achievement of that objective".[5] Moreover, a large gap has been indicated between the rights that international human rights law guarantees to non-citizens and the realities they must face as, in many countries, there are still institutional and endemic problems confronting non-citizens.[6]

In the framework of management of the phenomenon of irregular migration it is important to guarantee protection for the security of the European Union's borders from illegal entries on the one hand, and on the other it is important to guarantee the protection of these migrants' human

2 Art. 2 para. 1 of the Universal Declaration of Human Rights, UN General Assembly Resolution A/RES/217 (III) of 10 December 1948.

3 *Fitzpatrick*, The Human Rights of Migrants, in: Aleinikoff/Chetail (eds.), in: Migration and International Legal Norms, The Hague 2003, 171–172.

4 Commission on Human Rights Resolution 1999/44 on the Human Rights of Migrants of 26 April 1999, 55th session.

5 The mandate of the Special Rapporteur on the Human Rights of Migrants was created in 1999 by the Commission on Human Rights, pursuant to resolution 1999/44.

6 *Weissbrodt*, The Protection of Non-Citizens in International Human Rights Law, in Cholewinsky/Perruchoud/Macdonald (eds.), International Migration Law: Developing Paradigms and Key Challenges, The Hague 2007, 228–232.

rights, although, in the light of what is underlined above, their status is irregular. The greatest difficulty for the European Union is finding the right balance between the two aspects,[7] especially in the context of the external dimension.

The EU has been transformed into a supranational organisation that "is founded on the values of respect for human dignity, freedom, democracy, equality, the rule of law and respect for human rights ...".[8] As regards the issue of whether the EU could be regarded as a human rights organisation, A. von Bogdandy considered that "human rights, though important, should not be understood as the raison d'être of the Union".[9] S. Peers indi-

---

7 The EU has adopted some major pieces of legislation to manage the phenomenon of irregular immigration considering the security of the borders and the protection of human rights of irregular migrants (all legislations and their references will be better treated in this current Charter): the so-called "Facilitation Package" comprises Council Directive 2002/90/EC, OJ L 328, 5.12.2002, 17–18, setting out a common definition of the crime of facilitating unauthorised entry, transit and residence, and Framework Decision 2002/946/JHA, OJ L 328, 5.12.2002, 1–3, establishing criminal sanctions for this conduct. The package is complemented by Council Directive 2004/81/EC, OJ L 261, 6.8.2004, 19–23, providing for the granting of a residence permit to trafficked or smuggled persons who cooperate with the competent authorities (on trafficking, see also fact sheet on "Judicial cooperation in criminal matters" 4.2.6). In May 2015, the Commission adopted the EU Action Plan against migrant smuggling (COM (2015) 285 final). The "Return Directive", 2008/115/EC, OJ L 348, 24.12.2008, 98–107, sets out common EU standards and procedures for returning irregularly resident third-country nationals. The first report on its implementation was adopted in March 2014. In September 2015, the Commission published the EU action plan on return, which was followed by the adoption, in October 2015, of the Council conclusions on the future of the return policy. In March 2017, the Commission adopted a renewed action plan on a more effective return policy in the EU, and in September 2017, it published its updated "Return Handbook", OJ L 348, 24.12.2008, 98–107. The Directive 2009/52/EC, OJ L 168, 30.6.2009, 24–32, specifies sanctions and measures to be applied in Member States against employers of illegally resident third-country nationals. The first report on the implementation of the directive was submitted on 22 May 2014 (COM (2014) 286 final). At the same time, the EU is negotiating and concluding readmission agreements with countries of origin and transit with a view to returning irregular migrants and cooperating in the fight against trafficking in human beings. These agreements include reciprocal cooperation commitments between the EU and its third-country partners. For these agreements mentioned see p.79 footnote 221 of Chapter II.

8 *Von Bogdandy*, The European Union as a Human Rights Organization? Human Rights and the Core of the European Union, Common Market Law Review 37 (2000), 1307, 1338.

9 *Von Bogdandy*, Common Market Law Review 37 (2000) (fn. 8), 1307, 1338.

cated three principal sources of human rights protection in the EU legal framework: the European Convention on Human Rights (ECHR), the EU Charter and the general principles of EU law.[10]

The Council of Europe was founded in 1949 as an international organisation with the aim of promoting human rights, democracy, the rule of law, as well as cultural identity in Europe. It advocated its mission by composing norms and standards and opened them for signature to its members, and it became a major regional institution committed to fighting human rights violations. Among these, the most pivotal instrument is the European Convention on Human Rights (ECHR).[11] The signatory states of the Convention are 47,[12] including all 28 Member States of European Union.

The European Convention was not, *per se*, exceptional and innovative, as it was in many aspects similar to other international instruments on human rights but what was "extraordinary" was its "enforcement machinery",[13] which allowed its effective implementation through the possibility, granted either to a State or an individual, of filing a petition with the European Commission of Human Rights,[14] and with the subsequent establishment of an effective judicial authority of the European Court of Human Rights to adjudicate the cases brought before it.[15]

This important tool has as its scope of application to include *all persons within the jurisdiction* of the contracting parties, thus the Convention cov-

---

10 *Peers*, EU Justice and Home Affairs Law 3rd end, Oxford University Press, Oxford 2011, 96.

11 European Convention for the Protection of Human Rights and Fundamental Freedoms, 4 November 1950, CETS No. 5.

12 As indicated in http://conventions.coe.int/treaty/Commun/CherchSig.asp?NT=005&CM=&DF=&CL=ENG (accessed on 1 November 2013), as of 1 November 2013 the Member States were: Albania, Andorra, Armenia, Austria, Azerbaijan, Belgium, Bosnia and Herzgovina, Bulgaria, Croatia, Cyprus, Czech Republic, Denmark, Estonia, Finland, France, Georgia, Germany, Greece, Hungary, Iceland, Ireland, Italy, Latvia, Liechtenstein, Lithuania, Luxembourg, Malta, Moldova, Monaco, Montenegro, Netherlands, Norway, Poland, Portugal, Romania, Russia, San Marino, Serbia, Slovak Republik, Slovenia, Spain, Sweden, Switzerland, the former Yugoslav Republic of Macedonia, Turkey, Ukraine and the United Kingdom.

13 See, in these terms, *Janis/Kay/Bradley*, European Rights Law, Text and Materials, 3rd edition, Oxford.

14 The Commission was given the right to hear complaints submitted by individuals in 1955, with the consent of the interested State.

15 With Protocol No. 11 to the Convention, a permanent European Court of Human Rights was established.

ers citizens and non-citizens alike, among which also irregular migrants[16]. Closer scrutiny of the Convention has proven that only a limited set of basic rights is guaranteed to everyone under the convention, notwithstanding the impression that the ECHR conveys of being an inclusive and all-embrancing agreement.

Drzemczewski[17] said "in reality it must be admitted that the classical approach of distinguishing between aliens and nationals continues to exist ... after all, it is not difficult to draft provisions, which are noble, objective and non-discriminatory in purpose and yet whose practical effect is at times quite marginal". The non-derogable rights relate *inter alia* to the right of life (Article 2 ECHR), as well as the prohibition of torture, slavery and servitude (Articles 3 and 4(1) ECHR).[18] Some provisions explicitly concern non-nationals: for instance, concerning irregular migrants, state parties may derogate from the right to liberty in cases where the lawful arrest or detention shall either prevent unauthorised entry into the country, or shall ensure the capture of a person against whom action is being taken with a view to deportation or extradition.[19]

Moreover, Article 1 of Protocol No. 7 determines procedural safeguards relating to the expulsion of illegally staying aliens, and Article 4 of Protocol No. 4 prohibits the collective expulsion of aliens. Article 16 ECHR expressly permits the contracting parties to impose restrictions on the political activity of aliens; nothing in Article 10, 11 and 14 ECHR shall be interpreted otherwise in this respect.[20]

A. Wiesbork argued that the most important rights of the ECHR concerning the treatment of foreigners are Article 8 on the right to family life, Article 9 on the freedom of thought, conscience and religion and Article

---

16 See Art. 1 ECHR on the notion of "jurisdiction" under Art. 1 ECHR, see *M. Gondek*, Extraterritorial Application of The European Convention on Human Rights: Territorial Focus in the Age of Globalization?, Netherlands International Law Review 52 (2005), 3.

17 *Drzemcewski*, The Position of Aliens in Relation to the European Convention of Human Rights: a General Survey, in: Council of Europe (ed.), Human Rights of Aliens in Europe, Dordrecht 1985, 351–399.

18 See Art. 15 ECHR on derogation in time of emergency.

19 Art. 5 para. 1 (f) ECHR.

20 *Eisele*, The External Dimension of the EU's Migration Policy. Different Legal Position of Third-Country Nationals, in the EU: A Comparative Perspective, [in: Guild/Mitsilegas (eds.), Immigration and Asylum Law and Policy in Europe,] Leiden 2014.

14 on the principle of non-discrimination.[21] These rights are related to fundamental aspects of the life of the person: and they are very important for a foreigner because their correct exercise contributes significantly to the integration of the person in the new country.

Concerning Article 14 mentioned above, it provides one of the most relevant principles in the issue of protection of human rights of irregular migrants: the prohibition of discrimination. The Article specifically provides that "the enjoyment of the rights and freedoms set forth in this Convention shall be secured without discrimination on any ground such as sex, race, colour, language, religion, political or other opinion, national or social origin, association with a national minority, property, birth or other status". This provision is not a free-standing provision in that it cannot be invoked alone but applies only in combination with other rights protected under the Convention. However, it does not presuppose the breach of such rights.[22]

Protocol No. 12 covers the same, non-exhaustive, grounds as listed in Article 14 ECHR in respect of the enjoyment of any right set forth by law.[23]

In 2009 the European Union recognised, under the Treaty of Lisbon, the rights, freedoms and principles set out in the EU Charter of Fundamental Rights (EU Charter) which considerably adds to the fundamental rights protection in the EU.[24] The EU Charter acknowledges that the Union is founded on the indivisible, universal values of human dignity, freedom, equality and solidarity and that it is based on the principles of

---

21 *Wiesbrok*, Legal Migration to the European Union, Leiden 2010, 209–210; as right of potential relevance for migrants the author indicates: the freedom to move within a state (Art. 2 para. 1 of Protocol No. 4); the freedom to leave a state (Art. 2 para. 2 of Protocol No. 4); the prohibition of expulsion of nationals (Art. 3 para. 1 of Protocol No. 4); the right to enter the territory of one's own state (Art. 3 para. 2 of Protocol No. 4); the procedural rights for lawful residents as regards expulsion (Art. 1 of Protocol No. 7).

22 ECtHR, *Van Raalte v. The Netherlands*, Appl. No. 20060/92, judgment, 2 February 1997, 24 EHRR 503, para 33.

23 The expression "any right set forth by law" relates to any legal right recognised in domestic or international law and to the acts or omissions of public authorities. Thus, Protocol No. 12 provides greater protection than Art. 14 ECHR which aims to ensure equal treatment within the ambit of rights contained in the Convention only.

24 Charter of Fundamental Rights of the European Union, *OJ C* 83, 30 March 2010, 389.

democracy and the rule of law.[25] This legal tool is applicable also for irregular migrants.

Another important legal tool for the protection of irregular migrants within the European Union is The European Social Charter and irregular migration. It was drafted in 1961 under the auspices of the Council of Europe as a counterpart to the International Covenant on Economic, Social and Cultural Rights (ICESCR) of the UN framework to guarantee social and economic human rights in Europe and it entered into force in 1965.[26]

The revised European Social Charter (ESC) introduced a general prohibition of discrimination in its Article E laying down that "The enjoyment of the rights set forth in this Charter shall be secured without discrimination on any ground such as race, colour, sex, language, religion, political or other opinion, national extraction or social origin, health, association with a national minority, birth or other status". Therefore, it means that the Charter is valid also for irregular migrants.

However, the ESC´s most significant contribution to protecting irregular migrants derives from its vibrant case law. For instance, in the *IFHR (International Federation of Human Rights) vs France* (complaint No. 14/2003, decision of 8 September 2004) the European Committee on Social Rights held "that legislation or practice which denies entitlement to medical assistance to foreign nationals, within the territory of a State Party, even if they are there illegally, is contrary to the Charter". The decision of this case represents the importance of the correct application of this right and its application which must be guaranteed to everybody independently from their status.

Finally, there is another important Convention to mention, The European Convention for the Prevention of torture and inhuman or degrading treatment or punishment which is applicable to irregular migrants in some contexts (especially in terms of their detention on arrival, during their stay or in preparation for their expulsion from the country) and The Convention on Action against Trafficking in Human Beings (ETS 197) makes an important contribution to the protection of a particularly vulnerable group, among irregular migrants as well.

25 See Recital 2 of the Preamble to the EU Charter.

26 European Social Charter CETS No. 035 of 18 October 1961/CETS No. 163 of 3 May 1995 (revised); *Harris*, A Fresh Impetus for the European Social Charter, International and Comparative Law Quarterly 41 (1992), 659.

III. *Irregular migration: roots and definition of this category in the European Union.*

Irregular migration has become an issue to be found worldwide in policies as diverse as trade agreements, development policies, military strategies and international relations.

The concept of "irregular migration" is a legal, political and social construct of the twentieth century, which has only gained prominence during the latter third of that century. It is a blurred concept, loaded with ideological import and highly politicised.[27]

Preliminarily, it is important to underline that while legal systems and most public discourses usually adopt the concept of illegality in referring to this phenomenon, employing such terms as "illegal immigrants" or, in shorter form "illegal", the social sciences prefer to refer to "undocumented" or "irregular" immigrants. This is done to avoid any discriminatory connotation, to prevent further criminalisation and to emphasise that it is not the immigrant as a human being who is illegal but his or her mode of entry and stay or work.

Irregular migration came for the first time into discussion at an EU level in 1976, when the European Commission presented a proposal for a directive on the harmonisation of laws in EU Member States in order to combat irregular migration and illegal employment.

Irregular migration as a phenomenon, was neglected by the literature until the 1990s. As highlighted by Portes and De Genova,[28] irregular migration has, for a long time, been approached as a problem, leading research to adopt a policy perspective and envisage solutions. Since the 1990s, researchers have tried to adopt a more comprehensive perspective.

The birth of the idea of "irregular immigrants" can be associated with the emergence of the post-First World War modern nation-state. Thus, it was determined less by increasing migration than by the political processes of nation building. These processes defined the extent of the state's territory, its national borders, national space, and so nationality and membership were reconstructed and deserving and undeserving individuals defined and members created.

It is relevant when talking about irregular migrants at European level, to classify these migrants according to the European Union (EU) legisla-

---

27 *Düvell*, Illegal immigration in Europe. Beyond control?, London 2006.

28 *Portes*, Illegal immigration and the international system: lessons from recent legal Mexican immigrants to the United States, Social Problems 26 (1979), 425–443.

tion. There is a lack of a precise definition of irregular migrants or the status of irregularity at European Union level. There is just a definition of "illegal stay" provided by Directive 2008/115/EC, better known as the Return Directive. First of all, the Treaty on the functioning of the European Union, in Article 20, 1 paragraph (ex Article 17 of TEC) states that "... Every person holding the nationality of a Member State shall be a citizen of the Union. Citizenship of the Union shall be additional to and not replace national citizenship".

In the Schengen Code, Article 2, (5) outlines who are persons enjoying the Union right of free movement:

> "(a) Union citizens within the meaning of Article 20(1) TFEU, and third-country nationals who are members of the family of a Union citizen exercising his or her right to free movement to whom Directive 2004/38/EC of the European Parliament and of the Council[29] applies; (b) third-country nationals and their family members, whatever their nationality, who, under agreements between the Union and its Member States, on the one hand, and those third countries, on the other hand, enjoy rights of free movement equivalent to those of Union citizens".[30]

For completeness, in the Schengen Code, in paragraph 6 of Article 2, there is a definition of third-country national: "'third-country national' means any person who is not a Union citizen within the meaning of Article 20(1) TFEU and who is not covered by point 5 of this Article".

Moreover, paragraph 7 outlines "'persons for whom an alert has been issued for the purposes of refusing entry' means any third-country national for whom an alert has been issued in the Schengen Information System (SIS) in accordance with and for the purposes laid down in Articles 24 and 26 of Regulation (EC) No. 1987/2006 of the European Parliament and of

---

29 Directive 2004/38/EC of the European Parliament and of the Council of 29 April 2004 on the right of citizens of the Union and their family members to move and reside freely within the territory of the Member States amending Regulation (EEC) No. 1612/68 and repealing Directives 64/221/EEC, 68/360/EEC, 72/194/EEC, 73/148/EEC, 75/34/EEC, 75/35/EEC, 90/364/EEC, 90/365/EEC and 93/96/EEC (OJ L 158, 30.4.2004, 77).

30 Regulation (EU) No. 2016/399 of the European Parliament and of the Council of 9 March 2016 on a Union Code on the Rules governing the movement of persons across borders (Schengen Borders Code), OJ L 77, 23.3.2016, 1-52 (which repealed and replaced the Regulation (EC) No. 562/2006).

the Council",[31] "persons for whom an alert has been issued for the purposes of refusing entry" as any third-country national for whom an alert has been issued in the Schengen Information System (SIS) in accordance with and for the purposes laid down in Article 96 of the Schengen Convention.

Finally, Directive 2008/115/EC[32] on common standards and procedures in Member States for returning illegally staying third-country nationals, offers a positive definition of "illegal stay": "... means the presence on the territory of a Member State, of a third-country national who does not fulfil, or no longer fulfils the conditions of entry as set out in Article 5 of the Schengen Borders Code or other conditions for entry, stay or residence in that Member State".

Therefore, an "irregular migrant" is a migrant who, at some point in his migration, has contravened the rules of entry or residence. The term "irregular" is widely understood as a very broad concept and can refer to both stocks and flows of migrants.[33]

There are many adjectives – "irregular", "illegal", "undocumented", "unauthorised" or "clandestine" – which are combined with the nouns "migrants", "immigrants", "aliens" or "foreign nationals"; while expressions like "sans-papiers" and "clandestinos" have acquired an international use.[34]

The derived expression "illegal migrants" is considered demeaning and discriminatory by human rights advocates, since "no human being is illegal". Technically, the term in question designates the act of entering a country in violation of national law and is confined to illegal border crossing, referring only to a flow and not to a stock of persons.

Another term frequently used with the meaning of "irregular migrant" described above, is "undocumented migrant". It has the implicit meaning of a migrant who is not in possession of the required residence papers. It

31 Regulation (EC) No. 1987/2006 of the European Parliament and of the Council of 20 December 2006 on the establishment, operation and use of the second generation Schengen Information System (SIS II) (OJ L 381, 28 .12.2006, 4).

32 Directive 2008/115/EC of the European Parliament and of the Council of 16 December 2008 on common standards and procedures in Member States for returning illegally staying third-country nationals.

33 *Tryandafyllidou*, Irregular migration in Europe: myths and realities, Farnham 2010; *Koser*, Irregular Migration, State Security and Human Security, paper prepared for the policy analysis and research programme of the Global Commission for International Migration, September 2005.

34 The discussion of terminology is based on the *Clandestino* Project Research: Report on Methodological Issues, edited by *Kraler/Vogel* and prepared by *Jandl/Vogel/Iglicka*, in November 2008.

refers to people who enter or stay in a country without legal authorisation. Of course, not everyone residing in a state that is not his own needs explicit authorisation to do so as, for example, in the case of an EU national who has free movement rights within the EU, and it is necessary to interpret "unauthorised" as not authorised according to the law.[35]

There are certain groups of people that have shifted status during the last few years, as well as some people who are in possession of residence documents but not of the correct documents justifying their stay.[36]

The category of irregular migrants includes not only undocumented people but also people who are in possession of forged papers or people who have assumed false identities with real papers. They may live the life of a regular migrant unless they are discovered by the authorities.[37] It also includes the migrant who is "tolerated" on the State's territory: technically, toleration is a suspension of an expulsion order and not in itself a legal status. Toleration does not have a legalising effect and does not change the unlawful presence of the tolerated alien. An example of that is the category of *duldung* in Germany.

IV. European Union legislation on irregular migration: management of the phenomenon.

The trend of migratory flows towards the Member States facing the Mediterranean has gradually decreased, passing – according to data provided by the UNHCR – from about 363 thousand in 2016, to 172 thousand in 2017, to over 139 thousand in 2018 (of which 25 thousand arrived by land: about seven thousand in Spain and 18 thousand in Greece).[38] In the first two months of 2019, total landings in the EU amounted to over 8,500, of

35 *Triandafyllidou*, Irregular migration in Europe: myths and realities, Farnham 2010.

36 *Triandafyllidou*, Irregular migration in Europe: myths and realities, Farnham 2010.

37 In the Netherlands, persons without a residence status working in regular tax-paying jobs are called "white illegal". Their life may be very similar to the life of legal residents and citizens, involving regular jobs and free movement in the public sphere, or it can be similar to the life of migrants without any status. If the quality of the papers is so poor that the migrant does not dare to show them anywhere, these papers are not much different from having no papers at all.

38 European Union policies on migration matters, dossier documentation for the activity Assembly of the European Union, Italian Senate of the Republic and Italian Chamber of Deputies, 4 March 2019.

which 260 in Italy, 3,300 in Greece, and about 5,000 in Spain; to these data must be added about 900 land arrivals in Spain and 1,500 in Greece.[39]

The measures originally contained in the European Agenda on Migration and the subsequent initiatives that represent its coherent development are inspired by the so-called "Global Approach to Migration", which consists of a combination of instruments that concern: actions within the internal dimension of the migration policy; activities at the EU's external borders, strengthening external action.[40] This approach has been constantly reaffirmed in the recent key passages more relevant to the Union's policy in this sector, in particular, in the conclusions of the European Councils, which in 2018 addressed the issue of the migration crisis in priority.

The European Union has adopted various regulatory instruments to counter the phenomenon of irregular immigration. Following an examination in particular of the tools applied in relation to the external dimension, a contextual will be provided below.

Irregular migrants, in all aspects of their life, as human beings, have the right to see their fundamental rights protected. However, as already explained, because of the lack of a legal status recognised by States, they have serious difficulties asserting their rights and in particular this is evident in the phase of entry into a State.

Indeed, this is a very delicate and difficult phase in which their rights often collide with the interests and policies of the European Union States of destination. The analysis of the level and effectiveness of protection of this category of migrants in this phase is very relevant and currently also widely discussed at European Union level as a result of serious incidents of violations of human rights.[41]

There are various migratory routes into Europe: the main ones are Eastern Mediterranean, Western Mediterranean and Central Mediterranean.

---

39 European Union policies on migration matters, dossier documentation for the activity Assembly of the European Union, Italian Senate of the Republic and Italian Chamber of Deputies, 4 March 2019.

40 European Commission, Communication COM (2015) 0240 final, Communication from the Commission to the European Parliament, the Council, the European Economic and Social Committee and the Committee of the regions: A European Agenda on Migration.

41 *Savino*, La crisi migratoria tra Italia e Unione Europea: diagnosi e prospettive, Naples 2017; *Klein*, Maritime Security and the Law of the Sea, Oxford 2011, 75; *Y. Tanaka*, The International Law of the Sea, Cambridge 2012, 85; *Monzini*, Il Traffico di Migranti per via marittima, cit. 45; *Fischer-Lescano/Tillman/Tohidipur*, Border Controls at Sea: Requirements under International Human Rights and Refugee Law, International Journal of Refugee Law 21 (2009), 290.

The individual migratory routes are used for different reasons and trends change constantly.

In its analysis of the Eastern Mediterranean route, FRONTEX noted that people smuggling has become an important industry in Turkey, with networks active around Istanbul, Izmir, Edirne and Ankara.[42] The vast majority of migrants on this route arrived in the EU at one of the Greek islands in the Aegean. The nationalities of facilitators vary, though they frequently mirror the nationality of their customers. The Central Mediterranean route is used by smuggler networks established in Libya, from where they cross the Mediterranean Sea.[43] The sea is usually crossed in old, often unseaworthy, fishing boats or small rubber dinghies, usually with insufficient fuel and without proper navigation systems. In 2015 there were various fatal accidents resulting in considerable loss of life.[44] The destination on this particular route is usually Malta or Italy (Lampedusa or Sicily). The Western African route is, according to FRONTEX, one of the least developed migration/smuggling routes.[45] It runs from Northern/Western Africa to the Canary Islands.

In this frame, it is important to underline the existence of the Protocol against smuggling of migrants by land, air and sea[46] attached to the United Nations Convention against transnational organised crime.[47] Indeed, another relevant aspect related to irregular migration is that, more and more often, the migrant transport organisation from the country of origin to the one of the Member State, or from a transit country to the Member States, is run by criminal organisations. Thus, the fight against irregular migra-

42 European Parliament, Briefing, Implementation Appraisal, (2016), Combatting migrant smuggling into the EU. This briefing is one in a series of "Implementation Appraisals" on the operation of existing EU legislation in practice.

43 European Parliament, Briefing, Implementation Appraisal, (2016), Combatting migrant smuggling into the EU. This briefing is one in a series of "Implementation Appraisals" on the operation of existing EU legislation in practice.

44 European Parliament, Briefing, Implementation Appraisal, (2016), Combatting migrant smuggling into the EU. This briefing is one in a series of "Implementation Appraisals" on the operation of existing EU legislation in practice.

45 European Parliament, Briefing, Implementation Appraisal, (2016), Combatting migrant smuggling into the EU. This briefing is one in a series of "Implementation Appraisals" on the operation of existing EU legislation in practice.

46 The Protocol was approved on behalf of the EU by Council Decision 2006/616 and by Council Decision 2006/617.

47 See *Conforti*, in: Carta (ed.), Immigrazione, Frontiere Esterne e Diritti Umani, Roma 2009.

tion often has the characteristics of the fight against organised crime.[48] Migrants become subjects of exchange for these organisations and therefore can be considered as victims of organised criminal activity.

The Protocol imposes more far-reaching obligations (Art. 10), because it has as its object all practices connected to irregular migration, also previous to the transport, with particular attention to the methods to use in order to recognise false travel identity documents.

Other important provisions are those which guarantee protection of the migrants' human rights. They are intended to guarantee their life and the right not to be subjected to torture in the country of destination but also prohibit them being subjected to any cruel, inhuman or degrading treatment, and to ensure adequate protection from each form of violence (Art. 16, para. 1, 2, 3 and 5). Special mention was made for the special needs of children and women (Art. 16, para. 4).

The Protocol also provides specific norms on the irregular migrants (Art. 18). The obligation of receiving the irregular migrant is of the country of origin or of the state where the migrant has title to reside permanently. The States of origin allow the state of receiving to return the migrant: for the realisation of that they are obliged to guarantee all information on the identity of the migrant and issue the travel documents and the transport necessary to consent the return on their territory.[49]

The mechanism of contrast of irregular flow by sea mentioned above has had an important impact, under the profile of protection of human life on the sea and humanitarian protection of irregular migrants. It increased the risks run by the criminal organisation in determining major caution with respect to the action of contrast to the unification in public services which act on the sea.

According to Europol, over 90% of the more than one million irregular migrants entering the EU in 2015 used some form of "facilitation service" which was generally provided by smuggling networks.[50] Often, migrants are forced to work illegally throughout their journey to pay off their debts

---

48 *Mitzman*, Il rimpatrio dei migranti irregolari, in: M. Savino (ed.), La crisi migratoria tra Italia e Unione Europea: diagnosi e prospettive, Editoriale Scientifica, Naples 2017.

49 Protocol against the Smuggling of Migrants by Land, Sea and Air, supplementing the United Nations Convention against Transnational Organized Crime, United Nation, New York 2004.

50 *Europol*, study: Migrant Smuggling in the EU, February 2016.

to the smugglers.[51] With this Protocol the scope is to reduce the risk of smuggling and thus, consequently, the risk of violation of the above-mentioned irregular migrants' human rights.

To support the Member States most exposed to migratory flows, the EU, especially after the resumption of landings starting in 2015, reinforced the action of surveillance of the external borders, which resulted in missions dictated also by humanitarian concerns, in order to save human lives at sea.

Currently there are four operations in the Mediterranean: the Poseidon, Themis and Indalo missions of the European Border Guard and Coastal Agency (Frontex) respectively with Greece, Italy and Spain; and the operation EUNAVFOR MED Sophia in the context of the common security and defence policy.[52]

The military naval mission EUNAVFOR MED Sophia, aimed at contributing to the dismantling of migrant trafficking networks and trafficking in human beings in the south-central Mediterranean was launched with the EU Council decision of 22 June 2015.

The mission is carried out by adopting systematic measures to identify, stop and destroy boats and used vehicles suspected of being used by smugglers or traffickers, in accordance with applicable international law, including UNCLOS and UN Security Council resolutions. The mandate of the operation has been extended several times, most recently by the EU Council of 21 December 2018, until 31 March 2019. The operation after this latter date was extended, however, on the condition that it uses only air assets and this aspect has raised criticisms because the operation will not be able to effectively implement the function of rescuing life, and thereby guaran-

---

51 *Connel Davidson*, Troubling freedom: Migration, debt, and modern slavery, Migration Studies 1 (2013), 176–195.

52 From February 2018, operation Themis (within Frontex) replaced the previous Triton mission. It operates in the central Mediterranean, assisting Italy with particular regard to the flow of migrants from Algeria, Tunisia, Libya, Egypt, Turkey and Albania. Compared to the previous mission launched in 2014, Themis has a broader mandate: the operation continues to deal with the search and rescue of migrants at sea but, at the same time, has a reinforced focus on law enforcement activities (contrast this with drug and arms trafficking, illegal fishing and so on), including intelligence activities and other measures aimed at identifying terrorist threats (with particular regard to the phenomenon of foreign fighters) at the external borders. The Italian government has announced that the most important novelty in replacing the mission concerns the fact that the rescued migrants must be landed in the port closest to the point where the rescue was carried out.

tee the protection of fundamental rights such as the right of life of the migrants who arrive through this path, namely, irregular migrants.

Indeed, the main problematic aspect in the framework of the EU maritime operations described above seems to be the lack of protection of the human rights of the migrants, most of whom are irregular, within the operations. Indeed, the previously described operations are deployed with a security approach which has the main purpose of surveying borders and detecting irregular entry.

On the face of it, the issue is complicated, considering the complex framework and high number of actors who are involved in controlling maritime borders. There is a complex judicial framework of international legislation regarding sea rescue, which it is important to mention: the 1974 International Convention on the Safety of Life at Sea (SOLAS); the 1979 International Maritime Search and Rescue Convention (SAR); and the 1982 United Nations Convention on the Law of the Sea (UNCLOS).

Art. 98, para. 1 (obligation to provide assistance) of UNCLOS and Chapter V, Regulation 33 (distress situation: obligation and procedures), paragraph 1 of the SOLAS, state that every State shall require of the master of a ship flying its flag the rescue of people in danger without any distinction of status or nationality and it must also guarantee assistance until disembarkation in the nearest place of safety. With the SAR Convention, the seas were divided into research and rescue areas. With the formation of research and coordination centres, the identified sea areas fall under the responsibility of the coastal state and are subject to the control and power of that state.

In 2012 to combat the lack of human rights protection, the independent position of FRONTEX Fundamental Rights Officer (FRO) was created. The FRO' s role is to monitor, assess and make recommendations on the protection and guarantees of fundamental rights in all FRONTEX activities and operations. On a similar note, the European Ombudsman, Emily O'Reilly, announced on 22 October 2014 that her office has opened an investigation into how FRONTEX ensures respect of fundamental rights in the context of forced returns under the agency's joint return operations (JROs).

The inquiry also looks at FRONTEX's cooperation with national monitoring bodies as per Article 9(1b) of the FRONTEX Regulation[53] and Arti-

53 Regulation (EC) No. 2007/2004 of 26 October 2004, O.J.L. 349, 25 November 2004, 1-11.

cle 8(6) of the Return Directive.[54] Ms O'Reilly highlighted that "by their very nature, forced return operations have the potential to involve serious violations of fundamental rights. Through this investigation, I want to find out how FRONTEX is equipped to deal with potential violations and how it minimises the risk of such violations."[55]

Whether and under what circumstances a state that is party to a particular human rights treaty (or under a customary law obligation) owes legal obligations under that treaty (or customary rule) to a person who is not within the territory of that State is a difficult question and in many respects the critical issue for the international law on migrant smuggling.

Commentators have identified the growing shift towards extraterritorial immigration control as motivated largely by a desire to avoid the substantive and procedural guarantees to which migrants, including those who have been smuggled, are entitled.[56] Even if this does not hold true for all smuggling-related interventions at sea, it is clearly essential to examine whether States are indeed able to shift or minimise their obligations in this way and, if so, under what circumstances. International human rights treaties generally specify their scope of application as extending to every person within their territory and/or under their jurisdiction.[57]

The notion of being under the jurisdiction of a State has been interpreted by the Human Rights Committee in connection with the International Covenant on Civil and Political Rights (ICCPR) as meaning that a State Party must respect and ensure the rights laid down in the Covenant to anyone within its *de facto* jurisdiction, that is, persons who are "within the power or effective control of that State Party, even if not situated within the territory of the State Party".[58] It further confirmed that enjoyment of Covenant rights is not limited to citizens of States Parties but must also be available to all individuals, regardless of nationality or statelessness, such as asylum seekers, refugees, migrant workers and other persons, who may

---

54 Directive 2008/115/EC, 16 December 2008, O.J.L. 348, 24 December 2008, 98-107.

55 European Ombudsman, Press release No. 20/2014, 22 October 2014.

56 See generally *Ryan*, Extraterritorial Immigration Control: What Role for Legal Guarantees?, in: Ryan/Mitsleagas (eds.), Extraterritorial Immigration Control: Legal Challenges, Leiden 2010.

57 For instance International Covenant on Civil and Political Rights, 999 UNTs 171, adopted 16 December 1996, entered into force 23 March 1976 (ICCPR), at Art. 2 para. 1; Convention against Torture and Other Cruel, Inhuman or Degrading Treatment or Punishment, 1465 UNTS 85, adopted 10 December 1984, entered into force 26 June 1987, at Art. 2.

58 UN Human Rights.

find themselves in the territory or subject to the jurisdiction of the State Party. This, therefore, applies to irregular migrants.

Although not explicitly adopting the "power and control" test,[59] the International Court of Justice has generally affirmed that provisions of human rights treaties will apply to actions of a State outside its territory even where the terms of the treaty do not envisage such extraterritorial application.[60]

At regional level, the most substantial jurisprudence has emerged from consideration of the scope of application of the European Convention on Human Rights. The starting point is an acceptance of the essentially territorial nature of this instrument and a corresponding reluctance to interpret the Convention as being applicable to all State Party conduct everywhere. The focus has accordingly been on establishing the parameters of exceptions. Although earlier cases of the European Court of Human Rights emphasised effective control over territory,[61] judgments have moved towards recognition of the exercise of power and authority over individuals as sufficient to establish jurisdiction.[62]

One case, involving scenarios of relevance to the issue of smuggling by sea, deserves brief mention: in the 2012 case of *Hirsi Jamaa v. Italy* (high seas interception and push-back to Libya of smuggled Somalia and Eritrean nationals by the Italian coast guard), the Court found that Italy had exercised both *de jure* and *de facto* jurisdiction over the applicant, specifically stating its view that "The removal of aliens carried out in the context of interceptions on the high seas by the authorities of a State in the exercise of their sovereign authority, the effect of which is to prevent migrants from

59 *Gallagher/David*, The international law of migrant smuggling, Cambridge 2014.

60 Legal Consequences of the Construction of a Wall in the Occupied Palestinian Territory (Advisory Opinion), 2004, ICJ Rep 136 (Israeli Wall Advisory Opinion), at para. 111. See also Armed Activities on the Territory of the Congo (Democratic Republic of the Congo v. Uganda), (2005) ICJ Rep 168, para. 216.

61 Most famously ECtHR, *Bankovic and Others v. Belgium and Others*, Appl. No. 52207/99, judgment, 12 December 2001, 44 EHRR SE5. For further analysis of this case references to the extensive and largely critical literature.

62 Most recently by the European Court of Human Rights in ECtHR, *Al-Skeini and Others v. United Kingdom*, Appl. No. 55721/07, judgment, 7 July 2011, 53 EHRR 18; ECtHR, *Al-Jedda v. United Kingdom*, Appl. No. 27021/08, judgment, 7 July 2011, 53 EHRR 23. For earlier examples of the same approach see ECtHR, *Ilascu and Others v. Moldova and Russia*, Appl. No. 48787/99, judgment, 8 July 2004, 40 EHRR 46, paras. 312, 314; and ECtHR, *Issa and Others v. Turkey*, Appl. No. 31821/96, judgment, 30 March 2005, 41 EHRR 27, para. 71.

reaching the borders of the State or even to push them back to another State, constitutes an exercise of jurisdiction…".[63]

The Court held that Italy's actions violated fundamental rights, including the prohibition on torture and inhuman or degrading treatment or punishment and the prohibition of collective expulsion of non-nationals, despite the relevant actions occurring outside Italy's territory. Critically, the fact that this was billed as a search and rescue operation, that the Italian authorities had not boarded the vessels, and that they had not used weapons, did not affect the Court's judgment on the point of jurisdiction and extraterritorial application of the European Convention on Human Rights. The ruling does appear to be, in the words of one commentator "a resounding endorsement of the responsibility of States for their migration control activities at sea".[64]

It is reasonable to argue that extraterritorial human rights obligations will arise "when a State exercises control, power or authority over people or situations located outside its sovereign territory in a way that could have an impact on the enjoyment of human rights by those people or in such situation".[65] There can be little doubt that interception or rescue of a migrant smuggling vessel on the high seas or in the territory of another State, which involves conduct such as boarding the vessel, altering its course, or detaining persons on board fall within this "power, control or authority" test.[66]

This leaves unanswered the question of whether States owe extraterritorial human rights obligations to smuggled migrants at sea who are not intercepted or rescued.

The right to life, recognised in all major human rights instruments, extends to all persons, including those who are smuggled by sea and their smugglers, irrespective of legal status, nationality, conduct, or any other consideration.[67] The Migrant Smuggling Protocol makes explicit reference to the international legal obligation on States to preserve and protect the

63 ECtHR, *Hirsi Jamaa v. Italy*, Appl. No. 27765/09, judgment, 23/02/2012, para. 180.

64 *Costello*, Courting Access to Asylum in Europe: Recent Supranational Jurisprudence Explored, Human Rights Law Review 12 (2012), 287, 300.

65 *De Schutter/Eide/Khalfan/Orellana/Salomon/Seiderman*, Commentary to the Maastricht Principles on Extraterritorial Obligations of States in the Area of Economic, Social and Cultural Rights, Human Rights Quarterly 34 (2013), 1084, 1090.

66 *Gallagher/David*, The international law of migrant smuggling, Cambridge 2014.

67 See, as example, ICCPR, at Art. 6 para. 1: "Every human being has the inherent right to life".

right to life of smuggled migrants.[68] Coercive actions that threaten or result in loss of life whether deliberate (such as the pushback of an unseaworthy vessel) or accidental (such as occurred in the situation that was the subject of the Xhavara case[69]) would appear to be in violation of the positive obligations attached to the right to life.[70] Intentional failure of a State to come to the rescue of smuggled migrants or migrant smuggling vessels that are in distress, would also constitute a clear violation of this core human rights obligation.

The case analysed above, *Hirsi Jamaa v. Italy*, shows how the EU Member States must assume their legal responsibility for the protection of human rights of irregular migrants, even outside national and European borders, as ruled, in the specific case, by the European Court of human rights.

The European Union seems to be more focused on the application of a security-oriented policy. Indeed, as part of the strengthening of border management, this recalls the reform of the legal framework of Frontex, with which, in addition to the change of name (to the European Border and Coast Guard Agency), the body was given the rank of European Agency and its mandate was strengthened in the sense of reinforcing its role.

The European Commission has recently proposed an additional strengthening of the role of the Agency, in particular through the establishment of a permanent body of up to ten thousand border guards by 2020 (a term that the EU Council would extend to 2027), consisting of long-term or short-term operational personnel from Frontex and Member States, as well as reinforcing its mandate through greater powers by way of efforts to strengthen cooperation with third-party states and activities to repatriate irregular migrants[71].

---

68 Migrant Smuggling Protocol, Art. 16 para. 1: "*In implementing this Protool, each States Party shall take, consistent with its obligations under international law, all appropriate measures, including legislation if necessary, to preserve and protect the rights of persons who have been the object of conduct set forth in article 6 of this Protocol as accorded under applicable international law, in particular the right to life and the right not to be subjected to torture or other cruel, inhuman or degrading treatment or punishment* ".

69 European Court of Justice, C 424/01, ECLI:CE:ECHR:2001:0111DEC003947398, judgment, 11 January 2001.

70 For a consideration of State obligations to take positive measures to ensure the right to life, see *Nowak*, U.N. Covenant on Civil and Political Rights – CCPR Commentary, 2nd edition, Kehl 2005, 122-124.

71 European Commission COM (2018) 631 final, which would replace the regulation establishing the aforementioned Agency.

Member States will continue to have primary responsibility for managing their own borders, while the Agency and its staff will provide technical and operational assistance, subject to the agreement of the Member States concerned. It is also envisaged that the personnel of the permanent corps sent to a Member State may exercise, subject to prior authorisation by the host Member State, certain executive powers relating to the execution of border control or repatriation tasks, including the use of force or weapons.

Lastly, the EU has adopted a series of systems aimed at making the management of the EU external borders more efficient:

- The European Travel Information and Authorisation System (ETIAS), which screens travellers who are exempt from the visa requirement, for the purposes of security and the fight against irregular migration;
- The visa information system;
- The recently upgraded Schengen information system incorporating the databases of EU countries most used by law enforcement authorities and border authorities;
- The Entry/Exit System (EES), which records name, travel documents and data biometrics, among other things in order to identify irregular stays.

Moreover, the EU is considering measures to achieve a framework of interoperability of such information systems in order to interrogate them simultaneously, so as to cross-check biometric data and receive reports on multiple or false identities.

The limitations of the EU border agency, FRONTEX, have hindered its ability to effectively address and remedy the situation created by the refugee crisis: it is not able to purchase its own resources, it does not have its own operational staff and relies on Member State contributions, it is unable to carry out its own return or border management operations without the prior request of a Member State and it does not have an explicit mandate to conduct search and rescue operations. The above-mentioned new European Border and Coast Guard Agency has been strengthened and reinforced to address all these issues.

The Agency continues to coordinate forced return operations from Member States, but it now also has the possibility of proposing the organisation of returns on its own initiative and to provide support for voluntary departures of migrants, a procedure that best guarantees the human rights of migrants who are returned but not in a forced manner. Since January 2017, three return pools composed of escort, monitor and return specialists have been set up, and are available for deployment in the Member States, notably those facing particular pressure. When deficiencies are identified, the Agency will be empowered to require Member States to take timely corrective action. In urgent situations that put the functioning of the Schengen Area at risk and when deficiencies have not been remedied, the Agency will be able to step in to ensure that action is taken on the ground even where there is no request for assistance from the Member State concerned or where that Member State considers that there is no need for additional intervention. The new Agency will ensure Union standards for border management are implemented at all external borders. The external borders will be constantly monitored with periodic risk analyses and mandatory vulnerability assessments to identify and address weak spots. Liaison officers will be seconded to Member States where the borders are at risk. They will be fully integrated into the national information systems and able to relay the information back to the Agency. The Agency[72] will have a new mandate to send liaison officers and launch joint operations with neighbouring third countries, including operating on their territory.

Since 2015, the external dimension of EU migration policy has focused on finding a greater level of cooperation with third countries of origin and transit with respect to the goal of reducing irregular flows.

On the one hand, this policy translated into support for African states interested in migratory routes with regard to the elimination of the main factors of economic, social and political instability; on the other hand, in the request to the same third States to collaborate in a meaningful way with reference to greater control of their own borders, to strengthen the fight against the networks of migrant traffickers and to effectively comply with the obligations of readmission and repatriation of irregular migrants in Europe.

In this context, the European Trust Fund for Africa,[73] set up in November 2015 on the occasion of the EU–Africa Summit, which consists of a

---

72 The Agency's permanent staff will be more than doubled and for the first time, the Agency will be able to purchase its own equipment and deploy them in border operations at a moment's notice. A rapid reserve pool of border guards and a technical equipment pool will be put at the disposal of the Agency – meaning there will no longer be shortages of staff of equipment for Agency operations. Moreover, the Agency will include cross-border crime and terrorism in its risk analysis, process personal data of persons suspected to be involved in acts of terrorism and cooperate with other Union agencies and international organisations on the prevention of terrorism.

73 European Parliament resolution of 13 September 2016 on the EU Trust Fund for Africa: the implications for development and humanitarian aid (2015/2341(INI)), *OJ C 204, 13 June 2018, 68–75.*

volume of resources of over four billion euros, is considered an emergency. The largest contributing Member States to the Fund are Germany and Italy with a commitment of 182.5 and 112 million euros respectively.[74]

The approach followed with the Valletta agreement is also the basis of the new EU partnership framework, which has translated into pacts (migration compact) with priority third countries (Niger, Mali, Nigeria, Senegal and Ethiopia) with particular regard to the migration route that reaches Libya from the Sub-Saharan regions in view of the crossing of the central Mediterranean.

In the resolution of 14 March 2018, Preparing the Parliament's position on the post-2020 multi-year financial framework,[75] the European Parliament approved a series of indications with particular reference to the EU external action concerning third countries interested in migration flows: in particular, the resolution calls for a significant increase in appropriations, *inter alia* with reference to neighbourhood and development policies. The proposal was qualified as an initiative for a new "Marshall Plan for Africa to give hope to millions of Africans ready to go for lack of alternatives".

In summary, for the purposes of preparing the new multi-annual budget, the European Parliament called on the Union, *inter alia*, to develop and finance a policy asylum, migration and integration, considerably increasing the resources allocated for external action and addressing the root causes of migration and displacement in third countries, and to promote stability, in particular by safeguarding human rights abroad, conflict prevention and external development policies.[76]

---

74 The allocation of the Fund's resources is divided into three macro-regions: Sahel and Lake Chad (Burkina Faso, Cameroon, Chad, Ivory Coast, Gambia, Ghana, Guinea, Mali, Mauritania, Niger, Nigeria and Senegal), Horn of Africa (Djibouti, Eritrea, Ethiopia, Kenya, Somalia, South Sudan, Sudan, Tanzania and Uganda), and North Africa (Morocco, Algeria, Tunisia, Libya and Egypt). Thanks to the Fund, programmes are funded to: create economic development and work; support basic services for local populations (food and nutrition security, health, education); strengthen the stability and governance, in particular by promoting conflict prevention and combating human rights violations, and the rule of law; prevent irregular migration flows and fight against migrant trafficking networks.

75 European Parliament resolution of 14 March 2018 on the next MFF: Preparing the Parliament's position on the MFF post-2020 (2017/2052(INI)).

76 In particular, the communication of 12 September 2018 (COM (2018) 643) on a new Africa–Europe Alliance for Sustainable Investment and Jobs: Taking our partnership for investment and jobs to the next level includes a series of initiatives to: promote strategic investments and strengthen the role of the private sector, in particular by further reducing the risks associated with investment projects through the combination of grants and loans and the offer of guarantees; invest,

Another agreement adopted in order to manage the irregular flow is the EU–Turkey Declaration which is part of the external dimension of the migration policy concerning in particular the issue of irregular migration.

The unprecedented flow of migrants from Turkey to the Hellenic islands, mostly made up of Syrian citizens fleeing the conflict areas in Syria, has led the EU to negotiate a series of measures with Turkey that are mainly contained in the so-called EU–Turkey Declaration of March 2016.

The EU–Turkey Declaration provides, on the one hand, greater cooperation of the Turkish authorities in the fight against migrant smuggling and a repatriation program for irregular migrants in Turkey, and on the other, the resettlement of a part of Syrian asylum seekers in the European Union and initial financial support of three billion for 2016–2017 for refugees in Turkey and the local Turkish communities that welcomed them (the so-called Refugee Instrument in Turkey). Finally, the visa liberalisation process between the EU and Turkey and negotiations on Turkey's accession process to the European Union is expected to be relaunched.

Regarding the Eastern Mediterranean route, the European Council of 28–29 June 2018[77] underlined the need for further efforts to fully implement the EU–Turkey Declaration, prevent new crossings from Turkey and stop the flows. According to the EU–Turkey readmission agreement, bilateral readmission agreements should be fully implemented in a non-state discriminatory manner towards all Member States. More efforts are urgently needed to ensure rapid repatriation and prevent the development of new sea or land routes. Cooperation with partners from the Western Balkan region and their support remain essential to exchange information on migration flows, prevent irregular migration, increase border protection capacities and improve repatriation and readmission procedures in respect of the human rights legislations.

---

at continental and national level, in people through investments in education and skills, to strengthen employment and adapt skills to the job offer, also through scholarships and exchange programs, in particular in Erasmus + framework; strengthen the business environment and promote a climate more favorable to investments, especially by intensifying dialogue with African partners and supporting reforms in the sector; to fully exploit the potential of economic integration and trade: based on the implementation of the continental free trade area for Africa, the long-term perspective is to conclude an extensive intercontinental free trade agreement between the EU and Africa; mobilise a huge financial resources package on external financing, within the next EU 2021–2027 multiannual financial framework, considering Africa a priority region.

77 https://www.consilium.europa.eu/en/meetings/european-council/2018/06/28-29/.

In March 2018, the European Commission presented a package of initiatives, the fulcrum of which is represented by a proposal for a regulation (COM (2018) 252)[78] containing amendments to the visa code, aimed, among other things, at introducing a new mechanism to activate more restrictive visa treatment conditions when a partner country does not cooperate sufficiently for the readmission of irregular migrants.

In the European Union legal framework on irregular migration, one of the tools used to deal with this phenomenon is the return provision, which is hotly debated, especially concerning human rights.

The main tool at the EU's disposal is the aforementioned Return Directive of 2008,[79] which establishes a new approach to return which is now extended to the country of transit. Its implementation also covers undocumented non-EU citizens who have not yet reached the age of 18. It envisages the possibility of keeping irregular immigrants in detention in special or prison facilities, formalising this as one of the most important aspects of European Union policy in this area.[80]

The EU Return Directive, which entered into force in 2010, sets common standards and clear, transparent and common rules for the return of irregularly staying migrants, in full respect of fundamental and human rights. However, its inconsistent transposition into national legislation has had a negative impact on the effectiveness of EU return policy. Many Member States did not implement the Directive correctly as shown by several judgments of the European Court of Human Rights.

The return procedure, which also provides for the detention of irregular migrants before their return, is a case in which issues regarding the protection of human rights and their violation frequently arise. One of the most important innovations is the possibility of arranging the return of undocu-

78 Proposal for a Regulation of the European Parliament and of the Council amending Regulation (EC) No. 810/2009 establishing a Community Code on Visas (Visa Code) COM (2018) 0252 final – 2018/061 (COD), no longer in force since June 2019.

79 Directive 2008/115/EC of the European Parliament and of the Council of 16 December 2008 on common standards and procedures in Member States for returning illegally staying third-country nationals, OJ L 348, 24.12.2008, 98–107.

80 European Commission, Communication COM (2015) 0240 final, Communication from the Commission to the European Parliament, the Council, the European Economic and Social Committee and the Committee of the Regions: A European Agenda on Migration.

mented people not only to their country of origin, but also to a country of transit.[81]

One of the critical issues related to the fight against irregular migration is the checking and identification of those citizens who have reached the territory of a Member State without respecting the law. In this case, it is important to balance respect for people´s freedom with the right afforded to every state to authorise entry into its territory and to carry out verification activities. If a person´s identity is to be verified, it appears necessary to allow the competent authorities to keep the person in detention for a certain period of time, which should be both reasonable and no longer than strictly necessary to identify them.[82]

According to the Directive, a citizen without the legal stay requirements will be detained for the purpose of removal, but only:[83] *(a)* "to prepare the return and/or carry out the removal process; (b) unless other sufficient but less coercive measures, still capable of achieving the aim, can be applied effectively in a specific case".[84]

FRONTEX, as mentioned above, has a clear mandate, under its current legal basis, to provide the necessary assistance to Member States for organising joint return operations of irregular migrants. In addition, it shall identify best practices on the acquisition of travel documents and on the removal of irregularly present third-country nationals, including via cooperation with the authorities of third countries.

Within its current mandate, FRONTEX will provide, under the hotspot approach, substantial and increased operational support to the frontline Member States of Italy and Greece. This should enable these Member States' authorities to make a distinction early on between those that have a right to stay in the EU and those that need to be returned, and to carry out

81 Art. 3 para. 3, Directive 2008/115/EC of the European Parliament and of the Council of 16 December 2008 on common standards and procedures in Member States for returning illegally staying third-country nationals, OJ L 348, 24.12.2008, 98–107.

82 Articles 15 and 16, Chapter IV Directive 2008/115/EC of the European Parliament and of the Council of 16 December 2008 on common standards and procedures in Member States for returning illegally staying third-country nationals, OJ L 348, 24.12.2008, 98–107.

83 European Court of Justice C-61/11 PPU, ECLI:EU:C:2011:268, judgment, 28 April 2011, p. I-0000; European Court of Justice C-329/11, ECLI:EU:C:2011:807, judgment, 6 December 2011, p. I-0000.

84 European Court of Justice C-61/11 PPU, ECLI:EU:C:2011:268, judgment, 28 April 2011, p. I-0000; European Court of Justice C-329/11, ECLI:EU:C:2011:807, judgment, 6 December 2011, p. I-0000.

their swift return. The work of FRONTEX would focus on the nationals of those third countries that are a priority to return from the frontline Member States and would support those Member States in a number of stages (pre-return,[85] return operations[86] and capacity building[87]).

As anticipated previously, the return Directive is establishing minimum standards for the return systems of EU Member States. However, the margins of discretion contained in the Directive have led to an inconsistent application in Member States with a negative impact on the overall effectiveness of the EU's return policy.

---

85 Frontex experts will help frontline Member States register apprehended and arriving migrants, both documented and undocumented, whether they apply for asylum or not. They will screen newly arrived migrants, thus helping establish their presumed nationality and reducing the risk of nationality swapping. This would help quickly assess migrants, to identify those who are returnable and the ones who need assistance and protection. Frontex will provide support in the identification of migrants, which is one of the biggest challenges for return. This is because migrants frequently have no travel or identity documents and often do not cooperate in establishing their countries of origin, to hinder return. Frontex will coordinate the deployment of experts offered by Member States to help with the screening of migrants in the frontline States. These should have expertise on the presumed countries of origin of migrants present in the frontline Member States. To support identification and confirmation of the presumed nationality of migrants by the frontline Member State, Frontex will facilitate cooperation with the embassies or consular services of countries of origin of the migrants, to help obtain emergency travel documents. For this, it will, in particular, assist Member States in inviting task forces gathering immigration/consular officers from countries of return to carry out interviews for identification and to speed up the issuing of travel documents for return. Frontex will draw on the work of existing networks of experts working on return, as appropriate. It will, for instance, make use of the Best Practices developed by the European Integrated Approach on Return Towards Third Countries (EURINT).
To help increase the rates of voluntary return of irregular migrants from frontline Member States, the Member States' experts deployed should provide migrants with information about the assisted voluntary return options as well as about the prospects of forced return. The Commission supports assisted voluntary return programmes through AMIF, in cooperation with governmental and non-governmental actors, in particular the International Organisation for Migration (IOM).

86 After the identification of migrants and the issuing of travel documents for their return, Frontex will assist in organising, will coordinate and finance the joint return operations to swiftly bring the migrants to their countries of origin or transit. The joint return operations include migrants subject to forced returns and – if this is a feasible alternative – also voluntary returns. Frontex coordinated joint return operations may involve irregular migrants from just one frontline Member State, or from several Member States. In view of the needs of the frontline States, Frontex should prioritise returns to the main countries of origin of irregular mi-

The Commission has found, based *inter alia* on the results of the Schengen evaluation mechanism, that the legal framework provided for by the Directive has so far not been fully used by all Member States. A more rigorous and realistic interpretation of the Directive in full compliance with fundamental and human rights is even more necessary as the migratory challenges have made an effective and efficient EU return policy more important than ever.

After the Malta Summit of 3 February 2017 highlighted the need for a review of EU return policy, the Commission proposed a renewed EU Ac-

---

grants present and check the needs of other Member States for returns to these third countries. While Frontex does not yet have the capability and the capacity to charter the aircraft for the return operations or to assist the Member State with the chartering, it can support them by reimbursing the costs for joint return charters. In addition, Frontex will explore the possibility of rendering financial support to return operations carried out by frontline Member States to return migrants that have been refused entry in line with the Schengen Border Code, or who are present in an area near the EU/Schengen external border. This includes, for instance, those persons arriving irregularly by boat who are apprehended upon or shortly after arrival. According to Art. 2 para. 2 a of the EU Return Directive, Member States may choose not to apply this Directive to such migrants, and to apply national rules instead. The Frontex Code of Conduct applied during all joint return operations coordinated by Frontex shall ensure that return is carried out in a humane manner and in full respect of fundamental rights. Forced return monitors, from the pool established under the project Forced Return Monitoring (FReM) may be made available, to provide unbiased and neutral reporting of return operations. Frontex can finance the costs of providing monitors for return operations.

87 Frontex will continue providing training for escort leaders and escorts of Member States, helping for instance frontline States to establish pools of escorts close to the hotspots, to enable their swift deployment on return flights. Training includes theoretical as well as practical sessions, for instance focusing on the safety procedures on board the aircraft during critical situations. It will serve as a hub for exchanging operational experience and knowledge in return matters among Member States, through the network of national operational return experts, the Direct Contact Points on Return. Frontex is central to the system of return management in the EU, by helping coordinate the networks and projects funded at the EU level focusing on the readmission of irregular migrants and on their reintegration in their home countries – EURINT, the European Reintegration Instrument Network (ERIN) and the European Return Liaison Officers network (EURLO). Frontex should seek to increase synergies between these networks and enable them to work in a mutually reinforcing way. It should provide these networks with support, as appropriate – the making available of the web-based platform Frontex One-Stop-Shop (FOSS) to EURINT for the information exchange and sharing of best practices on the acquisition of travel documents between the project members is a good example of such support.

tion Plan on Return[88] and a set of recommendations to Member States on how to make return procedures more effective. The renewed Action Plan on Return and the Recommendation on making returns more effective when implementing the Return Directive focus on a better implementation of existing EU legislation. It is recommended that Member States:

- Improve the coordination among all the services and authorities involved in the return process in each Member State to ensure that all skills and expertise required are available for effective returns while respecting the rights of the returnees;
- Remove inefficiencies by shortening deadlines for appeals, systematically issuing return decisions that do not have an expiry date and combining decisions on the ending of a legal stay with the issuance of a return decision to avoid duplicate work;
- Tackle abuses of the system by making use of the possibility of assessing asylum claims in accelerated or, where considered appropriate, border procedures when it is suspected asylum claims are made merely to delay the enforcement of a return decision;
- Prevent absconding by detaining people who have received a return decision and who show signs they will not comply, such as refusal to cooperate in the identification process or opposing a return operation violently or fraudulently;
- Increase the effectiveness of return procedures and decisions by only granting voluntary departure if necessary and if a request is made and giving the shortest possible periods for voluntary departure, taking into account individual circumstances;
- Set up operational assisted voluntary return programmes by 1 June 2017 and ensure proper dissemination of information on voluntary return and assisted voluntary return and reintegration programmes.[89]

88 European Commission, COM (2017) 200 final, Communication from the Commission to the European Parliament and the Council on a more effective return policy in the European Union, on 2 March 2017.

89 Monitoring the effects of disparities between national voluntary return schemes (short term); funding through Asylum Migration and Integration Fund of assisted voluntary return programmes in cooperation with governmental and nongovernmental partners such as IOM; promoting best practices on voluntary return and reintegration programmes through the EMN to encourage Member States to develop an effective framework enabling irregular migrants to have easy access to voluntary return programmes; support for joint reintegration programmes to improve both the quality of the support provided to migrants and its cost efficiency.

Considering the renewed Action Plan on Return in more detail: It sets out steps at each stage of the return process to tackle key challenges for return both at EU level and in the cooperation with countries of origin and transit.

The action proposed at EU level includes:

- Increased financial support to Member States with EUR 200 million in 2017 for national return efforts as well as for specific joint European return and reintegration activities;
- Improving information exchange to enforce return by collecting real time information at national level and sharing it using the existing Integrated Return Management Application, as well as speeding up work on adopting the proposals to reform the Schengen Information System and Eurodac and to establish an EU Entry-Exit System (EES) and a European Travel Information System (ETIAS);
- Exchanging best practices to ensure reintegration packages are consistent and coherent among all Member States to avoid countries of origin favouring returns from countries offering higher reintegration packages or assisted voluntary return-shopping by irregular migrants;
- Offering full support to Member States by the European Border and Coast Guard Agency with the Agency called on to step up pre-return assistance, increase its return support unit staff and set up a commercial flight mechanism for financing returns by June, as well as step up the training of third-country authorities on return by October;
- Overcoming the challenges of readmission by working to swiftly conclude the negotiation of Readmission Agreements with Nigeria, Tunisia and Jordan and striving to engage with Morocco and Algeria.

Within the Partnership Framework, collective leverage in a coordinated and effective manner is employed through tailor-made approaches with third countries to jointly manage migration and further improve cooperation on return and readmission.[90]

Detention is a delicate issue in relation to human rights, but can be necessary for the successful preparation and organisation of return operations by ensuring that illegally staying third-country nationals do not abscond.[91] The detention period, with respect of human rights, should always be as

---

90 See also report on the implementation of the Partnership Framework: IP/17/402.

91 The Commission also sets out a number of criteria to assist Member States in assessing whether a risk of absconding exists. Objective circumstances for a risk of absconding include for example the refusal to cooperate in the identification process (e.g. by using false or forged documents), violent or fraudulent opposition to

short as possible and with a view to completing the return procedure successfully. However, the maximum period of detention used by several Member States is currently significantly shorter than the time needed to complete the return procedure. This has hindered the effective return of irregular migrants. The Commission therefore recommends that all Member States implement the possibility to make use of, in cases where it is necessary, the maximum detention period allowed for by EU law, in light of the individual circumstances of the case: a maximum initial period of detention of six months and the possibility of prolonging detention up to a maximum of 18 months when necessary. The Commission also recommends that Member States bring detention capacity for return in line with actual needs.

The Commission is recommending that Member States provide for the legal possibility, under national legislation, to make use of the detention periods allowed for by EU legislation in specific cases where it is necessary to allow for the completion of the return procedure. Detention should only be used if no other sufficient but less coercive measure can be applied effectively and when there is a risk of absconding. Detention periods should be adapted by judicial authorities in the light of the individual circumstances of the case.

Supporting Member States in the return of irregular migrants is one of the priority tasks of the European Border and Coast Guard. This role has been further strengthened since the Agency became operational under its new mandate on 6 October 2016.

A European Return Office within the Agency allows the deployment of European Return Intervention Teams composed of escorts, monitors and return specialists who will work to effectively return illegally staying third-country nationals. A uniform European travel document for return will ensure a wider acceptance by third countries.

The EU is negotiating and concluding readmission agreements with countries of origin and transit in order to repatriate irregular migrants and to cooperate in the fight against trafficking in human beings. The so-called mixed readmission committees monitor their implementation. These

---

a return operation, failure to comply with measures aimed at preventing absconding such as reporting to the competent authorities or staying at a certain place when required to do so and unauthorised secondary movements to another Member State. Indicative criteria to be taken into account by the relevant authorities should be an explicit expression not to comply with a return decision, non-compliance with a period for voluntary departure and an existing conviction for a serious criminal offence in an EU Member State.

agreements are linked to visa facilitation agreements, the aim of which is to provide the necessary incentives for readmission negotiations in the third country concerned without generating an increase in irregular migration.[92]

Another legislation that the European Union adopted to contrast irregular immigration is the so-called "facilitators package",[93] which includes the Council Directive 2002/90/EC aimed at establishing a common definition of the crime of facilitating the illegal entry, transit and stay and the framework decision 2002/946/JHA which establishes penalties for such conduct. The issue of trafficking is addressed by Directive 2011/36/EU concerning the prevention and repression of trafficking in human beings and the protection of victims. The package is completed by the Council Directive 2004/81/EC which provides for the issue of a residence permit to persons who are victims of trafficking or trafficking in human beings who cooperate with the competent authorities. In May 2015, the Commission adopted the EU action plan against migrant trafficking (2015–2020)[94] and, in line with the action plan, carried out a REFIT evaluation on the application of the existing legal framework, preceded by a public consultation. The Commission found that, at that time, there was insufficient evidence to prove the effective and continuous prosecution of individuals or organisations for humanitarian assistance and concluded that the EU legal framework for combating migrant smuggling in the current context remained essential. The Commission also noted that the revision of the facilitators' package would not bring any added value compared to its actual and full appli-

---

92 Since 2016, the European Union has signed six readmission agreements (Afghanistan, Guinea, Bangladesh, Ethiopia, Gambia and Ivory Coast). At present - according to the aforementioned communication of 4 December 2018 - there are therefore a total of 23 agreements in force (in addition to the cited third countries, these are agreements with Hong Kong, Macao, Sri Lanka, Albania, Russia, Ukraine, the former Yugoslav Republic of Macedonia, Bosnia and Herzegovina, Montenegro, Serbia, Moldavia, Pakistan, Georgia, Armenia, Azerbaijan, Turkey and Cape Verde).

93 EU legal framework against facilitation of unauthorised entry, transit and residence: the Facilitators Package (Directive 2002/90/EC and Framework Decision 2002/946/JHA), SWD (2017) 117 final. In addition, readmission agreements relating to Nigeria, Tunisia and Jordan are being negotiated. It is recalled that, during the November 2017 dialogue on migration, Morocco agreed to relaunch the negotiations on the readmission agreement, which has been pending for three years.

94 European Commission COM (2015) 0285 final, Communication from the Commission to the European Parliament, the Council, the European Economic and Social Committee and Committee of the regions EU Action Plan against migrant smuggling (2015-2020).

cation, while a general agreement on added value emerged which would instead bring non-legislative measures in support of State authorities, members, civil society organisations or other stakeholders, including cooperation with third countries. In its resolution of 5 July 2018, Parliament called on the Commission to draw up guidelines for Member States to prevent humanitarian assistance being criminalised and a hearing on the subject was held in September 2018.

Another important legal tool concerning the irregular immigration matter at European Union level is the Return Directive (2008/115/EC) which establishes the common EU rules and procedures applicable in the Member States for the return of illegally staying third-country nationals. The first report on its application was adopted in March 2014. In September 2015, the Commission published an EU action plan on return followed by the adoption of the conclusions on the future of return policy by the Commission, on October of the same year.

In March 2017, the Commission integrated the action plan with a communication entitled "A more effective return policy in the European Union – a renewed action plan" and a recommendation to make returns more effective. In September 2017, it published an updated version of its "manual on repatriation", which provides guidance on the exercise of duties for national authorities responsible for carrying out the tasks related to repatriation. Furthermore, in 2016, the Parliament and the Council adopted Regulation (EU) 2016/1953[95] concerning the establishment of a European travel document for the repatriation of third-country nationals whose stay is irregular. In September 2018 the Commission proposed a targeted review of the Return Directive, which includes a new border procedure for asylum seekers, clearer procedures and rules to prevent abuse, efficient voluntary repatriation programs to be set up in the Member States and clearer rules regarding detention. Subsequently, some considerations related to this Directive and its implementation by Member States, in compliance with the human rights legislations, will be conducted.

Finally, it is necessary to mention the main principle that protects the fundamental rights of the category of irregular migrants, which is that the obligation of non-refoulement relates to the actual risk of a person being subjected to a serious human rights violation or persecution as a result of

95 Regulation (EU) 2016/1953 of the European Parliament and of the Council of 26 October 2016 on the establishment of a European travel document for the return of illegally staying third-country nationals, and repealing the Council Recommendation of 30 November 1994, OJ L 311, 17.11.2016, 13–19.

his or her expulsion or return. As a result, States are prevented from returning smuggled migrants to a country that will, in turn, return them to a place where their life or liberty is in danger.[96] This principle is laid down by the 1951 Geneva Convention on refugee status and Art. 33 Principle of non-refoulement (Article 21 of Directive 2011/95 and Article 19 of the Charter of Fundamental Rights of the European Union).

V. Some final considerations

Concerning the protection of human rights of irregular migrants, from the analysis conducted thus far, it possible to affirm that the protection provided by several Conventions covers the category of irregular migrants in some cases. However, very often not a complete extension of the tools to protect the human rights of these persons is provided and very often in order to try to guarantee this extension, new interpretations are necessary. Given the lack of a specific status as a category of vulnerable individuals at international and European level, there is no specific legislation to protect the human rights of these migrants.

Irregular migrants in all aspects of their life, as human beings, have the right to see their fundamental rights protected. However, as already explained, because of the lack of a legal status recognised by States, they have serious difficulties asserting their rights and in the entry and the return phase, this is particularly evident.

The entrance is a very delicate and difficult phase in which their rights often collide with the interests and policies of the European Union States of destination. The analysis of the level and effectiveness of protection of this category of migrants in this phase is very relevant and currently also widely discussed at European Union level as a result of serious incidents of

96 This situation, generally referred to as "chain refoulement", has been described by UNHCR as follows: *"the risk that the person would be sent by the Third State to another State in which he or she would not receive effective protection or would be at risk of being sent from there on to any other State where such protection would not be available"*: UN High Commissioner for Refugees, *Summary Conclusions on the Concept of "Effective Protection" in the context of Secondary Movements of Refugees and Asylum-Seekers (Lisbon Expert Roundtable, 9–10 December 2002), Feb. 2003 (UNHCR, Summary conclusions on the Concept of "Effective Protection" in the Context of Secondary Movements of Refugees and Asylum-Seekers)*, para. 15 (c).

violation of human rights as reported previously, for instance, in the *Hirsi Jamaa v Italy* case.[97]

Concerning the readmission agreements, previously analysed, the effect of this tool is to recommend a coherent mobility package which should be offered to the negotiating third countries that, following the agreements with the EU, are establishing specialised detention facilities in their territories. In this case, there would be a risk of reducing the guarantees of the fundamental rights of these migrants. The condition of detention in territories outside the Union following agreements between the EU and third countries does not exempt the EU from complying with the principles of international and European human rights conventions.[98] A broader involvement of international bodies such as the UNHCR and the IOM in all situations similar to the one mentioned could constitute an element of greater guarantee of human rights performing a monitoring and control function.

The Return Directive, which represents the main tool for the managing of the return phase, has seen many violations of human rights in its implementation, however it has been interpreted more liberally than expected. It initially sought to guarantee a higher standard of protection of human rights. Indeed there have been several more CJEU judgments interpreting the Directive since then: *Celaj*, *Affum*, *Ouhrami*, *Gnandi* and *KA*.[99] For instance, the case law limits the use of ordinary criminal law to jail irregular migrants, requiring Member States to use the administrative detention rules in the Directive in most cases. The jurisprudence also establishes a limited right to a hearing for irregular migrants,[100] and in some extreme cases provides for a basis to *prevent* expulsion of irregular migrants, and secure their basic rights to health care in the meantime.[101]

97 ECtHR, *Hirsi Jamaa v. Italy*, Appl. No. 27765/09, judgment, 23 February 2012, para. 180.

98 *Borraccetti*, The EU, Migration and the Politcs of Administrative Detention, Abingdon 2014.

99 *Peers*, Lock 'em up: the proposal to amend the EU's Returns Directive, in EU Law Analysis, 12 September 2018, https://eulawanalysis.blogspot.com/2018/09/lock-em-up-proposal-to-amend-eus.html.

100 European Court of Justice, C 249/13, ECLI:EU:C:2014:2032, judgment, 25 June 2014.

101 European Court of Justice, C-542/13, ECLI:EU:C:2014:2032, judgment, 18 December 2014; European Court of Justice, C-562/13, ECLI:EU:C:2014:2453, judgment, 18 December 2014.

However, there is a Commission proposal[102] on the recast Return Directive which seems, for several commentators[103] and NGOs,[104] to guarantee lower fundamental rights standards in order to increase the number of deportations from the EU, although there is no evidence that this would make the EU's expulsion system any more effective. Anyway, this approach would represent a violation of human rights, for instance a massively expanded use of detention could not be justified. It appears that the Commission and Council favour a recast version of the Returns Directive that would risk both degrading fundamental rights standards and be ineffective, without considering potential alternatives and discarding the progress made by Member States in implementing such alternatives in the framework of the existing rules, as for example voluntary return procedure which is more respectful of the human rights of these migrants.

More in detail, for instance the first change in the proposal is to define "risk of absconding": the effect of such a definition is to make it easier to refuse a prospect of voluntary departure, and correspondingly easier to justify detention. The list of cases which might constitute a risk of absconding is long (there are sixteen factors listed) and non-exhaustive ("at least"). Some of the grounds are very broad ("illegal entry") and Member States will have to apply these criteria on a case-by-case basis.[105]

Another critical aspect is related to voluntary departure: Member States need no longer give a seven-day minimum of time for an irregular migrant to depart. The three cases where Member States can opt to refuse to give the irregular migrant a chance to leave voluntarily – risk of absconding, manifestly unfounded or fraudulent application for legal stay, and risk to public policy, public security and public health – are replaced by an obligation to refuse the chance of a voluntary departure in such cases. As noted

102 COM (2018) 634 final, proposal for a Directive of the European Parliament and of the Council on common standards and procedures in Member States for returning illegally staying third-country nationals (recast) A contribution from the European Commission to the Leaders' meeting in Salzburg on 19–20 September 2018.

103 *Peers*, Lock 'em up: the proposal to amend the EU's Returns Directive, in EU Law Analysis, 12 September 2018, https://eulawanalysis.blogspot.com/2018/09/lock-em-up-proposal-to-amend-eus.html.

104 As Statewatch in The revised Returns Directive: a dangerous attempt to step up deportations by restricting rights, *Jane Kilpatrick*, September 2019, http://www.statewatch.org/analyses/no-346-returns-directive.pdf.

105 *Peers*, Lock 'em up: the proposal to amend the EU's Returns Directive, in EU Law Analysis, 12 September 2018, https://eulawanalysis.blogspot.com/2018/09/lock-em-up-proposal-to-amend-eus.html.

by Steve Peers, the effect of this change is bolstered by including a wide definition of what might be considered as a risk of absconding.

Finally, another critical point is related to detention: three grounds for detaining irregular migrants are provided and anyway this list will become non-exhaustive. The first ground – risk of absconding – will be broadly defined, as mentioned before. The second ground, which was already broadly defined, will remain. It avoids or hampers the preparation of return or the removal process. The new ground is where the irregular migrant poses a risk to public policy, public security or national security.

Therefore, the proposal seems to place an emphasis on coercion at the cost of cooperation, despite a lack of evidence for the effectiveness of forced removals in increasing the overall number of returns and clear evidence of the harms to health and wellbeing caused by forced removals, especially with regard to the use of detention.

In conclusion, from what has been analysed until now and based on the reflections above, a security approach seems to continue to prevail on the need for protection of the human rights of irregular migrants, especially in the external dimension policy and in the tools used for the application of this policy. It would be an important step to consider these migrants explicitly within the category of vulnerable people, to guarantee the protection of their human rights, especially in the entry and return phase, where most violation occurs, as previously explained.

The External Dimension and Access to International Protection in the European Union: Resettlement and Humanitarian Visas

*Andrea Romano**

I. Introduction

Following the outbreak of the conflict in Syria and the subsequent crisis of European policies in the management of migratory inflows to the European Union, the issue of legal and safe access to the EU has gained a new momentum. The exponential increase in arrivals of migrants and refugees to European shores that has occurred since 2014,[1] has pushed both international organisations[2] and European institutions[3] to address the question of

---

* Dr Andrea Romano, PhD Sapienza University of Rome (2014), researcher and expert in refugee law. Section II and III are partly based on a previous work published by the author in Spanish: *Romano*, Los programas de reasentamiento de refugiados en la UE: tendencias actuales y repercusiones en España, in Anuario CIDOB de la Inmigración, 2018. Section IV relies on and updates *Romano/Zoeteweij*, X and X v. Belgium: the need for EU legislation on humanitarian visa, in Sui generis, 2017. This Chapter was finalised on 15 May 2020.

1 Eurostat data indicate that as of 2014 the number of international protection applications has undergone a significant change, registering 627,000 applications in 2014 and 1.3 million in 2015 and 2016, Eurostat, Asylum in the EU Member States, news release, 46/2017, http://ec.europa.eu/eurostat/documents/2995521/7921609/3-16032017-BP-EN.pdf/e5fa98bb-5d9d-4297-9168-d07c67d1c9e1.

2 The 2016 New York Declaration for refugees and migrants emphasised the need to "expand the number and range of legal pathways available for refugees to be admitted to or resettled in third countries". Cf UN General Assembly, New York Declaration for Refugees and Migrants: resolution adopted by the General Assembly, 3 October 2016, A/RES/71/1). Later on, the Global Compact on Refugees pushed for new efforts and strategy in the area of resettlement as well as for a "more systematic, organised sustainable and gender-responsible basis" as regards complementary pathways for admission to third countries (para. 94).

3 See the 2015 EU Agenda on Migration that reads as follows: "In addition to the relocation of those already on EU soil, the EU has a duty to contribute its share in helping displaced persons in clear need of international protection. This is a joint responsibility of the international community, with the United Nations High Commissioner for Refugees (UNHCR) given the task of identifying when people

how to enhance the access to international protection and to configure the issue of the legal and safe pathways as a key part of the process of reforming the Common European Asylum System (hereinafter CEAS).

Notwithstanding the relevance of such commitments, the access to international protection is still frustrated by a number of barriers. In the EU legal framework this is both due to structural shortcoming of the system of international protection in the EU asylum acquis as well as for the incomplete realisation of the external dimension of the EU migration and asylum policies, which has so fair failed to pursue its two-pronged objective,[4] i.e. to strengthen its external borders and to facilitate the access to international protection,[5] limiting itself to making relevant progress only on the first by creating a number of *non-entrée measures*, as renowned scholars defined them.[6]

Yet, a system that would ease prospective applicants to obtain access to international protection would entail a number of advantages. First, it would contribute to bringing the commitments of EU primary law – such as, *inter alia*, compliance with the international refugee regime (Art. 78 TFUE), the right to seek asylum (Art. 18 of the Charter) and the principle of solidarity among States as well as towards refugees and their hosting third countries (Art. 80 TFUE and Art. 3 para. 5 TUE) – closer to reality, strengthening the humanitarian pillar of the EU's external action and taking seriously into consideration the rights of vulnerable people displaced out of their countries of origin and in need of international protection. Second, it would (if not eliminate but at least) contribute to curbing the number of irregular arrivals in the EU, hence representing a further instrument to contrast irregular migration, as it has now been recognised by

cannot stay safely in their own countries. Such vulnerable people cannot be left to resort to the criminal networks of smugglers and traffickers. There must be safe and legal ways for them to reach the EU".

4 *The Stockholm Programme – An Open and Secure Europe Serving and Protecting the Citizens*, 2 December 2009, 17024/09.

5 Directive 2001/55/EC of 20 July 2001 on Minimum Standards for Giving Temporary Protection in the Event of a Mass Influx of Displaced Persons and on Measures Promoting a Balance of Efforts Between Member States in Receiving such Persons and Bearing the Consequences Thereof, 7 August 2001. See *Ineli-Ciger*, Time to Activate the Temporary Protection Directive, European Journal of Migration and Law, 18 (2016), 1–33.

6 *Hathaway*, The Emerging Politics of Non-Entrée, Refugees, 40, 1992.

scholars[7] and the EU Commission itself.[8] Third, a comprehensive system of access to international protection, apart from completing the realisation of the external dimension, would also contribute to ameliorating the internal asylum legal framework. In fact, by introducing a number of legal instruments that allow setting up legal and safe avenues to the EU from third countries, the EU will create a system to access international protection that is alternative to the Dublin rules. In particular, if under the Dublin Regulation the Member State that will grant international protection is determined on the basis of automatic rules, by introducing a set of measures that enable people to legally enter the EU, the link between the person in need of international protection and the State that will eventually guarantee its protection, would be carried out through different criteria, which consider the presence of connective elements between the State and the person in need of international protection (for example, the presence of family and relatives, private sponsors, previous study experience, training or work experience, language skills, etc.).

In the light of the renewed interest – at both the international and the EU level – towards the issue of legal and safe pathways and, this notwithstanding, the scarce degree of initiatives undertaken so far in the EU legal framework, the objective of this Chapter is to analyse whether a system of Europeanisation of such measures of the external dimension is both feasible and likely to be achieved. Naturally, whereas the establishment of an EU system of legal and safe pathways is assumed here as an improvement of international protection in the EU asylum acquis, it will also ensure that such a system will keep its complementary nature and will not represent an argument for the adoption of more restrictive policies towards the applications presented in the national territory.

This study will be conducted through the perspective of two particular instruments, namely resettlement and humanitarian visas, emphasising their (different) relevance in the current political context. Those instru-

7 See *Savino*, Refashioning resettlement: from border externalization to legal pathways for asylum, in: Carrera/den Hertog/Panizzon/Kostakopoulou (eds.), EU External Migration Policies in an Era of Global Mobilities: Intersecting Policy Universes, Brill 2018, 81.

8 European Commission, Managing migration in all its aspects: progress under the European Agenda on Migration. COM(2018) 798 final: "In view of the Union's policy to favour regular over irregular migration, it is important to note an increase in the number of people arriving via legal migration channels. Resettlement has eased some of the pressure on EU Member States at the external border and offered a safe and legal pathway to those in need of international protection".

ments are chosen for the existence of a considerable amount of legal material at the EU level – comprised of, *inter alia*, legislative proposals, non-binding measures, reports from EU institutions and jurisprudence – that allow the carrying out of a first assessment of whether the 2015 migration crisis has triggered a new phase of policies at the EU level characterised by a new engagement of EU institutions in tackling the dilemma of how to enable people in need of international protection to benefit from it in European countries.

II. EU resettlement policies

UNHCR defines resettlement as "the selection and transfer of refugees from a State in which they have sought protection to a third state which has agreed to admit them as refugees with permanent residence status".[9] Although resettlement programmes can be implemented according to different formulas, adjusted to the need of each crisis, the definition of UNHCR provides the essential feature of this instrument, allowing clarification of its differences from similar mechanisms. It can be said that both the subjective and objective aspects of resettlement are provided by such a definition. On the one hand, resettlement programmes usually refer to "refugees",[10] namely individuals whose refugee status has already been determined in the country of first asylum, usually by UNHCR – which represents the main player involved in resettlement operations. In this sense, they differ from similar programmes such as humanitarian admission programmes. In addition, though not included in the aforementioned definition, the beneficiaries of these programmes represent a smaller target within the refugee population, being those individuals who meet the criteria of vulnerability, established by UNHCR and by the resettlement States themselves.[11] On the other hand, as regards the objective aspect, these pro-

9 UN High Commissioner for Refugees (UNHCR), UNHCR Resettlement Handbook (2011), available at: https://www.refworld.org/docid/4ecb973c2.html, 3.

10 In the document cited in the previous note UNHCR refers to the following categories: people in need of legal and/or physical protection; survivors of violence and/or torture; medical needs; women and girls at risk; family reunification; children and adolescents at risk; absence of prospects for alternative durable solutions.

11 In certain cases, UNHCR has recognised the possibility of including stateless non-refugees and refugee relatives in resettlement programmes who, unlike the family member requesting family reunification, are not refugees.

grammes apply to individuals who are in a State (first country of asylum) different from that of origin. By resettlement, therefore, individuals will receive protection in a third State that agrees to admit them as refugees. This aspect differentiates resettlement programmes from humanitarian visas, through which a short-term protection is granted for humanitarian reasons, without determining – extraterritorially – the refugee status.

Resettlement is part of the so-called "durable solutions", a concept developed by UNHCR that conceives it as a last resort instrument that has to be applied when it is impossible either to facilitate the voluntary repatriation of refugees to their countries of origin or to ensure their integration into the State where they sought asylum. While it is true that only a limited percentage of the refugee population gain access to international protection by virtue of this instrument, since World War II, resettlement programmes have opened up remarkable solutions to alleviate the burden of several humanitarian crises.[12]

As per the legal framework that rules the adoption of resettlement programmes, it is clear that under international law these programmes are based on a discretionary decision of the State, since no positive obligation of resettlement can be imposed on States, such as recognises UNHCR itself and the prevailing legal doctrine.[13] Despite some specific indications in the 1951 Geneva Convention on the status of refugees,[14] in the UNHCR Statute (Article 2, para. F) and some relevant multilateral initiatives,[15] the main guidelines on resettlement are based on the soft law developed by UNHCR.[16] Yet, due to the expertise acquired by the UN agency in this area, its documents are of special relevance. In addition, it should be remembered that Article 35 of the Geneva Convention provides for an obligation of cooperation between the States parties to the Convention and the High Commissioner. It follows that the principles and policies promoted by UNHCR in the context of resettlement entail special authority,

---

12 *Troeller*, UNHCR Resettlement: Evolution and Future Direction, in International Journal of Refugee Law, 12 (2002), 85, 89.

13 *Hurwitz*, The Collective Responsibility of States to Protect Refugees, Oxford 2007, 151.

14 *Vedsted-Hansen*, Art. 28, in: Zimmermann, (ed.), The 1951 Convention Relating to the Status of Refugees and its 1967 protocol. A commentary, Oxford 2011.

15 See the Multilateral Framework of Understandings of Resettlement, 16 September 2004, http://www.unhcr.org/protection/convention/414aa7e54/multilateral-framework-understandings-resettlement-emforum20046em.html.

16 See the Resettlement Guidelines of 1994, the Resettlement Manual, published in 1997 and updated numerous times, and the annual report on global resettlement needs (Global Resettlement Needs).

and States should not arbitrarily depart from them, but only if alleging duly substantiated grounds.[17]

In order to analyse resettlement programmes in the context of the EU, it has to be acknowledged that, on the one hand, there exists a (limited) group of states that have adopted resettlement programmes for many years.[18] This is the case of those countries that already developed permanent resettlement programmes (Sweden, Denmark, Norway and Finland). On the other hand, in the vast majority of European countries, access to international protection through resettlement is a novelty that has only been recently consolidated.[19] It could be inferred that the EU has contributed to some extent to the progressive increase in the adoption of resettlement programmes at European level by means of a set of initiatives, which started in 2000 and culminated in the measures that will be examined below. Be that as it may, such an original discrepancy – i.e. between EU resettling countries and EU non-resettling countries – explains the absence of homogeneity that undermines EU resettlement policies, having a negative impact both on the law-making process of the adoption of European programmes in this area, and on the implementation of the plans adopted.

Following the entry into force of the Lisbon Treaty, resettlement programmes can be adopted on the basis of Article 78 para. 2 (g) TFEU that allows "partnership and cooperation with third countries for the purpose of managing inflows of people applying for asylum or subsidiary protection or temporary protection". Although the actions undertaken at the European level date back to the early 2000s,[20] the first EU initiative on resettlement was materialised by the adoption of Decision No. 281/2012/EU of the European Parliament and of the Council of 29 March 2012, whose

17 In this sense, *mutadis mutandis*, *Kälin*, Supervising the 1951 Convention Relating to the Status of Refugees: Article 35 and beyond, in: Feller/Türk/Nicholson (eds.), Refugee Protection in International Law UNHCR's Global Consultations on International Protection, Cambridge 2003, 613, 627.

18 *Perrin/McNamara*, Refugee resettlement in the EU: between shared standards and diversity in legal and policy frames, Migration Policy Centre, KNOW RESET, 2013/03, First Asylum Country Report, retrieved from Cadmus, European University Institute Research Repository, http://hdl.handle.net/1814/29400.

19 European Migration Network, Resettlement and Humanitarian Admission Programmes in Europe – what works?, Directorate General for Migration and Home Affairs, European Commission, 2016, retrieved from http://emn.ie/cat_publication_detail.jsp?clog=1&itemID=3007&t=6

20 *Van Selm et al*, Study on the Feasibility of Setting Up Resettlement Schemes in EU Member States or at EU Level, Migration Policy Institute, 2003.

features consisted in the identification of common priorities at European level for the resettlement of refugees, in the coordination of national resettlement schemes as well as in encouraging Member States to resettle refugees through EU funding.[21] The effects of this decision can be seen in the increase of European states that have incorporated resettlement programmes within their legislation or administrative action. As a matter of fact, following the entry into force of the Decision, the number of Member States adopting such programmes started to grow from only seven EU countries in 2007 to fourteen in 2012.

III. The EU's commitment to resettlement in the context of the migration crisis

Apart from the rise in the number of Member States that began to be familiar with the possibility of resettling refugees from third countries, at the EU level, beside the Decision already mentioned, no other concrete measure concerning resettlement had been undertaken prior to 2015. From this perspective, it may be said that the time for a new consideration of the role of resettlement in the EU arrived with the outbreak of the crisis in the management of migration and asylum. This has been the starting point for multiple initiatives in this area that will be outlined in the next sections by first bringing attention to the measures triggered since the adoption of the EU Agenda on Migration and then focusing on the EU Commission Proposal for a Union Resettlement Framework.

1. The measures undertaken following the 2015 European Agenda on Migration

In the European Agenda on Migration of 13 April 2015, the EU Commission proposed adopting new legal and safe pathways to the EU through an annual resettlement programme of 20,000 refugees. Soon after this communication, European engagements in this area materialised in the Council Conclusions of 20 July 2015 in which Member States committed to resettle 22,504 people in need of international protection from the Middle

---

21 *Moreno Lax*, External Dimension, in Peers/Guild/Acosta Arcarazo/Groenendijk/Moreno-Lax/Tomkin (eds.), EU Immigration and Asylum Law, vol. 3, Brill 2016, 617, 620; *Bokshi*, Refugee resettlement in the EU: the capacity to do it better and to do it more, Migration Policy Centre, KNOW RESET, 2013/04, EU Comparative Report, retrieved from Cadmus, European University Institute Research Repository, http://hdl.handle.net/1814/29398.

East, North Africa and the Horn of Africa. In a similar way as to the relocation Decision,[22] such a programme foresaw the allocation of a quota of people that each Member State undertook to resettle. As regards the subsequent effective implementation of this plan, it should be noted that the compliance rates by the Member States were much higher in the area of resettlement compared to the relocation programme. As of November 2017, according to the last report available from the European Commission, the average relocation compliance reached 30%.[23] By contrast, the resettlement compliance average reached 81%.[24] However, the existence of a considerable lack of homogeneity among European countries must critically be emphasised. Indeed, a group of States refused to perform any form of resettlement whatsoever (e.g., Bulgaria, Croatia, Cyprus, Hungary,

---

22 Council Decision (EU) No. 2015/1523 of 14 September 2015 establishing provisional measures in the area of international protection for the benefit of Italy and of Greece and Council Decision (EU) No. 2015/1601 of 22 September 2015 establishing provisional measures in the area of international protection for the benefit of Italy and Greece. The Section is limited on resettlement leaving out of the account the impact of the relocation decisions, as a number of factors differentiate the two programmes. A non-exhaustive list of such differences includes the institutional actors and the beneficiaries involved, as relocation is a measure of intra-EU distribution that applies to applicants for international protection, whereas resettlement programmes occur between EU Member States and third countries while targeting beneficiaries of international protection. In addition, as per the legal consequences of such measures, the second relocation Decision No. 2015/1601 was a mandatory initiative for Member States, when in fact resettlement programmes have been introduced so far by virtue of non-binding measures. Nonetheless, it is clear that resettlement and relocation are closely intertwined and actions in both areas should be performed in parallel, which implies – for instance – that bold initiatives in the field of resettlement should be accompanied by smooth and effective relocation procedures. Ultimately, the implications between both programmes represent, on a more general level, the links between the external and the internal dimension and the need to consider them as two faces of the same coin in addressing the current drawbacks of the EU in the field of migration and international protection.

23 European Commission, Communication from the Commission to the European Parliament, the Council, the European Economic and Social Committee and the Committee of the Regions on the Delivery of the European Agenda on Migration, (COM)558 final.

24 As of November 2017, 18,366 refugees out of 22,504 were resettled: see the Annex to the report from the Commission to the European Parliament, the European Council and the Council progress report on the European Agenda on migration resettlement, swd (2017) 372 final. It has to be taken into account, however, that the data are an excerpt from the EU Commission that aggregates in its figures the number of refugees resettled through the resettlement programme with Turkey.

Poland, Slovakia, Slovenia). In other cases, Member States only resettled less than 50% with respect to their initial commitment (Denmark, 48%; Spain, 44%; Portugal, 39%; Czech Republic, 13%).[25] Finally, another group of States complied with the quota allocated in the 2015 Conclusions (Belgium, Estonia, Finland, Germany, Iceland, Liechtenstein, Holland, Sweden, Switzerland, United Kingdom) or came close to it (Austria, 98%; France; 98%; Norway, 99%; Luxembourg, 86%; Latvia, 82%; Italy, 76%).

In addition to the 2015 Conclusions, a second resettlement programme, adopted in the context of the migration crisis, was the one included in the well-known statement between the Member States of the EU Council and the Republic of Turkey. As is known, this statement established a 1:1 scheme, on the basis of which, "for each Syrian returned to Turkey from the Greek islands, another Syrian from Turkey will be resettled in the EU, taking into account the vulnerability criteria of the United Nations".[26] This is a formula based on a debatable *do ut des* rationale (resettlement in exchange for return) that significantly moves away from the humanitarian objectives which inspire resettlement programmes. Indeed, far from representing an attempt to strengthen the legal implications of the principle of solidarity, the programme in question pursues a utilitarian objective, constituting the trade-off for Turkey to accept the return of Syrian citizens arriving irregularly in the Greeks Islands. Apart from the questionable logic that leads to the adoption of this programme, which mixes instruments belonging to the area of European asylum law with those that serve to curb irregular migration,[27] it is possible to show at least two problematic aspects that concern the beneficiaries of the programme: on the one hand, resettlement will be applied as a priority route to those who have not tried to arrive irregularly in Greece. In this way an element that should discourage irregular entry is introduced. Yet, it also represents a "double penalty", since not only were Syrian citizens who tried to arrive irregularly in Greece (temporarily) excluded from resettlement but they were also forced to re-

---

25 To compare the data, see the document cited in the previous note. The data refer only to the fulfilment of the commitments made in the 2015 Conclusions and do not take into account the number of resettled refugees based on the different resettlement plan with Turkey.

26 Council of the European Union, EU–Turkey statement, 18 March, 2016, https://www.consilium.europa.eu/en/press/press-releases/2016/03/18/eu-turkey-statement/

27 *Moreno Lax*, Life After Lisbon: EU Asylum Policy as a Factor of Migration Control, in: Acosta Arcarazo/Murphy (eds.), EU Security and Justice Law: After Lisbon and Stockholm, Oxford 2014, 146.

turn to Turkey.[28] On the other hand, the discriminatory potential of the measure in question can be highlighted, since it only applies to Syrian citizens, therefore excluding other nationals, such as Afghans and Iraqis who are, nevertheless, subject to removal from Greece to Turkey.

Finally, apart from the Union Resettlement Framework that will be analysed in more detail in the next paragraph, the last initiative undertaken by the EU Commission as a follow up of its 2015 Agenda on Migration remains to be examined. Following the 2017 EU resettlement plan and acknowledging the multifaceted importance of this instrument, in September 2017 the Commission issued a recommendation in order to ensure that "resettlement efforts can continue in the period between the end of the current EU resettlement schemes and the operationalisation of the Union Resettlement Framework". To this end, a new two-year resettlement plan was launched, with the objective of resettling 50,000 persons in need of international protection by October 2019 (later extended to December 2019). Member States failed again to meet that target, with 39,000 persons resettled by that deadline, which represents 78% of the initial pledge and indicates a slight inflection in comparison with the 2017 EU resettlement scheme (81% *supra*). At the time of writing, official disaggregated data per Member States are not available, yet media sources illustrate that the above referred discrepancy between resettling and non-resettling Member States is still frustrating the goal established by the EU Commission, with a group of States complying with their quota (Sweden, the UK), another scoring percentage of resettled people of around 80%, which is above the EU average (the Netherlands, France and Italy), and other States refusing to undertake resettlement operations.[29] The Commission announced that Member States have already pledged to resettle 30,000 persons in 2020.[30] Yet, if the reluctance of certain Member States to participate in EU-wide resettlement schemes is not tackled seriously, it is to be expected that such a target will not be met on this occasion either.

What is more, the EU efforts to bolster resettlement policies triggered by the adoption of the European Agenda on Migration stemmed also from the development of the EASO's role in the area of external dimension. As a

28 *Fernandez Arribas*, The EU–Turkey Agreement: A Controversial Attempt at Patching up a Major Problem, in European Papers, 3 (2016), 1097, 1102.

29 Data from Deutsche Welle, EU breaks promise of safe passage for 50,000 refugees, https://www.dw.com/en/eu-breaks-promise-of-safe-passage-for-50000-refugees/a-50803664.

30 European Commission, press release, 18 December 2019, retrieved from https://ec.europa.eu/commission/presscorner/detail/en/ip_19_6794.

matter of fact, the agency is a platform for coordinating the exchange of information among Member States and is tasked with monitoring and supporting activities in the context of resettlement operations from Turkey to the EU. Furthermore, EASO has become part of the EU–FRANK project and provides training on resettlement for officers from the EU+ countries.[31] In the future, should the Proposal for a European Agency for Asylum be adopted, the tasks of EASO will be further expanded. Article 35 para. 4 of the Proposal entrusts the agency with gathering information, monitoring resettlement to Member States and supporting their capacity building in that area. In addition – by virtue of an open clause – it sets out that the agency may coordinate actions between Member States and third countries, subject to an agreement of the third country and in agreement with the Commission. The proposed reform goes in the direction of strengthening the institutional design of the EU on resettlement, consolidating the legal basis for future resettlement operations coordinated by the EU.

2. *The proposal for a Regulation of the European Commission for a Union resettlement framework*

At the time of writing, the European Parliament and the Council are examining a remarkable Proposal from the European Commission aimed at adopting an EU Regulation on principles and rules relating to resettlement in the EU that would replace the existing temporary resettlement schemes analysed in the previous paragraph (European Commission: 2016).[32] The Proposal is part of the package presented by the Commission in July 2016 to reform the CEAS and its main objectives are to introduce and harmonise resettlement procedures adopted at national level. First of all, the legal source through which the Commission aims to introduce this new measure is appreciable, since the choice for a Regulation is coherent with

31 European Asylum Support Office, EASO External Action Strategy, retrieved from https://www.easo.europa.eu/sites/default/files/EASO-External-Action-Strategy.pdf.

32 The text refers to the version as it stands in the Commission's initial proposal, including some proposed modifications submitted by the Parliament and the Council. For a more timely analysis of the different positions of these institutions, see *Radjenovic*, Resettlement of refugees: EU framework, Bruxelles: European Parliamentary Research Service, 2017, 10, retrieved from http://www.europarl.europa.eu/RegData/etudes/BRIE/2016/589859/EPRS_BRI(2016)589859_EN.pdf.

the objective of achieving greater convergence among national resettlement models. As per the content, the Proposal introduces a permanent resettlement mechanism at European level that should be articulated in different phases. In a first phase, the Commission would be called on to approve a General Resettlement Plan every year. Subsequently, on the basis of this plan, the Council should determine through an implementing act the following aspects: the total number of refugees to be resettled, the participating Member States (since participation in the resettlement plan is voluntary) and the countries from which the resettlement plan would be carried out. Finally, in the third phase, the Commission could approve specific resettlement programmes (targeted Union resettlement schemes, in the English version), specifying the exact number of refugees to resettle and from which geographical areas. Unlike the Conclusions of 20 July 2015, the proposal does not provide for a distribution key, thus leaving the number of refugees to be resettled every year to the discretion of Member States.

The new instrument introduces two resettlement procedures: the ordinary and the expedited one, which differ – *inter alia* – both for its beneficiaries and the time-frame of their implementation. The ordinary resettlement programme is addressed to individuals who meet the requirements established for international protection and who, therefore, will be beneficiaries of either refugee status or subsidiary protection. Such a procedure can last up to eight months, extendable for another four months. On the other hand, the expedited programme is aimed at those individuals who meet, at least, the requirements established for the recognition of subsidiary protection, as enshrined in Article 15 of Directive 2011/98. Once resettled in the country of destination, they may apply for refugee status. In this case, the resettlement time frame is reduced to four months. In the definition of the country of destination, Member States may express a preference within a list of aspects provided for in Article 10 of the Proposal (family or social ties, or elements that may facilitate integration into the country of destination). The realisation of both procedures is funded by the Asylum, Migration and Integration Fund (AMIF). Member States will obtain EUR 10,000 per resettled refugee, provided that the resettlement is carried out in accordance with the common Union Resettlement Framework. It is also to be stressed that the proposal establishes certain exclusion clauses. The first clause affirms that individuals who have committed international crimes or serious crimes cannot access the resettlement programmes, which, obviously, is related to Article 1 F of the 1951 Geneva Convention. The second clause sets out a much broader margin of discretion, excluding from the programme those individuals who represent a danger to public order, security and public health or even to the international relations of the Member State that examines the resettlement request. Finally, a clause that takes into account the background of the "migratory history" of refugees is introduced: it excludes those for whom an alert has been issued in the Schengen Information System and who have entered or attempted to enter irregularly into one of the EU countries in the five years prior to the time their application is processed. This is a provision that finds its predecessor, *mutatis mutandis*, in the Declaration with Turkey, as previously seen. As regards the question of the countries and regions from which resettlement would take place, the definition by the Commission and the Council of the so-called geographical priorities becomes crucial: among the criteria that allow European institutions to include a third country in the area of geographical priorities, there is the "effective cooperation with the Union in the field of migration and asylum" (Article 4 of the Proposal), which consists in the adoption of policies aimed at counteracting irregular flows and strengthening their capacity to receive people in need of international protection.

After having synthetically outlined its main features it has to be acknowledged that the Proposal presents a number of debatable aspects on which both UNHCR and several NGOs have focused their attention (ECRE, 2016). To begin with, two factors must be problematically considered: the voluntary nature of resettlement – which leaves Member States free to adhere to the programme to a greater or lesser degree – and the absence of any indication of how many refugees would be resettled yearly. In this way it is not possible to foresee if the Proposal is capable of achieving its main objective, namely, the promotion of legal and safe pathways to the EU. It is true that there is no obligation under international law for States to resettle refugees. Yet, the binding nature of the annual resettlement plan could have been established at least at a minimum percentage. For the purpose of determining such a minimum percentage, UNHCR documents and in particular the figures identified in its annual report on Global Resettlement Needs could have been taken as a point of reference. It should be added that the idea of a binding framework in this area is not completely unknown in the EU context, since the European Parliament advocated for the introduction of binding measures in the field of resettlement in its Resolution of 12 April 2016 (European Parliament, 2016). What is of striking concern is the procedures: the lack of an emergency procedure along with the ordinary and the expedited procedure. UNHCR, in its Handbook on Resettlement, acknowledges that States adopt a procedure that allows resettlement within a maximum period of 24 hours for those individuals who urgently need protection.[33] It is also critical to define the exclusion clauses and in particular the provision that automatically leaves out refugees for whom an alert has been issued in the Schengen Information System, or who have entered or attempted to enter irregularly into the EU. The automatic effect and lack of consideration of the individual situation of the migrant should be reconsidered. Furthermore, the provision in question is even more arbitrary if one considers the lack of homogeneity of the CEAS. Take as an example the case of Afghans, whose recognition rate of international protection is extremely low in Bulgaria (1.7%) compared to the overall percentage of the EU (55.7%) or even more compared to Italy (Italy, 97%). Now, if applicants from Afghanistan after having entered irregularly in Bulgaria are removed to their country without their application being examined, they would not be able to be resettled in any other EU country in the next five years, although the recognition rate of this nationality is considerably high in Europe.[34] Finally, some doubts need to be raised regarding the issue of geographical priorities, defined on the basis of the cooperation of third States with the EU compared to irregular migration. Although this is an optional criterion that the European institutions will be free to ignore, this seems to reproduce the logic that has inspired the Statement with Turkey to the extent that resettlement is conceived and used as an instrument for conditioning migration policies of non European States.

This notwithstanding, the Proposal also presents a number of positive aspects. Apart from being noticeable that this matter would be ruled by virtue of a Regulation for the first time, the Proposal introduces a permanent channel for access to international protection that is alternative to the criteria of the Dublin mechanism. Unlike other systems such as those existing in Canada or the United States, under the EU legal framework on asylum the access to international protection is relevant only insofar as the applicant reaches the borders or the territories of the Member States. In the absence of such contact, EU law does not provide for any form of access to international protection. In addition, the Proposal would introduce an annual and permanent resettlement plan, whose importance, among other aspects, will also be to encourage non-EU resettling states, i.e. those ones that do not have national resettlement plans or have just introduced them.

33 UN High Commissioner for Refugees (UNHCR) (fn. 10), 344.

34 Eurostat, First instance decisions on applications by citizenship, age and sex Annual aggregated data, 2018, retrieved from http://appsso.eurostat.ec.europa.eu/nui/show.do?dataset=migr_asydcfsta&lang=en. The data mentioned in the main text refers to 2016.

All in all, the proposal seems to entail more shadowy areas than light and needs to be corrected both in its ultimate rationale and specific provisions. Indeed, the balance between the State interests to maintain control upon the arrival of asylum seekers and the principle of solidarity promotes the prevalence of a utilitarian and non-solidarity approach to resettlement in the EU. It would be appropriate to go back to the original purpose of this instrument in order to regain its traditional objective of easing access to international protection.

IV. Visa policies as a humanitarian instrument

Beyond the progressive establishment of a bold EU resettlement policy, the lack of pathways to access international protection under EU law could be also addressed with a U-turn on the visa policy of the EU and its Member States. A generous visa policy for potential applicants for international protection would ease access to international protection of especially vulnerable people in need of urgent or immediate protection. By contrast, a restrictive visa policy would make it hard for these people to access international protection in view of the lack of other, more tailored, pathways to international protection.

A discourse on the potential benefits of visas as instruments to facilitate access to international protection has to stem from the awareness that visas are among the most efficient and primary instruments to implement and outsource border controls[35], i.e. their implementation entails also the effect of preventing individuals from accessing international protection. In the context of the European Union, they have also added a vital dimension to the external policy of the EU, with visa liberalisation or facilitation being used as incentives for third countries to cooperate with the European Union in its migration management.[36] This has the effect that third countries bordering the European Union amend their immigration laws to reflect EU norms, thus functioning as a buffer for the European Union, as

35 See *Meloni*, EU Visa and Border Control Policies: What roles for Security and Reciprocity?, in: Bigo/Carrera/Guild (eds.), Foreigners, Refugees or Minorities: Rethinking people in the context of Border Controls and Visas, Farnham 2013, 151 ff., dealing with visa as a remote form of control.

36 *Thym*, Towards International Migration Governance? The European Contribution, in: Van Vooren/Blockmans/*Wouters* (eds.), The EU and Global Social Governance, Oxford 2013, 289, 296.

occurred in Balkan countries in the course of the last decade.[37] The EU visa policy is therefore an essential instrument in the EU migration management toolkit.

The EU acquired competence in regulating the movement of third-country nationals through the Treaty of Amsterdam. The legislative measures taken in this regard are, among others, the Visa Code Regulation,[38] which establishes the procedures and conditions for Member State authorities issuing visas for short stays in and transit through the territories of Member States, and a separate Regulation listing the non-EU countries whose nationals are required to hold a visa to enter the EU,[39] among which some of the countries that are the main sources or transit countries of refugees are included.[40] This makes it increasingly difficult for potential refugees to obtain a visa sanctioning their regular entry into the country where they wish to make their application for international protection.[41]

Be that as it may, visa policies can also be implemented to the benefit of protection seekers. Such a visa policy could, for example ease, suspend or lift visa obligations for nationals of countries whose application for international protection display high recognition rates. This might be a temporary or permanent measure to allow people in need of protection to safely and legally reach the EU. Alternatively, protected entry mechanisms could be put in place, and visas could be provided to people who have obtained international protection from a Member State while still in a third coun-

37 See for instance Agreement between the European Community and the Republic of Serbia on the facilitation of the issuance of visas, 18 September 2007 entered into force on 1 July 2008. On the negative effects for asylum seekers, see *Chachipe Rights & Justice*, Selective freedoms. The Visa liberalisation and restrictions on the right to travel in the Balkans, 2012, retrieved from https://romarights.files.wordpress.com/2012/07/chachipe_visa_liberalisation_report_270612.pdf.

38 Regulation (EC) No. 810/2009 of the European Parliament and of the Council of 13 July 2009 establishing a Community Code on Visas (Visa Code).

39 Regulation (EC) No. 539/2001, amended by Regulation (EC) No. 1289/2013.

40 Regulation (EC) No. 539/2001, Annex I.

41 Numbers of irregular entries of asylum seekers among Member States are extremely high. As scholars put it: "There were 1,321,560 asylum claims during the year [2015], according to the International Organisation for Migration. Frontex says at least 800,000 of these claims consisted of irregular entries", *Noll/Gammeltoft-Hansen*, Humanitarian Visas Key to Improving Europe's Migration Crisis, Raoul Wallenberg Institute, 2016, retrieved from https://rwi.lu.se/app/uploads/2016/04/Humanitarian-Visas-policy-brief.pdf.

try, or to people who wish to travel to a Member State in order to submit a claim for international protection on arrival.[42]

1. *Humanitarian visas: the EU legal framework and the national approach*

As is known, the possibility of issuing visas to people who are in need of international protection and who request to be admitted to the territory of a Member State in order to lodge an application for international protection has been debated in the context of the interpretation of Article 25 of the Visa Code. According to that provision, Member States *shall* issue humanitarian visas to applicants who do not fulfil certain entry conditions laid down in the Visa Code and the Schengen Borders Code, if this is necessary on humanitarian grounds, for reasons of national interest or because of international obligations. The visa that the Member State should issue in case it decides to apply Article 25 of the Visa Code is a so-called Visa with Limited Territorial Validity (LTV), which grants the visa holder the right to stay exclusively in the issuing Member State.

However, neither the visa code nor any other instrument of European Union law provides guidance on how this Article should be applied in practice, therefore a number of Member States have developed their own legislation and practices. Evidently, the degree of protection offered under the schemes varies considerably from one State to another and a wide spectrum of inclusive/protective variables may be identified. Comparative studies by legal scholars, EU institutions and NGOs have documented positive outcomes.[43] The 2014 report from the EU LIBE Committee recognises three different approaches among Member States implementing some kind of humanitarian visa scheme; there are those that issue LTV on humanitarian grounds, in accordance with Article 25 para. 1 of the Visa Code, but there are others that issue type C or type D visas on similar

---

42 See for this account *Moreno Lax*, Europe in Crisis: Facilitating Access to Protection, (Discarding) Offshore Processing and Mapping Alternatives for the Way Forward, Red Cross, EU Office, 2016, 1, 34 ff., distinguishing between collective and individual solutions.

43 *Noll/Fagerlund/Liebaut*, Study on the feasibility of processing asylum claims outside the EU, European Union: European Commission, 2002, retrieved from https://ec.europa.eu/home-affairs/sites/homeaffairs/files/e-library/docs/pdf/asylum-study_dchr_2002_en_en.pdf; *Jensen*, Humanitarian Visas: option or obligation?, Study for the LIBE Committee, Brussels 2014, *Hein/De Donato*, Exploring avenues for protected entry in Europe, Report from the Consiglio Italiano per i rifugiati Milan 2012.

grounds.[44] For instance, visas on humanitarian or asylum/humanitarian grounds may have an explicit basis in the law (which is the case in the Netherlands, Spain and Switzerland), or work as a *de facto* or informal procedure, with States allowing third-country nationals to apply for a tourist visa and then submit an international protection request upon having entered the territory of the State.[45] Furthermore, differences also exist as to the place from which these pathways may be accessed by protection seekers, as some States restrict the possibility of applying for a protected entry procedure in embassies or consular representations in third countries, whereas others also include countries of origin.[46] It is also important to examine and compare the extent to which the State from which a humanitarian visa is requested takes over responsibility for the safety of the applicant during the assessment procedure of the application, because whereas some States do offer protection during the assessment procedures, others do not. Finally, some of the States mentioned here have decided to suspend or put a cap on the humanitarian visa procedure, as it resulted in the arrival of more applicants for international protection than their domestic asylum system – and their domestic politics – was able to handle.[47]

---

44 *Jensen* (fn. 43) 42. It is worth remembering that the Common Code on Visas (CCV) provides for two general categories of visas, namely type "C", which are uniform EU visas released for short-term stays and valid throughout the Schengen Area. By contrast, type "D" are national visas valid for longer periods within the State of issuance and with restrictions on travelling to other Schengen States. The CCV also provides a further visa establishing in Art. 25 that States may issue visas on humanitarian grounds with limited territorial validity (LTV), i.e. providing the beneficiary only the right to stay in the country issuing the visa. This is the type of visa that Syrian applicants requested at the Belgium embassy in the case at stake in the ruling European Court of Justice, C-638/16 PPU, ECLI:EU:C:2017:173, judgment, 7 March 2017 – X and X v. État belge.

45 This is the case of LTV in Italy and short/long-term visas issued in France, see *Jensen* (fn. 43), respectively at 44 and 45.

46 *Noll/Fagerlund/Liebaut* (fn. 43).

47 This is the case for Switzerland and Austria, for example. For Switzerland see *Thränhardt*, Kann Deutschland vom neuen Schweizer Asylverfahren lernen?, in Zeitschrift für Ausländerrecht und Ausländerpolitik, 2016, 331, where he mentions that numbers have dropped considerably from 4,722 in 2014 to 1,721 in 2015. Later, in 2016 the issuance of humanitarian visas to Syrians was suspended by the Swiss authorities, see http://www.swissinfo.ch/eng/politics/humanitarian-visas_asylum-checks-to-be-tightened-on-injured-syrians-and-iraqis/42304404. Austria decided in 2003 to reserve humanitarian visa only for family members of recognised refugees; proposals are presently in the pipeline to abolish the humanitarian D-type visa completely. See http://www.ecre.org/austria-proposals-to-restrict-humanitarian-visas-and-family-reunification/.

This short overview of Member State laws and practices with regard to humanitarian visas clearly shows that there is no consistency among Member States in this respect. This results in a situation in which persons in need of international protection might feel that they are participating in a lottery when they choose the legal pathway to access international protection in Europe – and that, in turn, inspires many of them to attempt a risky journey towards the borders of Europe rather than putting their hopes on an equally risky walk down the legal pathway. The existing, wide divergences among Member States' laws and practices in regard of humanitarian visas has a number of negative consequences in terms of different waiting times, uncertain outcome of the application depending on the Member State processing the request, possibilities of protection while the examination is conducted, etc. In addition, the exercise of broad discretionary powers by consular or other responsible authorities seems a common trend and this puts at risk basic principles of EU administrative law, such as the principle of good administration enshrined in Article 41 of the Charter.

Both the Luxembourg and the Strasbourg Court have been called in to address such problems. In the famous case X and X, the CJEU was asked to interpret Article 25 of the EU Visa Code in order to determine whether an application for a visa with limited territorial validity such as the one in question fell within the scope of the Code, and as a result thereof within the scope of application of the Charter of Fundamental Rights of the European Union. Notwithstanding the affirmative Opinion of Advocate General Mengozzi to that question, the Court came to the conclusion that the Visa Code and therefore the Charter does not apply to such applications as the intention of the applicants to lodge an application for international protection once in the country that issued the visa. A similar case was adjudicated by European Court of Human Rights,[48] which declared inadmissible the application by stating that Belgium did not have jurisdiction over a consular decision on the issuance of a visa to a third-country national and therefore the rejection of the visa request did not trigger the application of the Convention. The outcome of the decision was already anticipated by

48 ECtHR, *M.N. et autres c. Bélgique*, Appl. No. 3599/18, 26 April 2018. See on this case *Schmalz*, Will the ECtHR Shake up the European Asylum System?, *Verfassungsblog* (30 November 2018), https://verfassungsblog.de/will-the-ecthr-shake-up-the-european-asylum-system/ and *Gatta*, La "saga" dei visti umanitari tra le Corti di Lussemburgo e Strasburgo, passando per il legislatore dell'Unione europea e le prassi degli Stati membri, 12 June 2019, Dirittifondamentali.it.

the legal doctrine,[49] albeit some authors suggested that the jurisprudence of the Court did not prevent it from recognising Article 3 as setting out a positive obligation for Member States to issue a visa in exceptional circumstances such as the ones at stake in the case of MN and others.[50] Be that as it may, Courts cannot be left to handle a matter that due to its magnitude and complexity falls within the responsibility of EU policy makers and legislators, who are better placed to introduce a clear and comprehensive legislative framework on humanitarian visas in EU law, also with a view to harmonising differing Member State practices in this area.

2. *The failure of the European Parliament's proposals for an EU humanitarian visa scheme and the need to reactivate it*

In this regard, it is worth noting that the LIBE Committee of the EU Parliament has long advocated for the opportunity to stress the protective function of visas, in line with its previous positions on the need to create legal pathways to the EU.[51] In spite of the number of proposals advanced to that end, every attempt so far has failed. When the EU Commission adopted its 2014 proposal to reform the visa code – limiting it to financial,

49 See *Schmalz* (fn. 36) who, nonetheless, states that "one can expect that [the Court] acknowledges the substantial theoretical, historical and political weight of the questions involved". See also *Stoyanova*, M.N. and Others v Belgium: no ECHR protection from refoulement by issuing visas, *EJIL: Talk* (12 May 2002), https://www.ejiltalk.org/m-n-and-others-v-belgium-no-echr-protection-from-refoulement-by-issuing-visas/.

50 See already *Moreno Lax*, Asylum Visas as an Obligation under EU Law: Case PPU C-638/16 X, X v État belge (Part II), *EU Migration and Law Blog* (21 February 2017), http://eumigrationlawblog.eu/asylum-visas-as-an-obligation-under-eu-law-case-ppu-c-63816-x-x-v-etat-belge-part-ii/. *Reyhani*, Expelled from Humanity. Reflections on M.N. and Others v. Belgium, *Verfassungsblog* (6 May 2020), https://verfassungsblog.de/expelled-from-humanity/. See also *Gatta*, (fn. 36), 40–45.

51 Resolution (EU) No. 2015/2095, European Parliament Resolution on the situation in the Mediterranean and the need for a holistic EU approach to migration, 12 April 2016. Besides non-binding resolutions adopted in the context of the Mediterranean tragedies, it is worth also remembering that the European Parliament has recently adopted a draft report on the proposal of the EU Commission on a Union resettlement framework, with a view to bolstering the humanitarian rationale of resettlement, which is at the present time overshadowed and undermined by the ambiguous proposal of the EU Commission.
http://www.europarl.europa.eu/sides/getDoc.do?type=TA&reference=P8-TA-2016-0102&language=EN&ring=A8-2016-0066

technical and logistical aspects[52] – the EP proposed a number of amendments of the proposed recast visa code with a view to developing the humanitarian potential of the visa code.[53] Most importantly, the European Parliament's report proposed that "the issuing of a visa to a person seeking protection constitutes a means of allowing such person to access the territory of the Member States in a safe manner" (Amendment 7). What is more, it included in its amendments a provision enabling third-country nationals to apply for humanitarian visas at consulates or embassies of one of the Member States. In case of a positive assessment of their visa application, asylum-seekers would have had the possibility to safely travel to the Member State concerned and lodge an application for international protection (Amendment 95). In line with this amendment, the European Parliament also proposed exempting beneficiaries of humanitarian visas from the ordinary short-stay visas' validity by stating that Member States "shall grant an exemption from the standard 90 days validity in any 180 days" and issue visas for a period of 12 months, which would also be renewable (Amendment 96). Furthermore, the EP made reference to the case law of the ECtHR[54] emphasising that Member States have "certain obligations even outside the[ir] territory when they exercise jurisdiction" (Amendment 7) and listed expressly a number of international obligations that bind Member States' activity.

Yet due to the Commission and Council's opposition to the provisions for humanitarian visas, the Parliament withdrew the amendments. Nevertheless, the LIBE Committee endeavoured in further initiatives but all of them eventually collapsed.[55] In particular, requested by virtue of a non-binding resolution of the EU Parliament to submit a proposal on European humanitarian visas, the Commission refused to follow it up, on the grounds that the (above-described) Union Resettlement Framework would

---

52 COM (2014) 164 final, 1 April 2014.

53 Draft report on the proposal for a regulation of the European Parliament and of the Council establishing a Union Resettlement Framework and amending Regulation (EU) No. 516/2014 of the European Parliament and the Council, COM(2016)0468.

54 The European Parliament makes reference to the judgment ECtHR, *Hirsi Jamaa and Others v. Italy*, Appl. No. 27765/09, judgment, 23 February 2012.

55 For a short overview of the initiatives undertaken by the EU Parliament see: Legislative Train, 12.2019. 8 Towards a new policy of migration, available at: http://www.europarl.europa.eu/legislative-train/api/stages/report/current/theme/towards-a-new-policy-on-migration/file/proposal-for-a-regulation-on-establishing-a-european-humanitarian-visa.

represent a sufficient instrument to the objectives of the EU Parliament.[56] Such a conclusion is disappointing for it downplays the different requisites, objectives, functions and nature between resettlement and humanitarian visas as explained before (see *supra*).[57] The LIBE Committee's proposals aimed at introducing for the first time a protected entry procedure based on individual demands and would have filled a crucial gap in the field of EU asylum law, contributing to address the above-mentioned issues of national divergences of humanitarian visas.

V. Conclusion

With the failure of the EP proposal it remains to be seen whether other legal pathways to access to international protection in the EU will be advanced. In this respect, an increasing interest towards the use of private sponsorship programmes and the EU action that might be undertaken in this area is noticeable, as it is demonstrated by a number of documents issued by the EU Commission[58] and the growing involvement of EASO.[59]

---

56 See *ivi*: "The Commission's answer welcomed Parliament's interest in safe and legal avenues to the EU for third-country nationals needing international protection, but highlighted its Union Resettlement Framework proposal as sufficient, as it has the potential to achieve the objective pursued by the Parliament's initiative', and qualified creating a subjective right to admission as 'politically not feasible'. It also noted that it would consider including in the evaluation of the application of the regulation establishing a Union Resettlement Framework, an assessment on whether additional measures for admission to the territory of the Member States for persons in need of international protection are needed."

57 Resettlement is namely a rather collective instrument managed almost entirely by UNHCR, and rarely offers the possibility to individuals of spontaneously submitting an application (self referrals).

58 In 2018 the EU Commission issued the Communication from the Commission to the European Parliament and the Council, Enhancing legal pathways to Europe: an indispensable part of a balanced and comprehensive migration policy, COM(2018) 635 final, Brussels 12 September 2018. See also the Study on the feasibility and added value of sponsorship schemes as a possible pathway to safe channels for admission to the EU, including resettlement, final report, October 2018.

59 See the EASO Pilot Project on Private Sponsorship Programmes, European Commission. The EASO's website section on external dimension states that "EASO's activities in the field of complementary pathways started in 2017 through a pilot project on Private Sponsorship Programmes (PSP), which involved interested Member States and relevant stakeholders. The pilot project complemented the European Commission's study on the feasibility and added value of private sponsorship schemes as a possible pathway to safe channels for admission to the EU,

Yet, however appreciable might be the use of this kind of legal pathway, it would be pointless for the EU to leave action in the area of humanitarian visas out of account. As a matter of fact, the lack of "intermediaries" (NGOs or international organisations, such as UNHCR) between protection-seekers and the Governments that characterise other legal pathways make humanitarian visas a powerful instrument of protection for (especially vulnerable) people in need of asylum, offering them the possibility to spontaneously self-refer their cases to consulates or embassies of Member States in order to obtain access to international protection in the EU. In addition, it would have to be seen whether once the ECJ excluded the situation that Member States may be compelled under the Charter to issue humanitarian visas in order to ensure compliance with the principle of non-refoulement, such obligations do exist under the ECHR, other international treaties or will arise in the EU legal framework by virtue of future reforms.

Be that as it may, the overall picture seems to be that the Europeanisation of the asylum external action on the one hand will continue to be primarily constrained to the so-called *non-entrée measures*, an area that entails to relevant incentives for Member States.[60] On the other hand, the declaration of commitments of the EU institutions in the area of legal and safe channels during and after the 2015 crisis will probably remain on paper in the near future, with the only action that has some chance of being adopted the Union Resettlement Framework. The measures adopted in the area of resettlement throughout the crisis reveal an increasing awareness of Member States regarding the need to strengthen the use of this instrument and the Proposal for a Union Resettlement Framework is to be welcomed insofar as it establishes a permanent channel of entry into the EU from third countries. However, the actions undertaken demonstrate structural deficiencies of the EU legal framework, the most striking of which is the enduring discretionary nature of resettlement programmes. Keeping resettlement as an instrument whose activation is fully conditioned to the will of the States has a number of negative implications, among which is the lack of homogeneity as regards the national compliance of EU resettlement programmes. In addition, the risk that resettlement policies might be used as a trade-off for bolstering the fight against irregular immigration must be highlighted and closely monitored, as border and migration con-

---

including resettlement." https://www.easo.europa.eu/operational-support/external-dimension.

60 In this sense, *Schmalz* (fn. 36).

trol-related interests are squeezing this domain with the risk of undermining the humanitarian, complementary and solidarity potential that is co-essential to the ambition of ensuring legal pathways for international protection.

Development and Cooperation in the Field of Migration

Claudia Pretto[*]

I. From "decolonisation" to the "management of migration" in the European Union policy

Interaction as interdependence between the African continent and the Member States of the European Union continues even after the so-called "decolonisation" in the phenomenon of mixed migratory flows towards Europe precisely from those same "decolonised" countries.[1]

The question that seems to be always on the table is whether the European Union really can leave those territories that it had previously colonised to be free to pursue self-determination and if all the instruments and policies on cooperation and development could be classed as self-determination or whether behind them colonialism and hegemonic perspective and power still exist.

Here the object of this analysis is in particular the European Union's migration policy in the context of development cooperation with a reflection on the right to self-extermination and what the real purpose of the EU policies is: to promote a world of global wellness and protection of human rights or continue to exert hegemonic control over the territories that were formerly colonies to exploit them for the EU's own benefit? The question will obviously remain open, but this analysis intends to examine it starting from analysis of these migration and development cooperation policies.

In the context of European Union policy, the term *EurAfrica* has completely disappeared, a term that was taken up instead in Sarkozy's speech,[2] but which was not intended to give redundancy. The word *EurAfrica* is in-

---

* PhD in Comparative Legal studies (University of Bari, 2011) and lecturer in migration law at the University of LUMSA.

1 *Van Mol/de Valk*, Migration and Immigrants in Europe: A Historical and Demographic Perspective, in: Garcés-Mascareñas/Penninx (eds.) Integration Processes and Policies in Europe. IMISCOE Research Series, Cham 2016, 31.

2 See: *Tasche*, The Project of a Union for the Mediterranean – pursuing French Objectives through the instrumentalization of the mare nostrum, in: Centre international de formation européenne, 356 (2010/2), 53, "What France wants with Africa is co-development, shared development ... What France wants with Africa is to

dicative because it highlights how in reality in the construction of its own politics, identity and action, the European Union conceives the close connection with the African continent, a close connection which in the context of migration and migration policy appears clearly.[3]

As a matter of fact the European Union has gradually transformed its policy of decolonisation into a policy of controlling external borders, changing processes of decolonisation into cooperation. The European Union has begun, as also highlighted by international bodies, to perceive migration towards its own territory as a problematic migration, as an attack on its own security and of course the African countries start to be part of the reasoning for controlling migratory flows from the origin: the country of departure and/ or transit. In this way the policy of externalisation is strictly connected to the policy of development and cooperation.[4]

Today the European Union could define its own policy on the theme of migration as a Fortress Europe policy, as the entry, stay and access to European territory legislation, as it is known, is both European and nationally restrictive. There is a fear of mass influx, already feared by UNDP[5].

Already in the 1994 report on human development, the UNDP had used irregular and mass migration[6] as an example of a transnational threat to an international public good – that is, human security, a prerequisite for peace between nations. In the same report, it was emphasised that effective action to control migration flows could not be reduced to forms of administrative cooperation, aimed at preventing departures, necessitating a concrete commitment on the part of the recipient states of the flows in combating welfare differentials, which constitute the first cause of uncontrolled migration.[7]

The European Union's policy on migration in recent years seems to have been based on a single key to understanding: security guaranteed by

---

prepare the advent of 'Eurafrica', a great common destiny which awaits Europe and Africa."

3 *Hansen/Jonsson*, Demographic Colonialism: EU–African Migration Management and the Legacy of Eurafrica, Globalizations 8 (2011), 261.

4 *Keukeleire/Delreux*, The Foreign Policy of the European Union, Basingstoke, Palgrave Macmillan, 2nd edition, 2014, 27–29.

5 UNDP (2009) Overcoming barriers: Human mobility and development, Human Development Report 2009.

6 UNDP (1994) Human Development Report, March 1994, http://hdr.undp.org/sites/default/files/reports/255/hdr_1994_en_complete_nostats.pdf

7 *Kaul/Grunberg/Stern*, Defining Global Public Goods, in: Kaul/Grunberg/Stern (eds.) Global Public Goods: International Cooperation in the 21st Century, New York 1999, 509, 509 ff.

the blocking of arrivals, limitation of the flows themselves. This interpretation does not seem to have proved successful as, on the one hand, the arrivals of people from third countries in the territory corresponding to the European Union have never stopped, and on the other hand this policy seems to create more and more risk of human rights violation.[8]

The European Union deals with immigration challenges in the context of the broader "Freedom, security, justice" area. It is important to underline this fact, as it helps us understand the point of view from which to start: immigration problems must be addressed from the perspective of allowing wider freedom for individuals, while at the same time safeguarding safety and security compliance with the rules of cohabitation (in this sense, reference is also made to the citizenship form). Precisely for this reason the European Union Treaty mentions solidarity among Member States and in all policies – Art. 80 TFEU on the Principle of Solidarity and Fair Sharing of Responsibility – but such solidarity does not seem to be expressed as fairness towards third-country nationals and third countries themselves.[9]

If on the one hand, the European Union aims to avoid controls as much as possible at internal borders, on the other hand it guarantees a control and surveillance action at its external borders. However, the two aspects are connected, as it is precisely to achieve the first objective essential to achieve the second: the abolition of internal border controls assumes that such controls will be strengthened at the external borders. Hence the need for a common asylum, visa and refugee policy: without rules, States with more permissive legislation could be the entry point for flows, and also large numbers of people, who could then circulate freely among all Member States. On the contrary, the Union wants to make sure that the criteria for accessing its territory are shared.[10]

---

8 On missing and dead people in the European Mediterranean area see: UNHCR, Dead and missing in 2019 (estimate): 1,071, last updated 8 October 2019, https://data2.unhcr.org/en/situations/mediterranean, accessed 11 October 2019.

9 *Mitsilegas*, Solidarity and Trust in the Common European Asylum System, in Comparative Migration studies, CMS 2 (2014), 181; *Moreno-Lax*, Solidarity's Reach: Meaning, Dimensions, and Implications for EU (External) Asylum Policy, in: Maastricht Journal of European and Comparative Law 24 (2017), 740, 740 ff.; *Thym/Tsourdi*, Searching for solidarity in the EU asylum and border policies: Constitutional and operational dimensions, in: Maastricht Journal of European and Comparative Law 24 (2017), 605, 605 ff.

10 See among all Fine, All at Sea, Europe Crisis of Solidarity in Migration, October 2019, https://www.ecfr.eu/page/-/all_at_sea_europes_crisis_of_solidarity_on_migration.pdf.

The European Union has therefore endowed itself with controlling and protecting its own external policy boundaries, the sphere of development cooperation with third countries could be connected to the externalisation of migration policies. In this policy, the European Union has not taken a method of checks and balances on human rights and effective safeguards in the event of violations but has limited itself to exchanging fake economic support policies with false promises to control migration from third countries.

The objective is to reduce or avoid irregular migrants' arrivals by signing agreements with third countries which have the role of activating policy to reduce or not allow migrants' departure to Europe. The agreements with African countries have in fact the purpose of tariffs so that migrants require protection and asylum in third countries, while asylum procedures are not those of the Common European Asylum System.[11]

Migration and mobility are increasingly vital dynamics and they seem to create controversial areas of governance. It is undeniable that the European Union aims to manage the migration flows coming from the African countries, therefore, this is the pre-eminent migration management objective.

European Union actions in the migration area consists of proposing and implementing immediate and longer-term measures focusing on the internal and external dimensions of its migration policy and on the EU's external borders.

The EU's external migration policy is part of the general EU approach on migration and is complementary to EU foreign policy and development cooperation. It is based on common goals set by the Member States and it is clearly reflected in the Common European Asylum System (CEAS).[12]

Cooperation with third countries is covered under the global approach to migration and mobility (GAMM), through which the EU has engaged in political dialogue and has established partnerships with third countries. The challenges that the EU has confronted since the recent unprecedented, uncontrolled arrival of large numbers of refugees and irregular migrants,

11 Human Rights Watch, Towards an Effective and Principled EU Migration Policy Recommendations for Reform, June 2018.

12 *Guild/Costello/Garlick/Moreno-Lax/Mouzourakis*, New Approaches, Alternative Avenues and Means of Access to Asylum Procedures for Persons Seeking International Protection, PE509.989 (Brussels), available at: https://www.europarl.europa.eu/RegData/etudes/STUD/2014/509989/IPOL_STU(2014)509989_EN.pdf.

exposed a series of deficiencies and gaps in EU policies on asylum, external borders and migration.

Moreover, only a very few countries, based on their geographical position, are responsible for essentially all asylum claims submitted within the EU, and we know these countries are Greece and Italy. To render the legal framework more efficient, harmonised, fairer and more resistant to future migratory pressures, it needs to be reformed. One of the first urgent measures after the migration wave in 2015 was intended to alleviate the migratory pressure on Greece and Italy, who have borne the brunt of the influx, and for this reason the "new non-legal instrument" of "hotspots approach" has been introduced.[13]

The declared "hotspot approach" aimed to "relocate"[14] eligible applicants for international protection – nationalities with an overall asylum recognition rate of 75 % or higher in EU Member States – to other Member States, thus ensuring fair and balanced distribution and sharing of responsibility for asylum-seekers in the EU: the so called "relocation" procedure.

The European Court of Justice concerning the principle of solidarity among Member States argues that the Council, when adopting the decision in question, was in fact required to give effect to the principle of solidarity between Member States, which applies under Article 80 TFEU when EU migration policy is implemented.[15] Because the relocation decision

---

13 On the so-called "hotspot approach" see: *Penasa*, L'approccio "Hotspot" nella gestione delle migrazioni: quando la forma (delle fonti) diviene sostanza (delle garanzie) efficientismo e garantismo delle recenti politiche migratorie in prospettiva multilivello, Rivista della Associazione Italiana dei Costituzionalisti, 2017 vol. 2.
The article analyses the main characteristics and issues raised by the "hotspot approach", implemented within the legal and institutional arrangements introduced at the European and national levels in order to handle the migration phenomenon. After having discussed the existing European regulatory framework, criticisms of the Italian approach to "hotspots" are analysed, with a specific view on its compatibility with constitutional principles.

14 Council Decision 2015/160/EU of 22 September 2015 establishing provisional measures in the area of international protection for the benefit of Italy and Greece.

15 European Court of Justice, C-643/15, C-647/15, ECLI:EU:C:2017:631, judgment, 6 September 2017 – Slovak Republic and Hungary v. European Council, annulment of Council Decision 2015/1601/EU of 22 September 2015 establishing provisional measures in the area of international protection for the benefit of Italy and Greece (OJ 2015 L 248, 80, "the contested decision").

represents a concrete expression of the principle of solidarity, it can impose the legal obligation of solidarity.

The Court therefore highlights that the duty of solidarity in this domain of EU law is enforceable when it is transformed into a valid, legally binding obligation through the process of the adoption of concrete measures in accordance with a treaty-based legislative procedure. According to the Court, this principle imposes a legal obligation on EU Member States to act for the benefit of other Member States even when such actions are not in their own interest.[16] This finding echoes its previous pronouncement that a state cannot breach EU rules for the sake of the protection of its own conception of national interest.

However, not all Member States were willing to participate in the scheme, reflecting contrasting attitudes in public opinion and difficulties in balancing solidarity and responsibility between different EU countries.[17] Furthermore, reducing irregular migration necessitates an effective policy on return and readmission of irregular migrants.

The Commission, due to the low return rates, has therefore been focusing on improving its own capacities through the renewed return action plan and proposed revision of the return directive and has been concluding readmission agreements or practical arrangements with countries of origin and transit from Africa and Asia. Uncontrolled migratory flows also exposed weaknesses in the management of the EU's external borders.

A key element in the EU's support for its Member States has been the operational support provided under the hotspot approach. This includes identifying and registering every asylum seeker arrival, as well as providing adequate reception conditions and capacity. Although the fingerprinting of migrants has progressed and, according to the Commission figures, has reached close to 100%, reception conditions remain a serious concern.

In fact years 2017 and 2018 saw a significant fall in detected illegal border crossings along the EU's external borders, mainly on the eastern and central Mediterranean migratory routes, but the overall pressure on Europe's external borders remains relatively high. Besides, the journey to the EU can be extremely dangerous, and smugglers frequently expose migrants

16 European Court of Justice, C-39/72, ECLI:EU:C:1973:13, judgement, 7 February 1973 – Commission of the European Communities v. Italian Republic.

17 *Goldner Lang*, Human Rights and Legitimacy in the Implementation of EU Asylum and Migration Law, in Human Rights, Democracy, and Legitimacy in a World of Disorder, Cambridge University press 2018, 256.

to life-threatening risks.[18] Preventing the loss of lives, notably in the Mediterranean Sea, necessitates search and rescue operations as well as fighting human trafficking and smuggling networks.

II. UN Global Compact approach and human rights[19]

Migration is a macro-critical policy issue on a global scale. It should not just be considered as a political legal issue, a question of borders and access to the territory. Migration is connected to development and demographic sustainability. Looking at migration as an all-round phenomenon, the United Nations Development Programme (UNDP) predicted that with a zero-migration scenario, in the developed world, by 2025, only New Zealand and Ireland will still have growth in their working age population, as all other countries experience a severe decline.[20] The view of the migration issue only as a matter of border control and protection from new arrivals leads to blindness and a closure with respect to the real future of society. One way, amongst others, to counterbalance the decline or stagnation in population growth is to open legal channels to migration, and this calls for a global solution.

Migration and mobility have the potential to act as powerful enablers for economic, social and environmental development in low- and middle-income countries of origin and destination. Migration and mobility are important livelihood strategies in developing countries, and migrants almost always multiply their incomes when moving. However, weak governance frameworks make migrants particularly vulnerable to violations of their fundamental freedoms, human and other rights.

Migrants disproportionately suffer the human, social and economic costs of migration. Furthermore, over ten million refugees find themselves in protracted situations in developing countries – i.e. displaced for over five years without achieving a durable solution.

---

18 Question for written answer E-006479-17 to the Commission Rule 130, Bizzotto, September 2017: failure of the migrant relocation mechanism confirmed — urgent Commission action needed, http://www.europarl.europa.eu/doceo/document/E-8-2017-006479_EN.html.

19 On 10 and 11 December 2018, the city of Marrakesh hosted the Intergovernmental Conference to Adopt the Global Compact for Safe, Orderly and Regular Migration.

20 UNDP, Human Development Report 2016, http://hdr.undp.org/sites/default/files/2016_human_development_report.pdf.

In their formal speeches, politicians declared an urgent need to replace irregular migratory flows, which have caused so much suffering and extreme human rights violations, with legal channels for migration. As European Commission President Jean-Claude Juncker said in his State-of-the-Union speech in 2017: "Irregular migration will only stop if there is a real alternative to perilous journeys".[21] A correct and effective policy of development cooperation and the possibility of legal and safe entry also through humanitarian visas therefore seem to be the only possible solutions to prevent the useless loss of life.

At the high-level meeting to address the flows of refugees and migrants, held on 19 September 2016, the United Nations General Assembly adopted the New York Declaration for Migrants and Refugees (New York Declaration for Refugees and Migrants). In the Declaration, Member States recognised the need for a comprehensive approach to human mobility, strengthening global cooperation and committing to:

- Protecting the safety, dignity, human rights and fundamental freedoms of all migrants, regardless of their status, at any time;
- Supporting countries in the rescue, reception and reception of refugees and migrants;
- Integrating migrants through humanitarian assistance and development programs – addressing the needs and abilities of migrants and those of the receiving communities;
- Fighting xenophobia, racism and discrimination against migrants;
- Developing, through state-guided processes, principles and guidelines on the treatment of migrants in vulnerable conditions;
- Strengthening global governance on migration, with the entry of IOM within the United Nations and with the development of the Global Compact for a safe, orderly and regular migration.[22]

In his State of the Union speech on 13 September 2017, in Strasbourg, European Commission President Jean-Claude Juncker said: "The global flow of refugees and migrants is one that poses challenges, opportunities and obligations for countries around the world, which the UN itself has been investigating in some depth".

21 See information European Commission Speech, 13 September 2017, https://europa.eu/rapid/press-release_SPEECH-17-3165_en.htm.

22 Global Compact for safe, orderly and regular migration – GCM, https://www.iom.int/global-compact-migration.

A real opportunity and challenge in migration context is how to ensure that the different interests and needs are addressed within a strong human rights framework. As a matter of fact, if we take into consideration the declaration on the development of European Union policy and its effective implementation, there is an evidence of a big gap in human rights protection.

Article 3 of the Treaty on European Union (TEU) binds the EU, as a non-state actor, to align itself with United Nations norms in its role in promoting and protecting human rights through all its actions, bearing the most vulnerable particularly in mind, while also addressing Realpolitik concerns.[23]

A common concern to both the UN and the EU is respect for the human rights of migrants, asylum-seekers and refugees. How can security concerns be addressed while developing a proactive immigration policy to tackle, on the one hand the needs of third-country nationals, while on the other, addressing Europe's demographic concerns – as Europe is aging and young workers are needed to pay for older retired workers' pensions? How can the commitments made on 19 September 2016 in the UN's Declaration on Refugees and Migrants be implemented effectively? Of special concern is the vulnerable situation of unaccompanied and separated child migrants. Such concerns raise questions, such as how to strike the right balance between liberty and security. A key agreement was reached on 19 September 2016 in New York, during the 71st regular session of the UN General Assembly (UNGA 71).

One of the main outcomes of the General Assembly in 2016 was a declaration demanding greater international cooperation on managing migration, which was widely endorsed, including by the EU. The Global Compact for Migration (GCM) was adopted by a vast majority of UN Member States on 10 December 2018, at a conference in Marrakech, Morocco. Refugee movements and migration are at the centre of global attention as a result of record levels of displacement, human suffering, the socio-economic impact on host communities, and the complex political ramifications in many countries. An unprecedented mass movement to the EU of asylum-seekers and migrants of all ages began in 2014, reached a peak in 2015, and then continued in 2016 and into 2017.

According to the United Nations Refugee Agency (UNHCR) and the International Organisation for Migration (IOM), human mobility has nev-

23 *Piris*, The Lisbon Treaty: a legal and political analysis, Cambridge University Press 2010, 72.

er been as high. A coordinated and effective protective response is essential, and that requires both a gender- and child-sensitive dimension. Over 258 million migrants around the world are living outside their country of birth. This figure is expected to grow for several reasons including population growth, increasing connectivity, trade, rising inequality, demographic imbalances and climate change.

Migration provides immense opportunity and benefits – for the migrants, host communities and communities of origin. However, when poorly regulated it can create significant challenges. These challenges include reception capacity and support for migrants in host countries overwhelmed by the unexpected arrival of large numbers of people, and the deaths of migrants undertaking dangerous journeys.

As evidenced by doctrine on the subject, the whole system of the global compact, which moreover follows the experience and objectives of the European Union's actions and policies on development and migration and the relations created with third States, remains merely a recognition on the literal level of the rules on international law, an empty list of concrete implementation methods that will lead to an effective development of participation and growth in the governance of the area of migration also of the so-called third countries.[24]

To be effective in international cooperation, any State can sufficiently achieve the objective of effective management of the phenomenon alone. Due to its nature as a global phenomenon, there should be composite and inclusive decision-making processes at the interstate and international level with all the actors involved. Fair international cooperation is a shared responsibility between States and it is a declination of collective responsibility. If the human person were always placed at the centre of international cooperation and development policies, this same person should not then be forced into illegal migration but should be able to access legal and safe migration.

The Global Compact for Migration deals with: the elimination of poverty, food security, health, education, inclusive economic growth, infrastructure, urban and rural development, the fight against unemployment, the fight against gender discrimination, the prevention of environmental disasters, the protection of the rule of law and human rights. These are all areas on which it is necessary to act to protect those who, not returning to inter-

---

24 *Vitiello*, Il contributo dell'Unione europea alla governance internazionale dei flussi di massa e dei rifugiati e migranti: spunti per una rilettura critica dei Global Compacts, Diritto immigrazione e cittadinanza, 2018 vol. 3.

national protection cases, find themselves forced to abandon themselves to forced migration.

There is therefore a need, and it emerges from the Global Compact itself to act against underdevelopment by protracting people's rights. Even to return safely to their country seems to be the only possible solution in the perspective of global migration and human rights protection. The possibility of access to a redistribution in other countries could be a solution in line with the rights and freedoms exercises. Those who are not refugees under 1951 Refugee Status Convention or who are not entitled to subsidiary protection[25] remain linked in the only possible movement of return.[26] This is in contrast with the need for human presence in the face of the population descent as shown by the UNDP reports cited.[27]

A further element of the global pact that would seem to endorse a lower redefinition of international protection standards for mass refugees is the call for complementarity between international protection and the defence of national security by the States, which is followed by the full recognition of the predisposition of forms of cooperation aimed at filtering refugees suspected of threatening national security at the border.

The Global Compact induces the international community to take action to promote the effective enjoyment of this right in compliance with the obligation of non-refoulement, whose function is reduced to guarantee access to information and decent decentralisation.

Harsh is the silence of the Global Compact with respect to the human right to leave any country, even one's own, pursuant to Article 12 of the ICCPR, a right that is closely connected to the right to return to one's own country. In a perspective of progressive development of the right to migrate, the model that the pact proposes is that of a weak right to exit – since international cooperation is not aimed at making effective a "right to escape" from persecution or abuse – and strongly in entry, or in relation to the return of the refugee. To the extent that voluntary return becomes the main solution to the refugee problem, relations between the "producer" states of refugees and the countries of destination change.

---

25 EASO Qualification for International protection Directive 2011/95/EU, A Judicial Analysis, December 2016, https://www.easo.europa.eu/sites/default/files/QIP%20-%20JA.pdf .

26 Noll, Rejected Asylum Seekers: The Problem of Return, in International Migration, IOM, 1999, p. 267.

27 Note 17, UNDP, Human Development Report 2016, http://hdr.undp.org/sites/default/files/2016_human_development_report.pdf .

III. Through the steps of the European policy on cooperation and development in the context of migration

Development cooperation is a fundamental part of the European integration process from the beginning, and already the Treaty of Rome (1957) with the creation of the "European Development Fund" aimed at aiding territories overseas.[28] In the early sixties, with the adoption of the decolonisation policy, the European Member States agreed to share the costs for the reconstruction of the former colonies that had obtained independence. Politics then gradually extended to a greater number of developing countries in Asia, Latin America and Europe itself.

The Lisbon Treaty further strengthened the legal basis for EU development cooperation. It is clearly stated that the primary objective of the development cooperation policy of the Union is the reduction and ultimately the eradication of poverty. This goal must be respected when the Union implements policies that may be of interest to developing countries. This implies the need for a full development policy.

The Cotonou Agreement between the EU and the countries of Africa, the Caribbean and the Pacific (ACP) was signed in 2000. It is a trade and aid agreement which, to date, constitutes the most important partnership between ACP and EU countries and has a duration of 20 years. This agreement provides for an intense collaboration between countries aimed at eradicating poverty and integrating ACP countries into the world economy.[29]

It is necessary also to mention the Rabat Process in the context of cooperation and dialogue with third countries. This process was first launched at the first Euro-African Ministerial Conference on Migration and Development in Rabat in July 2006.

It brings together governments of 55 European and African countries from North, West and Central Africa, together with the European Commission and the Economic Community of West African States (ECOWAS).

---

28 For a historical overview on the European Union's international cooperation and development approach, see: https://ec.europa.eu/europeaid/historical-overview-eu-cooperation-and-aid_en.

29 The Cotonou Agreement was signed in Cotonou on 23 June 2000, revised in Luxembourg on 25 June 2005 and then revised again in Ouagadougou on 22 June 2010. For the most recent, amended and updated version, see: http://www.europarl.europa.eu/intcoop/acp/03_01/pdf/mn3012634_en.pdf.

The Rabat Process's objective was to enhance dialogue and cooperation on migration more broadly, through all the areas that concern the theme of migration: legal migration and mobility; prevention of irregular migration and measures to counteract it; migration and development; international protection, as well as to identify common priorities in order to develop operational and practical cooperation.

The Rabat Process has been designed as an intergovernmental dialogue to create a solid dialogue between the EU and countries in North, West and Central Africa, and has fostered enhanced cooperation through the implementation of bilateral, sub-regional, regional and multilateral initiatives, to ensure cooperation and support at the political and technical level.

Among the examples of concrete cooperation at the regional level, we can refer to the Seahorse Atlantic Network, which enabled information exchange between authorities along the Western African coast in order to prevent irregular migration and cross-border crime.

The EU–Africa Summit in 2014 gave new impetus to cooperation on migration: In addition to the declaration on migration and mobility, an Action Plan 2014–2017 was also adopted, focusing on the following priorities: trafficking in human beings; remittances; diaspora; mobility and labour migration (including intra-African mobility); international protection (including internally displaced persons) and irregular migration.

The EU also envisages continued funding in the area of migration under the 11th European Development Fund which should be signed in the first half of 2015.

As part of the Sahel Regional Action Plan, the EU declared the will to reinforce the development migration nexus and mainstream migration into the EU and Member States' collective actions based on the Global Approach to Migration and Mobility and the Rabat Process.[30]

With the Sahel programme, we are also reminded that the Khartoum Process was launched at a Ministerial Conference in Rome in November 2014. The objective was to establish a long-standing dialogue on migration and mobility aimed at enhancing the current cooperation, including through the identification and implementation of concrete projects. In the first phase, activities concentrated on addressing trafficking in human beings as well as smuggling of migrants.

---

30 *Lopez*, Performing EU agency by experimenting the 'Comprehensive Approach': the European Union Sahel Strategy, Journal of Contemporary African Studies 2017; *Venturi*, The EU and the Sahel: A Laboratory of Experimentation for the Security–Migration–Development Nexus, in: Isituto Affari Internazionali – Papers, 2017.

The Khartoum Process is led by a Steering Committee comprised of five EU Member States (Italy, France, Germany, UK, Malta), five partner countries (Egypt, Eritrea, Ethiopia, South Sudan, Sudan) as well as the European Commission, the European External Action Service and the AU Commission on the African side.

On 20 April 2015, the Council adopted the Sahel Regional Action Plan 2015–2020 which provides the overall framework for the implementation of the EU Strategy for Security and Development in the Sahel, as adopted and revised in its Conclusions on 21 March 2011 and 17 March 2014, respectively.

The Action Plan provides a solid basis for reinforcing the EU's focus around four domains that are highly relevant to the stabilisation of the region, namely prevention and countering radicalisation; creation of appropriate conditions for youth; migration, mobility and border management; the fight against illicit trafficking; and transnational organised crime.

People move to escape poverty and conflict, to seek protection from persecution or serious harm, or to build a better life.

For individuals, migration can be one of the most powerful and immediate strategies for poverty reduction. In the absence of employment opportunities, many youth seek better opportunities by migrating.

The Sahel Regional Action Plan will focus on this link between migration and development. In addition, the EU is focusing on prevention and fighting against irregular migration, smuggling and trafficking in human beings; promoting international protection and organising mobility and legal migration.

The situation in Niger, as a major transit country, is requiring strengthened efforts, notably to reinforce and accompany the actions already launched by the Common Security and Defence Policy (CSDP) and its mission, EUCAP Sahel Niger.

Youth Economic growth is necessary to create employment and significantly reduce widespread poverty and income inequalities that continue to prevail across the Sahel. More effort is needed to create job opportunities throughout all sectors, for youth. The EU will provide relevant aid for youth, including education and training as well as job creation, and ensure equal opportunities for boys and girls. An example of such assistance is the empowerment of mainstream youth through identification of indicators to monitor and promote education and youth employment to offer alternatives to illegal activities/extremist actions. Further analysis on how to support youth as agents for positive change will also be provided.

The EU would like to build youth migrant resilience, inviting them not to leave their countries of origin, promoting economic and employment opportunities.

A further strengthening of the multilateral dimension of the European Neighbourhood Policy could also add value to cooperation on migration. Neighbourhood countries are both countries of origin and of transit. Migration management requires solid regional frameworks. Their strengthening in the Southern Neighbourhood would provide the basis for a more systematic engagement with the existing regional forums and regional migration dialogues and programmes.

Using the aforementioned instruments, the European Union Emergency Trust Fund for Africa (EUTF), the Migration Partnership Framework and the Refugee Facility for Turkey, the European Union and individual Member States provided funds to stop migration of certain people from taking place on or across European territory.[31]

These funds are aimed at guaranteeing strong collaboration on migrants' readmission, training of police and border officials, and the improvement of biometric systems. While many projects are actioned through the European Commission, some also take a lead in funding and supporting border externalisation efforts through bilateral agreements with non-EU countries.

Turkey's attack against Kurdish people in the Rojava area is evidence of the failure of this kind of collaboration with third countries, giving millions of euros without any effective check on respect for the Rule of Law and Human rights obligations.[32]

---

31 See, for example: The 2018 Annual Report of the European Union Emergency Trust Fund for Africa https://ec.europa.eu/trustfundforafrica/sites/euetfa/files/ar_2018_en.pdf.

32 See, for example: UN report details massive destruction and serious rights violations since July 2015 in southeast Turkey, https://www.ohchr.org/EN/NewsEvents/Pages/DisplayNews.aspx?NewsID=21342; Human Rights Watch report, Turkey/Syria: Civilians at Risk in Syria Operation Key Concerns Include Unlawful Attacks, Treatment of Displaced People, Arbitrary Arrests, 11 October 2019.

IV. *Global Approach on Migration and Mobility, and partnerships as main instruments*[33]

Since the Treaty of Amsterdam, the European Union has created several instruments in the field of cooperation and development.[34]

The most elaborate bilateral cooperation frameworks under the Global Approach on Migration and Mobility (GAMM)[35], Mobility Partnerships (MP)[36] and the Common Agendas for Migration and Mobility (CAMM) could be considered a political framework for comprehensive, enhanced and tailor-made dialogue and cooperation with partner countries.

However, there are two particular differences: first, establishing an MP would include the negotiation of visa facilitation and readmission agreements, the MP could be defined as international agreements between the EU and third countries and the negotiation is based on separated dialogue and specific dialogue with each third country.[37]

These agreements and policies obviously cannot be in violation of principles such as the non-refoulement sanctioned by Article 33 of the 1951 Geneva Convention and, as is known, the common law binding principle for any state. They must not violate the non-refoulement and access to protection for the persons who cease in the light of the obligation to respect

---

33 On 10 and 11 December 2018, the city of Marrakesh hosted the Intergovernmental Conference to Adopt the Global Compact for Safe, Orderly and Regular Migration.

34 *Strik*, The Global Approach to Migration and Mobility, Groningen Journal of International Law 2017, 310.

35 Communication from the Commission to the European Parliament, The Council, The European Economic and Social Committee of the Regions, The Global Approach to Migration and Mobility – SEC(2011) 1353.

36 Overview of the EU Mobility Partnership Instrument Summary of the Initiatives in Georgia and Moldova, International Centre for Migration Policy Development (ICMPD), May 2016.

37 See, for example, https://ec.europa.eu/home-affairs/e-library/documents/policies_en?policy=468
International agreements:
Sub-Saharan African Countries
28 May 2009 – Agreement between the European Community and the Republic of Seychelles on the short-stay visa
28 May 2009 – Agreement between the European Community and the Republic of Mauritius on the short-stay visa
27 May 2008 – Mobility partnership between the EU and Cape Verde Mobility partnership between the EU and Cape Verde.

the hierarchy of sources and the obligations assumed in terms of fundamental human rights by the States and by the European Union itself.

The principle initially enshrined in Article 33 of the 1951 Convention relating to the Status of Refugees as prohibiting expulsion or refoulement to a country where the life or liberty of the person concerned would be threatened on the basis of the five grounds enumerated by the Convention. The Convention later became part of the fundamental principles of human rights. Article 3 of the Convention against Torture prohibits State Parties, from expelling or returning a person to a country where there are substantial grounds for believing that he would be subjected to torture. Subsequent jurisprudence, using the prohibition of torture and other inhuman and degrading treatment or punishment, as well as the right to life and physical integrity (respectively enshrined in articles 7 and 6 of the Covenant at the international level) International Covenant on Civil and Political Rights) subsequently extended the scope of the principle. The principle is also enshrined in the International Convention for the Protection of All Persons from Enforced Disappearance.[38]

Mobility Partnerships used to be built on the scheme: legal migration and mobility, asylum, border management and prevention of irregular migration, and migration and development.

Typical actions or activities covered in a Mobility Partnership are:

- Legal migration and mobility promotion of a better framework for legal migration and mobility, including through circular and temporary migration schemes as well as better information and protection of migrants, including pre-departure training;
- Informing potential migrants on opportunities for legal migration and on requirements for legal stay, as well as on the dangers of undocumented migration and illegal work;
- Institutional and administrative capacity-building of partner countries' authorities in legal migration management, through improvement of the regulatory framework, technical assistance, training, exchange of experts and best practices, etc.

---

38 *Hathaway*, The Rights of Refugees under International Law 2005, 363, 367; *Allain*, The Jus Cogens Nature of Non-refoulement, International Journal of Refugee Law 533 (2001), 533; *Goodwin-Gill*, The Right to Seek Asylum: Interception at Sea and the Principle of Non-refoulement', International Journal of Refugee Law 23 (2011), 443, 443 f.; Inter-American Court of Human Rights Advisory Opinion, Juridical Condition and Rights of the Undocumented Migrant, Concurring Opinion of Judge A.A. Cançado Trindade, OC-18/03, 41.

Mobility Partnerships are referred to as: "the most complete framework for bilateral cooperation between the European Union and its partners, based on mutual offers of commitments and project initiatives covering mobility, migration and asylum issues".[39]

The Global Approach to Migration and Mobility (GAMM) is, since 2005, the overarching framework of the EU external migration and asylum policy. The framework defines how the EU conducts its policy dialogues and operational cooperation with third countries, based on clearly defined priorities which reflect the strategic objectives of the EU, and is embedded in the EU's overall foreign policy framework, including development cooperation. It is also important to underline that the GAMM aims to develop mutually beneficial partnerships in line with both the interests of the EU and of partner countries (which is needed to ensure effective management of migration flows).

The GAMM is focused on four thematic priorities: (1) better organising legal migration and fostering well-managed mobility; (2) preventing and combating irregular migration and eradicating trafficking of human beings; (3) maximising the development impact of migration and mobility; (4) promoting international protection and enhancing the external dimension of asylum. The protection of human rights is a cross-cutting priority.

The GAMM is implemented through several political instruments (regional ones and bilateral policy dialogues and action plans), legal instruments (visa facilitation for some third countries national and readmission agreements in the light of the EU return directive[40]), operational support and capacity-building (including via EU agencies, e.g. FRONTEX, EASO and ETF, and technical assistance facilities such as MIEUX and TAIEX) as well as the wide range of programme and project support that is made available to third-country administrations and other stakeholders, such as civil society, migrant associations and international organisations.

The GAMM implementation is a common and shared responsibility of the Commission, EEAS (including EU Delegations) and Member States, in accordance with their respective competences as set out in the Treaties.

---

39 European Commission, Migration and Home Affairs, Mobility partnerships, visa facilitation and readmission agreements, http://ec.europa.eu/dgs/home-affairs/what-we-do/policies/international-affairs/easternpartnership/mobility-partnerships-visa-facilitation-and-readmission-agreements/index_en.htm.

40 Directive 2008/115/EC of the European Parliament and of the Council of 16 December 2008 on common standards and procedures in Member States for returning illegally staying third-country nationals.

General background on migration and development Almost all developing countries are significantly affected by population movements.

Based on its Global Approach to Migration and Mobility (GAMM) – the predominant framework of the EU external migration and asylum policy – the EU is moving to design more and more agreement with African countries on migration and mobility at bilateral, regional and continental levels.

On the basis of its Global Approach to Migration and Mobility (GAMM) – the overarching framework of the EU external migration and asylum policy – the EU is running a broad dialogue with countries on the African continent on migration and mobility at bilateral, regional and continental levels: Continental level, with the African Union. A key political declaration on migration and mobility was endorsed by the Heads of State and Government at the EU-Africa Summit in April 2014.

The Global Approach to Migration and Mobility reaffirms the joint commitment of the parties, on the one hand third countries, on the other the European Union itself, to "combat", among other things, irregular migration and to address all its relevant aspects, including prevention, strengthening migration and border management, migrant smuggling, repatriation and return, as well as addressing the root causes of irregular migration and strengthening cooperation to tackle human trafficking and offer international protection.

In 2011, the global approach was evaluated. Following this, the Commission underlined the need to further strengthen external migration policy and in November 2011 published the Communication on the Global Approach to Migration and Mobility, COM (2011) 743 final on a new impetus for the EU's external migration policy. The renewed GAMM focuses on four main priorities: improving the organisation of legal migration and facilitated mobility, preventing and reducing irregular migration in an effective and humane manner, enhancing the synergies between migration and development, and strengthening the migration systems, protection, the external dimension of migration and asylum.

Throughout the document, as well as in numerous EU acts and instruments, the demarcation between legal and illegal, regular and irregular immigration is identified as simply identifiable, since from this point the approach of the European Union does not always know how to respond to the reality of the condition of the migratory flows that are mixed by nature of the human condition. These might include those who find themselves perhaps migrating with a visa that does not then allow the actual possibility of remaining in a Member State, or those who are in a condition of entry for reasons of study and must ask for asylum after finding themselves to be a refugee in a place, or whoever discovers that they are a victim of trafficking when they believed they had entered on a regular visa for work.

V. *European Union and cooperation and development in migration: a paternalism approach?*

As a matter of fact, Africa and Europe have different narratives, approaches and perceptions of migration – and they have different important links with the development processes. The interest in the migration flows are different and a fair policy would be a correct balance of all the different needs.

Respect of human rights is a cross-cutting priority for this policy framework, but due to the legal nature of GAMM, of course the effectivity of this cross-cutting priority seems to be at risk. GAMM is implemented through several political instruments (bilateral and regional policy dialogues and action plans), legal instruments (such as visa facilitation and readmission agreements), operational support and capacity building as well as programme and project support made available to third countries and other stakeholders, e.g. civil society and international organisations.

The open question is whether the European Global approach on migration and mobility is useful to guarantee the effectivity of human rights?

In the context of cooperation and development policy the European Union seems to fail because, while on the one hand, for example trafficking in human beings is not eradicated, on the other, even countries with which it has activated bilateral agreements do not seem to use the funds obtained for people's access to resources because they are not forced to rely on smugglers and traffickers' networks.[41]

In the analysis in particular of the different instruments of cooperation and development with the countries of the MENA area, a hegemonic relationship of the European Union emerges so that in fact migrants are stopped. Think of the agreements with Niger without any verification of effective access to equal rights and protections.[42]

From the lack of respect for equitable economic participation and governance within its own borders, the European Union appears to be trans-

41 See, for example, the UNODC Global report on trafficking in persons 2018, https://www.unodc.org/unodc/data-and-analysis/glotip.html

42 *Parkes*, Nobody move! Myths of the EU migration crisis, EU Institute for Security Studies, December 2017.

posing the same dynamics to the level of third countries. Therefore, the development cooperation that should be aimed at preventing trafficking in human beings, for example, is declined with the mere request for control and management of flows by third countries so that the arrivals of migrants in Europe are not excessive and are manageable.[43]

Some third countries at the first step refused to sign readmission agreements for some time because these agreements brought third countries to respect the governance of the European Union in migration. Within these agreements there is cooperation on expelling "illegal and unwanted migrants". The European Union exploited the extremely fragile and uncertain political context in some third countries and finally succeeded in obtaining what are the European Union objectives and priorities.[44]

The European Neighbourhood Policy always recalls the same dynamics of hegemony and control. This emerged clearly following the Arab springs and with what emerged and was encountered in Libya.[45] There are countries like Niger which have accepted the bilateral agreement but cannot guarantee fair access to effective protection for all migrants. Tunisia, on the other hand has rejected these agreements for long time, pointing out that it has no intention of playing the role of controller of the borders of Europe in exchange for money and support.[46]

The European Union continued to operate according to the logic of normative empire towards neighbouring countries.[47] This entails a continuation of the basic idea that neighbouring countries should gradually accept a pre-defined set of European Union rules and practices, without being able to participate in the decision-making process and responding to the main European Union objective: manage migration not from the perspective of the Rule of Law but from a hegemonic point of view.

---

43 *Del Santo*, Normative Empire Europe: The European Union, its Borderlands, and the Arab Spring, JCMS 2016, 215.

44 *Wolff*, The Politics of Negotiating EU Readmission Agreements: Insights from Morocco and Turkey, Perspective on European Politics and Society 16 (2014), 69.

45 *Papa*, Externalizing EU Migration control while ignoring the human rights of migrants: is there any room for the international responsibility of European States?, Questions of International Law, 56 (2019), 1; *Pascale*, Is Italy Internationally Responsible for the Gross Human Rights Violations against Migrants in Libya?, Questions of International Law, 56 (2019), 35.

46 *Del Sarto, Limam*, Periphery under Pressure: Morocco, Tunisia and the European Union's Mobility Partnership on Migration, EUI Working Paper RSCAS 2015/75.

47 *Markard*, The Right to Leave by Sea: Legal Limits on EU Migration Control by Third Countries, European Journal of International Law 27 (2016), 591–616.

This point of view always recalls the colonialist approach, with an incapacity to understand that migration, fair cooperation and development policies could be to the benefit of every country and human being. To insist on limiting the right to leave as prescribed in Article 12 ICCPR and on eroding the cornerstone of human rights by asking to stop migrants by any means could in the end lead to the legitimisation of violence and a lack of democracy that Turkey itself is showing in its military and political action.[48]

As a matter of fact, in cooperation and development issues, the European Union seems unable to learn from history and improve its dynamics of paternalism rather then defend the rule of law and human rights in any policies and actions.

48 *Guild*, To protect or to forget? The Human Right to Leave a Country, EU Immigration and Asylum Law and Policy Droit et Politique de l'Immigration et de l'Asile de l'UE, December 2017.

PART TWO

THE EUROPEAN UNION'S "GATEKEEPERS": COUNTRY FOCUS

EU–Turkey Relations in Migration Matters

Ülkü Sezgi Sözen[*] and Chad Heimrich[**]

I. Introduction

The relationship between the European Union (hereinafter, the EU) and Turkey has never been straightforward as the past 50 years have clearly demonstrated. This continues to be the case in migration matters which, in recent years, have become the main focus in EU–Turkey relations. For most of the 20th century, Turkey was a state-sponsored immigration country due to its population. Emigration from Turkey did not begin until 1961. Until the 1990s, the main incentive for this was economic migration, in particular labour migration to Europe. Over the last two decades, Turkey has been an immigration and transit country in terms of both asylum seekers and irregular migration.[1] Due to an unprecedented migration flow, Turkey currently accommodates 3,542,250 registered Syrian asylum seekers alongside other immigrants who, registered or unregistered, stay in Turkey and/or use it as a transit country en route to Europe. [2]

Hand in hand with these developments, the balance of the relationship between the EU and Turkey was once again challenged and put to the test – a relationship that is characterised by an awareness of mutual dependency, but equally by a certain distanced attitude. In order to understand this fragile balance and make the connection to the external dimension of the EU's migration and asylum policies towards Turkey and its effects on their relationship, this chapter seeks to give an overview of the developments between the EU and Turkey and to answer the question of how Turkey became the EU's gatekeeper in migration matters.

---

* PhD candidate at the Universität Hamburg, Albrecht Mendelssohn Bartholdy Graduate School of Law.

** Legal Trainee at District Court Kassel.

1 *Baldwin-Edwards*, Migration in the Mediterranean and Middle East, in: Marshall (ed.), The Politics of Migration, London 2006, 184.

2 See for more statistics regarding Syrian asylum seekers in Turkey: UNHCR Operational Data Portal, retrieved from: https://data2.unhcr.org/en/situations/syria/location/113, accessed: 05 November 2019.

Firstly, Turkey's EU journey will be outlined from a historical perspective in order to understand the dynamics in the relationship between the EU and Turkey. Secondly, special attention will be given to the EU–Turkey Readmission Agreement as a milestone in migration matters and as the official starting point of Turkey's gatekeeper role in this relationship. Thirdly and lastly, the content and legal nature of the EU–Turkey Statement will be elaborated, before addressing our perspective on the question of how Turkey became the EU's gatekeeper in migration matters in order to open some further discussions in this regard.

II. Turkey's EU journey: a rocky path

In order to get an understanding of the dynamics in the relationship between Turkey and the EU in recent years – and more specifically, its implications on the external dimension of the EU's migration policies – a look at the past is indispensable. The complexity of this doubtlessly "special" relationship differs from the EU's cooperation with other third countries. Three dimensions of the relationship between Turkey and the EU will be distinguished and further explored in the following.[3]

Firstly, in the 1960s, the priority was cooperation in economic and trade affairs in order to strengthen, and to some extent formalise through the setup of an agreement, links with Turkey. A milestone was reached in 1963 with the signing of the "Agreement Creating an Association Between the Republic of Turkey and the European Economic Community", commonly referred to as the "Ankara Agreement".[4] On a primary level, the Agreement intended a greater cooperation in economic and trade matters between the parties through the establishment of a customs union. At the same time, the parties had affirmed not to limit their relation to the facilitation of movement of goods, workers and services, but to take a step further and "examine the possibility of the accession of Turkey to the Community" (Art. 28 of the Ankara Agreement).[5] Originally seen as a progres-

3 See *Ott*, EU-Turkey Cooperation in Migration Matters: A Game Changer in a Multi-layered Relationship?, CLEER Papers 4 (2017), 1, 8 ff.

4 Agreement establishing an Association between the European Economic Community and Turkey.

5 See also the preamble to the Ankara Agreement: "Recognizing that the support given by the European Economic Community to the efforts of the Turkish people to improve their standard of living will facilitate the accession of Turkey to the Community at a later date."

sively thinking idea, the realisation could not match the high expectations particularly on the side of Turkey to become an integral part of the EU's internal market and, possibly, a full member. The customs union was not set up until 1995 and the aim, expressed in the Agreement and the 1970 Additional Protocol,[6] to establish free movement rights for economically active persons has seen no progress since the 1980s. In fact, Turkish workers today still need to rely on the provisions of the Additional Protocol and Decision 1/80 of the Association Council to establish rights to work and reside.[7] In addition, in 1982, some countries such as Germany, France and the Benelux introduced visa requirements for Turkish citizens in fear of uncontrolled numbers of Turkish people moving and settling in these countries.[8] This stood in strong contrast to the objective of (visa-)free movement, and even the Court of Justice in its decision in *Demirkan* abated the hope of Turkish citizens for a visa-free regime through case law.[9] There, the Court held, that the standstill clause in Art. 41 para. 1 of the 1970 Additional Protocol – i.e. obliging the parties to refrain from restrictions to the freedom of establishment and the freedom to provide services – does not prohibit the introduction of visa requirements by EU Member States for Turkish citizens. A central point of the Court's reasoning was the "solely economical purpose" of the Ankara Agreement, concluding that there is no right of Turkish citizens to visa-free travel to the EU, if it is not for the active provision of services on the territory of Member States.[10]

---

6 Additional Protocol and Financial Protocol, annexed to the Agreement establishing an Association between the European Economic Community and Turkey.

7 *Sözen*, EU-Turkey readmission agreement: Not a "carrot" but more a '?', Turkish Migration Conference 2015 Selected Proceedings, London 2015, 55.

8 *Sözen*, Turkish Migration Conference 2015 Selected Proceedings (fn. 7), 55.

9 European Court of Justice, C-221/11 ECLI:EU:C:2013:583, judgment, 24 September 2013 – Demirkan/Bundesrepublik Deutschland

10 European Court of Justice, C-221/11 ECLI:EU:C:2013:583, judgment, 24 September 2013, paras. 50 and 63 – Demirkan/Bundesrepublik Deutschland; see for a comment on the decision *Hatzopoulos*, Turkish service recipients under the EU-Turkey Association Agreement: Demirkan, Common Market Law Review 51 (2014), 647; *Sözen*, C-221-11 Demirkan Decision from the European Court of Justice, Istanbul Culture University Law Review 13 (2014), 171-185; for an overview about the jurisprudence of the European Court of Justice in this field: *Tezcan/ Idriz*, Free Movement of Persons Between Turkey and the EU: to Move or not to Move? The Response of the Judiciary, Common Market Law Review 46 (2009), 1621; *Wiesbrock*, Political Reluctance and Judicial Activism in the Area of Free Movement of Persons: The Court as the Motor of EU-Turkey Relations?, European Law Journal 19 (2013), 422.

Secondly, the dynamics of EU–Turkey relations are characterised by the long-standing interest to demonstrate affiliation to the Western powers through full membership in the EU. Despite a rejected attempt to join the European Economic Community in 1987, partially because of critics with regards to the country's conflicts with Greece and Cyprus, accession talks did not come to a complete stop and EU officials recognised Turkey's "general opening towards Europe".[11] A turning point in otherwise long and arduous accession discussions was reached at the Helsinki Summit in 1999, where Turkey was officially awarded candidate status, and the formal opening of accession negotiations occurred in 2005. Following the 2015 political instabilities, the proclaimed state of emergency as well as changes in the political and judicial system in Turkey, in 2019 negotiations came to a standstill. Referring to the European Council conclusions of 26 June 2018, EU institutions stated that "Turkey has been moving further away from the European Union", serious concerns about deficits in fundamental rights, the rule of law and constitutional changes affecting the judiciary were raised.[12] Whether negotiations will be resumed in the near future is unclear and in the current political climate, highly unlikely. It certainly constitutes a major push-back in Turkey's membership ambitions.

Thirdly, the EU–Turkey relationship has, in recent years, turned towards alternative cooperation measures in fields that could not sufficiently be part of the accession process or that have urgently called upon the parties to find common solutions.[13] The prime example for those so-called "joint interests" is the field of migration. Some would even argue that migration has become the central motor in EU–Turkey relations, overshadowing political disruptions such as the Gezi Park protests in 2013 that have caused heavy criticism of Turkey's internal politics.[14] The outbreak of the Syrian Civil War and the rising number of migrants transiting Turkey in an attempt to reach EU soil have urged the EU to undertake necessary measures to intensify the cooperation with third countries as part of its

---

11 *Aksu*, A Historical Background to Turkey-Europe-Relations, in: Aksu (ed.), Turkey-EU Relations: Power, Politics and the Future, Cambridge 2012, 1, 10.

12 See also: Press statement following the 54th meeting of the Association Council between the European Union and Turkey, Brussels, 15 March 2019, retrieved from: https://www.consilium.europa.eu/en/press/press-releases/2019/03/15/press-statement-following-the-54th-meeting-of-the-association-council-between-the-european-union-and-turkey-brussels-15-march-2019/, accessed: 31 October 2019.

13 *Ott*, CLEER Papers 4 (2017) (fn. 3), 11.

14 *Hauge/Eralp/Wessels/Bedir*, Mapping milestones and periods of past EU-Turkey relations, FEUTURE Working Paper September 2016, 1, 20.

wider migration policy. Turkey as the often so-called "key strategic partner" has become the prime partner for the EU in tackling the "migration crisis". In a sense, Turkey's ambitions to become a full member of the EU were boosted by the EU's dependency on Turkey's cooperation, significantly improving the country's bargaining position, or at least in theory.

In that context, the 2013 EU–Turkey Readmission Agreement and the 2016 EU–Turkey Statement are of particular importance to demonstrate the current state of the relationship dynamics.

III. The EU–Turkey Readmission Agreement

It was repeatedly emphasised on the side of the EU that a comprehensive and encompassing approach to migration requires – by its nature – efficient cooperation with countries of origin and of transit when it comes to combatting irregular migration. Policies of return, removal and repatriation were considered an imperative part of efficient migration policies, both to strengthen the external borders of the EU and, at the same time, to discourage migrants from irregularly entering a Member State's territory.[15] In conformity with the EU's "Global Approach to Migration and Mobility" (GAMM), which intended to formulate a "comprehensive framework to manage migration and mobility with partner countries in a coherent and mutually beneficial way through policy dialogue and close practical cooperation", EU readmission agreements (EURA) were considered the primary tool to achieve such cooperation, particularly with countries that produce a steady and high flow of migrants.[16]

Bilateral readmission agreements of Member States with third countries were no novelty. In 2001, Greece and Turkey signed a bilateral readmission agreement. The implementation, however, turned out to be highly dysfunctional with a high number of rejections of as well as severe delays in accepting readmission requests.[17] Disputes between Turkish and Greek border officers on the origin of third-country nationals also reinforced the

---

15 *Icduygu/Aksel*, Two-to-Tango in Migration Diplomacy: Negotiating Readmission Agreement between the EU and Turkey, European Journal of Migration and Law 16 (2014), 337, 340.

16 See for further comments on this issue *Hampshire*, Speaking with one voice? The European Union's global approach to migration and the limits of international migration cooperation, Journal of Ethnic and Migration Studies 42 (2016), 578.

17 *Sözen*, Turkish Migration Conference 2015 Selected Proceedings (fn. 7), 58.

lack of efficiency.[18] The malfunctioning of the bilateral readmission agreement supported the urge at EU level to push for an EU–Turkey Readmission Agreement.[19]

A first hurdle was the question of competence for the conclusion of EURAs. In the 1990s, this was still impeded by the lack of an EU competence in the field of migration. Only with the Treaty of Amsterdam in 1999, the abolition of the pillar structure and the creation of the Area of Justice, Freedom and Security, the EU obtained implied powers to act externally *vis-à-vis* third countries in matters regarding irregular immigration (Art. 63 para. 3 (b) of the Treaty Establishing the European Community).[20] With the entry into force of the Lisbon Treaty in 2009, Article 79 para. 3 of the Treaty on the Functioning of the European Union (TFEU) confers on the EU the explicit power to "conclude agreements with third countries for the readmission to their countries of origin or provenance of third-country nationals who do not or who no longer fulfil the conditions for entry, presence or residence in the territory of one of the Member States." Albeit not explicitly ruled out, this would then *de facto* prohibit Member States from concluding readmission agreements with those third countries, who have concluded such agreements with the EU. A – in principle – shared competence transforms into a *de facto* exclusive competence of the EU by exercise, as there would be no remaining margin of action left to Member States (pursuant to Article 2 (2) TFEU). This, however, does not impact bilateral agreements that were concluded before the EURA, meaning that, in the case of Turkey, the Greece–Turkey Readmission Agreement is still in force and remains applicable law.

Despite their popularity, a look at the existing EURAs shows that negotiating such agreements can at times be very lengthy due to the lack of incentives for the country concerned.[21] Most times – even though the obligations are reciprocal – EURAs will apply in cases where the third country is

18 *Dimitriadi/Kaya/Kale/Zurabishvili*, EU-Turkey Relations and Irregular Migration: Transactional Cooperation in the Making, FEUTURE Online Paper No. 16 March 2018, 1, 7; see also *Wolff*, The Politics of Negotiating EU Readmission Agreements: Insights from Morocco and Turkey, European Journal of Migration and Law 16 (2014), 69, 92.

19 *Icduygu/Aksel*, European Journal of Migration and Law 16 (2014) (fn. 15), 340.

20 On the situation before the Lisbon Treaty: *Billet*, EC Readmission Agreements: A Prime Instrument of the External Dimension of the EU's Fight against Irregular Immigration. An Assessment after Ten Years of Practice, European Journal of Migration and Law 12 (2010), 45, 59. For more details: *Sözen*, Turkish Migration Conference 2015 Selected Proceedings (fn. 7), 56 ff.

21 *Icduygu/Aksel*, European Journal of Migration and Law 16 (2014) (fn. 15), 343.

under the obligation to readmit migrants. The reluctance of the third country is also reinforced by the fact that EURAs include clauses to readmit third-country nationals that have purely transited the territory of the readmitting state. This significantly broadens the scope of these agreements and, at the same time, becomes a strong discouraging factor. Hence, agreeing to readmit not only its own nationals, but also third-country nationals and stateless persons bears the high risk for transit countries such as Libya, Morocco or Turkey to experience an increase of irregular migrants who eventually become "stuck" in the readmitting state.[22]

Turkey's reluctance to negotiate was based mainly on two aspects: firstly, the fear arose of becoming a "buffer zone" between the EU and the conflict zones in the Near and Middle East,[23] and secondly, the lack of concrete commitments by the EU on visa liberalisation.[24] The latter caused concerns about the credibility of promises made on the EU side and an unequal treatment compared with the Western Balkan candidate countries, who were offered visa facilitation agreements relatively quickly.[25] It became clear that the conclusion of an EURA would stand and fall with the opening of a visa liberalisation dialogue.[26] The negotiations of the agreement, which started in 2005, were characterised by a high reluctance on the side of Turkey to agree on the readmission of third-country nationals. Turkey demanded to postpone the conclusion of the agreement until it could enter bilateral agreements with countries of origin.[27] Negotiations came to a stop in 2006 following the freezing of accession talks on eight chapters of the EU's acquis, which was the reaction to Turkey's objection to opening its ports and airports to vessels and aircrafts coming from the Republic of Cyprus.[28] With the resumption of negotiations in 2010, Turkey repeated its request to – in parallel to the conclusion of the EURA – open a visa liberalisation dialogue to ultimately achieve a visa-free regime.[29] Countries such as Germany and France opposed the idea of lift-

---

22 *Icduygu/Aksel*, European Journal of Migration and Law 16 (2014) (fn. 15), 343.
23 *Burc Aka/Özkural*, Turkey and the European Union: A Review of Turkey's Readmission Agreement, The European Legacy 20 (2015), 255, 263.
24 *Ott*, CLEER Papers 4 (2017) (fn. 3), 13.
25 *Wolff*, European Journal of Migration and Law 16 (2014) (fn. 18), 86.
26 *Ott*, CLEER Papers 4 (2017) (fn. 3), 14.
27 *Wolff*, European Journal of Migration and Law 16 (2014) (fn. 18), 90.
28 *Icduygu/Aksel*, European Journal of Migration and Law 16 (2014) (fn. 15), 353.
29 *Icduygu/Aksel*, European Journal of Migration and Law 16 (2014) (fn. 15), 353; Republic of Turkey Ministry of Foreign Affairs, No. 57.25, February 2011 Press Release Regarding the Conclusions of the EU Justice and Home Affairs Council, re-

ing visas in return for the conclusion of the EURA, as they feared that migration from Turkey to the EU Member States would increase.[30]

Finally, in 2013, in alignment with the signature of the EURA, the EU and Turkey launched the visa liberalisation dialogue. Based on requirements set out in the "Roadmap towards a visa-free regime with Turkey", Turkey's legislation and administrative practices need to comply with EU standards in the fields of document security, migration and border management, public order and security and fundamental rights as well as specific conditions on the readmission of irregular migrants including to "fully and effectively implement the EU–Turkey Readmission Agreement in all its provisions".[31] While Turkey made significant progress until 2016, fulfilling 66 of 72 total requirements, no progress was detected from then until 2019.[32]

The final EURA contains reciprocal obligations to readmit own nationals (Articles 3 and 5) as well as third-country nationals and stateless persons (Articles 4 and 6) for those who do not, or who no longer, fulfil the conditions in force for entry to, presence in, or residence on, the territory or the requesting state. With regards to Turkey's readmission of third-country nationals and stateless persons, Article 4 para. 1 subpara. c specifies that the obligation to readmit arises once these persons have "illegally and directly entered the territory of the Member States after having stayed on, or transited through, the territory of Turkey". This provision, however, pursuant to Article 24 para. 3 was only to become applicable three years after the entry into force of the agreement, unless Turkey had concluded bilateral readmission agreements with the country of origin of the concerned persons. This was meant to release the pressure on and the fear of Turkey to become responsible for a large number of third-country nationals. At the same time this provided Turkey with the chance to step up its own read-

---

trieved from: http://www.mfa.gov.tr/no_-57_-25-february-2011_-press-release-regarding-the-conclusions-of-the-eu-justice-and-home-affairs-council.en.mfa, accessed: 31 October 2019.

30 *Bürgin*, European Commission's agency meets Ankara's agenda: why Turkey is ready for a readmission agreement, Journal of European Public Policy 19 (2012), 883, 894.

31 Roadmap Towards a Visa-Free Regime with Turkey, retrieved from: https://ec.europa.eu/home-affairs/sites/homeaffairs/files/what-is-new/news/news/docs/20131216-roadmap_towards_the_visa-free_regime_with_turkey_en.pdf, accessed: 31 October 2019.

32 European Commission, Turkey 2019 Report, retrieved from: https://ec.europa.eu/neighbourhood-enlargement/sites/near/files/20190529-turkey-report.pdf, accessed: 31 October 2019.

mission efforts with countries of origin.[33] The EURA entered into force on 1 October 2014, hence, Articles 4 and 6 would only enter into force as of 1 October 2017. In the light of the number of irregular migrants reaching its peak in 2015 and the EU–Turkey Summit on 29 November 2015, a decision was reached to activate those two provisions as of 1 June 2016.[34]

The implementation of the EURA, however, remained – more than three years after the entry into force of all provisions, including those on the readmission of third-country nationals – unsatisfactory.[35] In the European Commission's 2019 Turkey Report, the inconsistent implementation of the provisions concerning Turkish nationals was criticised. Furthermore, it states, that Turkey insists on the lifting of visa requirements for short-term stays and only in return, will apply readmissions to third-country nationals. Readmissions on the basis of the bilateral Greece–Turkey Agreement have also been halted.[36] In addition, NGO reports have indicated frequent human rights and international refugee law violations by Turkey, for instance, through collective expulsion of asylum seekers back to their countries of origin. Although the EURA stipulates in Article 18, the so-called non-affection clause, that the agreement does not affect the parties' obligations under international law, for instance the 1951 Geneva Convention on the Status of Refugees or the European Convention of Hu-

---

33 Bosnia-Herzegovina (2012), Moldova (2012), Nigeria (2011), Russian Federation (2011), Yemen (2011), Pakistan (2010), Ukraine (2005), Kyrgyzstan (2003), Syria (2001), Greece (2001), Romania (2004).

34 See reference to this decision in European Commission, First Report on the progress made in the implementation of the EU–Turkey Statement COM (2016) 0231, 4; European Commission, Proposal for a Council Decision [...] on a Decision of the Joint Readmission Committee [...] for the application of Articles 4 and 6 of the [Readmission] Agreement [...] as of 1 June 2016, retrieved from: https://ec.europa.eu/transparency/regdoc/rep/1/2016/EN/1-2016-72-EN-F1-1.PDF, accessed: 31 October 2019; see also: European Commission, Fact Sheet Implementing the EU–Turkey Statement – Questions and Answers (15 June 2016), retrieved from: http://europa.eu/rapid/press-release_MEMO-16-1664_en.htm, accessed: 31 October 2019.

35 See for more information European Commission, Turkey 2019 Report, 46, retrieved from: https://ec.europa.eu/neighbourhood-enlargement/sites/near/files/20190529-turkey-report.pdf, accessed: 31 October 2019.

36 European Commission, Turkey 2019 Report, retrieved from: https://ec.europa.eu/neighbourhood-enlargement/sites/near/files/20190529-turkey-report.pdf, accessed: 31 October 2019.

man Rights,[37] the claims of human rights shortcomings continue.[38] It also seemed problematic that there does not exist a substantial safeguard with regards to third-country nationals returned to Turkey on the basis of the EURA.

IV. The EU–Turkey Statement

The dysfunctionality of the EURA with Turkey and the challenge facing the largest influx of asylum seekers and refugees since the end of World War II led to a change in the mindset of European leaders. Internal policies such as the Dublin system on the attribution of responsibility for asylum seekers collapsed and countries at the EU external borders such as Greece, Italy or Spain have become over-burdened, resulting in a failure to conduct appropriate asylum procedures in line with Directive 2013/32/EU (Asylum Procedures Directive) and to provide reception facilities that meet minimal human needs. Within those agitated times and considering Turkey as a "key strategic partner" in the resolution of the high influx of migrants crossing the Aegean Sea, German chancellor Angela Merkel suggested a close collaboration with the Turkish authorities to get the situation under control.[39] Following the set-up of a Joint Action Plan in Octo-

---

37 Turkey became a state party to the European Convention of Human Rights in 1954 and to the Geneva Convention in 1961 with a geographical limitation. According to the Geneva Convention, geographical limitations refer to people fleeing from Europe. Corresponding to the wishes of the governments in charge, the 1951 Convention has given the State Parties the possibility of limiting their obligations to those who would become refugees as a result of events occurring only in Europe (Art. 1 para. B.1.). Europe, here, refers to the members of the European Council.

38 See, for critics regarding some claims on human rights, *Gossalin*, Two years on, deal continues to fail thousands of people seeking asylum, in: Medicins Sans Frontières, retrieved from: https://www.msf.org/euturkey-two-years-deal-continues-fail-thousands-people-seeking-asylum, accessed: 31 October 2019; *Gogou*, The EU-Turkey deal: Europe's year of shame, in: Amnesty International, retrieved from: https://www.amnesty.org/en/latest/news/2017/03/the-eu-turkey-deal-europes-year-of-shame/, accessed: 31 October 2019; *Human Rights Watch*, Greece: A Year of Suffering for Asylum Seekers, retrieved from: https://www.hrw.org/news/2017/03/15/greece-year-suffering-asylum-seekers, accessed: 31 October 2019.

39 See European Council, European Council meeting (15 October 2015) – Conclusions (EUCO 26/15) 1–5; European Commission, Fact Sheet: EU-Turkey joint action plan (Brussels, 15 October 2015) (MEMO/15/5860); see also Die Bundeskanzlerin, Regierungserklärung von Bundeskanzlerin Merkel (Berlin, 15 October

ber 2015 which envisaged financial support for Syrians falling within the Turkish Temporary Protection Scheme and, in more general terms, a strengthened cooperation in order to combat irregular migration, a series of meetings have been held to concretise actionable points to enforce co-operation. On 18 March 2016, a third meeting took place, where both sides expressed their intention to jointly tackle the issue of irregular migrants arriving on the Greek islands by stepping up efforts to effectively return migrants who do not qualify for international protection and at the same time "burden-share" Syrian refugees through a resettlement scheme from Turkey to the EU.

This statement, which was largely inspired by a policy proposal by Gerald Knaus, Chairman of the European Stability Initiative,[40] sets out a number of action points to achieve the overall aim of "end[ing] the irregular migration from Turkey to the EU".[41] First of all, as from 20 March 2016, "all new irregular migrants crossing from Turkey into Greek islands [...] will be returned to Turkey".[42] Ensuring that this takes place in conformity with EU and international law, all arriving migrants must be given the chance to individually apply for international protection in Greece in line with the obligations of the Asylum Procedures Directive. The system was based on the presumption that irregular migration would decrease, once migrants understand that they were to be "quasi-automatically" returned to Turkey and this would thus discourage migrants from crossing the Aegean in the first place. In return, and as a burden-sharing measure, the EU will resettle one Syrian refugee in the EU for each Syrian returned to Turkey.[43] This so-called "1-on-1-scheme" was envisaged to work on a vol-

---

2015), retrieved from: https://www.bundeskanzlerin.de/Content/DE/Regierungserklaerung/2015/2015-10-15-regierungserklaerung.html;jsessionid=D6C2244A81E46BE01918C3D2C7D6A75B.s4t2, accessed: 31 October 2019.

40 *Knaus*, "Why people don't need to drown in the Aegean – ESI policy proposal summary" (17 September 2015), retrieved from: http://www.esiweb.org/rumeliobserver/2015/09/17/why-people-dont-need-to-drown-in-the-aegean-esi-policy-proposal-summary/, accessed: 31 October 2019.

41 Council of the EU, EU-Turkey statement (18 March 2016), retrieved from: https://www.consilium.europa.eu/en/press/press-releases/2016/03/18/eu-turkey-statement/pdf, accessed: 31 October 2019.

42 Council of the EU, EU-Turkey statement (18 March 2016) (fn. 41).

43 Council of the EU, EU-Turkey statement (18 March 2016) (fn. 41).

untary basis, similarly to the scheme agreed on by Member States in July 2015.[44]

Clearly, Turkey's commitment to the Statement did not come at no cost. The parties, furthermore, agreed on action points which – unlike the above mentioned – are not connected to the combat of irregular migration but more broadly refer to EU–Turkey relations in general. Firstly, it was envisaged to accelerate the progress made in relation to the visa liberalisation roadmap and to lift visa requirements for Turkish citizens by the end of June 2016.[45] Secondly, financial commitments under the Facility for Refugees in Turkey shall be made available for Turkey and an additional three billion euros shall be disbursed by the end of 2018.[46] And thirdly, progress with regards to the accession process shall be achieved by the opening of Chapter 33 on financial and budgetary provisions.[47]

Turkey's incentive to agree to take back irregular migrants arriving in the Greek islands was mostly the prospect of a visa-free regime for Turkish citizens, but a closer look at the EU–Turkey Statement shows that it only repeats what has already been promised during the negotiations for the EURA. The lifting of the visa requirement remains under the condition that Turkey fulfils all benchmarks of the visa liberalisation roadmap and the European Parliament and the Council approve a corresponding proposal by the Commission.[48]

Despite the repeated appraisal by EU officials of the success in implementing the EU–Turkey Statement and the significant reduction of sea and land crossings through Turkey, the legal controversies around it have not ceased. Following the release of the Statement, the predominant question concerned the nature of the statement as either an international and legally binding agreement or a purely political and not legally binding statement. This opened the floor for the public and academic debates with different points of view.

On the one hand, from an EU law perspective, the EU–Turkey Statement did not follow the EU procedure for negotiating and concluding international agreements with third countries, which is governed by Arti-

---

44 Council of the EU, Outcome of the Council Meeting Justice and Home Affairs (Brussels, 20 July 2015), retrieved from: http://www.consilium.europa.eu/media/22985/st11097en15.pdf, accessed: 31 October 2019.

45 Council of the EU, EU-Turkey statement (18 March 2016) (fn. 41).

46 Council of the EU, EU-Turkey statement (18 March 2016) (fn. 41).

47 Council of the EU, EU-Turkey statement (18 March 2016) (fn. 41).

48 See *Ott*, CLEER Papers 4 (2017) (fn. 3), 24.

cle 218 TFEU.[49] Admittedly, the form of the statement as a press release does seem to argue in favour of a political statement, which was not intended to produce legal effects. For this reason, it could be argued that the Statement is not an international agreement within the meaning of Article 216 TFEU.

On the other hand, according to the case law of the International Court of Justice (ICJ), from an international law perspective, the designation of a treaty does not depend on its form, but on whether the parties expressed their consent to abide by contractual obligations.[50] Whether such an intention exists depends on the terms used and the context in which the text was written. The Statement does not use terms such as those typically used in international law to indicate obligations arising from the results, model verbs such as "shall" or commitment appropriations such as "should". Instead, the more vague term "will" is used. For this reason, some academics argue that the Statement shall not be regarded as a treaty within the meaning of the Vienna Convention on the Law of Treaties.[51]

Yet, even if the Statement could not be regarded either as a treaty or as an international agreement and it is not challengeable in court, its individual elements are legally binding and their implementation in practice could be challenged.[52] In an attempt to obtain some clarity on the legal nature and the authorship of the Statement as well as to challenge its imple-

49 Pursuant to Art. 218 para. 6 (a)(v) TFEU, the Council shall adopt a decision concluding an agreement covering areas relating to the ordinary legislative procedure, such as asylum and immigration, only with the assent of the European Parliament. The question of the competent EU organ to conclude the EU–Turkey Statement was further explored by *Fernandez Arribas*, The EU-Turkey Statement, the Treaty-Making Process and Competent Organs. Is the Statement an International Agreement?, European Papers 2 (2017), 303, 306–308.

50 International Court of Justice, *Maritime Delimitation and Territorial Questions between Qatar and Bahrain, Jurisdiction and Admissibility*, judgment, 1 July 1994, para. 24; compare with International Court of Justice, *Aegean Sea Continental Shelf (Greece v. Turkey)*, judgment, 19 December 1978, para. 95.

51 *Peers*, The Draft EU/Turkey Deal on Migration and Refugees: Is It Legal?, retrieved from: http://eulawanalysis.blogspot.com/2016/03/the-draft-euturkey-deal-on-migration.html, accessed: 31 October 2019; see also *den Heijer/Spijkerboer*, Is the EU-Turkey Refugee and Migration Deal a Treaty?, retrieved from: http://eulawanalysis.blogspot.com/2016/04/is-eu-turkey-refugee-and-migration-deal.html, accessed: 31 October 2019.

52 *den Heijer/Spijkerboer*, Is the EU-Turkey Refugee and Migration Deal a Treaty?, retrieved from: http://eulawanalysis.blogspot.com/2016/04/is-eu-turkey-refugee-and-migration-deal.html, accessed: 31 October 2019; see for this conclusion *Babická*, EU-Turkey Deal Seems To Be Schizophrenic, retrieved from: http://migrationon-

mentation in practice, two Pakistani and one Afghan national (*NF*, *NG* and *NM*) who had previously made applications for asylum in Greece and were about to be returned to Turkey on the basis of the EU–Turkey Statement, launched an action for annulment to the General Court. In their applications, they requested the Court to annul the "alleged agreement", whereas the European Council was arguing against the admissibility of the action and further denied that an international agreement, requesting the procedure of Art. 218 TFEU, had been concluded on the meeting on 18 March 2016.

The Court ultimately followed the European Council and declared that the Court lacks jurisdiction to rule on the legality of the Statement on the ground that it cannot be attributed to the European Council or any other EU body.[53] Taking into account the phrasing of the Statement as well as the context and circumstances of its occurrence, the Court did not see sufficient evidence that the Statement could be attributed to an EU body. Instead, the Court held that, even supposing it were a legally binding international agreement, "that agreement would be an agreement concluded by the Heads of State or Government of the Member States of the European Union and the Turkish Prime Minister".[54] An appeal lodged against the General Court's orders was declared "manifestly inadmissible" by the ECJ on the grounds of an insufficiently reasoned appeal.[55] It is hence unlikely that the ECJ will, on another occasion, pronounce itself on the legality of the EU–Turkey Statement.

---

line.cz/en/eu-turkey-deal-seems-to-be-schizophrenic, accessed: 31 October 2019; *Gatti*, The EU-Turkey Statement, retrieved from: https://www.ejiltalk.org/the-eu-turkey-statement-a-treaty-that-violates-democracy-part-1-of-2/, accessed: 31 October 2019.

53 General Court (EU), T-192/16, ECLI:EU:T:2017:128, order, 28 February 2017 – NF/European Council; T-193/16, ECLI:EU:T:2017:129, order, 28 February 2017 – NG/European Council; T-257/16, ECLI:EU:T:2017:130, order, 28 February 2017 – NM/European Council.

54 General Court (EU), T-192/16, ECLI:EU:T:2017:128, order, 28 February 2017, para. 72 – NF/European Council; T-193/16, ECLI:EU:T:2017:129, order, 28 February 2017, para. 72 – NG/European Council; T-257/16, ECLI:EU:T:2017:130, order, 28 February 2017, para. 72 – NM/European Council. For a comment on the decision see *Carrera/den Hertog/Stefan*, It wasn't me! The Luxembourg Court Orders on the EU-Turkey Refugee Deal, CEPS Policy Insights 15 (2017); *Idriz*, The EU-Turkey deal in front of the Court of Justice of the EU: An unsolicited Amicus Brief, Asser Policy Brief 3 (December 2017).

55 European Court of Justice, joined cases C-208/17, C-209/17, C-210/17, ECLI:EU:C:2018:705, order, 12 September 2018 – NF, NG, NM/European Council.

Besides the question of its legal nature, also the content of the Statement has caused controversial debates as to its compliance with international law. The underlying rationale of the Statement can be summarised as an attempt to "unburden" EU Member States, in particular Greece, from the continuous influx of asylum seekers crossing the Aegean by returning them – by means of an expedited procedure – back to Turkey as their country of transit. Yet on which grounds? The Statement proposes to return all new arrivals to Turkey based on the assumption that Turkey is a "safe third country". While from a practical perspective the benefit of this approach might appear appealing, from a legal point of view, the question of whether Turkey can actually be considered a safe third country must be asked. Article 38 of the Asylum Procedures Directive sets out that Member States may apply the safe third-country concept provided, *inter alia*, the following principles are respected in the third country: the principle of non-refoulement in accordance with the Geneva Convention and the possibility for the person concerned to request refugee status and, if found to be a refugee, to receive protection in accordance with the Geneva Convention. With regards to Turkey, the fulfilment of these criteria might – to say the least – be doubted.

Firstly, Turkey – albeit state party of the 1951 Geneva Convention relating to the Status of Refugees and its 1967 New York Additional Protocol – retains a geographical limitation to the Convention in the sense that it only recognises those fleeing from Europe as refugees. The wide majority of people that would be returned under the EU–Turkey Statement could not obtain refugee status in Turkey, but only "temporary protection" under the 2013 Law of Foreigners and International Protection. Similarly, under the 2014 Turkish Temporary Protection Regulation, Syrian nationals are granted so-called temporary protection, allowing them – as the name suggests –only to remain for a limited time in Turkey instead of allowing them the full range of rights of refugee status under the Geneva Convention. This is particularly relevant with regards to access to housing, education and the labour market. The temporary protection scheme assigns residence rights to a group of people purely on the basis of their origin, instead of individually assessing a person's right to asylum.[56]

---

56 *Poon*, EU-Turkey Deal: Violation of, or Consistency with, International Law?, European Papers 1 (2016), 1195, 1202; *Eksi*, The New Turkish Law on Foreigners and International Protection, Baden-Baden 2014, 91; *Ineli-Ciger*, Protecting Syrians in Turkey: A Legal Analysis, International Journal of Refugee Law 29 (2017), 555–579.

Secondly, NGOs have repeatedly warned that persons returned to Turkey may be subject to indirect refoulement in the sense that they might be returned to their countries of origin.[57] In the 2017/2018 Amnesty International Report on Turkey, repeated practices of collective forced expulsions of Syrian and Iraqi refugees and asylum seekers were detected, substantialising the claim that Turkey is in breach of non-refoulement and, hence, cannot be deemed to be a safe third country.[58]

EU officials continuously praise the success of the implementation of the EU–Turkey Statement as the EU's principal and most effective response to the "migration crisis".[59] While it is true that after the Statement the number of new arrivals on the Greek islands have significantly decreased, not much progress was detected with a view to the returns to Turkey. Between April 2016 and December 2018 approximately 1.800 individuals were returned to Turkey on the basis of the EU–Turkey Statement. This constitutes two per cent of the absolute number of arrivals of migrants during this period.[60] This is largely corroborated by the fact in the months after the Statement, Greek Asylum Appeal Committees have, in a majority of the cases, refused to consider Turkey as a safe third country and

57 *Poon*, European Papers 1 (2016) (fn. 56), 1201; *Poon*, Non-Refoulement Obligations in the EU-Turkey Deal and Italy-Libya Memorandum of Understanding, retrieved from: https://internationallaw.blog/2019/06/20/non-refoulement-obligations-in-the-eu-turkey-deal-and-italy-libya-memorandum-of-understanding/#_ftn14, accessed: 06 November 2019; Danish Refugee Council, Hundreds of Thousands of Syrians Risk Being Pushed to Return in 2018 Despite Ongoing Violence, retrieved from: https://drc.ngo/news/hundreds-of-thousands-of-syrians-risk-being-pushed-to-return-in-2018-despite-ongoing-violence, accessed: 06 November 2019. On the third anniversary of the EU–Turkey Deal, 25 NGOs denounced the EU–Turkey Deal in an open letter, retrieved from: https://www.hrw.org/sites/default/files/supporting_resources/open_letter_eu_turkey_deal.pdf, accessed: 06 November 2019.

58 Amnesty International, Turkey Report 2017/2018, retrieved from: https://www.amnesty.org/en/countries/europe-and-central-asia/turkey/report-turkey/, accessed: 06 November 2019.

59 See for instance European Commission, Seventh Report on the Progress made in the implementation of the EU–Turkey Statement, COM (2017) 470 final, retrieved from: https://ec.europa.eu/neighbourhood-enlargement/sites/near/files/20170906_seventh_report_on_the_progress_in_the_implementation_of_the_eu-turkey_statement_en.pdf, accessed: 06 November 2019.

60 ESI, The EÚ–Turkey Statement three years on (15 April 2019), retrieved from: https://www.esiweb.org/pdf/ESI%20core%20facts%20-%20EU-Turkey%20Statement%20three%20years%20on%20-%2015%20April%202019.pdf, accessed: 06 November 2019.

hence hindered the full extent of returns back to Turkey.[61] However, in a long-awaited decision by the Greek Council of State on 22 September 2017, the Court did not find a risk of refoulement for the Syrian applicant nor any threat for the person's life or freedom in Turkey.[62] The Council of State, moreover, found that Turkey fulfils the criteria of a safe third country set out in Article 38 of the Asylum Procedures Directive. In the end, by a majority of one vote (12 against and 13 in favour), the Court decided not to refer the case to the ECJ under the preliminary reference procedure. After the General Court's Orders in *NF*, *NG* and *NM*, this is another missed chance to finally obtain clarity on a highly contested measure where it is much needed.

V. Conclusion

Despite the complexity and the various dynamics of EU–Turkey relations, with view to Turkey's role in the EU's external dimension policies in migration matters, three "milestones" were identified which show the transition of Turkey from an associated privileged partner of the EU to a key strategic partner which can be considered a gatekeeper of the EU's external borders.

A first milestone was reached in 1963 with the signing of the Ankara Agreement, which made Turkey an associated privileged partner of the EU. Following the example of Greece who had become the first associated country in 1961, and ultimately achieving full membership in 1981, Turkey also pursued the aim of fully acceding to the EU. Whilst the Ankara Agreement certainly paved the way to bring together Turkey and

61 See for an analysis of the decisions of Greek Asylum Appeal Committees: *Gkliati*, The EU-Turkey Deal and the Safe Third Country Concept before the Greek Asylum Appeals Committees, movements 2 (2017).

62 See for a comment on the decision: AIDA, Greece: The Ruling of the Council of State on the Asylum Procedure post EU-Turkey Deal (4 October 2017), retrieved from: http://www.asylumineurope.org/news/04-10-2017/greece-ruling-council-state-asylum-procedure-post-eu-turkey-deal, accessed: 06 November 2019; EDAL, A critical approach of the concept of Turkey as a safe third country under the scope of the EU–Turkey "Common Statement" as interpreted by the Greek Council of State and two different Independent Appeal Committees (10 July 2018), retrieved from: https://www.asylumlawdatabase.eu/en/journal/critical-approach-concept-turkey-safe-third-country-under-scope-eu-turkey-%E2%80%9Ccommon-statement%E2%80%9D, accessed: 06 November 2019.

the EU, the prospect of full membership seems today – more than 50 years after the Ankara Agreement – highly unlikely, at least in the near future.

With a view to migration, the EU has in light of the increasing numbers of asylum seekers and irregular migrants in the first two decades of the 21st century, intensified its efforts to externalise migration policies, for instance, through a readmission agreement with Turkey. Readmission agreements have become a primary tool of the external dimension of EU migration and asylum policies. The conclusion of the EU–Turkey Readmission Agreement certainly constitutes a second milestone in EU–Turkey relations in migration matters and can be seen as the (official) starting point of Turkey's role as a gatekeeper at the EU's external borders.

In March 2016, with the "release" of the EU–Turkey Statement a third milestone was reached, as it demonstrated a paradigm shift from hard to soft law. While readmission agreements have a clear legal basis in Article 79 (3) TFEU and clearly constitute legally binding instruments, the EU–Turkey Statement's legal nature has caused many controversies in jurisprudence and academia. We have argued that the content of the statement as well as the vocabulary used speak in favour of a non-legally-binding political statement, which nonetheless causes legal effects as it *de facto* declares Turkey a safe third country despite the imminent risk of violating the principle of non-refoulement. By creating such a soft law instrument, the EU not only circumvents its own system of judicial protection – as the unsuccessful challenge in *NF*, *NG* and *NM* has shown – it also sets a dangerous precedent for the EU's accountability when cooperating with other third countries. While from a purely practical point of view the EU–Turkey Statement has led to a massive decrease of new arrivals on the Greek islands, from a legal perspective the use of soft law in human-rights-sensitive areas such as migration inheres big risks of failing effective judicial protection and a shift of responsibility from the EU to the third country concerned. The EU–Turkey Statement did in fact create another layer on an already complex relationship between the EU and Turkey and confirms Turkey's role as a gatekeeper at the external borders of the EU.

The European and International Response to the Human Rights Situation of Migrants in Libya: The Humanitarian Evacuation Programmes Run by the African Union, the European Union and the United Nations

*Francesco Luigi Gatta**

I. Introduction

The Mediterranean Sea has always been a context for human mobility and migration. For centuries thousands of persons have travelled across its waters and entered in contact with other populations for the most different reasons. Nowadays, it continues to be a bridge between the "South" and the "North", with migratory flows towards Europe that have been intensifying during the last decades.

The increase of trans-Mediterranean mobility in the recent period has been accompanied by the progressive proliferation of an articulated and widespread system of irregular migration channels to Europe. A deeply rooted and prosperous "business" associated with a growing mortality rate: a combination which, according to the International Organisation for Migration (IOM), has made the Mediterranean crossing the world's deadliest route for migrants.[1]

Migratory pressure against European borders, in particular, has been intensifying from 2011 onwards, in the wake of significant international events such as, on the one hand, the so-called "Arab Spring", giving rise to turmoil and instability in some of the North-African countries and, on the other, the outbreak of the war in Syria, provoking millions of refugees. As a consequence, migratory flows towards Europe have grown exponentially, leading to the so-called "refugee crisis", which reached its peak in 2015, when an estimated one million migrants irregularly entered the territory

---

* PhD in EU Law (Universities of Padua and Innsbruck) and research fellow at the Université Catholique de Louvain.

1 IOM, Four decades of cross-Mediterranean undocumented migration to Europe: A review of the evidence, Geneva 2017. According to the report, between 2000 and 2017 (30 June), 33,761 migrants died or went missing in the Mediterranean Sea during their journeys.

of the European Union (EU).[2] Accordingly, migration has emerged as a common, urgent and long-lasting challenge in the EU, gaining prominence and becoming one of the main concerns for European policymakers and a top priority on the EU political agenda.[3]

In this scenario, the EU and its most affected Member States have been forced to step up cooperation at the international level in order to deal with incoming migratory flows, to this end especially engaging in dialogue and collaboration initiatives with countries of origin and transit. In this framework, Libya plays a crucial role in the overall geo-political context of the Southern Mediterranean, representing a country of pivotal importance in terms of migratory channels towards Europe. The "strategic" geographical location at the centre of the North-African coast, indeed, makes Libya a major transit area and a significant pole of attraction for migrants wishing to reach the EU.

The situation of persistent instability of the Libyan country, moreover, has created an ideal breeding ground for the migrant-smuggling business, whose proliferation has been facilitated by a complex array of factors, including long-lasting insecurity and territorial fragmentation, political divisions, rivalries and absence of State authority, democratic control and rule of law. In this complicated context, Libya, as one of the main gateways to the European territory, receives a considerable inflow of migrants, who are turned into a profitable source of income for the human-being-smuggling industry. At the same time, migrants seeking to depart for Europe remain trapped in Libyan detention centres, where they are systematically subjected to widespread and severe violations of their human rights.

2 For detailed data on migratory flows in the EU during 2015, see Frontex, Annual Risk Analysis for 2016, 2499/2016, Warsaw 2016. For an analysis of the reasons and the features of the European migration crisis, among others, see *Carlier/Crépeau*, De la "crise" migratoire Européenne au Pacte Mondial sur les Migrations: Exemple d'un mouvement sans droit?, Annuaire Français de Droit International 1 (2017), 461; *Atak/Crépeau*, Managing migration at the external borders of the European Union: Meeting the human rights challenges, Journal Européen des Droits de l'Homme – European Journal of Human Rights 5 (2014), 591, 601; *Bossuyt*, The European Union confronted with an asylum crisis in the Mediterranean: Reflections on refugees and human rights issues, Journal Européen des Droits de l'Homme – European Journal of Human Rights 5 (2015), 581, 598.

3 According to the data of the December 2018 Eurobarometer, migration represents a major concern for European citizens as 40% of them consider it the main challenge to be addressed by the EU, followed by other issues such as terrorism (20%) and the economic situation (18%). For the detailed data and statistics, see European Commission, Autumn 2018 Standard Eurobarometer: Positive image of the EU prevails ahead of the European elections, Press Release, IP/18/6896.

Against this background, this chapter explores the operational responses put in place by the EU in cooperation with other international actors in order to cope with the humanitarian and migration crises generated by the situation in Libya. More specifically, following a brief reconstruction of the historical background of the Libyan crisis (paragraph II), leading in particular to the systematic violation of migrants' human rights especially due to their arbitrary and unlawful detention in Libyan detention centres (paragraphs II. 1. and II. 2.), attention is then devoted to the EU's responses to the situation in Libya (paragraph III). In so doing, the focus is especially put on the multilateral collaboration developed by the EU with the United Nations (UN) and the African Union (AU), with particular regard to the Joint Trilateral Task force on migration and Libya established at the end of 2017 (paragraphs IV and V). In the framework of such triangular cooperation, the chapter analyses the concrete initiatives put in place by the AU-EU-UN Task Force to protect and evacuate migrants from Libyan detention centres, namely the Voluntary Humanitarian Returns run by the IOM (paragraph V. 1.) and the Emergency Transit Evacuation Mechanism managed by the UNHCR (paragraph V. 2). Finally, the chapter proposes an overall assessment of the trilateral cooperation between the mentioned international organisations (paragraph VI).

II. Background of the crisis in Libya

In order to better grasp the various reactions to the situation in Libya put in place by the EU and its international partners, it is worth briefly recalling and tracing the country's recent historical and political context, as it acted as breeding ground for the subsequent development of the humanitarian and migration crises.

A former Italian colony, Libya gained independence in 1951, being governed in the form of monarchy. The king's authority, however, did not last long, as in 1969 it was overthrown by a *coup d'état* organised by military formations, whose leader, Muammar Gaddafi, took control of the country. As "permanent leader", he pursued a strategy of centralisation of power, essentially establishing restrictive control over all possible forms of opposition, thereby ensuring his stable command over political, military and economic aspects of the life of the country. The national economy, in particular, was placed under strict control: as one of the major oil-producing African countries, Libya's oil infrastructure was subjected to nationalisation, as well as other resources and activities, including the mining industry and the banking sector.[4]

During the following decades, between the 1970s and the 1990s, while Libya's attractiveness in terms of possibility of employment and business increased, gathering unemployed youth from around the region, on the international scene, by contrast, the African country became gradually marginalised, due to Gaddafi's alleged support for international terrorism. Reactions came from the international community as the Libyan situation led to the imposition of UN-sponsored sanctions, voted by the UN Security Council ("UNSC") in its Resolution 748/92, and including, among other measures, an arms embargo and restrictions related to oil production.[5]

Following a period of substantial isolation during the 1990s, Libya regained consideration by the international community; the sanctions regime was lifted in 2003 and dialogue and cooperation initiatives were resumed with European countries. Italy was particularly active in this respect, engaging in collaboration in a variety of areas, including the fight against terrorism, organised crime and illegal immigration.[6] This Italian–Libyan partnership was later reinforced through the conclusion, in 2008, of a Treaty of Friendship and Cooperation, signed by Gaddafi and Prime Minister Berlusconi and aimed especially at curbing irregular migration flows towards Italy and Europe.[7]

In parallel, dialogue and negotiations with Libya were also conducted by the EU, which, before the 2011 uprisings, still considered the African country a relatively reliable partner and quite an attractive market for European business activities. In 2009 the European Commission and the

4 For a more detailed analysis of the Libyan historical context, including the evolution of its economic and political structure, among others, see *Toaldo*, Migrations through and from Libya: A Mediterranean challenge, IAI Working Paper 15 (2015); *Varvelli*, Europe and the Libyan crisis: A failed State in the backyard?, ISPI Analysis 237 (2014); *Baldwin-Edwards/Lutterbeck*, Coping with the Libyan migration crisis, Journal of Ethnic and Migration Studies 2018, 2241.

5 UNSC, Resolution 748/92, 31 March 1992, UN doc. S/RES/748 (1992).

6 *Accordo per la collaborazione nella lotta al terrorismo, alla criminalità organizzata, al traffico illegale di stupefacenti e sostanze psicotrope e alla immigrazione clandestina*, signed in Rome on 13 December 2000. The agreement was later accompanied by the adoption of two protocols signed in Tripoli on 29 December 2007. On this topic, see *Giuffre*, State responsibility beyond borders: What legal basis for Italy's pushbacks to Libya?, International Journal of Refugee Law 24 (2012), 692, 700; *Pacella*, Coperazione Italia-Libia: Profili di responsabilità per crimini di diritto internazionale, Diritto Penale Contemporaneo, 4 (2018), 5, 7.

7 The Treaty was signed in Bengasi on 30 August 2008 and ratified in Italy with the Law n. 7/2009.

European External Actions Service (EEAS) issued the "Libya Strategy Paper and National Indicative Programme 2011–2013", outlining the EU's strategy in that country and identifying priority areas of cooperation, including, in particular, "fighting illegal migration in the Mediterranean or terrorism, developing Libya's energy resources in hydrocarbons and renewable energies, creating the bases for successful investment in new sectors, improving fundamental freedoms and human rights".[8]

The year 2011 represented a breaking point: cooperation initiatives were interrupted in the wake of the turmoil and instability provoked by the Arab Spring and popular insurrections spread out in the North-African region. In Libya, protests against Gaddafi's authoritarian regime led to a severe repression and an escalation of violence, giving rise to gross and systematic human rights violations. Reactions soon came from the international community: on 26 February 2011, the UNSC, unanimously adopting Resolution 1979/2011, demanded the end of hostilities by invoking the principle of the "responsibility to protect", imposed economic sanctions and referred the matter to the International Criminal Court (ICC) for investigation.[9] The EU, for its part, aligning itself with the UN, launched its sanctions regime by adopting a Council Decision implementing the UNSC Resolution and further widening its scope.[10]

Later on, due to the persistent situation of coercion and violence, more severe measures were put in place. By passing Resolution 1973/2011, the UNSC, considering the situation in Libya "a threat to international peace and security", authorised all necessary steps to protect civilians and to immediately establish a ceasefire and an end to violence against them.[11] The Resolution further strengthened the sanctions regime, the assets freeze and the embargoes, also imposing a no-fly zone over the country. UN-NATO military intervention soon followed, eventually leading to the fall of Gaddafi in October 2011.

8 EEAS, Libya Strategy Paper and National Indicative Programme 2011–2013, Brussels 2011, 6.

9 UNSC, Resolution 1970/2011, 26 February 2016, UN doc. S/RES/1970(2011).

10 Council Decision of 28 February 2011 implementing the UN Security Council Resolution on Libya of 26 February (UNSCR 1970/2011), 7081/11.

11 UNSC, Resolution 1973/2011, 17 March 2011, UN doc. S/RES/1973(2011), 2.

1. The "new Libya" and the development of the migration and humanitarian crises

The events following Gaddafi's removal from power soon proved that Libya's "new era" was to be characterised by great instability, disorder and huge difficulties in the transition to and the restoration of democracy and peace. Following the military intervention which toppled the regime and the subsequent situation of power vacuum, elections were held in July 2012, with Libyan people voting for the General National Congress, an institutional body enjoying full legislative authority and the power to appoint a new interim government.[12]

Despite the elections and the launch of the institution-building process, Libya's situation of instability remained critical, with a sharp deterioration of security conditions. Emblematically, the 2011 terrorist attack on the US consulate in Benghazi, in the context of which the Ambassador to Libya and other members of the US diplomatic services lost their lives, made clear that the road to pacification and restoration of order was paved with enormous difficulties and obstacles.

The following years, indeed, were characterised by increasing security challenges, especially fuelled by the emergence of a widespread phenomenon: the presence and the proliferation in Libya of terrorist groups, armed militias and rival tribes in conflict with one another to take control of various areas and portions of the territory.[13] As a result, 2013 and 2014, in particular, were marked by the severe deterioration in the country's security environment, with an escalation of violence and multiple episodes of assassinations, kidnappings, bombings and fights over energy supplies and resources. The situation in the country increasingly attracted attention from the international community, becoming a central matter of concern. At the 2013 G8 Summit in Northern Ireland, participating world leaders put the situation in Libya among the main priorities on the international agenda by stating their commitment to "leading international support for Libya's security and democratic transition".[14]

12 For an analysis of the electoral outcomes, see *Varvelli*, ISPI Analysis 237 (2014) (fn. 4), 1, 2 f.

13 For an analysis of the phenomenon of armed groups and militias in Libya, see *El Kamouni-Janssen/De Bruijne*, Entering the lion's den: local militias and governance in Libya, Netherlands Institute of International Relations, Clingendael Report, October 2017.

14 G8 Summit, 17–18 June 2013, 2013 Lough Erne G8 Leaders' Communique, para. 7.

The establishment of the new Libyan Government of National Accord did not lead to a substantial change in the circumstances. Formed in January 2016 and led by Prime Minister Fayez Mustafa Serraj, the new government was based on the Libyan Political Agreement concluded in Skhirat (Morocco) on 17 December 2015 and facilitated by the mediation efforts put in place by the UN in order to overcome the critical situation of instability in the country. Serraj's government was recognised as the sole legitimate government of Libya by the UN, the AU and the EU, together with the vast majority of its Member States.[15]

Despite the support received from the international community, this government has been far from being in a position of full control of Libyan territory. The situation of the country is still characterised by widespread instability, rivalries and violence, providing the ideal conditions for the migrant smuggling business to grow and prosper in parallel with the deterioration of human rights.

2. *The migrant issue and the Libyan detention centres*

In the highly fragmented scenario described above, Libya's human rights situation soon collapsed. Migrants, in particular, have been among the most affected victims of serious human rights violations, perpetrated in a context of organised crime and state of impunity, where smuggling and trafficking networks took advantage of the situation of disorder and uncertainty, gaining control of migratory routes through the country and towards Europe.

Libya, indeed, is both a destination and transit country for migrants, and in recent years has become the most important human trafficking route linking central and northern Africa with Europe. According to the UN Office on Drugs and Crimes and its 2018 Global Study on Smuggling of Migrants, as regards the Central Mediterranean route, Libya represents

15 See UNSC, Resolution 2259/2015, 23 December 2015, UN Doc. S/RES/2259(2015) and the Statement on Libya issued by France, Germany, Italy, the United Kingdom, the US and the EU at the Ministerial Meeting held in Paris on 13 March 2016. The statement is available on the official website of the Italian Ministry of Foreign Affairs, at https://www.esteri.it/mae/it/sala_stampa/archivionotizie/comunicati/2016/03/ministerial-meeting-in-paris-france_0.html.

the main departure point of flows, with about 90% of migrants heading to Italy and Europe departing from there.[16]

In such context, the so-called Central Mediterranean route through Libya has turned into a matter of major concern for the EU, which has engaged in a number of initiatives towards the containment and prevention of departures of migrants. In this regard, the technical and financial support provided to the Libyan Coast Guard to stop migratory flows has been particularly controversial. Trained and funded by Italy with the full backing of the EU,[17] the Libyan Coast Guard, by performing activities of restrictive control of maritime borders and deterrence of departures from the Libyan coasts, has produced a significant impact on the numbers of migratory movements along the Central Mediterranean route.[18] Whether blocked in Libya before departure or brought back there following interception at sea, thousands of migrants have been placed in detention facilities. As a result, detention conditions therein, which were already way below acceptable human rights standards, further worsened.

Against this backdrop, the UNHCR in 2016 clearly certified that "the situation of migrants in Libya is a human rights crisis".[19] Besides human rights violations related to interception at sea, with illegal conducts amounting to collective expulsions or refoulement practices, migrants stuck in the country and trapped in detention centres have been systematically subjected to abuses, violence and dire living conditions.

As reported by the UNHCR, Libya provides a largely insufficient level of protection for migrants and asylum seekers, both in terms of legal regime and practice. As for the first aspect, at international level, Libya is not party to the 1951 Geneva Convention relating to the status of refugees or its 1967 Protocol. It has ratified the 1969 Convention governing the specific aspects of refugee problems in Africa, however, its implementation at

---

16 United Nations Office on Drugs and Crimes, Global Study on Smuggling of migrants 2018, UNODC, New York, June 2018, 145.

17 See, in particular, European Council, Malta Declaration by the members of the European Council on the external aspects of migration: addressing the Central Mediterranean route, Press Release 43/17, 3 February 2017, para. 6, letter i); EEAS, Strategic Review of EUBAM Libya, EUNAVFOR MED Op Sophia & EU Liaison and Planning Cell, EEAS (2017) 530, para. 163.

18 For an overview of the Italy-Libya cooperation and the migration control activities delegated to the Libyan Coast Guard, see *Mancini*, Italy's new migration control policy: stemming the flow of migrants from Libya without regard for their human rights, Italian Yearbook of International Law 28 (2019), 259.

19 UNHCR, "Detained and dehumanised". Report on human rights abuses against migrants in Libya, 13 December 2016, 1.

domestic level is lacking, as no legislation concerning the right to asylum and asylum procedures has been adopted. Libya is party to other international instruments, including, among others, the Convention against Torture and other Cruel Inhuman or Degrading Treatment or Punishment, the International Covenant on Civil and Political Rights and the 1979 International Convention on Maritime Search and Rescue. Their respect and implementation, however, remain highly problematic.[20] At domestic level, Libya lacks a comprehensive migration governance framework. Existing laws and regulations contain significant gaps and fall short of international standards. In particular, under Libyan legislation, dating back to Gaddafi's regime or before but still in force today, illegal entry or stay in the country is a criminal offence punishable with imprisonment.

As for the practice, particularly since 2014, Libyan justice system and law enforcement functions have been severely hampered by persistent fighting and insecurity. Human rights violations have multiplied yet remain unpunished and not properly addressed. Abuses have been repeatedly committed without any concrete and effective remedy for the victims. Criminal networks of smugglers and traffickers have proliferated, running the business of illegal migration. Migrants are turned into a profitable source of income, being subjected to labour exploitation and selling. Once apprehended by smugglers, they are either forced to work in inhuman conditions to earn their onward transport or deprived of their personal liberty and subjected to extortion, being compelled to ask for additional money from their families. Even in the event that they manage to depart, they are later intercepted by the Libyan Coast Guard, sent back to the country and placed in detention.

Besides forced labour and exploitation, further abuses and human rights violations have been reported, including, in particular, torture and ill-treatment. Conditions of migrant women are particularly worrisome, being often exposed to rape and sexual violence. Children are also deprived of their parents and are left without the proper assistance that their vulnerable conditions would require. When falling into the criminal smuggling machinery run by armed groups, ultimately, migrants in transit through Libya are substantially defenceless, being subjected to serious human rights viola-

20 For a detailed analysis of Libya's relevant legal framework, both at domestic and international levels, see UNHCR, "Detained and dehumanised". Report on human rights abuses against migrants in Libya, 13 December 2016, 8–10.

tions and yet basically lacking any form of legal, social or medical assistance.[21]

According to the information gathered by various international observers, including the UNHCR and the UN Support Mission in Libya (UNSMIL),[22] abuses against migrants mostly take place in detention centres across Libyan territory, where they are arbitrarily deprived of their personal liberty for undefined periods of time, usually in inhuman and degrading living conditions. Detention takes place in breach of the most basic international and domestic legal standards: incarceration occurs without any substantive or procedural guarantees, including identification, formal registration or legal process; access to legal remedies is denied and the period of detention is indefinite, ranging from days up to several months, without any review by competent judicial authority. Prior to imprisonment, documents are usually confiscated, as well as money and other personal belongings.

Conditions of detention are appalling and inhuman, as Libyan centres are characterised by several problems such as severe overcrowding, malnutrition, lack of access to sanitation facilities leading to infectious diseases, scarce light and ventilation. The situation possibly gets even worse when it comes to unofficial places of detention. Indeed, besides government-run immigration detention facilities, mostly managed by Libya's Department for Combatting Illegal Migration, unofficial places of detention are in function under the control of armed groups and smugglers. Scattered across Libya, these centres usually serve as "connection houses", where traffickers and criminal gangs hold migrants intercepted and captured while transiting through the country in the attempt to depart for Europe. Often located within farms, warehouses or other buildings guarded by armed groups, these places accommodate migrants for undefined periods of time, before transfer onto the next location.[23]

While several international observers have stigmatised the widespread conditions of precariousness and extreme vulnerability of migrants that are on the Libyan territory in transit to Europe, the systematic violation of their human rights has been acknowledged also by the jurisprudence, with relevant decisions coming from both national and international courts.

---

21 Ibidem.

22 UNSC Resolution 2009/2011, 16 September 2011, UN doc. S/RES/2009(2011).

23 UNHCR, "Detained and dehumanised". Report on human rights abuses against migrants in Libya, 13 December 2016, 14–17.

At the international level, in particular, the situation in Libya has been referred to the ICC by the UNSC with the above-mentioned Resolution 1970/2011 and it is currently under investigations for war crimes and crimes against humanity. The Prosecutor of the ICC, furthermore, has reiterated on many occasions the existence in Libya of a situation of systematic violation of migrants' rights, due to inhuman and unlawful practices such as torture, slavery and forced labour, rape and sexual violence, human trafficking and arbitrary and indefinite detention.[24] In 2019 the Office of the Prosecutor has also received a Communication regarding the crimes against humanity allegedly committed by the EU and its Member States in the framework of their migration policy conducted in the Mediterranean and in Libya between 2014 and 2019.[25]

The risks faced by migrants in Libya had been acknowledged also by the European Court of Human Rights ("ECtHR"), in particular in a number of cases lodged against Italy. First addressed in 2010 in the case *Hussun*,[26] the issue of migrants' human rights in Libya was later analysed by the Grand Chamber in its 2012 landmark judgment *Hirsi Jamaa*.[27] The Court of Strasbourg, in dealing with migration control practices carried out under the Italian–Libyan bilateral agreements to combat irregular migration, unanimously declared Italy's violation of the European Convention on Human Rights (ECHR) for arbitrarily returning migrants intercepted at sea to Libya, thereby exposing them to the risk of torture and ill-treatment.

More recently, in 2018, another application to the ECtHR was introduced against Italy with regard to the so-called "pull-back" practices carried out by the Libyan Coast Guard, aimed at preventing migrants from heading to Europe and taking them back to Libya.[28] The case addresses po-

---

24 ICC Prosecutor *Fatou Bensouda*, Statement to the United Nations Security Council on the Situation in Libya, pursuant to UNSCR 1970 (2011), 8 May 2019; ICC, Office of the Prosecutor, Seventeenth report of the Prosecutor of the International Criminal Court to the United Nations Security Council pursuant to UNSCR 1970 (2011), 8 May 2019, notably, para. 5 ff.

25 Communication to the Office of the Prosecutor of the International Criminal Court pursuant to the Article 15 of the Rome Statute, *EU migration policies in the Central Mediterranean and Libya (2014–2019)*, available online.

26 ECtHR, *Hussun and Others v. Italy*, Applications nos. 10171/05, 10601/05, 11593/05 and 17165/05, judgment, 19 January 2010.

27 ECtHR (Grand Chamber), *Hirsi Jamaa and Others v. Italy*, Appl. No. 27765/09, judgment, 23 February 2012.

28 ECtHR, *S.S. and Others v. Italy*, Application no. 21660/18, introduced on 3 May 2018, communicated to the Italian Government on 26 June 2019. At the time of writing, the application is pending before the first section of the ECtHR.

tential human rights violations occurred in border management operations carried out under the Memorandum of Understanding concluded in 2017 between Italy and Libya.[29] The applicants allege several human rights violations with regard to the aggressive conduct of the Libyan Coast Guard, funded, trained and equipped by Italy, invoking, in particular, a breach of various provisions of the ECHR: Article 2 (right to life), 3 (prohibition of torture) and 4 (prohibition of slavery and forced labour).

The Court of Justice of the EU, for its part, has indirectly confirmed the situation of systematic infringements of human rights in Libya with some decisions adopted in the framework of the EU's Libya sanctions regime.[30]

Judicial assertions of the serious human rights violations suffered by migrants in Libya have been made also at national level and, notably, in Italy. In particular, in 2017, for the first time, the Assize Court of Milan acknowledged the inhuman and degrading conditions of the Libyan migration detention centres, sentencing a Somali national to life imprisonment for the crimes committed as member of the criminal network which managed the detention centres of Bani Walid and Sabratha, located near the Libyan coasts.[31] In 2018, the Assize Court of Agrigento further confirmed the atrocities perpetrated in the Libyan detention centres by condemning a Gambian national to ten years of imprisonment for holding migrants in slavery in the detention centre of Sabratha.[32]

More recently, in 2019, the Court of Rome has confirmed the seriousness of the human rights situation of migrants in Libya, by ordering the Italian Minister of Foreign Affairs to issue a visa on humanitarian grounds

---

29 The Memorandum of Understanding was signed in Rome on 2 February 2017 between the Italian Government and the UN-backed Libyan Government of National Accord headed by al-Sarraj. For an analysis of the content of the Memorandum and its implications in terms of migration control, see *Mancini*, Italian Yearbook of International Law, 28 (2019), (fn.18); *Palm*, The Italy-Libya Memorandum of Understanding: The baseline of a policy approach aimed at closing all doors to Europe?, EU Migration Law Blog, 2 October 2017.

30 European Court of Justice, C-168/17, ECLI:EU:C:2019:36, judgment, 17 January 2019 – SH.

31 Assize Court of Milan, judgment of 10 October 2017. For an analysis of the judgment, see *Battarino*, I campi di raccolta libici: un'istituzione concentrazionaria, Questione Giustizia, 2 (2018); *Bernardi*, Una condanna della Corte d'Assise di Milano svela gli orrori dei "centri di raccolta e transito" dei migranti in Libia, Diritto Penale Contemporaneo, 4 (2018), 207.

32 Assize Court of Agrigento, judgment of 22 June 2019, No. 1/2018.

pursuant to the EU Visa Code[33] in favour of a Nigerian unaccompanied minor in Libya who was in urgent need of medical treatment, thereby allowing him to legally and safely travel to Italy, have access to a proper health care and join the mother who was residing there.[34]

III. The EU responses to the crisis in Libya

The turmoil provoked by the "Arab Spring" and the following disorders triggered in the Southern Mediterranean neighbouring countries pushed European policymakers to discuss strategies and define actions to be taken. Measures adopted by the EU in such problematic and fragile geo-political context have taken different forms, addressing both immediate needs and longer-term goals to be achieved in various areas.

In particular, the need for action was first expressed in the 2011 Joint Communication "Partnership for democracy and shared prosperity with the Southern Mediterranean",[35] envisaging the adoption of an incentive-based approach (so-called "more for more") in order to foster cooperation with specific African countries and accompany their democratic transition following the uprising of the "Arab Spring". As for Libya, the Communication expressed the intention to discuss "a shared commitment to the values of democracy, the rule of law and respect of human rights".[36]

The need to promote and restore such values and principles was expressed also by Bernardino Léon, specifically appointed as EU's Special Representative for the Southern Mediterranean, with the aim of "strengthening democracy and institution building, the rule of law, good gover-

---

33 Regulation (EC) No. 810/2009 of the European Parliament and of the Council of 13 July 2009 establishing a Community Code on Visas (Visa Code), Art. 25 para. 1 (a).

34 Ordinary Tribunal of Rome, Order of 21 February 2019, X v. Ministry of Foreign Affairs and Ministry of Health. For an analysis of the decision, see *F.L. Gatta*, A "way out" of the human rights situation in Libya: the humanitarian visa as a tool to guarantee the rights to health and to family unity, Cahiers de l'EDEM, August 2019.

35 European Commission/High Representative of the Union for Foreign Affairs and Security Policy, A Partnership for Democracy and Shared Prosperity with the Southern Mediterranean, Joint Communication to the European Parliament, the Council, the European Economic and Social Committee and the Committee of the Regions, COM(2011) 200 final, 8 March 2011.

36 Ibidem, 8.

nance, respect for Human Rights and fundamental freedoms, peace and regional cooperation".[37]

In such a context, from the point of view of European leaders, the interest in stabilising Libya has been of pivotal importance, with the Libyan crisis increasingly framed as mainly a migratory and humanitarian problem. The necessity to prioritise the migration issue linked to Libya, indeed, has been repeatedly affirmed by the EU institutions over the years and especially during the peak of the so-called refugee crisis in 2014 and 2015. In the October 2014 Council Conclusions on Libya, for example, European policymakers clearly expressed their strong political interest and commitment to assisting the country.[38] In 2015, following the shipwreck occurred off the coasts of the island of Lampedusa on 9 April, where hundreds of migrants lost their lives, in the extraordinary meeting held a few days later, on 23 April, the Council of the EU, noting that "instability in Libya creates an ideal environment for the criminal activities of traffickers", agreed to take action in order "to strengthen our presence at sea, to fight the traffickers, to prevent illegal migration flows and to reinforce internal solidarity and responsibility".[39] Later in 2015, the Council reiterated that "the EU cannot accept the continuing tragic loss of life at sea of migrants departing from Libya. The irregular movement of people across Libya and through its borders has a dramatic effect on the lives of too many people, and destabilises countries on both shores of the Mediterranean. The challenges posed must be addressed in a comprehensive manner".[40]

Similar assertions concerning the migration issue linked to Libya have come from the Commission,[41] and the European Council, which, particularly in the Malta Declaration, adopted in early 2017 during the Maltese

---

37 Council Decision 2011/424/CFSP, of 18 July 2011, appointing a European Union Special Representative for the Southern Mediterranean region, Art. 2 (b). The mandate of the Special Representative was later extended by the Council Decision 2013/307/CFSP of 24 June 2013.

38 Council of the European Union, Council conclusions on Libya; Foreign Affairs Council meeting, 20 October 2014, para. 10.

39 Council of the European Union, Special meeting of the European Council – Statement. Foreign Affairs and Home Affairs Council meeting, 23 April 2015, para. 2.

40 Council of the European Union, Council conclusions on Libya. Foreign Affairs Council meeting, 16 March 2015, para 13.

41 European Commission/High Representative of the Union for Foreign Affairs and Security Policy, Migration on the Central Mediterranean route. Managing flows, saving lives, Joint Communication to the European Parliament, the European Council and the Council, JOIN (2017) 4 final, 25 January 2017.

Presidency of the Council of the EU, emphasised that "efforts to stabilise Libya are now more important than ever".[42]

Against this background, different measures have been adopted by the EU to cope with the Libyan migration and humanitarian crises, including diplomatic initiatives, financial tools and operational measures, such as the operations EUBAM Libya[43] and EUNAVFOR MED.[44] In addition to autonomously led actions, the EU has also been involved in multilateral cooperation initiatives with relevant international actors. In this respect, in particular, dialogue and collaboration have been developed in order to address the humanitarian profile of the Libyan crisis and, specifically, the issue of migrants trapped in detention centres. To this end, as the following paragraphs will illustrate, the EU has specifically engaged in cooperation programmes with the AU and the UN.

IV. AU–EU–UN trilateral cooperation to cope with the Libyan situation

Reactions to the Libyan migration and humanitarian crises have come from different contexts, involving a multiplicity of stakeholders. In general

---

42 European Council, Malta Declaration by the members of the European Council on the external aspects of migration: addressing the Central Mediterranean route, Press Release 43/17, 3 February 2017, para 5.

43 Council Decision 2013/233/CFSP, of 22 May 2013, on the European Union Integrated Border Management Assistance Mission in Libya (EUBAM Libya). For an analysis of the operation and its main features, see *Ivashchenko-Stadnik/Petrov/Ranieri/Rieker/Russo/Strazzari*, How the EU is facing crises in its neighbourhood: evidence from Libya and Ukraine, EUNPACK Paper, 31 March 2017, 16–19; *Loschi/Ranieri/Strazzari*, The implementation of EU Crisis Response in Libya: bridging theory and practice, EUNPACK Working Paper, January 2018, 9–10; *Baldwin-Edwards/Lutterbeck*, Journal of Ethnic and Migration Studies 2018 (fn. 4), 9.

44 Council Decision (CFSP) 2015/778, of 18 May 2015, on a European Union military operation in the Southern Central Mediterranean (EUNAVFOR MED); Council Decision (CFSP) 2015/972, of 22 June 2015, launching the European Union military operation in the southern Central Mediterranean (EUNAVFOR MED). For a detailed analysis of the mission EUNAVFOR MED, see *Baldwin-Edwards/Lutterbeck*, Journal of Ethnic and Migration Studies, 2018 (fn. 4), 9–11; *Blockmans*, New thrust for the CSDP from the refugee and migrant crisis, CEPS Special Report 142 (2016), 4–8; *Ivashchenko-Stadnik/Petrov/Ranieri/Rieker/Russo/Strazzari*, EUNPACK Working Paper, January 2018, 27–32; *Strauch*, When stopping the smuggler means repelling the refugee: international human rights law and the European Union's Operation to combat smuggling in Libya's territorial sea, Yale Law Journal 126 (2017), 2421.

terms, international responses to crises and conflict situations in Africa have become complex over the years, involving a variety of interventions, carried out by multiple actors operating under different mandates and with different objectives. In this articulated and evolving framework, the EU has been increasingly dealing with the UN and the AU for the stabilisation of its Southern maritime borders, progressively developing and consolidating an interesting form of trilateral cooperation in migration-related matters.

Partnerships and joint actions in the field of crisis management had already been discussed between the EU and the UN before the outbreak of the recent migration crisis in the Mediterranean. In particular, with the "Joint Declaration on UN–EU Cooperation in crisis management" released in 2003, the two organisations expressed the commitment to further develop their "positive cooperation" and "examine ways and means to enhance mutual coordination and compatibility" as regards planning, training, communication and sharing of best practices.[45] In a following Joint Statement of 2007, the UN and the EU, besides reaffirming the willingness to intensify their already existing cooperation, specifically addressed the opportunity to involve also the AU, so as to broaden the collaboration and better focus on crisis management in Africa.[46]

Later on, the EU expressed its support to UN peacekeeping activities in 2012, also pointing out the need to strengthen the coordination with the UN with regard to the assistance provided to the AU. To this end, coordination initiatives and information-sharing between the respective delegations were suggested, as well as yearly trilateral coordination meetings to discuss common benchmarks, goals, actions and strategies.[47]

In 2015, the EU and the UN released the Joint document "EU–UN Priorities for 2015–2018", laying down seven common priorities, among which, they included the objective of ensuring "support to the African peace and security architecture", thereby expressing the necessity to "move towards closer trilateral cooperation among the UN/EU/AU".[48]

45 Joint Declaration on UN–EU cooperation in crisis management, 12510/03, New York, 24 September 2003, para 3.

46 Joint Statement on UN–EU cooperation in crisis management, Brussels, 7 June 2007, para. 3.

47 EEAS, Plan of Action on Enhancing EU CSDP Support to UN Peacekeeping, EEAS 01024/2/12 REV 2, 4 July 2012, para. 58.

48 EEAS, Strengthening the UN–EU Strategic Partnership on Peacekeeping and Crisis Management: Priorities 2015–2018, 7632/15, 27 March 2015, para. 2 (b).

The UN, for their part, have explicitly acknowledged the crucial importance of the engagement of regional partners in crisis management and their relevant contribution alongside UN-driven operations.[49] In particular, the African context is considered the most vivid example of fruitful cooperation between the UN and regional organisations, like the AU, as well as the EU, especially in terms of their active involvement throughout the various phases of the conflict and crisis management.

The first contexts where all three organisations have collaborated, operating alongside one another simultaneously or consecutively, are represented by the coordinated responses to crises and conflict situations in Somalia, Mali and the Central African Republic. The international responses to these conflict situations have showed the growing potential of the triangular cooperation between the UN, the EU and the AU. Building on these previous experiences, thus, the three organisations have recently undertaken a new form of trilateral cooperation in order to specifically deal with the humanitarian and migration crisis in Libya.

V. *The Tripartite Task Force on migration and Libya*

The issue of migrants trapped in Libya and held in detention centres in inhuman living conditions has attracted growing attention within the international community, thereby calling for an effective response to tackle the matter. The issue, in particular, came to the table of the AU–EU Summit held in Abidjan in November 2017, where dialogues and negotiations were being carried out as regards the management of the humanitarian and migration crises generated by Libya's situation of great instability. In the final Joint Declaration of the AU–EU Summit, European and African leaders emphasised the importance of looking for long-term solutions to deal with the Libyan migration crisis, highlighting the need "to address the root causes of irregular migration and forced displacement" and "to promote a […] multidimensional approach to migration that takes place in a safe, orderly and regular manner".[50]

In the margins of this Abidjan AU–EU Summit, a tripartite meeting was also held between the representatives of the two regional organisations and

49 UNSC, Partnering for peace: moving towards partnership peacekeeping, Report of the Secretary General, 1 April 2015, UN doc. S/2015/229.

50 AU, Final Declaration: Investing in youth for accelerated inclusive growth and sustainable development, Abidjan, 29 November 2017.

the UN to discuss the dramatic conditions of migrants and refugees kept in detention and victims of the abuses perpetrated by smugglers. In this context, the leaders of the three organisations agreed to join forces and adopt a common approach to the migrants' situation in Libya. To this end, they decided to establish a joint AU–EU–UN Taskforce specifically focused on the migration-related issues linked to the Libyan crisis and with the mandate to organise and coordinate trilateral cooperation efforts and ensure the implementation of the common objectives agreed upon by the three organisations.[51]

Such AU–EU–UN triangular cooperation was initially established with the view to addressing a broad variety of migration-related issues, including both regular and irregular migration, human rights protection, humanitarian assistance and support to local authorities. The Taskforce, in particular, was endowed with the mandate to coordinate both long-term strategies and immediate and urgent interventions.

As for the immediate actions, the focus was put on the organised humanitarian evacuation of migrants and asylum seekers trapped in the official detention centres run by the UN-endorsed Libyan Government of National Accord, with the view to finding durable solutions by either repatriating them in their home countries or resettling them outside Libya. Interventions in this respect were meant to be based on the existing work of specialised actors as the IOM and UNHCR, so as to benefit from their expertise and experience on the ground, as well as to ensure continuity in their on-going projects and operations.

The long-term objectives set by the EU–AU–UN Tripartite Task Force were identified, on the one hand, in the improvement of conditions of migrants and asylum seekers present in Libya, and, on the other, in fighting smuggling and human-trafficking activities and dismantling the related criminal networks. According to the Task Force, such long-term actions and strategies had to be carried out also in close coordination with key countries of origin, transit and destination.

In order to pursue the aforementioned common goals, the EU, the AU and the UN recognised the need to strengthen and further develop their collaboration, emphasising, in particular, the necessity to "upgrade in a

51 European Commission, Joint press release of the United Nations, the African Union and the European Union, Statement/17/5029, Abidjan, 29 November 2017.

systematic manner their trilateral cooperation and to meet on a regular basis at the highest political level, notably in the UN General Assembly".[52]

After the Abidjan Summit, the formal launch of the AU–EU–UN Tripartite Task Force took place on 4 December 2017 in Addis Ababa, and was followed, few days later, by a meeting in Brussels between the representatives of the three organisations to discuss further steps to be taken for the work of the Task Force on migration and Libya. Members of the IOM and UNHCR also joined the discussions, so as to better plan and organise actions on the ground.[53] The role played by the UN specialised bodies was considered decisive for the positive outcome of the concrete operations in Libya, as was later highlighted by the EU, which expressed its strong appreciation for the work of the IOM and UNCHR, underling how they contributed to the creation of "an unprecedented mechanism for cooperation".[54]

At the summit in Brussels, first of all, the importance of the trilateral cooperation was reaffirmed: the multilateral tripartite collaboration on Libya and migration was defined as "a turning point" creating "a completely different dynamic" in the area of migrants' protection.[55] The need to engage in dialogues and collaboration initiatives with Libyan authorities was also reiterated, so as to "build a stronger security architecture in the region".[56] Secondly, concrete actions and interventions were discussed, also focusing on a clear division of tasks between the involved actors. In particular, concerning the immediate actions agreed in the margins of Abidjan Summit, that is to say, the urgent evacuation of migrants inside Libya, two different mechanisms of organised and protected transfer were agreed.

On the one hand, an emergency Voluntary Humanitarian Return (VHR) operation, managed by the IOM and aimed at safely returning migrants from Libya to their home countries, also and especially focusing on their reintegration; on the other hand, an emergency Evacuation Transit

---

52 Ibidem.

53 Meeting of the Joint AU–EU–UN Task Force to address the migration situation in Libya, Joint press release, Brussels, 14 December 2017; see also EEAS, Remarks by Federica Mogherini following the meeting at political level of the European Union – African Union – United Nations – Task Force, Brussels, 14 December 2017.

54 EEAS, Remarks by HR/VP Federica Mogherini at the high-level panel event on migration and structural transformation in Africa during the 2018 UN General Assembly, New York, 25 September 2018.

55 EEAS, Remarks by Federica Mogherini following the meeting at political level, 14 December 2017.

56 Meeting of the Joint AU–EU–UN Task Force, 14 December 2017.

Mechanism (ETM), under the UNHCR's guidance, targeting those individuals present in Libya and unable to be returned to their countries of origin and needing international protection. At the Brussels meeting, finally, the European Commission announced the decision to supply EUR 100 million funding to support the two programmes managed by UNHCR and IOM.

The willingness to further develop the trilateral cooperation was later confirmed on the occasion of the AU–EU–UN Trilateral Meeting, held at the UN headquarters in New York in September 2018, in the margins of the 73rd meeting of the UN General Assembly. In the Joint Statement adopted by the leaders and representatives of the three international organisations clearly emerges the commitment to promote "an effective multilateral system" with the view of "tackling global challenges through international cooperation".[57]

While maintaining their *ad hoc* initiatives in support of complex and delicate country situations, the three international organisations also agreed to take their cooperation forward, aiming at successfully addressing common global challenges and achieving ambitious goals in terms of stronger economic integration, security and conflict prevention, inclusive and sustainable growth, response to climate change, empowerment of youth and education, and protection of human rights.[58]

With specific regard to the trilateral cooperation on Libya and migration, the three organisations welcomed the progress made in addressing the Libyan migrants' crisis and expressed satisfaction for the work done by the Tripartite Task Force established in Abidjan in November 2017.[59] In the Joint Statement, however, while appreciation is shown with regard to the operations of evacuation of migrants and their following voluntary return and reintegration in the home countries, at same time, further efforts are requested and encouraged to dismantle trafficking and criminal networks.[60]

In general terms, moreover, albeit explicitly recognising the positive potential of the cooperation between the AU, the EU and the UN, the leaders of the three organisations have proven to be well aware of the political, legal and institutional challenges behind such trilateral collaboration. In the

57 Third African Union – European Union – United Nations Trilateral Meeting, Joint Communiqué, New York, 23 September 2018, para. 2.

58 Ibidem.

59 See also EEAS, EU, UN and AU take their cooperation forward, Press release, 24 September 2018.

60 Ibidem, para. 3.

Joint Statement, indeed, they acknowledge "the need for a clear definition of roles", as well as the necessity to "enhance collaboration, coordination and planning" between their respective efforts, especially in terms of effectiveness and coherence between their concrete actions.[61]

The need for further efforts in the assistance of migrants caught in Libyan detention centres has been recently reiterated by the Tripartite Task Force in its *ad hoc* meeting held in Addis Ababa in April 2019.[62] While noting the progress made by the programmes implemented by the IOM and UNHCR, the Task Force called for more efforts and more work to be done, underlining the existence of serious problematic issues: on the one hand, the presence of still more than 7,000 migrants and refugees held in Libyan detention centres and, on the other, the growing number of internally displaced persons in need of assistance and protection.

1. *The Voluntary Humanitarian Returns run by the IOM*

Voluntary Humanitarian Returns (VHR) essentially target migrants held in Libyan detention centres and wishing to return home. IOM plays a crucial role in this respect, not only in the organisation of the concrete transfer of migrants away from Libya, but also and especially in assisting them as regards a safe return to their home country with the view to facilitating their positive reception and reintegration in the local communities. Accordingly, VHR programmes allow migrants who decide to return to their countries of origin to do so in a safe and dignified manner, providing an opportunity to restart their lives in their original communities after being subjected to abuses and violence along unsafe and risky African migration routes.

The IOM's engagement in this kind of VHR operations is not new, being in place even long before the AU–EU–UN trilateral cooperation was agreed at the 2017 AU–EU Summit in Abidjan. The IOM, indeed, has been acting as a facilitator of repatriation processes with operations dating back to 2006 and targeting the return of migrants not only from Libya, but also from a number of several other countries across Africa and along the Central Mediterranean route.

61 Ibidem, para. 7.

62 The AU–EU–UN Task Force meeting calls to rescue stranded migrants and refugees in Libya, Press release 060/2019, Addis Ababa, 18 April 2019.

However, before the establishment of the AU–EU–UN trilateral cooperation on migration and Libya, the success in humanitarian return programmes has been modest, with only limited results obtained in practice.[63] Previous VHR programmes run by the IOM, in fact, were often undermined by the scarce level of cooperation of the involved actors, including Libyan authorities and the governments of the countries of origin where the migrants had to be repatriated. Further practical obstacles, including the lack of coordination and the shortage of economic resources, coupled with delays and slow procedures, determined modest and unsatisfactory outcomes in terms of successfully assisted and repatriated individuals.

Building on the enhanced trilateral cooperation between EU, AU and UN, IOM-driven VHR initiatives have regained momentum, significantly improving the positive impact of the programmes and allowing to boost the number of returned people and to accelerate the repatriation procedures. The joint work of the Tripartite Task Force, indeed, has played a decisive role in positively addressing and overcoming a number of challenges faced in the evacuation of migrants. Each of the involved actors has contributed to overcoming practical and organisational difficulties that had undermined the success of VHR operations in the past.

More specifically, the AU has played an essential role in the active interaction with the African countries of origin of the migrants targeted by the VHR programmes. Establishing and maintaining contacts with the governments of the countries of origin have been decisive for a closer cooperation on repatriating their nationals, especially in addressing issues such as provision of consular and diplomatic services, identification, release of relevant documentation and timely issuance of visas so as to allow returns of people to their home countries.[64]

The AU, moreover, has played a fundamental role in the dialogue with the Libyan authorities and the Government of National Accord. Their cooperation, indeed, has been necessary, especially to grant IOM staff, NGOs and other international partners unrestricted access to the official detention centres in Libya. As starting point, indeed, VHR programmes have targeted official detention centres only, as they are more easily identifiable and accessible, also and especially with the support of the Libyan UN-

63 For an overview of the voluntary humanitarian returns carried out by the IOM and the challenges faced during the years, see *Abderrahim*, Advancing the impossible? Progress of the joint African, European and International response to the migration crisis in Libya, ECDPM, Discussion Paper No. 229, September 2018, 6.

64 IOM, UN Migration Agency moves to relieve plight of migrants trapped in Libya, Backing AU–EU Plan, IOM, 12 January 2017.

recognised government. According to the IOM, the enhanced VHR programme launched under the AU–EU–UN trilateral cooperation has helped reduce the number of detained migrants in official Libyan detention centres from around 20,000 in October 2017 to nearly 4,000 in March 2018.[65]

While VHR programmes have contributed to positively evacuate migrants from official detention centres, thereby alleviating the pressure in their reception capacity and mitigating problems of overcrowding and poor detention conditions, on the contrary, migrants held in unofficial centres still remain subject to severe human rights violations. These irregular places of detention, indeed, being under the strict control of militias and armed groups, are difficult to locate, and remain less reachable and often impossible to be evacuated, with the consequence that individuals held in detention there still suffer from unlawful and inhuman practices, including torture, forced labour and other severe forms of violence.[66]

The contribution of the AU has been also important, together with the logistical support provided by the UN, to interact with Libyan authorities to get access to the territory, establishing camps and facilities, as well as to allow evacuation airplanes to land in airports across the country.[67]

The EU, for its part, has played its role mainly by deploying its diplomatic and financial capacities. Besides promoting relationships, dialogues and consultative processes with African countries and the AU, the EU has funded most of the returns carried out by the IOM. Already before the launch of the VHR programme based on the AU–EU–UN trilateral cooperation and specifically targeting Libya, the EU was engaged in protection and humanitarian evacuation operations under the EU–IOM Joint Initiative on Migrant Protection and Reintegration.[68] Launched in December 2016 and funded through the EU Emergency Trust Fund for Africa,[69] the EU–IOM Joint Initiative had a broader scope of action, involving different

65 IOM, Voluntary Humanitarian Returns from Libya continue as reintegration efforts step up, IOM, 13 March 2018.

66 *Abderrahim*, ECDPM, Discussion Paper No. 229, September 2018, (fn.63) 8.

67 Ibidem.

68 More details about the EU–IOM Joint Initiative for Migrant Protection and Reintegration maybe found online, in the official website of the EU–IOM Joint Initiative https://migrationjointinitiative.org.

69 The EU Emergency Trust Fund for Africa was launched by European and African partners at the Valletta Summit on Migration in November 2015, with the aim to address root causes of instability, forced displacement and irregular migration. On 12 November 2015, the Constitutive Agreement to officially establish the Fund was signed by the European Commission, 25 EU Member States, Norway and Switzerland.

areas of activity including protection and voluntary return assistance for vulnerable and stranded migrants; support for sustainable reintegration in their countries of origin; data collection on migratory routes, trends and flows; and information for migrants and local communities about the risks of unsafe and dangerous journeys along African migratory routes illegally managed by traffickers and smugglers.[70]

The financial support provided by the EU has been crucial also with regard to the VHR initiative launched by the Tripartite Task Force established in November 2017. The immediate focus of the organism established under the AU–EU–UN cooperation, indeed, was to reach the objective of the successful voluntary repatriation, by February 2018, of at least 15,000 migrants identified in Libyan government-controlled detention centres.[71] According to the data of the IOM, out of the nearly 15,000 migrants evacuated from Libya between the launch of the Task Force and February 2018, the vast majority of them (over 10,000) were repatriated with EU financial support.[72]

Overall, in 2017 and 2018, the joint work of the AU, the EU and the UN has supported more than 39,000 migrants to return to their countries of origin under the IOM-led VHR initiatives.[73] In 2019, voluntary repatriations have been slowed down and hampered by the backdrop of continuing armed conflict in Tripoli. In particular, as reported by the IOM, operations on the ground have been affected by the escalation in violence in the capital, with an impact on the functioning of the only airport in the city and on the availability of flights out of the country.[74] Despite security constraints and operational difficulties, however, repatriations have continued and, according to the data, as for April 2019, 3,175 migrants have been evacuated from Libyan official detention centres and returned home via the VHR programme run by the IOM.[75]

70 For detailed information and statistics on migratory flows, trends and routes towards Libya, see IOM, Displacement tracking matrix, Libya's migrant report, round No. 21, July–August 2018, IOM Libya 2018.

71 Meeting of the Joint AU–EU–UN Task Force to address the migration situation in Libya, 14 December 2017.

72 IOM, Voluntary Humanitarian Returns from Libya continue.

73 EEAS, AU–EU–UN Task Force, one year on – joint work delivers results, EEAS, Press release, 4 December 2018.

74 IOM, IOM Voluntary Humanitarian Return Assistance to Migrants Continues Amid Conflict in Tripoli, IOM Press release, 26 April 2019.

75 IOM, IOM Assists 160 Migrants with Voluntary Humanitarian Return Despite Ongoing Armed Conflict, IOM Press release, 12 April 2019.

2. The Emergency Transit Evacuation Mechanism managed by the UNHCR

When the Trilateral Task Force on migration and Libya was established, providing "a way out" for asylum seekers and refugees stranded in Libya was one of the key objectives to be urgently achieved through the AU–EU–UN cooperation. In fact, although international sources indicate that the vast majority of migrants traveling to or passing through the Libyan territory are individuals in search of better economic and living conditions, persons fleeing persecution, civil wars and conflicts and potentially eligible for international protection have also been reported. One of the main concerns of the trilateral AU–EU–UN cooperation was thus providing assistance to protection seekers stuck in Libyan detention centres with the view to evacuate and subsequently resettle them elsewhere.

While VHR programmes discussed above mainly target migrants fleeing from difficult living conditions who remained trapped in Libya, being led by the IOM with the view of their repatriation to the respective countries of origin; asylum seekers and people in need of international protection who cannot return to their countries of origin are evacuated from Libya via the ETM mechanism, specifically managed by the UNHCR.

Such UNHCR-driven programmes essentially encompass two different phases and movements: the initial, assisted evacuation of asylum seekers and refugees from Libya, followed by their subsequent resettlement to specific host countries which previously gave the availability to receive and resettle them. So conceived, this evacuation mechanism in view of resettlement is aimed in particular at targeting individuals deprived of liberty and imprisoned in Libyan official detention centres, where severe human rights violations have been widely reported.[76]

Similarly to the VHR programmes led by the IOM, effective coordination between all the involved actors had proven to be equally essential in order to fulfil the various necessary phases of the ETM mechanism: Libyan authorities, having the role to grant unhindered access for UNHCR staff to the official detention centres and camps, so as to allow identification and registration of asylum seekers; the AU, working in close cooperation with African countries of origin to provide adequate consular services to their nationals stuck in Libya, including timely release of documentation needed for the returns; the UN, providing logistical support and sustaining the UNHCR in organising and orchestrating all the procedural steps; finally,

---

76 UNHCR, "Detained and dehumanised". Report on human rights abuses against migrants in Libya, 13 December 2016.

the EU, on the one hand, contributing by making available funds and economic resources and, on the other, encouraging its Member States to make available places for resettlement and receive refugees resettled from Libya.[77]

As in the case of VHR initiatives run by the IOM, ETM programmes run by the UNHCR were already in place, but, following the establishment of the trilateral AU–EU–UN Task Force, they received a significant acceleration due to the joint efforts and the additional financial, diplomatic and political energies provided by the three organisations. According to the UNHCR, in particular, between September 2017 and April 2018, over 1,300 refugees and asylum seekers had been evacuated from Libya and resettled to other countries, including EU Member States, such as Italy and Romania.[78]

Refugees moved out from Libya are resettled not only outside Africa, especially in Europe or Canada, but also within other African countries. In effect, finding resettlement places could entail long waiting periods, coupled with lengthy procedures to process asylum applications once a host country eventually gives its availability for resettling people. For these reasons, asylum seekers evacuated from Libya may be temporarily hosted in other African countries, where they wait, in suitable protected conditions, for the processing of their applications and the conclusion of the relevant resettlement procedures. This is done through the cooperation between the UNHCR and particular partner countries, on the basis of specific agreements. Examples in this respect may be found in the cooperation initiatives launched between the UNHCR and Rwanda and Niger to accept to temporarily host asylum seekers evacuated from Libya during the processing of their applications and the conclusion of the resettlement procedures.

More specifically, cooperation with Niger has been in place since 2017, under an *ad hoc* agreement signed between the UNHCR and Niger's Government to implement ETM programmes and provide temporary shelter in Niger to people needing international protection, while waiting for al-

---

77 For an overview of the resettlement initiatives carried out in the European Union, see *F.L. Gatta*, Legal avenues to access international protection in the European Union: past actions and future perspectives, Journal Européen des Droits de l'Homme – European Journal of Human Rights (JEDH), (3) 2018.

78 UNHCR, UNHCR flash update LIBYA. 31 March – 6 April 2018, UNHCR Report, 6 April 2018.

ternative, long-term solutions in third countries.[79] Cooperation on ETM operations with Rwanda is more recent, as in September 2019, the Rwandan Government, the UNHCR and the AU signed a Memorandum of Understanding to set up a transit mechanism for evacuating refugees out of Libya.[80] Under the agreement, Rwanda will receive and provide protection to refugees and asylum-seekers who are currently being held in official detention centres in Libya; the AU will provide assistance with evacuations, strategic political support with training and coordination, and help to mobilise resources; the UNHCR will provide protection services and necessary humanitarian assistance, including food, water, accommodation, education and healthcare.[81]

According to the UNHCR's data, updated to May 2019, overall, since November 2017, 3,612 refugees and asylum-seekers have been evacuated from Libya via ETM operations. The vast majority of individuals (2,782) were destined to Niger, under the specific agreement concluded between the UNHCR and the government.[82] Outside Africa, 426 refugees have departed on resettlement from Libya directly to Europe (Romania, France, Italy, the Netherlands, Norway and Sweden) and Canada.

VI. Concluding remarks

The AU–EU–UN trilateral cooperation certainly represents a positive example of enhanced multilateral collaboration aimed at providing international responses to global issues and at achieving strategic objectives. The Tripartite Task Force on migration and Libya, in particular, constitutes an encouraging and fruitful experiment, which has already led to the achievement of good results, showing a promising potential to do even more.

The operations put in place on the ground under the guidance of specialised bodies such as the IOM and UNHCR have allowed a tangible response to be offered to the Libyan crisis and the situation of migrants. The AU–EU–UN, thus, signal a new momentum in their cooperation on mi-

---

79 On this topic, see UNHCR, 131 refugees evacuated out of Libya to Niger, amidst ongoing conflict in Tripoli, UNHCR Press release, 20 June 2019; ASGI, The "Emergency Transit Mechanism" program and the resettlement from the Niger. Legal analysis, current and future concerns, November 2018.

80 UNHCR, Joint Statement: Government of Rwanda, UNHCR and African Union agree to evacuate refugees out of Libya, 10 September 2019.

81 Ibidem.

82 UNHCR, UNHCR Update Libya, 3 May 2019.

gration, improving their relationships and bringing collaboration initiatives to a new level. The work of the Tripartite Task Force on migration and Libya has benefited from an enhanced network of cooperation, involving a good combination of efforts coming from the EU, the UN and their specialised agencies, and the AU, which has played a fundamental role in fostering the dialogue with African governments and, especially, with the Libyan authorities.

The VHR and ETM programmes run by the IOM and the UNHCR have received a significant improvement since the launch of the trilateral international cooperation on migration and Libya. Economic, political, diplomatic and organisational joint efforts have given a considerable impulse to humanitarian and assistance operations on the ground, whose outcomes have been positively increased. The process of evacuation of migrants from Libyan detention centres, in particular, has showed a good combination of functions and tasks, facilitated in their performance by the funding and economic resources made available especially by the EU, the diplomatic actions and political pressure mainly exercised by the AU with the African governments, the logistical and operational capacities provided by the UN and UNHCR and IOM.

In spite of the progress made, however, at the same time a number of challenges and problematic questions have emerged, especially in terms of cooperation, coordination and organisational aspects, also and especially in light of the involvement of a variety of actors operating at different levels and through different means. With regard to the VHR and ETM operations carried out in Libya by the IOM and UNHCR, in particular, a number of operational challenges have affected the implementation of the joint response provided by the AU, the EU and the UN.

First, evacuations of migrants from Libyan detention centres are slowed down by the lack of an effective and rapid provision of the necessary consular services. In addition to delays in carrying out the relevant procedures, it has been highlighted that many African countries do not have proper consular and diplomatic capacities to efficiently deal with sometimes complex procedures, involving multiple procedural steps such as identification, screening, timely issuance of documents to allow repatriation and/or resettlement.[83] Due to the insecurity situation in Libya, many countries do not have a consular representation in Tripoli, or, if they do, the number of competent diplomatic authorities has been considerably reduced, with an impact on consular procedures. The lack of financial resources also plays

83 *Abderrahim*, ECDPM, Discussion Paper No. 229, September 2018 (fn. 63), 9.

an important role. For example, rapid and advanced consular services, including through the use of online platforms and IT apparatuses, would allow speeding up of the processing of applications and carrying out of procedures, but they are not always available or affordable.

Second, in order to be evacuated outside Libya, migrants need not only consular services from their countries of origin, but also an authorisation to leave the country by the Libyan Government. The Libyan legal framework concerning immigration is complex and challenges have been reported in authorising the exit of people from the country.[84] From an operational point of view, moreover, taking migrants out of Libya has proven to be difficult due to security conditions. Criticalities have emerged, in particular, with regard to transportation both inside and outside Libya, especially in terms of access to airports, which has been complicated due to clashes between armed groups and militias.

Third, and more generally, a number of issues have been pointed out with regard to the overall effectiveness of the evacuation programmes themselves. It has been highlighted that, if it is certainly true that VHR operations evacuating migrants from Libya help to mitigate the pressure on Libyan authorities, reducing the number of people in detention centres, yet moving a significant amount of persons in a short period of time to the countries of origin may put their reception capacities under considerable strain. Consequently, national authorities, as well as NGOs and other international organisations operating on the ground, may be put under pressure by the inflow of additional numbers of migrants, especially due to their often already limited availability of resources. This may also lead to tensions, as exemplified by the case of the ETM programme in Niger discussed above: difficulties in the management of incoming refugees induced the Niger's government to suspend the agreed evacuation programme with UNHCR for some months, before accepting additional persons from Libya.[85]

Fourth, complex challenges for African receiving countries may arise also with regard to the effective capacity to support, provide proper assistance and reintegrate evacuated migrants. African countries of origin may suffer from shortages in resources and reception capacities, being often unable to support people coming back from Libya, both in terms of immedi-

84 UNHCR, "Detained and dehumanised", Report on human rights abuses against migrants in Libya, 13 December 2016.

85 *Abderrahim*, ECDPM, Discussion Paper No. 229, September 2018 (fn. 63), 12.

ate assistance, such as medical care and housing, and long-term support, as regards reintegration perspectives, education and employment.

Additionally, it has been underlined that returned people usually find themselves in a very delicate and vulnerable situation, which receiving countries are often not prepared to handle. Migrants evacuated from Libyan detention centres, indeed, are often traumatised and have suffered from severe forms of violence and exploitation. They also face the risk of remaining jobless and marginalised, as, once returned home, they are often subjected to harsh judgment and negative consideration from their original societies.

Finally, with regard to ETM programmes run by the UNHCR, despite the progress made, it has been highlighted that the level of commitment in terms of resettlement remains still largely insufficient in relation to the concrete needs. European countries, in particular, would need to increase their efforts and offer bigger numbers of resettlement places. Also it has been pointed out that the EU itself, despite unlocking financial resources and funds, should put more pressure on its Member States to encourage their commitment to resettle refugees from Libya.

In general terms, ultimately, the AU–EU–UN trilateral cooperation may certainly be considered as a positive step forward in addressing the Libyan crisis. While it appears too soon to formulate a comprehensive judgment on the overall action of the Tripartite Task Force on migration and Libya, as results will be better measurable in the long-term, yet, for the future, the trilateral cooperation will need to evolve, becoming more organised and focused more on addressing structural problems rather than having a mere emergency approach.

The complexity of the situation in Libya surely gives rise to significant challenges. However, international coordinated efforts will need to address solutions for systemic problems, such as those of both official and unofficial Libyan detention centres, where unacceptable human rights violations are in place. The migrant smuggling business, which continues to proliferate, will also need to be addressed in a more systematic manner.

In this context, the EU, in particular, is called upon to play a leading role, in supporting international initiatives, such as the trilateral cooperation with the AU and the UN, but also and especially in re-thinking its own migration policies. While economic resources and funding are flowing from Brussels towards Libya and other African partners, practices as the externalisation of border controls, the crackdown on departures from Libyan coasts, the interception of migrants by the Libyan Coast Guard – trained and funded with European resources – and their subsequent deprivation of liberty in the detention centres represent problematic issues that need to be addressed by the EU and its Member States. Last but not least, in reforming its migration policies, the EU should develop a credible and organic system of legal and organised mobility to access international protection in the European territory. Otherwise, the illegal migration business and the smuggling industry will inevitably continue to grow and prosper.

Balkan Migration to the EU: From Countries of Origin to Countries of Transit and to a Chaotic Exterior Guardian of the Schengen Area!

Arolda Elbasani and Senada Šelo Šabić***

I. Introduction

Since the end of the cold war, conflict-ridden Balkan states have provided probably the most consistent pool of illegal migration and asylum seekers in Europe. Waves of Balkan migration tipped the scale during the eruption of ethnic violence, civic disorder and state collapse that marked the dissolution of Yugoslavia. The influx of Yugoslav refugees in the early 1990s led to the development of the Common European Asylum System (CEAS), which today finds itself under significant pressure. Two decades later, around 2015, Balkan countries reemerged forcefully on the map of current European migration and asylum policy, this time around both as a major even if declining source of asylum seekers and a transit route for massive waves of Middle Eastern migrants seeking asylum in select European destinations. This chapter summarises the shifting trends and challenges of migration from the Balkans as well as European policy responses to those challenges during the period 2000 to the present. The starting point coincides with the extension of the EU enlargement strategy and specific EU tools to manage migration from the Balkans while keeping the region within the orbit of European integration.

The argument proceeds in two main sections. Following the introduction, section II analyses EU policies to manage Balkan trends of migration – particularly the visa liberalisation process, within the framework of EU enlargement strategy. Seen as a device to offer citizens and governments in the region concrete benefits of integration, the visa liberalisation process which occurred in 2009–2010 did not prevent rising asylum applications from specific Balkan countries. Although the rate of general asylum appli-

* PhD at the European University Institute (2007), visiting scholar at the NYU and senior analyst for the Wikistrat Consulting Network.

** PhD at the European University Institute (2003) and a senior scientific associate at the Institute for Development and International Relations in Zagreb.

cations has been in steep decline since its peak in 2014–2015, it remains an ongoing challenge. Cases like Kosovo and Albania continue to rank high among countries providing the highest number of asylum seekers in countries that maintain a generous asylum system. In response, the EU Commission has adopted an annual system of monitoring visa abuses. Meanwhile, specific EU members have advocated for *ad hoc* solutions which range from blocking the visa liberalisation process for the next country in line, Kosovo, to offering legal pathways to select EU member countries for Balkan citizens.

Section III explores the more recent phenomena of the Balkans' return to the map of European integration, this time around as transit countries for migrants leaving Middle Eastern wars. In this case too, the EU policy solutions have shifted depending on alternate trends of migration via the Balkan route. Initially, the most affected EU member countries opted for *ad hoc* restrictive policies towards incoming migrants, creating confusion and uncertainty at key border points, a situation which culminated in a common EU solution to close the southern entry by negotiating a deal with Turkey in 2016. The deal has curtailed the massive wave of migration, but also pushed still-incoming migrants towards more dangerous channels. Although the EU has offered the most affected countries substantial technical and financial aid to manage migration and enforce border controls, while fostering the promise of European integration, some of the Balkan states find themselves hosting increasing numbers of migrants. In the context of weak Balkan states as well as poor economy and rule of law, the clustering of migrants within Balkan countries risks degrading the region into a chaotic and uncertain external guardian of the Schengen Area.

II. EU policies to manage Balkan migration

1. Visa liberalisation and the asylum challenge

As of the early 2000s, the EU has extended its membership perspective to all the Western Balkan (WB) countries left out of the previous wave of enlargement. Different policies, which were outlined under the Stabilisation and Association Process, were designed to facilitate reforms and bring the WB closer to Europe.[1] Ever since, while working in parallel with govern-

1 *Elbasani*, European Integration and Transformation in the Western Balkans, Abingdon 2013; *Qorraj/Jusufi*, The EU Stabilisation and Association Agreement for the

ments in the region, the EU has tried to reach out to citizens of these countries with the aim of generating bottom-up support for the reforms those countries needed to undertake. Ensuring people-to-people contact as a way to create stronger bonds between the WB and the rest of Europe has been partially impaired by the existence of visas which presented an effective hurdle for more frequent travels from the WB to the Schengen Area. The Thessaloniki Summit of 2003 already endorsed the lifting of visas for WB citizens.[2] The debate evolved around the issue of how will Balkan citizens believe in a European future if they cannot travel freely into most parts of the EU?[3] The debate, however, was not without misgivings on both sides. Some worried about the abuse of the visa-free privilege, while others criticised self-defeating EU policy which punishes ordinary WB citizens – exactly those pro-European forces advocating reforms in their respective countries.

In order to lift visas for the WB, the EU listed a set of reforms targeting specifically the areas of the rule of law and security: fighting organised crime and corruption, ensuring border protection, combating illegal migration, and granting safety of identification documents, among others. Negotiations for the Visa Liberalisation and Readmission Agreements with the WB were launched in November 2006.[4] In the course of a year during the period September – November 2007, the Agreements were signed between the Commission and five WB countries, approved by the Parliament, adopted by the Council and ratified by the respective countries.

In November 2008 the European Commission adopted Visa Liberalisation Guidelines, a document that lists conditions that need to be met by targeted Balkan countries. These guidelines were more specifically tailored to the situation in each country, but envisaged reforms and specific policy actions in common areas including readmission and reintegration, document security, border control and migration management, maintenance of public order and security, and ensuring protection of fundamental rights

Western Balkans: Between Challenges and Opportunities, Croatian International Relations Review 81 (2018).

2 European Commission, Declaration. EU–Western Balkans Summit. Thessaloniki, 21 June 2019, available at: http://europa.eu/rapid/press-release_PRES-03-163_en.htm, accessed: 24 June 2019.

3 European Stability Initiative, The Western Balkans and visa-free travel, available at: https://www.esiweb.org/index.php?lang=en&id=495, accessed: 15 June 2019.

4 The negotiations were launched with five WB countries except Kosovo which declared independence in 2008.

(related to the freedom of movement).[5] Kosovo was given the Visa Liberalisation Roadmap in 2012 and negotiations were still ongoing in 2019. The dialogue on visa liberalisation between the Commission and five WB countries (Albania, Bosnia and Herzegovina, North Macedonia, Montenegro and Serbia) lasted from 2008 to 2010. Visas for Serbia, North Macedonia and Montenegro were lifted in December 2009. A year later, in December 2010, Albania and Bosnia and Herzegovina (BiH) were granted visa-free regimes too.

Granting visa-free travel is recognised as one of the most tangible benefits for Balkan citizens. This became clear in the case of BiH. Failing to fulfill the necessary criteria by December 2009, BiH, together with Albania, was not granted a visa-free regime like the other countries in the region. Bosnian politicians blamed a complicated state structure and each other for their failure to deliver necessary reforms. However, when it became clear that the usual blame game would not work and that they would be collectively punished by angry citizens, BiH politicians got their act together and in a matter of months implemented a few remaining conditions.[6]

The success of visa liberalisation, measured in terms of Balkan countries implementing sensitive and often technically and politically demanding reforms, was used as an inspiration to be repeated in some other policy areas. However, the visa liberalisation model of facilitating reforms was not easily repeatable. This is also due to the fact that it is difficult to find a policy area that is so directly affecting citizens, that is region-wide and allows for measurement and thus comparison.[7] Also, the EU was able to exert direct and unyielding pressure because it possesses clear regulations in terms of conditions that need to be implemented if a country wishes to qualify for visa-free status. Unlike many other policy areas, this one is detailed, straightforward, measurable and non-negotiable.

While WB citizens felt the immediate effect of visa-free travel, the EU can count on long-term benefits of bringing the Balkans closer and creating stronger links among people. A short-term effect of visa liberalisation, however, was a significant increase in asylum applications and illegal resi-

---

5 *Trauner/Kruse*, EC Visa Facilitation and Readmission Agreements: A new Standard EU Foreign Policy Tool? Paper presented at the ECPR Fourth Pan-European Conference on EU Politics, 25–27 September 2008, Riga.

6 European Commission, Enlargement Strategy and Main Challenges 2011–2012, available at: https://ec.europa.eu/neighbourhood-enlargement/sites/near/files/pdf/key_documents/2011/package/ba_rapport_2011_en.pdf, accessed: 14 June 2019.

7 An exception to this may be the roaming free service, a benefit citizens immediately feel.

dence of Balkan citizens in EU countries. Asylum applications rocketed, making a historical high in the years 2014 and 2015, and causing consternation in a number of EU countries, principally Germany. Although not being the primary destination for all WB countries in the beginning, as of 2015 Germany received 75% of the overall asylum seekers from the Balkans.

Table 1. Main destination of asylum seekers from WB6 between 2008 and 2018

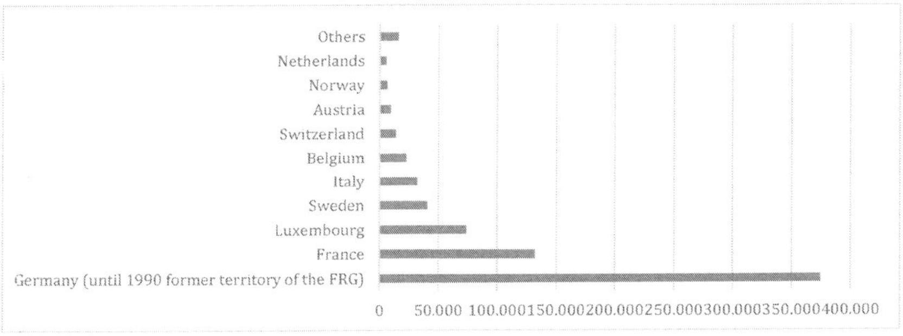

Source: *Eurostat,* Asylum and first time asylum applicants by citizenship, age and sex Annual aggregated data, 2019.

Table 2: Evolution of the applications of asylum seekers from WB6 to the EU: Total and first time applicants

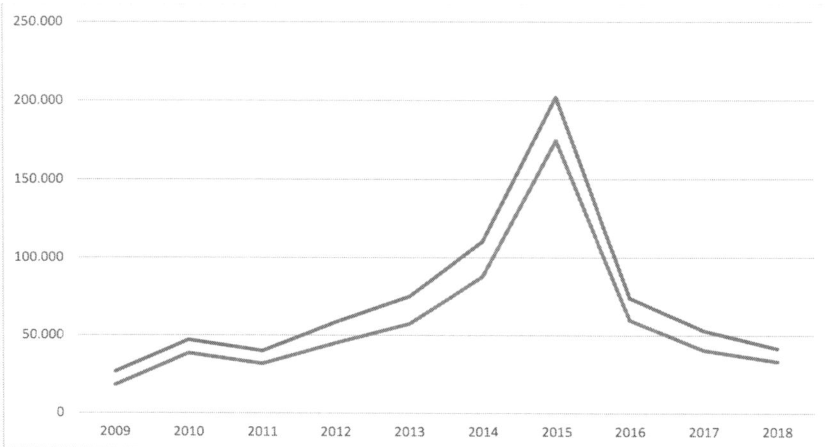

Source: *Eurostat,* Asylum and first time asylum applicants by citizenship, age and sex Annual aggregated data, 2019.

Table 3: Evolution of the applications of asylum seekers from WB6 to the EU: Total and first time applicants

Applicants to the EU	2009	2010	2011	2012	2013	2014	2015	2016	2017	2018
WB Applicants	26.460	46.835	39.765	58.275	74.820	110.140	201.875	73.930	52.800	41.365
WB 1st Time applicants	17.890	38.255	31.495	44.830	57.160	87.610	174.350	59.575	40.255	33.010

Source: *Eurostat,* Asylum and first time asylum applicants by citizenship, age and sex Annual aggregated data, 2019.

Table 3 shows the rates of asylum application from WB countries in the period between 2009 and 2018. The data shows that after visa liberalisation was introduced, a significant increase in the number of asylum applications and irregular migration followed. However, there is no conclusive evidence that the upsurge of asylum application from the WB registered in the few years following the introduction of visa-free regime can only be attributed to visa liberalisation. Instead, a combination of factors seemingly facilitated increasing asylum registrations. The reasons for emigration include pull factors such as economic deprivation, a high rate of unemployment (in particular that of youth), poor health care, low-quality education, and little social benefits; and pull factors such as the presence of the diaspora, cash benefits, access to illegal labor market, begging, and length of asylum procedure.[8] As we see from Table 4, the spike in the asylum applications did not result in any significant number of recognition of claims. Most applications were rejected with only a fraction of applicants receiving a status of refugee or humanitarian protection.[9]

Table 4: First instance decisions on asylum applications from WB6

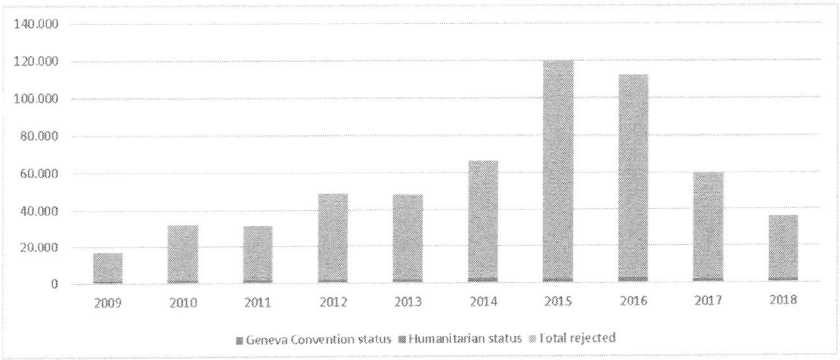

Source: *Eurostat,* First instance decisions on applications by citizenship, age and sex Annual aggregated data, 2019.

A specific characteristic of WB asylum spike was seasonality. For example, the rate of asylum applications rose in Serbia after 2009 and it reached 42% of overall WB asylum applications in the EU in 2013. In this case it was primarily Roma population, for whom the attraction of asylum financial assistance and the possibility to spend a winter in a collective accommodation centre was a justified incentive to make the trip and try their luck in the EU.[10] The rate dropped after the Serbian government started to implement measures that controlled exit from the country, ran information

8 European Asylum Support Office (EASO), Asylum Applicants from the Western Balkans: comparative analysis of trends, push-pull factors and responses – Update, May 2015, available at: https://www.easo.europa.eu/sites/default/files/public/Asylum-Applicants-from-the-Western-Balkans_Update_r.pdf, accessed: 15 June 2019.

9 *Koelbl/Kuntz/Mayr,* What Is Driving the Balkan Exodus?, available at: https://www.spiegel.de/international/europe/western-balkan-exodus-puts-pressure-on-germany-and-eu-a-1049274.html, accessed: 21 June 2019.

10 *Ristic,* Serbia Tops Germany's Asylum Seekers List, available at: https://balkaninsight.com/2013/01/16/serbia-leads-german-asylum-seekers-list/, accessed: 15 June 2019.

campaigns, and after applicants received repeated rejections in a speedy procedure.

In general, however, a rise in asylum applications rose for all countries in the years following the introduction of visa-free regime in 2009 and 2010. Preferred destination for citizens of Serbia, Bosnia and Herzegovina and North Macedonia was Germany. Albanians seemingly targeted mostly France, Sweden, the UK or Belgium, while Montenegrins opted for France, Luxembourg or Sweden. Since 2015, Germany topped the list as the principal destination country for most WB migrants.

2. *Remaining problematic countries and data on asylum seekers*

In 2015, Albanians remained the second group of asylum seekers in Germany after Syrians while Kosovars followed as the third group. This was the fifth year of the implementation of visa-free regime for Albania and the asylum application rates were not significantly subsiding. Kosovars, even if exempt from the visa liberalisation process, would still find a way to register for asylum in countries of choice. Only during the period November 2014 – March 2015, 57,945 Kosovars requested asylum in Germany.[11] The rate of illegal immigration was even higher, at approximately 75,000.[12]

Many Kosovar citizens were misled by smugglers who managed to convince them that they could get protection and a chance to start a new life in rich European countries.[13] For this goal they were prepared to sell their property and leave everything only to fail and be returned home after their asylum application was rejected. This, however, did not stop many from applying several times, an approach that the European Commission demanded the WB countries take measures to prevent.

Even as asylum applications from four WB countries showed a sharp decline, Albania and Kosovo remain somewhat an exception. The percentage

11 *Qosaj-Mustafa*, Policy Paper No. 1/15 – March 2015, Kosovar Institute for Policy Research and Development, available at http://www.kipred.org/repository/docs/1_April_2015_Kosovo_to_EU_The_Challenge_of_Irregular_Migration_FINAL_680809.pdf, accessed: 15 June 2019.

12 European Stability Initiative, New facts and figures on Western Balkan Asylum Seekers, 2015, available at https://www.esiweb.org/pdf/New%20facts%20and%20figures%20on%20WB%20asylum%20claims%206%20April%202015.pdf, accessed: 21 June 2019.

13 *Bytyci/Than*, Dramatic surge in Kosovars crossing illegally into EU, available at: https://www.reuters.com/article/us-kosovo-eu-migrants/dramatic-surge-in-kosovars-crossing-illegally-into-eu-idUSKBN0L811120150204, accessed: 21 June 2019.

of Albanian citizens seeking asylum has reduced significantly, but at a slower pace than has been the case with other countries from the region. Data from March 2019 show that Albanian citizens accounted for the highest percentage of asylum applications in France (44%). They also constitute 16% of asylum applications in Greece and 12% in the United Kingdom.[14]

In the spring of 2019, the Belgium parliament passed a resolution requesting the re-institutionalisation of visas for Albania. In April 2019, the Dutch Parliament also asked its government to request the European Commission to suspend visa-free travel for Albania. In June 2019 the same parliament with two-thirds majority decided to block the opening of negotiations with Albania, as recommended by the Commission. Specifically, the Dutch parliament suggested that Albania did not sufficiently advance in fighting organised crime and corruption, and thus cannot start negotiations for EU membership.[15]

Table 5: Evolution of asylum applications from Albania by destination country

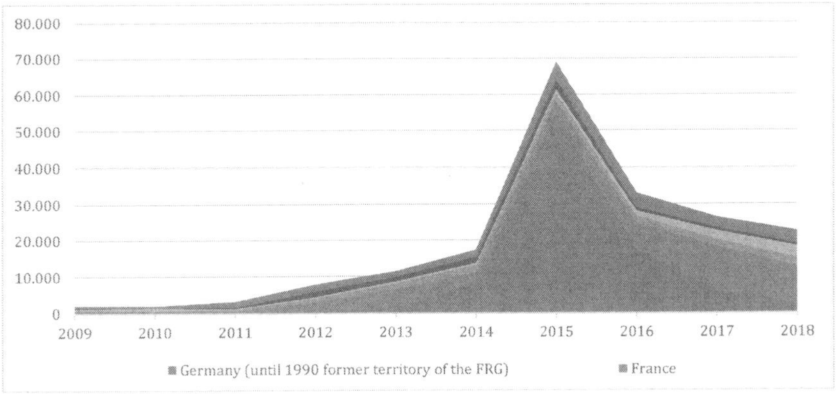

Source: *Eurostat,* Asylum and first time asylum applicants by citizenship, age and sex Annual aggregated data, 2019.

14 Eurostat, Asylum and Migration Visualizations, available at https://ec.europa.eu/eurostat/web/asylum-and-managed-migration/visualisations, accessed: 21 June 2019.

15 "Dutch Parliament Votes Against Opening EU Accession Negotiations with Albania", Exit portal (12 June 2019). https://exit.al/en/2019/06/12/dutch-parliament-votes-against-opening-eu-accession-negotiations-with-albania/.

Table 6: Evolution of asylum applications from Kosovo by destination country

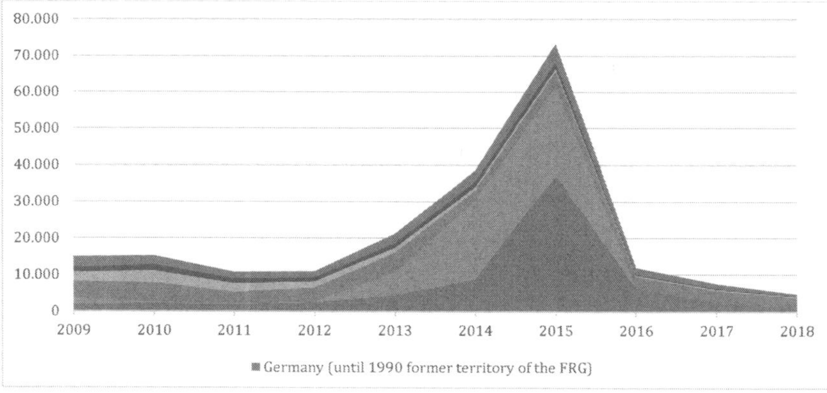

Source: *Eurostat,* Asylum and first time asylum applicants by citizenship, age and sex Annual aggregated data, 2019.

In 2016, in response to the remaining problems with WB countries, and expecting further challenges by granting Moldova a visa-free status while preparing to do so for Georgia and the Ukraine, the Commission adopted a monitoring mechanism to evaluate countries' commitment to policies that guarantee continuation of visa-free regime.[16] Hence, in addition to regular annual reports on the countries fulfilling visa liberalisation benchmarks, the Commission also publishes annual reports on the visa suspension mechanism that monitors possible abuses of visa-free travel regulation. The reports would allow the Commission to suggest temporary re-introduction of visas for countries whose citizens have been found to abuse/violate the visa-free regime.

3. *A new strategy of integration – facilitating work permits*

To address labor shortage in their countries, as well as unemployment and economic hardship in the WB, Germany has opened its market much more generously for workers from this region. As of 1 January 2016 Germany simplified procedures for issuing residence permits on the basis of

16 European Migration Network (EMN), Impact of Visa Liberalisation on Countries of Destination, 2019.

employment for citizens of the Western Balkans. In effect, it created a legal labor channel for immigration from the WB, decoupling this procedure strictly from asylum application. Although qualified as safe countries, which would prevent their citizens from asking for asylum, WB citizens could still qualify to get a job contract if a German or EU citizen has not applied for the job.[17] The regulation was part of a broader initiative in Berlin to offer legal pathways to those in need of protection while reducing the numbers of people seeking asylum. Those who would otherwise arrive and enter the asylum system or stay in a country without any legal status will be incentivised to try to receive a legal work permit from home, rather than embark across borders irregularly.

One prerequisite for granting residence on the basis of employment is that a person did not receive any benefits under the Asylum Seekers Benefits Act in 24 months prior to the job application. The other condition is that a person is offered a job before the residence permit is issued. This decision on the simplification of legal labor migration is intended to run until 2020, but in the current economic situation of a shortage of workforce, it may well be extended.[18] The policy has been largely successful. Between 2015 and 2017, about half of all visas were issued in Bosnia-Herzegovina (26.1%) and Kosovo (25.2%), followed by Serbia (18.4%), FYR Macedonia (17.7%), Albania 9.1% and Montenegro 3.5%.[19] What is interesting in the context of WB legal labor migration is that Germany allows for employment both of skilled and unskilled force. This is in contrast to usual labor migration requirements where countries seek qualified workers. Roughly one half of permits issued in 2016 and 2017 in Germany were for the category of helpers (unskilled workers), while skilled workforce accounts for 45%. The remaining permits were issued to specialists and highly educated workforce. Because of the regulation, Bosnia and Herzegovina is among the top four countries from which workers came to Germany in 2017. The

---

17 *Bither/Ziebarth*, Creating Legal Pathways to Reduce Irregular Migration? What We Can Learn from Germany's 'Western Balkans Regulation', Migration Strategy Group (2018).

18 *Buck*, Germany looks to foreign workers to tackle labour shortage, available at: https://www.ft.com/content/c1626f0c-a6f2-11e8-8ecf-a7ae1beff35b, accessed: 22 June 2019.

19 *Hoffmeyer-Zlotnik*, Developments in Germany in the context of visa liberalisation, European Migration Network (EMN), 2019, https://ec.europa.eu/home-affairs/sites/homeaffairs/files/11a_germany_visa_liberalisation_en.pdf.

remaining three were India, China and the US.[20] While regional unemployment has declined since 2010, it remains at 21 per cent, with inactivity particularly high among women, the less educated, and youth.[21] Combined with always-simmering ethnic tensions, such rates of unemployment may still provide fertile ground for ongoing migration from the region.

Table 7: First residence permits given to WB citizens in European countries

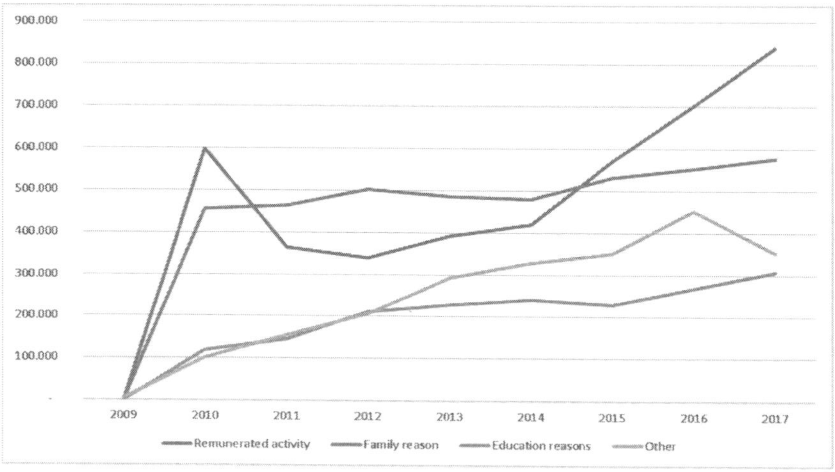

Source: *Eurostat,* First permits by reason, age, sex and citizenship, 2019.

III. Balkan transit routes: externalising challenges of European migration

Escalating Middle Eastern conflicts since 2015 have triggered new waves of massive migration towards Europe via the Balkans, placing Balkan countries on the map of the main sources of European migration anew, this time around as transition countries. During the peak period of Middle Eastern conflict in 2015–2016, and to some extent still in the present, migrants escaping war and human rights abuses generally targeted European

20 Germany's Federal Ministry of the Interior, Building and Community, Skilled immigrants: an asset to our country, 2018,https://www.bmi.bund.de/EN/topics/migration/immigration/labour-migration/skilled-immigration/skilled-immigration.html.

21 World Bank Group, Western Balkans Labor Market Trends 2019, 2019.

countries perceived as safe places of asylum. Balkans – all countries bordering the EU and enjoying the EU visa liberalisation regime, but not bound by EU asylum legislation or sharing an appealing asylum system themselves – offered the easiest path to reach European destinations.[22] The Balkan transit routes, however, kept shifting and developing depending on policy changes at the EU level and cascading Balkan governments' responses. Meanwhile, the very connotation of the Balkans as transit countries proved complex because there will always be a certain number of persons interested in remaining there and seeking some form of protection, especially as the designation and circumstances of travel routes are subject to change.[23]

1. Balkans transit routes that connect Middle Eastern migrants with selected European destinations

Initially, Germany's open borders approach to migration and European policy makers' failure to take a common approach towards incoming migration helped expand the Balkan routes as the most convenient way to reach European destinations. The path which usually began in Turkey, then winds through either Bulgaria or Greece, and then further north via North Macedonia and Serbia to Slovenia or Hungary had as ultimate destinations Germany or Austria. Eighty per cent of the almost one million refugees that found shelter in Germany in 2015 passed through this route.[24] In 2015, 600,000 registered at the Presevo camp, on the border between Serbia and North Macedonia, alone. Most of those passing migrants refused to register for asylum in any of the Balkan countries. The data shows that most migrants, instead, opted for asylum "shopping strategies". Out of a total of 590,816 persons who expressed the intention to seek asylum in Serbia during 2015 and 2016 only 1,157 (0.2%) submitted a formal

22 *Weber*, The EU–Turkey Refugee Deal and the Not Quite Closed Balkan Route, Friedrich Ebert Foundation, 2017.

23 *Kilibarda*, Obligations of Transit Countries Under Refugee Law: A Western Balkans Case Study, International Review of the Red Cross 90 (2017), 211–239.

24 *Mandić*, Anatomy of a Refugee Wave: Forced Migration on the Balkan Route as Two Processes, Europe Now Journal (2017), available at: https://www.europenowjournal.org/2017/01/04/anatomy-of-a-refugee-wave-forced-migration-on-the-balkan-route-as-two-processes/.

application.[25] In North Macedonia too, out of 525,059 asylum-seekers recorded, only 2,660 (0.51%) persons submitted an application.[26] Meanwhile, during the period 2015–2016, 850,230 persons of Syrian and Iraqi origin were registered as asylum seekers in Europe, as compared to only 189,070 during the previous two years.[27]

Table 8: Main irregular migration routes through Western Balkans, March 2016

Source: Šabić /Borić, *At the Gate of Europe: A Report on Refugees on the Western Balkan Route* (Zagreb: Friedrich Ebert Foundation Croatia, 2016)

The Balkan governments proved willing to facilitate the transit – by providing medical and humanitarian assistance as well as transportation means usually with the help of humanitarian organisations – as long as Europeans kept the door open and financial assistance running.[28] Typically, however, they highlighted that those were measures of "hospitality" rather

25 *Petrović*, Right to Asylum in the Republic of Serbia, Belgrade Center for Human Rights, 2017, 11–12.
26 *Kilibarda*, International Review of the Red Cross 90 (2017) (fn. 23), 217.
27 Eurostat data.
28 *Greider*, Outsourcing Migration Management: The Role of the Western Balkans in the European Refugee Crisis (17 August 2017), available at: https://www.migrationpolicy.org/article/outsourcing-migration-management-western-balkans-eu-

than a legal obligation towards persons who did not request asylum in those countries. That migrants passed through different countries where they could have required asylum prior to transiting the Balkans, preferred "asylum shopping", and constituted a flow rather than individual cases made possible legal protections a tool vulnerable to governments' shifting policy urgencies. In September 2015, for example, the government of Serbia enacted a "Decision on Issuing a Certificate of Having Entered the Territory of Serbia." which circumvented the necessity of applying for asylum in the country in order to facilitate migrants' movement north. By November 2015, in the face of massive waves of migration both Serbia and North Macedonia introduced new measures – such as allowing migrants a 72-hour temporary permit in the country – in order to manage and reduce migrant flows.

Already in early 2016, the collapse of a common asylum system and restrictions taken from select European countries set off a domino effect of restrictions across the countries along the Balkan route, each trying to avoid responsibility for incoming or trapped migrants in their territory. As soon as Hungary started erecting a border fence, Slovenia and Croatia responded by imposing quotas and Austria and Germany began imposing their own restrictions. All the while, Serbia started expediting migrants' passage to its borders. Those individual and uncoordinated policy shifts aggravated further the situation at the Greek–North Macedonian border.[29] North Macedonia too in response resorted to building its own fence while using tear gas to counter protests and barrages on the border with Greece. Ultimately, the incoming waves of migrants were seen as a security and financial liability and all countries strategised about possible ways of shifting responsibility. Speaking for many Balkan leaders, then Serbian PM Vučić noted that "Serbia must not become a parking lot for Afghans and Pakistanis whom no one else in Europe wants". Soon enough the issue of migration also risked feeding into poor regional relations and potential conflicts: the closure of the Belgrade–Hungary route and the danger of overcrowding the Croatian border, for example, led the Croatian PM to blame neighbours for incoming migrants: "Until I see the Budapest–Belgrade axis stop burdening Croatia with refugees, I will remain convinced that [Serbia is] doing something behind our back". All the while, the shift

ropes-refugee-crisis; *Kilibarda/Kovačević*, Country Report: Serbia, Belgrade Centre for Human Rights and AIDA, 2017, available at: http://www.asylumineurope.org/reports/country/serbia.

29 *Šelo Šabić/Borić*, At the Gate of Europe: A Report on Refugees on the Western Balkan Route, Friedrich Ebert Foundation, 2016.

of Balkan politics towards incoming migration informed hard-core policies on the borders and contributed to sealing off, at least partially, the Balkan route. Quite often, police guarding borders all across the passage countries began using detention and violence, including the use of dogs and beatings, to deter or intimidate people attempting to cross.[30]

2. *EU solutions to shifting problems*

Massive flows of migration via the Balkans declined after the EU signed the 2016 deal with Turkey. Accordingly, migrants who irregularly arrived in the EU would be readmitted by Turkey in return for six billion euros in aid. Soon after the deal, arrivals by sea dropped from 856,000 in 2015 to 173,450 in 2016 and 29,718 a year later.[31] By 2019, 36 per cent of individuals who arrived in Europe came via the Eastern Mediterranean route (Cyprus, Bulgaria, Greece).[32] Accordingly, as of January 2019, out the 2,658 arrivals via the Eastern Mediterranean route, 78 per cent arrived in Greece by sea and the remaining 22 per cent were registered as land arrivals. Half of the registered population that arrived in the country by sea was of Afghan origin, followed by 17 per cent Palestinian nationals, nine per cent Syrian and eight per cent Iraqi nationals, resembling the order found among the total population registered in 2018.

Although the number of migrants taking the Balkan routes have decreased substantially, the routes have also shifted towards more dangerous irregular channels that rely on smuggling networks. The southern entry point changed at least partially from the Greek islands to Bulgaria's land border with Turkey.[33] Afterwards, migrants moved towards Greece, Albania, Montenegro and then Bosnia and Herzegovina, where thousands of migrants are now gathered trying to get to Croatia and then Italy.[34] Some of the migrants taking the more risky southern routes are pushed backwards, others are trapped in limbo in reception camps, and yet others are

---

30 *Greider* (fn. 28).

31 UNCHR data.

32 International Organization for Migration, Mixed Migration Flows in the Mediterranean, 2019, available at https://migration.iom.int/reports/europe—-mixed-migration-flows-europe-monthly-overview-january-2019?close=true.

33 *Weber* (fn. 22).

34 *Annibale*, The New Balkan Route, Jacobin (2018), available at: https://www.jacobinmag.com/2018/07/eu-migrants-refugees-balkan-route-frontex-dublin-schengen.

pushed to next-door countries, making the region a feeble, chaotic and unpredictable external guardian of the Schengen Area.

Given the lack of an overarching EU policy to manage the Southern Mediterranean border and illegal crossings, the EU has by and large preferred externalising the challenges of managing migration while offering various incentives to neighbouring countries, including aid to security sectors but also assistance to cover the social and material burden that comes with migration. Specifically, from the very start, the EU has provided a total EUR 31 million only in humanitarian assistance since the start of refugee crisis in 2015.[35] Accordingly, urgent humanitarian assistance includes: food, water, emergency shelter, sanitation, health care and warm clothing. Additional mid-term assistance seeks to assist in migration management capacities, adequate accommodation and basic services as well as education. In addition, the EU has allocated substantial aid to finance and assist security-related areas such as border control and smuggling activities. Part of the aid has gone directly to migration management centers including funding of migration camps and government capacities. Bosnia has been an important beneficiary. In 2018 alone, the EU promised EUR 1.5 million ($1.77 million) in humanitarian aid to address the increasing needs of refugees and migrants stranded in Bosnia. The year 2018 also saw the opening of the first and only reception center in Montenegro, thanks to a European Union grant of EUR 3 million.

Besides financial aid and technical support, the EU has offered renewed attention to the EU enlargement promise, which culminated in the 2018 strategy: a credible enlargement perspective for and enhanced EU engagement with the Western Balkans.[36] The renewal of the EU promise was directly connected to the security-related aspect of enlargement. Accordingly, "this firm, merit-based prospect of EU membership for the Western Balkans is in the Union's very own political, security and economic interest. It is a geostrategic investment in a stable, strong and united Europe based on common values." Back in 2017, the President of the European Commission, Jean Claude Juncker, had made it clear that integration of

35 European Commission, EU provides humanitarian aid for refugees and migrants in Bosnia and Herzegovina, available at: https://ec.europa.eu/neighbourhood-enlargement/news_corner/news/eu-provides-humanitarian-aid-refugees-and-migrants-bosnia-and-herzegovina_en.

36 European Commission, A credible enlargement perspective for and enhanced EU engagement with the Western Balkans, available at: https://ec.europa.eu/commission/sites/beta-political/files/communication-credible-enlargement-perspective-western-balkans_en.pdf.

the region is necessary to advance stability across the borders: "If we want more stability in our neighbourhood, then we must also maintain a credible enlargement perspective for the Western Balkans."[37]

Ultimately, the 2018 strategy foresees enhanced EU strategic and operational cooperation with the Western Balkans on migration and border management including "sharing of relevant information (such as risk analyses), enhancing border control, ensuring the effective implementation of readmission and return policies and the fight against irregular migration and migrant smuggling. Strengthening international and regional cooperation (including with EU agencies and the respective liaison officers in the region), and further consolidating border and migration management capacities is also necessary." The shared commitments include operational cooperation such as "the possibility of deploying and implementing joint operational activities of the competent national authorities of the EU Member States and of the Western Balkans countries together with the European Border and Coast Guard Agency." Thanks to a reinforced mandate agreement for the European Border and Coast Guard Agency (EBCGA), signed in October 2016, and following draft agreements with countries of the region, the Agency was able to provide assistance and carry out operational activities there.

Positive incentives are coupled with negative incentives that would entice countries to better manage illegal routes of migration. Among those, the EU has made sure to reinforce readmission agreement with the relevant countries. In July 2018, the European Court of Justice further ruled that the Dublin Regulation could be applied to arrivals during the migration crisis, meaning those who made it to any EU Member State other than Germany can be sent back to their point of entry into the European Union, in most cases Croatia, which could further challenge limited processing capacity in the region. The EU has also considered longer-term policy initiatives that delegate responsibility to the Balkan countries. In 2018, for example, Franz Lang, the head of Austria's Federal Criminal Police Office, suggested that EU countries had discussed setting up "portal centres" in countries outside the EU, where requests for asylum would be processed although the proposal was never operationalised into specific policies.

---

37 *Junker*, Opening Remarks by Commissioner Johannes Hahn on the presentation of the Western Balkans Strategy at the plenary session of the European Parliament, available at: https://ec.europa.eu/commission/commissioners/2014-2019/hahn/announcements/opening-remarks-commissioner-johannes-hahn-presentation-western-balkans-strategy-plenary-session_en.

Whether there will be portals or not, when considering the hybrid and weak state of democracy, economy and rule of law in the "third" Balkan countries where migrants are to be returned, the region risks becoming a dysfunctional and uncertain external guardian of the Schengen Area. More often than not, the policy of returning migrants to the point of entry leaves them trapped in the Balkans where they transit from, which in the present is mainly BiH. Generally, migrants caught in Italy and Slovenia are randomly subject to chain pushbacks, summarily handed over to Croatian police and forcibly expelled back to camps in Bosnia and Herzegovina, usually without having their asylum claims considered. By January 2019, BiH recorded 4,503 migrants and refugees residing in the country, five per cent more than the 4,291 reported at the end of December 2018.[38] An estimated 76 per cent of individuals were adult males, seven per cent adult females and 17 per cent were children, among which, one third were registered as unaccompanied and separated. Most of them were pushed back to the country from other European destinations. As a recent report observes, "nearly all in the camps in Bihać and Velika Kladuša had been pushed back into BiH from Croatia or Slovenia and nearly one third of those interviewed had experienced violence at the hands of the Croatian police."[39] Ultimately, BiH now finds itself struggling to accommodate thousands of people who are trying to reach wealthier EU countries. Others in the region too find themselves hosting an increasing number of refugees. In a May 2018 meeting with Austrian chancellor Sebastian Kurz, the Albanian prime minister contended that the number of "illegal" migrants in Albania rose from just 162 in January 2017 to 2,311 in 2018. Only a small number of asylum claims were approved in each country.

IV. Conclusions: migration as a facilitator and challenge of EU integration

Since the early 2000s, the EU has extended its enlargement policy to the Western Balkans left out from the previous Eastern enlargement. The framework of enlargement came with new instruments – particularly visa liberalisation – as a means to manage the Balkan migration while rewarding citizens and governments in the region with some of the concrete

38 International Organization for Migration (fn. 32).

39 Amnesty International, Croatia: EU complicit in violence and abuse by police against refugees and migrants, available at: https://www.amnesty.org/en/latest/news/2019/03/croatia-eu-complicit-in-violence-and-abuse-by-police-against-refugees-and-migrants/.

benefits of integration. The visa liberalisation process, however, has not been smooth and did not reduce the number of asylum seekers, which spiked in the period 2014–2015. In the face of an ongoing even though declining asylum problem, the EU commission has created a new mechanism of reporting annually about possible abuses of visa-free travel, a mechanism at work since 2017. Select EU member countries have also adopted *ad hoc* measures like blocking visa liberalisation with Kosovo in 2018; and suggesting a suspension of visa-free travel for Albania in 2019. Germany, instead has adopted the so-called Western Balkan Regulation, which since 2015 creates legal pathways for Balkan citizens to access the German labour market. Accordingly, those who would otherwise arrive and enter the asylum system or stay in the country without any legal status will be incentivised to receive a work permit before arriving.

Besides the remaining challenges of migration from the Balkans, this region has become one of the most beaten paths for migrants from the Middle East to reach targeted European destinations. The initial Balkan route which usually begins in Turkey, then continues via Bulgaria or Greece, then further north via North Macedonia and Serbia to Slovenia or Hungary, brought hundreds of thousands of migrants to their desired European destinations in 2015. Balkan governments facilitated the passage as long as Europeans, mainly Germany, kept the door open. Once the EU reached a deal with Turkey in March 2016, a domino effect set of restrictive policies followed that are being strengthened over the years. Apprehensive and fearful of a continued tide of migrant influx, the EU counts on Turkey to sustain the deal on the basis of which Turkey hampers illegal exit of migrants from its territory. On its own side, EU countries tightened border controls to prevent illegal entries. However, migration did not stop. Although overall numbers are much lower in 2019 than they were in 2015, migrants continue to use the Balkan routes. Only now, they take more dangerous and irregular channels. Criminals who profit from smuggling people, despite concerted efforts from law enforcement groups across countries to stop them, are attracted by high profits and thus willing to take risks.

Balkan governments in response to EU incentives tend to cooperate in ensuring border controls. However, they face difficulties in effectively managing migration, which, even if relatively low, poses a burden on their fragile domestic context. Public sentiment across the region has also changed in the course of the last few years. Ranging between relative indifference and empathy towards the plight of migrants, the sentiment has significantly shifted towards anger. Specifically, Balkan citizens tend to view suspiciously the activity of their neighbours who do not prevent migrants from crossing over as much as the EU for closing itself off and migrants for continuing to come even when many end up stuck in those countries. Bosnia and Herzegovina is especially hit hard due to Serbia and Montenegro not preventing efficiently the exit of migrants and sometimes pushing them forwards to BiH only to have Croatia push them back again. Sandwiched between neighbours who each care for their narrow interests further weakens BiH, which already struggles with internal functionality and institutional stability. In this sense, illegal migration pressure has a potential to seriously undermine the stability of BiH and to damage the relations with the neighbouring countries. An engaged and comprehensive framework for cooperation on migration from and through the Balkans is necessary to prevent such risks.

Morocco and Spain Bilateral Legal Relationship on Migration and Asylum Issues

Francisco Javier Donaire Villa[*]

I. The multiple (historical, geopolitical and legal) factors conditioning the current Spanish–Moroccan bilateral legal relationship on immigration and asylum

The Spanish–bilateral legal relationship on immigration and asylum issues with Morocco is currently framed within the homonymous policies of the European Union (EU). Legally, not only because of Spain's EU membership, but also because the latter has shared powers with its member States (save Ireland and, before Brexit, the United Kingdom) on immigration and asylum of third-country nationals. And factually, because Spain is the only EU member bordering Morocco by land, so, likewise, the only EU external land border with Africa lies, precisely, on that between Spain and Morocco, located around the Spanish cities of Ceuta and Melilla.

As far as Morocco is concerned, its status of a non-EU third country is the main legal factor determining its migration and asylum relationship with Spain, whereas the relevant migratory flows arriving in Spain from the territory and border waters of Morocco condition those relations, either as a country of origin, since one of the main migrant groups settled in Spain is precisely that of Moroccans (as will also be illustrated with figures below), or as a transit or a "bridge" State to the European Union through the access to Spanish external borders for significant flows of migrants structurally departing from Sub-Saharan Africa, and, at specific times, from other places in civil war or in serious unrest, like Syria or Libya during the so-called "immigrant crisis".[1]

---

* Tenured Associate Professor of Constitutional Law, Department of Public Law Faculty of Social and Legal Sciences, University Carlos III of Madrid, PhD in Law (University of Extremadura, 2000).

1 For further details on this subject, among many others, see *Arango/Mahía/Moya/Sánchez-Montijano*, Introducción: el año de los refugiados, Anuario CIDOB de la Inmigración 2015–2016, Barcelona 2016, 12.

The legal subordination of the Spanish immigration policy to that of the European Union, in particular with respect to Morocco, is perfectly compatible with the role of Spain as an outstanding actor in the global design of the said European policy in its projection towards the Maghreb and the Mediterranean. Such a role for Spain in the definition of EU policies towards both areas is due to the fact that those geopolitical scenarios have traditionally been the focus of special attention in the Spanish external action, for deep historical roots and motivations, since long before its membership of the European Communities (nowadays, the European Union) from the mid-eighties of last century onwards.

There has been a prolonged historical Spanish–Moroccan bond, first *de facto*, but further legally formalised since the eighteenth century (Treaties of Marrakech, 1767, of Aranjuez, 1780, and others that followed), which did not prevent, however, past wartime events on Moroccan soil, either to protect the Spanish cities of Ceuta and Mellilla ("Margallo War", in 1893–1894, the First Rif War of July–December 1909) or even to defend Morocco's territorial integrity (during the exercise of the Spanish Protectorate over Morocco, the Second Rif War, between 1921 and 1927, against the proclamation of the independent Republic of the Rif in the northern Moroccan zone), or other post-colonial incidents, like the Second Ifni War (October 1957 – April 1958) in enclaves still under Spanish administration (Ifni, Cape Juby and North-Western Sahara) after the end of the Protectorate in 1956, as well as the Spanish withdrawal from Western Sahara, following the Green March organised by Morocco, by the signing of the Madrid Tripartite Agreement of 14 November 1975 between Spain, Morocco and Mauritania. A significant turnaround in the bilateral relationship would take place with the democratic Spanish governments after the end of Franco's dictatorship, resulting in a first major fisheries agreement with Morocco in April 1981, and the move to a global policy of collaboration based on the principle of Spanish non-interference in Moroccan internal affairs, as well as on a new so-called "cushion of shared interests" doctrine, seeking to dampen bilateral tensions by promoting economic development and political and social stability in Morocco.[2]

2 On this new doctrine, as well as its intellectual authorship, as key elements of the Spanish external policy *vis-à-vis* the Maghreb area in general, and *vis-à-vis* Morocco, in particular, see *Artetxe Larrabide*, La Unión Europea y España en su relación con el Magreb: los casos de Marruecos y Argelia, Doctoral Thesis, País Vasco University, December 2015, 1, 92 and 95, as well as fn. 26, available at: https://addi.ehu.es/bitstream/10810/18490/1/TESIS_ARTETXE_LARRABIDE_AINTZANE.pdf.

On 1 January 1986, Spain joined the European Communities (currently, the European Union), with the consequent "communitarisation" of the Spanish foreign policy on Mediterranean affairs on areas transferred to the European supranational institutions (fisheries, trade policy and other fields), so that a significant part of the most complex issues in the bilateral relationship with Morocco passed to a multilateral framework. This was not yet the case with immigration, although, for it did not come under Community competence until the Treaty of Amsterdam (in force since 1 May 1999), within the framework of the new European policies relating to the so-called Area of Freedom, Security and Justice (AFSJ), a new global Union objective which supposed the abolition of intra-Community border controls and the adoption of compensatory measures including the harmonisation of national external border checks (with the Spanish–Moroccan frontier since then becoming one of the EU's external borders) and a European policy on immigration and asylum of third-country nationals, all of which are referred to in detail below in terms of their impact on the Spanish–Moroccan migratory relationship. Suffice it now to point out that the aforementioned new objective of the Union (the AFSJ), as well as the corresponding new Community powers for its achievement (although not exclusive, but shared with its Member States), as introduced in EU law by the Treaty of Amsterdam, have, since then and up to now, legally conditioned bilateral Spanish–Moroccan relations on migration and asylum.

Subsequent Spanish governments, according to the so-called "cushion of interests" doctrine, intensified ties of economic interdependence with Morocco through instruments of financial cooperation, while institutionalising a regular bilateral political dialogue with that country, the first and significant manifestation of which was the signing in 1991 of the Treaty of Friendship and Good Neighbourliness between Morocco and Spain.[3] As regards the multilateral external action with an impact on the bilateral relationship with Morocco, the Spanish Presidency of the EU during the first semester of 2002 promoted the implementation of Home and Justice Affairs issues within the Euro-Mediterranean Partnership, including in particular the fight against illegal immigration.[4]

A period of deterioration in the bilateral relationship was caused by the failure of the negotiations of the Fisheries Agreement between Morocco and the EU in April 2001, which particularly harmed Spain due to its important fishing sector. With a previous escalation of mutual accusations in

---

3 *Artetxe Larrabide* (fn. 2), 95.
4 *Artetxe Larrabide* (fn. 2), 95.

relation to Ceuta and Melilla, Western Sahara and illegal immigration, this period reached a climax with the Spanish military eviction in July 2002 of Moroccan police officers who had occupied Perejil Island shortly before. However, the initiatives launched by the European Commission (European Neighbourhood Policy, ENP) and France (Union for the Mediterranean) meant that Morocco, which demanded differential treatment from the EU, would see in this ENP an opportunity to improve relations with the EU and, indirectly, with Spain.[5] The by then newly elected Spanish government, for its part, threw itself on a novel draft of the advanced EU–Morocco Statute, whereby, within the asymmetric framework of the ENP, this North African country could achieve greater access to the EU market.

However, Spanish–Moroccan relations during this new phase were not exempt from incidences, such as the crisis brought about by the successive massive influxes of immigrants from Morocco climbing the Melilla fence in August 2010 and onwards. Nevertheless, from the end of 2011, the renewed Spanish government intensified bilateral relations with that of Morocco, holding a new Hispano–Moroccan summit after a four-year period of absence, as well as a visit by the King of Spain to Morocco.[6] All this opened a new stage of collaboration between the security forces of both countries in order to put an end to the arrival of irregular immigrants in territories under Spanish control near the Moroccan coasts and land. Such collaboration has recently been maintained and even increased during the Spanish government that emerged from the motion of censure in 2018, following a new royal Spanish visit to the King of Morocco, and since then Moroccan cooperation in the area of illegal immigration control has increased, with the number of irregular entries reduced by almost half (some 64,000 by the end of summer 2019, as will also be seen later).

II. The Spanish–Moroccan immigration situation. In particular, the factual and legal problem of "pushbacks" ("devoluciones en caliente") at the common borders with Morocco surrounding the Spanish cities of Ceuta and Melilla

As of 30 June 2019, there were 795,619 Moroccan persons with a registration certificate or residence card in Spain, so they are, after Romanian persons, the second largest immigrant group (specifically, 14.37%) of the total

5 *Artetxe Larrabide* (fn. 2), 102.
6 *Artetxe Larrabide* (fn. 2), 104.

of 5,535,079 foreign persons in such a situation in Spain.[7] It is also the oldest immigration that Spain has ever received, for labour reasons. It began in the mid-1980s towards the Spanish Mediterranean areas of intensive agriculture and irrigation. Nevertheless, Moroccan migrant workers found themselves, firstly, with a legal vacuum on immigration in Spain, and since 1985 (date of approval of the first Spanish Immigration Law), with a restrictive legal regime, but at the same time with an easy factual entry into the Spanish territory, together with visa exemption until 1991, when Spain acceded to the Schengen Area, thereby committing itself to the imposition of visa requirement.

Irregularity of Moroccan workers was the norm during the 1980s and the 1990s because of the lack of surveillance of borders and the virtual absence of inspections of irregular work in Spain. By contrast, the abandonment of the countryside by Spaniards gave place to a high demand for Moroccan migrant workers, either as farmers in the Spanish crop fields, or in the construction sector during the years of the real estate boom (or "real estate bubble", as it was later revealed to be by the economic crisis beginning in 2007). Irregularity, as well as the parallel demand of Moroccan workers in Spain, would motivate their major regularisations in 2000–2001.[8] On the other hand, and from the perspective of the destination of migratory flows, Spain has gone from being the main Mediterranean route for illegal immigration to presenting its collaboration with Morocco as a model to be followed in the EU.

In fact, in October 2019, irregular immigration figures were reduced by half, with 24,159 entries, representing a 50% drop in arrivals by land and sea for the first time since 2010, a reduction that can be explained to a large extent precisely by Morocco's collaboration, which avoided thousands of departures by sea and rescued from maritime waters more than 10,000 immigrant persons. However – despite representing a significant decrease of 42% compared to 2018 – 317 people still died or disappeared trying to

7 According to the figures provided by the Spanish Ministry of Labour, Migrations and Social Security, available at: http://extranjeros.mitramiss.gob.es/es/estadisticas/operaciones/con-certificado/201906/Residentes_Principales_Resultados_30062019.pdf.

8 *Amirah Fernández*, Relaciones Marruecos-España, Informe Elcano, Madrid 2015, 57, available at: http://www.realinstitutoelcano.org/wps/portal/rielcano_es/publicacion?WCM_GLOBAL_CONTEXT=/elcano/elcano_es/publicaciones/informe-elcano-19-relaciones-espana-marruecos).

reach Spain in the Strait of Gibraltar and the Alboran Sea.[9] In 2018, the irregular entries of more than 60,000 people, even more than those occurring during the "Cayuco crisis" in 2006, made immigration a political priority in Spain. Accusations were made by the political opposition to the President of the Spanish Government in the sense of generating a "pull effect" ("*efecto llamada*") as a consequence of governmental decisions such as the authorisation of port docking in Spain to the immigrants' sea rescue ship Aquarius in June 2017. By then, the Spanish Government shifted its policy towards irregular immigration, with the adoption of measures such as the "express" expulsion of Sub-Saharans who jumped the fences of Ceuta and Melilla, a further ban on the sailing of NGO vessels to rescue shipwrecked immigrants, and others.[10]

A recent study by the International Organisation for Migration (IOM) reveals that little more than half of newcomers intend to stay in Spain, with France being the second country of preference.[11] Morocco, backed by the European Union, has deployed its security forces to contain the migratory pressure towards Europe.[12] In addition, it has reactivated agreements with Spain that languished in the past, such as the one that allows Sub-Saharans who jump the fences of Ceuta and Melilla to be quickly returned. In addition, Moroccan security forces have intensified raids, forced relocations to the south of the country, and deportations.[13]

Over the last few years, Morocco has also involved itself in maritime actions, which it formerly ignored: the operations that Spain previously assumed through its Maritime Rescue Service in the Moroccan responsibility rescue zone – the so-called SAR (Search and Rescue) Area – are currently being carried out by the Royal Navy of Morocco by returning the shipwrecked persons to their embarkation point in Moroccan territory, which has meant assuming nearly a third of the almost 50,000 people who were in this situation in 2018, as well as the rescue of 8,000 castaways by Moroc-

9 *Martín*, El Gobierno alcanza la meta de reducir a la mitad la inmigración irregular, El País (16 October 2019), available at: https://elpais.com/politica/2019/10/15/actualidad/1571160471_893228.html.

10 *Martín* (fn. 9).

11 *Martín*, La entrada irregular de inmigrantes a España cae un 39% en lo que va de año, El País (16 August 2019), available at: https://elpais.com/politica/2019/08/15/actualidad/1565889744_365065.html.

12 *Martín* (fn 11).

13 *Martín* (fn 11).

co's Navy and Gendarmerie.[14] Nevertheless, clandestine migration networks have varied access points, now further away and at greater risk. (Until July 2019, there were 206 dead or disappeared persons, according to the IOM, which represents 1.4% of the total number of people trying to reach Spain by this means, in contrast to 1.1% during the same period of the previous year.[15]) Furthermore, the networks are now charging immigrants to enter waters under Spanish responsibility, which entails spending more time at sea[16].

The Government of Spain, in return, has been exerting political influence in recent years within the EU on behalf of Morocco as a strategic partner. Spain, which inaugurated cooperation models with African countries in Europe,[17] promoted the transfer, from the Union to Morocco, of EUR 140 million as compensation for its work in controlling illegal immigration at the border, to which a further transfer of EUR 30 million has been added from the Spanish Budget itself, and Spain continues to advocate the annualisation of a consignment of European funds to Morocco, in line with the agreements with Turkey and Libya to "block" clandestine immigration routes to the EU at other points in the Mediterranean.[18] This is yet another concrete example within a broader trend that has been described as the "externalisation"[19] or outsourcing[20] of the Union's migration

---

14 *Martín*, España deja en manos de Marruecos el rescate de pateras en sus aguas, El País (27 July 2019), available at: https://elpais.com/politica/2019/07/26/actualidad/1564157921_749346.html.

15 *Martín* (fn 14).

16 *Martín* (fn 11).

17 In detail on this issue, see *Asín Cabrera*, Las Asociaciones para la Movilidad con Cabo Verde, Marruecos y Túnez: un instrumento marco de diálogo, cooperación y coordinación entre la UE y terceros países, in: Donaire/Olesti (eds.), Técnicas y ámbitos de coordinación en el espacio de libertad, seguridad y justicia, Madrid 2015, 163.

18 In general, see *Asín Cabrera* (fn 17).

19 In this sense, among many others, *Boswell*, The 'External Dimension' of EU Immigration and Asylum Policy, International Affairs 79 (2003), 619; *Garcés*, Más externalización del control migratorio, CIDOB Opinión 450 (2016), available at https://www.cidob.org/es/publicaciones/serie_de_publicacion/opinion/migraciones/mas_externalizacion_del_control_migratorio; or *Menjívar*, Immigration Law Beyond Borders: Externalizing and Internalizing Border Controls in an Era of Securitization, Annual Review of Law and Social Science 10 (2014), 353.

20 *Donaire Villa*, Quo vadis? The European Union's Migration and Asylum Policy: Legal basis, Legal Challenges, and Legal Possibilities, in: Croucher/Caetano/Campbell (eds.), The Routledge Companion to Migration, Communication and Politics, New York 2018, especially 34, 41 ff.

policies, which intends to transfer the "barrier" to immigration to the countries of origin, or to those third States of last transit of flows of people moving towards the Union. The Agricultural Association and the Fisheries Agreements, respectively signed by the Union with Morocco, include the European injection of funds for the containment of migratory flows.[21]

Of the around half a million third-country nationals rejected at European Union level, almost 50 per cent of them are at Spanish borders, and of these, 97% are Moroccans trying to access European Union territory through Ceuta and Melilla, according to Eurostat figures.[22] In fact, Spain currently leads in border rejections at Union level and ranks third among its Member States in terms of the number of regular arrivals, with a share of 13% of the total.[23] The top number of refusals to enter Spain had occurred in 2008, with more than half a million, representing no less than 80% of the European Union's total, and although these figures decreased in the immediate years following the economic crisis, they picked up again in 2016, coinciding with the so-called "refugee crisis", in which the EU became the destination of hundreds of thousands of people from countries with serious security risks such as Syria and Iraq.[24]

Ceuta and Melilla are, as has already been said, the only land access points between Africa and the European Union. In normal times,[25] more than 32,000 people enter daily through its border posts, plus an unofficial

---

21 See in this sense, *Martín*, Marruecos contiene la inmigración irregular hacia España, El País (30 April 2019), available at: https://elpais.com/politica/2019/04/30/actualidad/1556651285_600474.html. On these Agreements, see *Donaire Villa* (fn. 20), 42–43, or *Góis/Faraone*, Reconstructing the Migration Communication Discourse. The Call for Contextual and Narrative Based Evidence in the Construction of Fear, in: Croucher/Caetano/Campbell (eds.), The Routledge Companion to Migration, Communication and Politics, 139, 144.

22 *Martín*, Ceuta y Melilla acaparan casi la mitad de los rechazos en frontera de la UE, El País (23 July 2019), citing Eurostat figures, https://elpais.com/politica/2019/07/17/actualidad/1563377797_776243.html.

23 *Martín* (fn. 22).

24 *Martín* (fn. 22).

25 At the very time of finishing this Chapter, CoVID 19 has determined the Moroccan decision to temporarily close frontiers with Spain. The closing has been officially announced as far as maritime and air communications are concerned, stressing that the measure was previously agreed with the Spanish authorities (See Maroc.ma, 12 March 2020, Marruecos decide, en concertación con las autoridades españolas suspender, hasta nuevo aviso, los vuelos aéreos y el tráfico marítimo de pasajeros desde y hacia España, available at: http://maroc.ma/es/news/marruecos-decide-en-concertacion-con-las-autoridades-espanolas-suspender-hasta-nuevo-aviso-los). As regards land borders with Spain at Ceuta and Melilla, that Moroccan deci-

daily number of vehicles ranging between fifteen thousand and twenty thousand, figures comparable to those of the busiest border in the world, the one at San Ysidro between the United States and Mexico.[26] Transit is high in both cases, due to travellers from the European Union to Morocco and other Maghreb countries, or also owing to frontier workers residing on either side of the border itself.[27] However, the border infrastructures of both cities, which date back to 1988, are obsolete and deteriorated, and the Spanish Government has endorsed a EUR 32 million plan to modernise them, with facial recognition systems among other technical measures to increase the security and speed of border verification procedures.[28]

This problem arises because of the fencing of Ceuta and Melilla after the Spanish accession to the European Communities (currently, the European Union) in 1986. From that moment on, both Spanish cities became the only way of land access from Africa to the EU, determining that these Spanish–Moroccan borders, which were permeable for years and always had intense local traffic, began to be fenced by the Spanish Government from 1993 onwards, in response to the growing number of unauthorised border crossings to the EU.[29] After the massive assaults on the fences in September 2005, secondary fences were installed and their height was increased from three to six metres, with tear-gas sprinklers and 3D detection cables in the intermediate space, surveillance cameras, thermal sensors, sound and movement sensors, as well as razor wire (the so-called "concertinas", removed in 2007, but relocated in 2013, and once again done away with in 2020). On the other side of the border, with EU funding, the Moroccan army has established numerous surveillance positions and military camps to monitor the southern approach to the border with Spain, which Morocco does not recognise as legitimate but a residue of colonial impositions.[30]

---

sion was not officially declared, supposedly due to the position of Morocco concerning sovereignty over those two cities, but, nevertheless, the Moroccan decision on the closing of land borders with both Spanish cities was likewise communicated to Spain's Police officers: El Confidencial (13 March 2020), Marruecos cierra fronteras terrestres con Ceuta y Melilla y se aísla de España, available at: https://www.elconfidencial.com/mundo/2020-03-13/marruecos-cierra-fronteras-con-ceuta-melilla-aisla-espana_2495836/.

26 *Martín* (fn. 22).

27 *Martín* (fn. 22).

28 *Martín* (fn. 22).

29 *Ribas*, Las vallas fronterizas de Ceuta y Melilla. ¿Un paisaje para el futuro?, available at: http://www.xavierribas.com/Contents/Texts/Texts/XRIBAS-Ceuta%20y%20Melilla_Cast.pdf.

30 *Ribas* (fn. 29).

Those who manage to jump the fences have the right, according to Spanish legislation, to be provisionally accommodated in a Centre for Temporary Stay of Immigrants (CETI, in Spanish), and to move freely through Ceuta or Melilla while the administrative procedure for their expulsion is being processed. Some of them are transferred to the Iberian Peninsula to be admitted to Foreigners Internment Centres (CIE, in Spanish) for a maximum of 60 days, after which they are deported to countries of origin if the procedure is completed, or otherwise they are released.[31] The fencing of Ceuta and Melilla is a dissuasive measure that, despite its not having managed to reduce migratory pressure, indeed has, at least, significantly reduced illegal entries, which has not prevented immigrants, however, from finding other ways to enter these cities.[32] After the second "jump" of the fence in Ceuta on 22 August 2018, Spain returned 116 migrants to Morocco in 48 hours.[33]

The Port of Melilla, on the other hand, is a common point of entry for Maghreb immigrants, mainly Moroccans and unaccompanied minors, who try to access the port security zone and reach vessels which connect Melilla with peninsular Spain to enter the territory of the EU irregularly.[34] In this way, 19,200 intrusions occurred in 2017, which motivated the rein-

---

31 On the Foreign Internment Centres (CIE) and the deprivations of liberty of foreigners in an irregular status with a view to their expulsion (in their various manifestations: expulsions, returns) in Spanish immigration legislation, see *Donaire Villa*, Detención e internamiento de extranjeros a efectos de expulsión. Régimen de los Centros de Internamiento de Extranjeros, in: Boza/Donaire/Moya (eds.), La nueva regulación de la inmigración y la extranjería en España. Régimen jurídico tras la LO 2/2009, el Real Decreto 557/2011 y la Ley 12/2009, Valencia 2012, 508. In relation to expulsions or returns of immigrants in an irregular status determining their arrests and internments, see *Moya Malapeira/Hernández Calero*, Los controles en frontera: denegación de entrada, orden de regreso y devolución, in: Boza/Donaire/Moya (eds.), La nueva regulación de la inmigración y la extranjería en España. Régimen jurídico tras la LO 2/2009, el Real Decreto 557/2011 y la Ley 12/2009, Valencia 2012, 192, 216–218.

32 See *Saceda Montesinos*, Evolución de las migraciones entre Marruecos y España (1999–2014): La gestión migratoria en Ceuta ante la encrucijada de intereses UE-Marruecos, Doctoral Thesis, Complutense University, Madrid 2016, available at: https://eprints.ucm.es/38046/1/T37328.pdf.

33 European Council on Foreign Relations, Madrid Office, Marruecos, la Unión Europea y el dilema migratorio", 2018, available at: https://www.ecfr.eu/madrid/post/marruecos_la_union_europea_y_el_dilema_migratorio.

34 El País (1 January 2019), Herido un menor en un intento de avalancha de inmigrantes en el puerto de Melilla, available at: https://elpais.com/politica/2019/01/01/actualidad/1546357975_881838.html.

forcement of the Melilla Port security zone with the installation of higher fences, cameras, a permanent surveillance post and "concertina" wire.[35]

The fact that Spain and Morocco are territorially contiguous has determined the legally problematic practice of the so-called "*devoluciones en caliente*" (pushbacks). These are situations in which persons who intend to make the irregular crossing of the border by land (the so-called "jump" of the Fence from the Moroccan territory surrounding one or another Spanish city) or by sea (swimming from Moroccan coasts to the nearby Spanish beaches of El Tarajal, in Ceuta, of the Cárabos, in Ceuta, or to the Spanish Isla de Tierra at low tide) are returned to Morocco's territory and handed over to Moroccan border officials by the Spanish police authorities without any previous processing of their expulsion procedures or without offering the immigrants the possibility of requesting international protection.[36] On one well-known occasion, on the Ceuta beach of El Tarajal in February 2004, anti-riot material was even used against the immigrants while they were still swimming in the sea,[37] which led to the opening of criminal judicial investigations against the agents, although they have since been archived.[38]

Spain has attempted to legalise this practice through the amendment of the Organic Law on Immigration carried out by Organic Law 4/2015, which introduced a new Additional Provision 10 in the former, according to which foreigners who are detected on the border line of the territorial demarcation of Ceuta or Melilla while attempting to overcome border containment elements to irregularly cross the border may be rejected in order to prevent their illegal entry into Spain, a rejection that will be carried out in compliance with international human rights and international pro-

35 El País (fn. 34).

36 See Asociación Andaluza Pro Derechos Humanos, Derechos Humanos en la Frontera Sur 2014, 46–47, quoting governmental sources.

37 La Vanguardia (20 March 2014), Interior admite que la Guardia Civil lanzó 145 pelotas de goma al mar en la tragedia de Ceuta, available at: https://www.lavanguardia.com/politica/20140319/54403831490/guardia-civil-145-pelotas-goma-tragedia-ceuta.html, or 20 Minutos (13 February 2014), La Guardia Civil disparó al agua para "disuadir" y la playa de Ceuta técnicamente no es España, available at: https://www.20minutos.es/noticia/2057090/0/ceuta-inmigrantes/muertos-sinpapeles/guardia-civil/.

38 See for example, Eldiario.es (26 January 2018), Archivada la causa de las muertes de 14 migrantes en Ceuta entre pelotas de goma de la Guardia Civil, available at: https://www.eldiario.es/desalambre/archiva-quince-inmigrantes-muertos-Tarajal_0_733527236.html.

tection standards to which Spain is a party.[39] As was said before, this legislative amendment aims to provide national legal coverage to pushbacks as a legislative overturning of the rejection of this practice at the highest Spanish judicial level (Supreme Court),[40] in order to give legislative coverage to the so-called "operational concept of border" that previously, and with the same purpose of justifying those border pushbacks, had been handled by the Spanish Ministry of Interior by means of administrative circulars addressed to the Police and Security Forces under its dependence.[41]

According to that so-called "operational concept of border", which took shape in 2014, by the Ministry of Home Affairs, addressed to its dependent police bodies which carry out border controls, it is only the internal fence and not the external one surrounding Ceuta and Melilla, which marks the line with which Spain as sovereign State delimits its national territory for the sole purposes of the legal status of aliens, such that immigrants not having crossed that internal line would not have entered Spanish territory and consequently would not be entitled to the guarantees enshrined in the Spanish legislation on immigration. This construction or understanding would allow border authorities to reject these immigrants in the previous lines of surveillance. To cut a long story short, according to this Ministry of Home Affairs interpretation, only once the interior fence has been overcome would Spanish territory be accessed, so that the immigrants rejected at the previous lines of surveillance would not be subject to pushback, because such a return would only be the consequence of an entry onto Spain's soil, and this would not occur, even illegally, in such circumstances, as far as the Spanish law on aliens is concerned.[42]

39 On this legal amendment, see *Bertomeu Navarro,* La inclusión del rechazo en frontera en la legislación española de extranjería. Análisis de la legalidad de las «devoluciones en caliente» acontecidas en la frontera sur española, in: Ugartemendía/ Labayle (eds.), La tutela judicial de los Derechos Fundamentales en el Espacio de Libertad, Seguridad y Justicia de la Unión Europea, Oñati 2016, 388.

40 Supreme Court of Spain (Tribunal Supremo), 1924/2003, ECLI: ES:TS:2003:1924, judgment, 20 March 2003; Supreme Court of Spain (Tribunal Supremo), 488/2007, ECLI: ES:TS:2007:488,judgment, 8 January 2007.

41 As it is pointed out by *Bertomeu Navarro* (fn. 39), 350 and footnotes 36, 37 f., or by *Acosta Sánchez*, Las fronteras terrestres de España en Melilla, Revista Electrónica de Estudios Internacionales. 28 (2014), 28. Both scholars refer, as sources of this administrative coinage of the operational concept of border, to the Order of Service 6/2014 of the Chief Colonel of the Command of the Civil Guard of Melilla entitled "Anti-intrusion device on the perimeter fence of Melilla and operational protocol of border surveillance", and in subsequent documents of the Ministry of Home Affairs.

42 *Bertomeu Navarro* (fn. 39), 351 and footnotes 39, 40 and 41.

Scholars consider that this operational notion of border goes against general international law, both customary and conventional (1950 Geneva Convention on the Status of Refugees), and also with regard to European conventional law, in particular Article 4 of Additional Protocol No. 4 to the European Convention on Human Rights,[43] a question that will be addressed below in this Chapter. For its part, the Spanish Ombudsman rejected the practice of pushbacks in its 2005 Annual Report,[44] even before the aforementioned governmental coinage of the so-called "operational concept of border".

In the sphere of the Spanish Judiciary, the same line of rejection reflects, for example, an Order of Melilla's Court of First Instance and Preliminary Investigation No. 2, dated September 11, 2014,[45] stating that "through the use of the operative concept of border there could have been a *de facto* abrogation of the international treaties signed between the two countries regarding the delimitation of border boundaries, since the Spanish legislation on aliens was not applied to those persons who on 18.06.14 and 13.08.14 assaulted the Melilla fence".[46] Nevertheless, the administrative and police practice for a long time by the Spanish border agents lies in the factual returning to the Moroccan agents of those who have jumped the fence without administrative procedure,[47] a *de facto* way,[48] to which this Additional Provision 10 of Law 4/2000 introduced by Organic Law 4/2015 intends to grant legal coverage.[49] With the parliamentary endorsement of the new Additional Provision 10 introduced to the Organic Law 4/2000 (the Spanish Aliens Act), the judiciary has maintained its previous criterion on the illegality of pushbacks, but at the same time acknowledging a coverage effect to this new legislative provision, which lies in the avoidance of the crime of prevarication for those police authorities deciding the

43 For example, *Carbó Xalabarder/Sanz Vilar*, Las devoluciones en caliente: ¿Una respuesta deshumanizada, Revista Jurídica de la Universidad Autónoma de Madrid 34 (2006), 379.

44 Defensor del Pueblo, Informe anual 2005, Madrid 2006, 1, 292, available at: https://www.defensordelpueblo.es/wp-content/uploads/2015/05/INFORME2005informe.pdf.

45 Melilla's Court No. 2 of First Instance and Preliminary Investigation, 866/2014,ECLI:ES:JPII:2014:14A, order, 11 September 2014.

46 This Order is available at http://www.poderjudicial.es/search/AN/openDocument/f03f9be202955f4a/20141001.

47 In this sense, see *Bertomeu Navarro* (fn. 39), 347 and footnote 39.

48 See *Bertomeu Navarro* (fn. 39), 354.

49 As it is pointed out by *Bertomeu Navarro* (fn. 39), 353.

rejection of persons at the border in situations of massive influx to the fence.

This is the case, for example, of the Order of the Provincial Court of Malaga, Section 7, of 7 April 2015:[50] "It is true that the text finally approved differs from the bill initially proposed in the Congress of Deputies, by introducing as a condition that the return or rejection at the border shall respect the minimums of humanitarian law, but in any case, it institutes, as has been said, the rejection at the border along with the other alternatives provided for in the Aliens Act, that is, expulsion, return and denial of entry. In conclusion, the contested administrative decisions follow the criterion adopted by the Directorate General of the Civil Guard for the massive influx of immigrants through the border fence of Melilla, which is but a manifestation coinciding with the policy of the Spanish State since the construction of the fence, that is, a way to provide a response to the conflict of the massive assaults of immigrants in favour of the security of the State's external borders, and with that, they address a hitherto unforeseen legal issue, such as the concept of the border within the framework of the border fences of the aforementioned cities, and the solution chosen seems to be in line with the legislative amendment currently being implemented in this area. In view of this, the contested resolutions, despite their objective contradiction with the legal system, at least with that in force at the time they were adopted, cannot be said to lack any reasonable explanation or to be manifestly arbitrary, and this prevents their inclusion within the criminal concept of article 404 of the Criminal Code".[51] The 10th Additional Provision of Organic Law 4/2000, introduced by Organic Law 4/2015, is currently in force, although it has been challenged before the Spanish Constitutional Court.[52]

---

50 Provincial Court of Malaga, Criminal Branch, Section 7, ECLI:ES: APML:2015:1A, order, 7 April 2015.

51 This judicial decision is available at: http://www.poderjudicial.es/search/AN/openDocument/98c55e6b9a68362b/20150527.

52 Constitutional Court (Spain), Spain's Official State Gazette No. 14, 16 June 2015, 50083, order, 9 June 2015, admitting to consideration the Action of Unconstitutionality No. 2896-2015, promoted by more than fifty Deputies of the Socialist, Plural Left, Progress and Democracy Parliamentary, and of the Mixed Parliamentary Groups of the Congress of Deputies against Organic Law 4/2015, on the Protection of Citizen Security. The Action includes the challenging to this 10th Additional Provision added by that same Organic Law to Organic Law 4/2000, on the Rights and Freedoms of Foreigners in Spain and their Social Integration (as it is officially named the Spain's Aliens and Immigration Act).

Notwithstanding this national legislative formalisation of what has come to be known as "border rejection", as a legal coverage of pushbacks, Spain was initially condemned by the European Court of Human Rights, on account of this practice (pushbacks or "*devoluciones en caliente*") carried out at the border with Morocco.[53] Significantly, the Court dispenses with the problem of determining whether or not the pushed-back foreigners were at the border, an issue which is finally circumvented in the European Court's reasoning, by stating as a *ratio decidendi* that, regardless of whether the foreigners are inside or outside that border, the determining factor is that those persons are under the *de facto* control of the Spanish authorities, and therefore these are as bound by the ECHR if they are outside the border as if they are inside it. On that premise, the ECtHR's Judgment reached the conclusion that the prohibition of collective expulsions contained in Article 4 of Additional Protocol No. 4 to the European Convention on Human Rights was violated and granted the equitable reparation requested by the appellants.

This ECtHR's judgment, however, had a partially dissenting particular vote which, although agreeing with the declaration of violation of the ECHR (Article 4), advocated to limit the judgment to such declaration in view of the moral hazard caused, and considering that the violation was not serious because the plaintiffs were not in an emergency situation resulting from persecution or from a threat to life, integrity or dignity, that the appellants crossed the border illegally and violently, and that the Spanish authorities subsequently examined the individual circumstances of each of the applicants, as required by the Convention, when they crossed the border again. This particular vote, finally, expressed concern that the ECtHR maintains its strict rules *vis-à-vis* the authorities in a situation of illegal behaviour or even violence.

In any case, this ECtHR's Judgment was not yet final because the Spanish Government requested its referral to the ECtHR's Grand Chamber in accordance with Article 43.1 of the ECHR, which was accepted by a College of five judges on 29 January 2018.[54] The ECtHR Grand Chamber's Judgment was further adopted on 13 February 2020,[55] overturning the ini-

---

53 ECtHR, *N.D. and N.T v. Spain*, Appls. Nos. 8675/15 and 8697/15, judgement, 3 October 2017.

54 In this sense, among others, *Sánchez Tomás*, Las devoluciones en caliente ante el Tribunal Europeo de Derechos Humanos (STEDH, AS. N.D. and N.T., of 3 October 2017), Revista Española de Derecho Europeo 65 (2018), 101, 101.

55 ECtHR, *N.D. and N.T. v. Spain*, Appls. Nos. 8675/15 and 8697/15, judgement, 13 February 2020.

tial ECHR Sentence, and finally stating that there was no infringement either of Article 4 of Protocol No. 4 (ban of collective expulsions) or of Article 13 (right to an effective remedy), in both cases, in a nutshell, because of the applicants' own illegal conduct (paragraphs 231 and 242, both with a common basis and an almost identical wording).

The Grand Chamber considers that in fact the applicants placed themselves in jeopardy and in an unlawful situation by deliberately participating in the storming of the Melilla border fences on 13 August 2014, in an attempt to enter Spain taking advantage of the group's large numbers, at an unauthorised location, and using force. They did not avail themselves of the existing legal procedures for gaining lawful entry to Spanish territory, in the view of the Grand Chamber, and consequently, in accordance with its settled case law, it considers that the lack of individual removal decisions can be attributed to the fact that the applicants, if they indeed wished to assert rights under the Convention, did not make use of the official entry procedures existing for that purpose, and was therefore a consequence of their own behaviour. With that being so, the Grand Chamber concludes that Spain cannot be held responsible for not making available a legal remedy against that removal, either. There are two Particular Votes, but both immaterial to this effect, for they considered the case unreceivable, based, either on Art. 37 of the ECHR (the first vote), or on the inapplicability of Art. 4 of Protocol 4 (the second vote).

In the brief time following this Judgement in which the present work has been written, there are still no scholarly books, chapters, or papers released on the subject, but it seems to have prompted firm rejection by some scholars on social networks (Twitter, LinkedIn, etc.) who criticise this decision by the ECHR's Chamber because it confuses illegality with a lack of rights, or because it allows unlawfulness to justify rightlessness. Prior to this sentence, human rights defenders had argued that the practice of pushbacks or hot returns at the border (with its recent legislative formalisation through the concept of rejection at the border enshrined since 2015 by the new 10th Additional Provision of the Organic Law on Foreigners) does not allow sufficient time to ensure proper processing of all files.[56] It is yet to be determined how the new doctrine of the ECHR's Grand Chamber on border pushbacks will influence the still-pending sentence of the Spanish Constitutional Court that will decide the aforementioned uncon-

56 European Commission, Communication, Progress Report on the implementation of the European Migration Agenda, COM (2019) 481 final (16 October 2019), 11.

stitutionality action filed against Organic Law 4/2105, which introduced the said 10th Additional Disposition to the Organic Law on Immigration, thereby giving legal national coverage to pushbacks: the legal (constitutional) parameter is of an exclusive internal nature, but the Spanish Constitution (Article 10.2) provides for its rules on fundamental rights to be interpreted according to international agreements signed by Spain on Human Rights, which obviously includes the ECHR, and on its basis, ECHR judgements.

Finally, it is to be noted here that, in recent years, Morocco has become a country of transit and even of destination for immigrants. To support Morocco in this situation, EU cooperation on migration has recently provided that country with EUR 238 million through the Africa Trust Fund. This has led Morocco, in cooperation with Spain, to contribute to a reduction in the number of arrivals through the Western Mediterranean, to the fighting against irregular migration and to the dismantling of criminal networks, as well as to the supporting of vulnerable people.[57] Spain, for its part, is one of the main beneficiaries of the EU's Asylum, Migration and Integration Fund and of the EU's Internal Security Fund's national programmes, including among the priorities of this financial support the reinforcement of the Asylum Office and the reception system, the integration of non-nationals, the sending of reinforced forces and teams to borders, and the returning of non-nationals in an irregular situation.[58]

Also, at the EU's initiative, with its logical impact on the Spanish–Moroccan relationship on migration issues, legal migration pilot projects designed by the Union's Member States together with the main partner countries of origin and transit are being developed, with the support of the European Commission.[59] At present, five pilot projects on legal migration with EU funding are being conducted for the purpose of implementing long-term circular mobility plans for young graduates and workers from certain partner countries, including Morocco, and to encourage the commitment of those partner countries with effective migration management.[60] In sum, the EU is working on its relations with Morocco in order to forge a closer, deeper and more ambitious partnership, which has also been reflected in the resumption of readmission negotiations between the

57 European Commission (fn. 56), 12.
58 European Commission (fn. 56), 11.
59 European Commission (fn. 56), 19.
60 European Commission (fn. 56), 29.

Union and Morocco.[61] Within this framework of European policies, the Spanish–Moroccan bilateral relationship is a paradigmatic example of the use of conditional development cooperation as a tool for outsourcing the control of borders and immigration, as can be seen at the very reading of the successive Africa Plans endorsed by the EU since 2006.[62]

III. The situation of asylum between Spain and Morocco: some figures, legal issues and a general factual background

In addition to what has already been said in general about the migratory situation between Spain and Morocco, it should be added here, in specific relation to asylum, that people who arrive at the land border at Ceuta or Melilla (once again, the only border of this type among the EU and Africa) fleeing from persecution in their State of origin, or in third ones, have two legal channels in Spain to file an application for international protection. This application is either carried out at the border post itself, at the Office located there for this purpose, where the much shorter border application procedure applies, or is later filed on Spanish soil, after having physically accessed it in an irregular situation in any way (cayuco, swimming, jumping fences, or hiding in vehicles, usually).

Physical features and characteristics make it possible for Syrians, Algerians, Palestinians or Tunisians to pass for Moroccans and thus reach the border post by circumventing Moroccan control, while Sub-Saharans generally do not have the possibility of reaching, from Moroccan territory, the Spanish border post where the Asylum Office is located, and all this has stimulated illegal trafficking by means of small boats ("*pateras*").[63] Out of the 2,391 files opened in the Asylum Office at the Beni Enzar border post (in Melilla) during 2018, none came from Africans of countries outside the Maghreb because of the enormous difficulties they encounter arriving at the Spanish border post due to the control of the Moroccan police,[64] since

61 European Commission, Communication, Progress report on the Implementation of the European Agenda on Migration, COM (2019) 126 final (6 March 2019).

62 Comisión Española de Ayuda al Refugiado (CEAR), Informe 2019: Las personas refugiadas en España y Europa, 1, 52, available at: https://www.cear.es/wp-content/uploads/2019/07/INFORME_CEAR_2019.pdf.

63 See in this sense, *Varo*, Ceuta y Melilla, vía cegada a los subsaharianos, El País (2 January 2019), available at: https://elpais.com/politica/2019/01/01/actualidad/1546372216_230031.html.

64 *Varo* (fn. 63).

they are already in an irregular situation in Morocco, which does not allow them a free transit to reach the Spanish border post to make their request for protection in the respective Office of Asylum and Refuge (OAR) at Ceuta (El Tarajal) or Melilla (Beni Enzar).[65]

The inactivity of the OAR, at least until very recently,[66] has been motivating that for Sub-Saharan immigrants the way to access the possibility of requesting international protection is irregular entry, either through "las vallas" (fences) of the respective Spanish cities in Africa that separate them from the surrounding Moroccan territory, or by swimming from adjacent Moroccan beaches, with the consequent physical risk in both cases.[67] The alternatives are to expose themselves to a pushback or to arrive at the Centre for Temporary Stay of Immigrants (CETI, in Spanish acronym) to file the corresponding application.[68]

In 2018, 6,494 applications for international protection were filed at a border post, that is, at airports, ports and at the land border offices of Ceuta and Melilla, which represented an increase of 5.6% compared to 2017, without any application for international protection being filed at the border post of Ceuta in 2018, as has been happening since the opening of that asylum office, while that of Melilla, by contrast, received 2,800 applications.[69] It is also worth mentioning that in recent years, following an annual growing trend, hundreds of applications for protection have been submitted by Moroccans (340 in 2016, 525 in 2017 and 1,310 in 2018). This

65 *Serrano,* Maleno: A ningún africano le han permitido pedir asilo en las oficinas de frontera de Ceuta y Melilla, Público (28 August 2017), available at: https://www.publico.es/politica/maleno-africano-le-han-permitido-pedir-asilo-oficinas-frontera-ceuta-melilla.html.

66 Ceutaldía (1 September 2019), Interior estrena la Oficina de Asilo del Tarajal para entrevistar a los migrantes llegados el viernes, on the occasion of the jump of the fence in the area of Benzú (Ceuta) by 155 people, availableat: http://www.ceutaldia.com/articulo/administracion/interior-estrena-oficina-asilo-tarajal-entrevistar-migrantes-llegados-viernes/20190901114618206124.html. See also CeutaTV (20 November 2019), La Oficina de Asilo del Tarajal no registró ni una solicitud durante el pasado año, available at: http://www.ceutatv.com/art/7703/la-oficina-de-asilo-del-tarajal-no-registro-ni-una-sola-solicitud-durante-el-pasado-ano.

67 Comisión Española de Ayuda al Refugiado (CEAR), Informe 2018: Las personas refugiadas en España y en Europa, 82–83, available at: https://www.cear.es/wp-content/uploads/2018/06/Informe-CEAR-2018.pdf.

68 See with more details, *Garcés Mascareñas*, El sistema de asilo español, ¿Derecho de protección garantizado?", CIDOB Opinión, February 2017, available at: https://www.cidob.org/content/download/66103/2021871/version/15/file/463_OPINION_BLANCA%20GARC%C3%89S_CAST.pdf.

69 Comisión Española de Ayuda al Refugiado (CEAR), (fn. 62), 66.

makes Morocco the ninth country of origin, in 2018, with the highest number of applications, alleging persecution either because of sexual orientation, or because they come from the Rif region, where in recent years there have been revolts in demand of social improvements, although only around 10% of applications culminate in the granting of refugee status.[70] With regard to unaccompanied minors, finally, the issue is analysed below, in the section on the Spanish–Moroccan bilateral agreements with migratory incidence.

IV. The European exceptional legal status of the Spanish–Moroccan borders at Ceuta and Melilla according to the Schengen acquis

Within the framework of the EU's shared powers with its Member States on immigration and asylum of third-country nationals, as well as on external border controls, which are dealt with elsewhere in this book, we can now highlight the "Schengen exception" at the Spanish–Moroccan border in Ceuta and Melilla. Although external border controls are currently governed, in the EU's derivative law, by the Schengen Borders Code (Regulation 2016/399 of 9 March 2016), significantly Article 41 of this very Regulation states that all its provisions shall not affect the special rules applying to the cities of Ceuta and Melilla, as defined in the Declaration by the Kingdom of Spain on those Cities included into the Final Act to the Agreement on the Accession of the Kingdom of Spain to the Convention implementing the Schengen Agreement of 14 June 1985.

In particular, Spanish Declaration III of that Final Act states the continuity of controls on goods and travellers entering the customs territory of the EEC from the cities of Ceuta and Melilla, but also the specific arrangements on visa exemptions for local border traffic between Ceuta and Melilla, on one hand, and the Moroccan provinces of Tetuan and Nador, on the other. For Moroccan nationals not residing in those two provinces, and also wishing to enter the territory of Ceuta and Melilla, the same Declaration foresees their subjection to the visa requirement, whose validity is limited to the aforementioned Spanish towns, and permitting multiple entries and exits ("*visado limitado multiple*").

Finally, this very Declaration also provides for the maintaining of checks on identity and documents by Spain pursuant to its national law on

70 Comisión Española de Ayuda al Refugiado (CEAR), (fn. 67), 77–78, and Comisión Española de Ayuda al Refugiado (CEAR), (fn. 62), 64.

sea and air connections departing from Ceuta and Melilla with sole destination to any other place on Spanish territory, as well the continuity of checks on internal flights or sea connections departing from Ceuta and Melilla with destination to any other Schengen-participant State.

V. *The Spanish–Moroccan bilateral legal framework on migration and asylum: agreements on labour, readmission of irregular immigrants and on unaccompanied minors*

The first Agreement to mention within the legal framework of bilateral relations between Spain and Morocco in the area of immigration and asylum is that of 13 February 1992 between the two countries, on the movement of persons in transit and the readmission of aliens who had entered illegally, which was in provisional application for twenty years, although Morocco has often declined to comply with it on the grounds of its lack of validity.[71] The signing thereof took place in direct response to the humanitarian crisis experienced in 1992 in Melilla, when more than 800 Sub-Saharans arrived in the city, at a time when the number of irregular immigrants to Spain was much lower than nowadays.[72] However, this Agreement was part of a greater context, which began with the approval of the first Spanish Law on aliens and immigration in 1985, the subsequent creation in 1987 of a Joint Consular Commission of the Spanish and Moroccan Ministers for Foreign Affairs (which would meet for the first time in February 1988) to deal bilaterally with migration issues, among others, and in particular, the regularisation of Moroccans illegally resident in Spain due to the previous lack of control and legislation of the latter country, the increase in irregular entries by sea ("pateras") and land from the former country, and the imposition of an entry visa in 1991 on Moroccan citizens as a consequence of Spain's then recent accession to the Schengen Area.[73]

The aforementioned bilateral Agreement began to be effective after three years, when the first three immigrants were readmitted by Morocco.

71 *González Vega*, El control de la inmigración irregular en España: compromisos y desarrollos, in: Del Valle Gálvez et al. (dirs.), Revista CIDOB d'Afers Internacionals, 111 (2007), 173, 182.

72 See *Moreno*, El acuerdo de inmigración entre España y Marruecos con el que el Gobierno de Sánchez justifica las devoluciones, ElFarodeCeuta.es (23 August 2018), available at: https://elfarodeceuta.es/acuerdo-inmigracion-espana-marruecos-gobierno-sanchez-devoluciones/.

73 In this sense, and more deeply, *Artetxe Larrabide*, (fn. 2), 288 ff.

Between 1992 and 2005, however, it was used 114 times, mainly with Maghrebi persons.[74] In 1996, 45 returns and readmissions were made, 27 in 1997, only one was carried out in 1998, while between 1999 and 2003, the Moroccan authorities did not readmit any person, which reveals the low use of this Agreement until 2019.[75] This Agreement, however, was reactivated in summer 2019, when on 23 July, 116 people were handed over by the Spanish police to the Moroccan *gendarmes* on the same night of their entry.[76] These people were mainly Moroccans, and as far as Sub-Saharans are concerned, they entered by sea onto the Spanish rocks bordering the Moroccan region of El Rif or the Chafarinas Islands. A similar situation occurred with the people who managed to circumvent the fence on 22 August, whose expulsion under this Agreement was processed directly by the Spanish and Moroccan Ministries of Home Affairs, with Spain taking responsibility for the transport costs of these people until they entered the neighbouring country, to where they were transported in buses guarded by Moroccan soldiers.[77]

On the other hand, in relation to labour migration flows between the two countries, mention should be made of the Labour Agreement of 25 July 2001, which would also be firstly in provisional application (for four years in this case), suspended during the so-called "Parsley Islet Crisis" in 2002, and which would be ratified again in 2003. Its activation took place in 2004, and its purpose lies in the joint management of seasonal labour movements. It began to be applied that same year with the recruitment at source of women for strawberry picking in Huelva, who were selected by the Moroccan National Agency for the Promotion of Employment and Skills (ANAPEC).[78]

The experience with this Agreement has become a model for the European Commission, the World Bank, and the International Organisation for Migration, because of its combining both the personal interests and the legal security of agricultural employers with those of the EU's own migrant workers involved, having received European aid through two successive projects: AENEAS, of the European Commission (Programme for Fi-

74 *Artetxe Larrabide*, (fn. 2), 288 ff.

75 *S. Moreno,* La historia del acuerdo de devolución de migrantes a Marruecos que Pedro Sánchez ha sacado del cajón, El Diario.es (25 August 2019), available at https://www.eldiario.es/desalambre/acuerdo-readmision-migrantes-Marruecos-magrebies_0_807369599.html.

76 *S. Moreno* (fn. 75).

77 *S: Moreno* (fn. 75).

78 *Amirah Fernández* (fn. 8), 62.

nancial and Technical Assistance to Third Countries in the Area of Migration and Asylum), and then through another European programme, M@res, devoted to border management, or also in Almeria and Lleida with the temporary recruitment at source in Morocco for agricultural work.[79] The economic crisis that began in 2007, which brought about the return of native Spanish workers to the agricultural sector, meant a reduction in hiring under this Agreement from 2009 onwards, but, in any case, since the incorporation of Romania and Bulgaria to the EU, Morocco is the only non-EU country in which this hiring of immigrants for the strawberry sector continues.[80]

This Agreement is part of the Spanish practice of signing bilateral international instruments for the shared management of labour migration flows, following the change of the Spanish paradigm from a traditional emigration country to an immigration one in the early 1990s. These instruments establish procedures to regulate the incorporation into the Spanish labour market of workers who are nationals of third countries for those jobs that the "national" labour force is unable to satisfy.[81] These Conventions, signed in the early 1990s with various countries (Dominican Republic, Ecuador, Romania, Colombia, Poland and Bulgaria, including Morocco), are relevant after the amendment of the Spanish Law on Foreigners carried out in 2003, for since then it is thereby provided for (Article 39.6) that seasonal job offers will be preferentially oriented towards countries with which Spain has signed flow regulation agreements, and although most of these agreements also include a chapter to regulate and facilitate the voluntary return of nationals who have come to work in Spain, the exception is precisely that signed with Morocco, which does not include the possibility of facilitating voluntary return.[82]

Last, but not least, it is necessary to highlight the Agreement between the Kingdom of Spain and the Kingdom of Morocco on cooperation in the field of the prevention of illegal emigration of unaccompanied minors,

---

79 *Amirah Fernández* (fn. 8), 62.

80 *Amirah Fernández* (fn. 8), 62.

81 More details are offered by *Pérez*, La perspectiva española de la dimensión exterior de la política de inmigración de la UE, in: CIDOB, La dimensión exterior de las políticas de inmigración en la Unión Europea. V Seminario Inmigración y Europa, Barcelona 2008, 145, 146, available at https://www.cidob.org/en/content/download/8381/85385/version/2/file/16_perez_cast.pdf.

82 So it is pointed out by *Terrón*, Migraciones y relaciones con países terceros, Documentos CIDOB2 (2004), 5, 9, available at https://www.cidob.org/es/content/download/2813/32106/file/doc_migraciones_2.pdf.

their protection and their concerted return, signed ad referendum in Rabat on 6 March 2007, and officially published in Spain five years later! The legal figure of the unaccompanied foreign minor is of relatively recent appearance in Spanish legislation, with the Government's Aliens and Immigration Regulation of 1996, which develops the Aliens and Immigration Parliamentary Act.[83] Legal powers and responsibilities over foster care in Spain are attributed to the Autonomous Communities (the Regions), while those relating to immigration, by contrast, are State-owned, there not being in Spain a specific State protective legislation to standardise protection conditions, protocols and procedures that the Autonomous Communities are providing to Unaccompanied Alien Minors (MENA, in Spanish acronym). Articles 35 of the Aliens Act and 92 of the current Aliens Regulation establish as a priority solution the return of MENA to their countries of origin.

The arrivals of minors in successive *pateras* (small precarious boats) to the Spanish peninsular coasts in the Tarifa area during 2003 (21 minors in one *patera* in September, and 16 and 49 respectively in two further boats in October) were the object of extensive media attention in Spain, and began to focus the agenda of Hispano–Moroccan bilateral relations, with Morocco's diplomatic representation expressing itself in the media in the sense of considering that the Moroccan minors did not have the legal capacity to take the decision to emigrate, and that there was an obligation to return them.[84] The regional governments, competent in Spain for the guardianship of these minors, aligned themselves with the Moroccan position, claiming that they had failed in the said minor's social integration.[85]

The media echo of the arrival of minors in *pateras* also led the State Attorney General's Office to issue Instruction 3/2003. This instrument provided for the returning to Morocco in 48 hours of non-national unaccompanied children under 16 years of age who had arrived in Spain, because that Instruction considered them *de facto* emancipated persons. To that end they, had to follow the same procedure as that for the expulsion of adults, unless the Prosecutor intervened, which was often by telephone

83 In this sense, among others, *Senovilla Hernández*, Los menores extranjeros no acompañados en Europa, Murcia 2008, 135.

84 El País (11 February 2003), Marruecos pide al Gobierno que le devuelva a los menores que emigran solos a España, available at: https://elpais.com/diario/2003/02/11/espana/1044918027_850215.html.

85 El País (12 February 2003), Las Comunidades Autónomas quieren devolver a los menores inmigrantes que pide Marruecos, available at: https://elpais.com/diario/2003/02/12/espana/1045004420_850215.html.

without seeing the minor, calculating the minor's age through procedures that were questionable as to the certainty of their results, such as the oseometric test.[86] In this context, the agenda of the High Level Meeting between Spain and Morocco held in December of the same year had as its axis the signing of the Memorandum of Understanding between the two countries on Assisted Repatriation of Unaccompanied Minors, which would take place in Madrid on 23 December.[87]

An attempt to develop a policy of repatriation of Moroccan minors would begin in 2004. The procedure had to start on the proposal of the regional governments in the exercise of each unaccompanied foreign minor's guardianship, with her or his return being carried out by the Central Government Sub-delegations in the Provinces. However, the effective returns, which from the outset of this policy were few in comparison with the proposals, progressively decreased even further.[88] Starting in 2005, the central government's Ministry of Social Affairs, as well as several Autonomous Communities (in the exercise of their aforementioned powers on protection of minors in general, and on that of unaccompanied foreign minors in particular), launched various projects and initiatives with a view to enabling the reception in Morocco of minors of that nationality returned from Spain, and to on-site training the staff of such centres for the protection of minors and children, providing to that effect investments in economic, material and human resources. These initiatives, which were not coordinated among themselves at the Spanish level, met with the opposition from associations for the protection of minors and children, and even from UNICEF, because of their stigmatisation of these minors as irregular immigrants and the risk that the repatriations thus carried out

86 As it is related by *Jiménez Álvarez*, Intrusos en la Fortaleza. Menores marroquíes migrantes en la Frontera Sur de Europa, Doctoral Thesis, Madrid Autonomous University, 249 and 250, available at: https://repositorio.uam.es/bitstream/handle/10486/6842/40064_Jimenez_Alvarez_Mercedes.pdf?sequence=1&isAllowed=y. See also, *Simón Navarro*, La protección de los menores no acompañados en España. Implicaciones constucionales, Doctoral Thesis, University of Santiago de Compostela, 2015, 162, available at: https://minerva.usc.es/xmlui/bitstream/handle/10347/15162/rep_1312.pdf?sequence=1&isAllowed=y, and Federación SOS Racismo, Menores en las fronteras: de los retornos efectuados sin garantías a menores marroquíes y de los malos tratos sufridos, 27, available at: https://www.observatoriodelainfancia.es/oia/esp/documentos_ficha.aspx?id=609.

87 See in this sense, *Jiménez Álvarez*, (fn. 86), 247.

88 Some figures appear in *Jiménez Álvarez*, (fn. 86), 252 ff.

could be processed collectively, without analysis of the particular situation and without consideration for the best interests of the minor.[89]

Centres for minors in Morocco were thus created by the Spanish Agency for International Development Cooperation and the Moroccan *Entraide Nationale*, in the cities of Nador and Beni Mellal, in order to support minors in vulnerable situations in that country, those who had abandoned their studies, and other cases. But also the Autonomous Communities of Catalonia, Madrid and Andalusia contributed to the construction of centres, although not in coordination with the State.[90]

The Catalonia–Maghreb Plan led to the signing of an Agreement between the Department of Social Action and Citizenship of the Catalonian Autonomous Government with Morocco's Ministry of Social Development, Family and Solidarity, on the social, cultural, economic and labour integration of Moroccan minors. The Agreement limited its action to minors residing in the Moroccan area of Tangier as an alternative to their emigration, as well as the assisted return of Moroccan minors who emigrated and resided in Catalonian Autonomous Government Centres.[91] This action, aimed at improving the management of migratory flows between Morocco and Catalonia, as well as preventing illegal migration, from 27 December 2006 for a period of three years, was co-funded by 50% from the European Commission's AENEAS Programme on financial and technical assistance in the field of migration from third countries,[92] whereas the Catalonian Autonomous Government committed itself to allocate EUR 1,012,313 of a total cost of EUR 2,012,313.[93] The financing from the Catalan side included the contribution from the State fund for the integration and reception of immigrants and their educational reinforcement.[94]

With regard to the Autonomous Community of Madrid, it was reported in 2005 that the Immigration Department of its Regional Government, also with funding from the EU's AENEAS Programme, intended to build two centres to repatriate minors in Morocco, one in Tangier and the other

89 Among others, *Jiménez Álvarez*, (fn. 86), 250 and 251.
90 See, in this sense, *Simón Navarro*, (fn. 86), 319.
91 Govern.cat (5 June 2007), El Govern aprova la signatura d'un conveni per a la promoció de la integració social, cultural, econòmica i laboral dels menors marroquins", Press Note, available at: https://govern.cat/salapremsa/notes-premsa/74263/govern-aprova-signatura-un-conveni-promocio-integracio-social-cultural-economica-laboral-dels-menors-marroquins.
92 Govern.cat (fn. 91).
93 Govern.cat (fn. 91).
94 Govern.cat (fn. 91).

in Marrakech, with a budget of three million euros. It was criticised at the time that the chosen locations in this project were areas of passage and little inhabited, where it did not seem that there were enough elements for children to socialise (their families, friends, schools, green areas, youth associations), so that because of the centres' geographical location at a border crossing, they seemed designed, rather than to welcome minors, to invite them to migrate afresh.[95]

Andalusia, which together with Catalonia and Madrid is another of the Spanish Autonomous Communities with the largest number of MENA from Morocco, has also carried out on-site actions in that country. For example, the regional government, through the Andalusian Agency for International Development Cooperation (AACID) rehabilitated and equipped with funds a network of five centres in the Moroccan region of Tangier–Tetouan–Al Hoceima, within the framework of a support programme for the Kingdom of Morocco's Policy on Protection to Minors, including a training programme in social engineering and management of centres which has benefited 300 workers of *l'Entraide Nationale*, a Moroccan government entity promoting social action policies and a beneficiary of AACID's collaboration.[96]

Let us return our focus again to the Spanish–Moroccan bilateral agreement on unaccompanied minors. This agreement proclaims as its general objectives (Article 1) the establishment of a joint framework to exchange data and information between the parties for the prevention of illegal emigration (from Morocco to Spain) of unaccompanied minors and the protection and return of such minors. In order to achieve those general objectives, it is planned to adopt preventive measures focused on the social and economic development of the areas of origin of such minors, in the fight against human trafficking networks, measures of assistance and protection for the Moroccan minors present on Spanish soil, and to favour the assisted return of these minors to their families or the institution of guardianship in the country of origin, together with their social reinsertion thereon (Article 2). Preventive measures include awareness-raising campaigns on

95 *Jiménez*, La perversión de la cooperación al desarrollo: los proyectos de reagrupación de los menores migrantes en Marruecos, Mugak 37 (2006), available at: http://mugak.eu/revista-mugak/no-37/la-perversion-de-la-cooperacion-al-desarrollo-los-proyectos-de-reagrupacion-de-los-menores-migrantes-en-marruecos.

96 Europa Press (21 October 2019), Andalucía aborda con la embajadora de Marruecos el proceso de identificación de los menores solos, available at: https://www.europapress.es/esandalucia/sevilla/noticia-ruiz-aborda-embajadora-marruecos-proceso-identificacion-mena-atencion-junta-20191021153013.html.

the risks involved in emigration, and actions to combat networks of illegal trafficking and exploitation of minors (Article 3).

For their part, the measures for the protection of Moroccan unaccompanied minors in Spain consist of their assistance by the competent Spanish authorities with the same level of protection as that supplied to nationals in accordance with international law, national State law and the law of the Spanish Autonomous Communities, including an additional commitment to inform the competent Moroccan authorities within one month of the illegal entry of each Moroccan unaccompanied minor into Spain about her or his situation (Article 4.1). The measures for the protection of Moroccan responsibility encompass the identification of the minor and of her or his family within three months of the delivery of the documentation and/or information on the minor by the competent Spanish authorities, as well as own issuance of such documentation proving her or his nationality (Article 4.2).

It is for the competent Spanish authorities to decide on the return of each unaccompanied minor to the country of origin in accordance with international law, in particular with the Convention on the Rights of the Child (Article 5.1). To this end, provision is made for cooperation between Spain and Morocco to guarantee the return of these minors to their country of origin, the conditions for effective family reunification or their transfer to a guardianship institution, always preserving the best and superior interests of the child (Article 5(2)). These obligations of cooperation between the parties also extend themselves to the establishment of a reception facility equipped with qualified human and material resources, public and private, or coming from NGOs working in the field of protection and repatriation of minors (Article 5.3). Protection and repatriation actions must be financed by Spain, which also co-finances prevention actions, particularly those aimed at promoting the socio-economic development of regions with high migratory potential (Article 7).

Despite the provisions of the Bilateral Spanish–Moroccan Agreement on unaccompanied minors in terms of cooperation *in situ*, and although the Spanish Law on Foreigners authorises the conclusion of agreements by the Autonomous Regions with the countries of origin, at present, with the exception of the Catalan attempt to dust off the aforementioned Catalonia–Maghreb Plan, the possibility of opening reception and training centres within Morocco is no longer considered a priority by Spain because of the fiasco caused by the different experiences attempted in the last decade. As already seen for the Madrid Regional Government, in a conclusion that now it is possible to generalise to all the Autonomous Communities, although Morocco initially accepted the idea of such centres, it later refused to use them for the purposes for which they had been built, alleging the "knock-on effect" of such places, where accommodation, food and training were given to young people in a country with serious shortcomings in this field; given that the system of protection of minors in Morocco is not prepared to provide adequate care for minors repatriated by Spain".[97]

Continuing with the effective implementation of the Spanish–Moroccan Agreement on unaccompanied minors, the current disuse of its provisions on return must hereby be highlighted. The latest available Annual Report of the Attorney General's Office points out in this sense that "once again, the repatriation of unaccompanied foreign minors shows itself as an anecdotal legal figure", attesting to this assertion with the data that "in 2018 three family repatriations of minors, all of them male and of Algerian nationality, have been successfully completed".[98] In general, the Spanish policy on unaccompanied foreign minors is oriented towards their return to the country of origin as provided for by United Nations texts (i.e. Declaration of the Rights of the Child and Convention on the Rights of the Child), according to which priority should be given to the development of the minor within his or her family, or in an environment in which his or her own traditions and cultural values have an important presence, all without prejudice to the fact that all these factors may not coincide, in which case the return would not be in the interest of the minor.[99]

In cases of return, a specific procedure called a "minor's repatriation" is regulated, as distinct from that for voluntary or forced returns within the general immigration regime, and which in this case serves the best inter-

97 *Jiménez* (fn. 95), quoting in this sense the Human Rights Watch's Report, Retornos a cualquier precio España insiste en la repatriación de menores extranjeros no acompañados sin garantías. Informe de Human Rights Watch, 2008, whose complete text may be downloaded at https://www.hrw.org/es/report/2008/10/17/retornos-cualquier-precio/espana-insiste-en-la-repatriacion-demenores-extranjeros. See also La Vanguardia, (12 February 2016), 2.200 Menores marroquíes están solos en España sin repatriación prevista, available at: https://www.lavanguardia.com/vida/20160212/302110875184/2-200-menores-marroquies-estan-solos-en-espana-sin-repatriacion-prevista.html.

98 Fiscalía General del Estado (Spanish Attorney General's Office), Memoria de la Fiscalía General del Estado 2019, 846, with data referring to 2018, available at:https://www.fiscal.es/documents/20142/a63c133c-dff3-6cf9-1a74-55d658be912a.

99 Punto Nacional de Contacto de la Red Europea de Migración en España (National Contact Point of the European Migration Network in Spain), Estudio sobre el régimen de los menores extranjeros no acompañados tras la determinación de su estatus España 2017, 1, 26, available at: http://extranjeros.mitramiss.gob.es/es/redeuropeamigracion/Estudios_monograficos/ficheros/2017/Estudio_REM_Regimen_MENAS_tras_determinacion_ES.pdf.

ests of the minor. In Spain, the procedure for the return of unaccompanied foreign minors falls within the jurisdiction of the central State's authority, which is vested with immigration powers, as already mentioned. Specifically, it is the central Government's Delegation in the respective Autonomous Community or its Sub-Delegation in the province, that processes and resolves the return of unaccompanied foreign minors. To this end, the central Government's Delegations or Sub-Delegations contact the diplomatic authorities of the minor's country of origin to obtain information about the child's circumstances therein.

The minor herself or himself, the Public Prosecutor's Office, as well as the entity that holds her or his legal guardianship, custody, provisional protection, or ward (usually, of the Autonomous Community of residence), participate in the processing of the respective dossier. It will be determined in it whether the minor should regroup with his family or be placed at the disposal of the protection services of the country of origin, by previously hearing the minor or his or her legal representative, the Public Prosecutor's Office, the entity that holds the legal guardianship, custody, provisional protection or ward (it must issue a report), and the corresponding Autonomic (Regional) Service for the Protection of Minors.

Prior to the relevant evidence, the Government Delegation or Sub-Delegation decides whether the minor should regroup with his or her family, or be placed under the child protection services of his country's responsibility, or, instead, remain in Spain. And this administrative resolution may be appealed before the Courts. The best interest of the minor must be inexcusably valued throughout the process, so that if the repatriation is against that best interest, it cannot be carried out and then the minor stays in Spain. If repatriation is decided, it is because it has been concluded that it is in the minor's best interest to regroup with her or his family, or to be placed at the child protection services in the country of origin.[100] In any case, nine months after the minor has been placed at the disposal of the Spanish competent services for the protection of minors, a residence permit in Spain will be granted for him or her, notwithstanding that, at a later time, his or her repatriation might be decided in the minor's best interest.[101]

---

100 Punto Nacional de Contacto de la Red Europea de Migración en España (National Contact Point of the European Migration Network in Spain) (fn. 99), 28.

101 Punto Nacional de Contacto de la Red Europea de Migración en España (National Contact Point of the European Migration Network in Spain) (fn. 99), 29 and 30.

However, as noted above, the practical experience in the implementation of bilateral regulations with Morocco, as well as those unilaterally enacted in Spain by either the central or the regional authorities, is that there are very few cases in which unaccompanied foreign minors are repatriated, with the majority of them remaining in Spain.[102] However, the issue is dealt with continuously by the Hispano–Moroccan Permanent Group, which has a Subcommittee on Minors. Beyond specific measures, there is a channel of communication and permanent collaboration between Spain and Morocco in which the priority is to seek the most appropriate measures to safeguard the best interests of minors. The notable increase in arrivals of unaccompanied foreign minors, most of whom come precisely from Morocco, reaching a total of 12,500 in 2018,[103] prompted the Spanish Government to undertake further negotiations with the Moroccan governmental authorities to reactivate the bilateral Agreement on unaccompanied foreign minors, while at the same time it has provided more funding to the Autonomous Communities for reception centres and other necessary resources.[104]

Finally, it is necessary to refer here to the opaquest practice, without prejudice to its effectiveness, of the Memoranda of Understanding between both countries on the legal issues that are dealt with in this Chapter. These are non-normative instruments, or at least, instruments different from the international Treaties *stricto sensu*. In fact, several of the aforementioned bilateral Agreements of a conventional and international nature signed between Spain and Morocco, currently in force, and having an impact on issues of a migratory dimension, find their antecedent in previous Memoranda of Understanding or non-regulatory international Agreements concluded between the governments (or members of the respective ministerial cabinets) of both countries.

This is specifically the case of the above discussed Agreements on readmission of immigrants in an irregular situation, and on unaccompanied

---

102 Punto Nacional de Contacto de la Red Europea de Migración en España (National Contact Point of the European Migration Network in Spain) (fn. 99), 6.

103 See La Vanguardia (1 January 2019), 2018 cierra con al menos 12.500 menores extranjeros solos, available at: https://www.lavanguardia.com/vida/20190101/453871183154/2018-cierra-con-al-menos-12500-menores-extranjeros-solos-mientras-el-gobierno-negocia-con-marruecos-su-retorno.html.

104 Plenary Meeting of the Spanish Government (Consejo de Ministros) (28 October 2019), Destinados 40 millones de euros a las Comunidades Autónomas para la ayuda y atención solidaria a los menores extranjeros no acompañados, available at: http://lamoncloa.gob.es/consejodeministros/Paginas/enclaces/261018-enlace-menores.aspx.

minors, which respectively had their precedents in the Spanish–Moroccan Agreement on seasonal workers signed in Madrid on 30 September 1999, and in the Memorandum of Understanding between the Kingdom of Spain and the Kingdom of Morocco on assisted repatriation of unaccompanied minors of 23 December 2003.[105] The aforementioned royal and ministerial visit of Spain to Morocco led to the signing in Rabat of eleven agreements on 13 February 2019,[106] among which is outstanding the Memorandum of Understanding for a Global Strategic Partnership stands out from a migratory perspective, which aims, as basic objectives, at consolidating a permanent dialogue and a concrete and mutually beneficial cooperation between the two countries.[107] Specifically, this Memorandum provides for the creation of a Global Strategic Partnership Council, chaired by the Ministers of Foreign Affairs of the two countries, as a framework for maintaining a permanent dialogue on all bilateral issues, including expressly that of migration.[108]

VI. Concluding remarks

If a basic conclusion can be drawn from the previous analysis of the bilateral Hispano–Moroccan legal relationship on immigration and asylum, it is the decisive current impact on that relationship of Spain's membership of the European Union, and more specifically, of the latter's competences impinging upon immigration and asylum. Spain is the gateway to Europe on African soil, and that African surrounding border soil is Moroccan. Such a decisive bearing by the European Union, however, is recent, since the competences of the latter, which are not exclusive, but shared with its Member States (Spain, among them), date precisely back to the amendments carried out over the last decade of last century (Treaties of Amsterdam, Nice and Lisbon), for those EU competences or powers did not form part, properly, of the ones initially conferred on the Community by its

105 On these Agreements, see *González Vega* (fn. 71), 182 ff.

106 *Benedito,* España y Marruecos estrechan lazos con 11 acuerdos bilaterales, Expansión (14 February 2019), available at: https://www.expansion.com/economia/2019/02/14/5c647e9d468aebf25f8b45aa.html.

107 Maroc.ma (14 February 2019), Marruecos-España: La Asociación Estratégica Multidimensional tiende a consolidar el diálogo permanente y la cooperación bilateral, available at: http://www.maroc.ma/es/news/marruecos-espana-la-asociacion-estrategica-multidimensional-tiende-consolidar-el-dialogo.

108 Maroc.ma (fn. 107).

Member States for the completion of the original Common Market, nor of their related policies (on Fisheries, or the Commercial Policy, mainly).

It is likewise to be underlined here that the very characteristics and limitations of this Union's competence also have repercussions on the bilateral legal migratory relations between Spain and Morocco. Those limitations chiefly lie in the reservation that the EU Treaty makes to the Member States of the power to decide on the volumes and causes of admission, in their respective national territories, of third-country nationals. Due to its not being a "Europeanised issue", those volumes and causes of admissions are to be decided by each Member State. In particular, that is an issue that Spain itself decides in relation to legal immigration, and accordingly is able to settle through international commitments with Morocco insofar as this does not affect the competences that the Union does hold over control of external borders, visas, or residence permits.

Also unclear are the Union's competences in external relations in the field of immigration and asylum beyond the few and materially isolated express titles provided for by the EU Treaty. However, the refugee crisis in recent years has led the Union to take up action, although mainly in the field of soft law, by linking its own development cooperation policy funds to the outsourcing to third countries of the control of migratory flows into the Union itself (to the countries of origin, or to countries of transit), and by integrating the external dimension of the EU's Area of Freedom, Security and Justice, particularly immigration and asylum issues, into initiatives with a direct impact on Morocco, and consequently on Spain, such as partnerships, mobility associations and, recently, the European Neighbourhood Policy.

Morocco is possibly the greatest exponent of the EU's external action aiming at the "outsourcing" of the control of external borders and of the management of migratory flows departing from third-country nationals towards the Union. This has resulted in issues such as the granting of an Advanced Status to Morocco, within the framework of the European Neighbourhood Policy, as well as the release of European financial resources to support border controls where there are migratory inflows to the Union (through Spain, by sea or by land, at the Spanish cities of Ceuta and Melilla at the border with Morocco). Besides the intensification of Spanish–Moroccan bilateral relations on immigration and asylum, the EU's own policies on these issues, in their concrete application to the land and sea divide between Spain and Morocco, bring with them new problems of respect for fundamental rights, which even "migrate" from the external borders of the Union to the external borders of the third countries themselves in neighbourly relations with the EU and, in particular, to Morocco's borders.

This intensification of the bilateral migratory legal relationship between Spain and Morocco within the framework of EU policies has brought with it the problem of pushbacks at the border dividing the two countries, which have resulted, as has already been seen, in the provisional condemnation of Spain by the European Court of Human Rights, and its further acquittal by the same Court's Grand Chamber. The aforementioned Court does not possess direct jurisdiction over Morocco, but it can have indirect jurisdiction, precisely through Spain, since the conditions in which immigrants are found in Morocco after being returned by the Spanish authorities at the border is a parameter of the legality of the latter's actions in the eyes of the ECtHR when applying the ECHR, and the same could be true for the Court of Justice of the European Union in application of the Charter, and even of the rights declared by the ECHR as general principles underlying the legal system of the EU.

Finally, it can be seen from the situation described in this Chapter that Spain, as a member State of the EU, has supported Morocco "from within" the former, basically because of (and for) the Moroccan change of role over the last few years in the reduction of effective arrivals of third-country nationals to Spanish soil (and, consequently, to that of the EU), as well as the active patrolling of its land and sea borders with Spain, by the Moroccan side. Not only have European Neighbourhood and assimilated EU policies been a "currency of exchange" that has also determined a "change of tone" in the Spanish–Moroccan bilateral legal relationship in the field of migration and asylum, but also in the general bilateral relationship between both countries, since in recent years Morocco has "turned a deaf ear", without renouncing, however, to one of its main international differences with Spain, the sovereignty of Ceuta and Melilla, or to the question of the Sahara, in favour precisely of migratory bilateral cooperation, with the decisive conditioning factor of the EU's neighbourhood, immigration and asylum policies.

Not only Morocco has benefited from these policies, in the specific field of financing the means and operations for border control and migratory flows, and more generally from the intensification of Morocco's trade relations with the EU (Advanced Statute, Fisheries Agreement). Spain has found that Morocco's active role has reduced the arrivals of third-country nationals from that country, as regards the specific field of migration and asylum. And also, Spain has found itself with a more intense and fluid overall bilateral relationship with its neighbouring country, although that has happened with immigration and refuge issues as bargaining chips.

PART THREE
NEW STRATEGIES AND CHALLENGES

The Integrated EU Hotspot Administration and the Question of the EU's Liability

Catharina Ziebritzki[*]

I. EU hotspots and the question of responsibility

EU hotspots are asylum processing centres at the EU external borders, consisting of a camp and an administrative complex, as well as, in some instances, a pre-removal detention facility.[1] Since March 2016, the EU hotspots in Greece, located on five Aegean islands, serve as centres for the implementation of the return policy under the EU–Turkey Statement.[2] At the beginning of 2020, more than 40,000 persons are staying in those camps, the total capacity of which amounts to about 7,500 persons.[3] As

---

* PhD candidate and research fellow at the Max Planck Institute for Comparative Public Law and International Law in Heidelberg. The author wishes to thank Anna Lübbe and the anonymous reviewers for their criticism and suggestions.

1 The approach of this chapter has been set out in *Ziebritzki*, Refugee camps at EU external borders, the question of the Union's responsibility, and the potential of EU public liability law, Verfassungsblog (5 February 2020). Part II.1 of this chapter partly relies on *Ziebritzki/Nestler*, 'Hotspots' an der EU-Außengrenze. Eine rechtliche Bestandsaufnahme, MPIL Research Paper Series (SSRN) No. 2017-17 (2017). As this chapter has been finalised in January 2020, it does not take into account any questions related to the outbreak of the Coronavirus pandemic. However, the controversial measures which were taken in response to the pandemic, and the ensuring aggravation of the reception conditions in the EU hotspots make it even more pressing to find an answer to the question of who is responsible for fundamental rights violations in those centres.

2 European Council, Press Release of 23 April 2015, available at: https://www.consilium.europa.eu/en/press/press-releases/2015/04/23/special-euco-statement/ [hereinafter: *EU–Turkey Statement*; all links last accessed on 20 February 2020]. This article focuses on the EU hotspot approach as implemented in Greece, i.e. in the centres located on Lesbos, Chios, Samos, Leros and Kos. The implementation of the hotspot approach in Italy differs considerably. The reason for the focus on Greece is that the implementation of the EU–Turkey Statement raises particular legal questions which are relevant to the Common European Asylum System more generally.

3 UNHCR, Factsheet Greece (January 2020), available at: https://data2.unhcr.org/en/documents/details/74134. Severe overcrowding has been a continuous issue since the establishment of the EU hotspots in 2015, see: European Union Agency for Fundamental Rights, Update of the 2016 Opinion of the FRA on fundamental

noted by the EU Agency for Fundamental Rights (FRA), processing asylum claims in facilities at borders, particularly when these centres are located in relatively remote locations, creates fundamental rights challenges that appear almost unsurmountable.[4] In other words, the EU hotspot approach inherently leads to a risk of fundamental rights violations. More specifically, FRA finds risks with regard to, *inter alia*, Art. 1, 4, 5 para. 3, 6, 7, 18 and 19, 20 and 21, 24, 25 and 26, 41 and 47 of the Charter of Fundamental Rights of the European Union (ChFR).[5] Two aspects deserve particular attention: The dire living conditions, arguably amounting to a violation of the prohibition of degrading or inhuman treatment, and the cases of deportation to Turkey, arguably amounting to a violation of the non-refoulement principle. The former concerns a considerable number of persons, and the latter is of structural relevance to the function of EU hotspots.[6]

Against this background, it seems quite obvious to ask: Who is responsible for fundamental rights violations occurring in EU hotspots? While accountability mechanisms in a broader sense can be understood as allocating responsibility,[7] this chapter focuses on judicial accountability. Hence, it more specifically asks the question: Who can be held responsible before

---

rights in the "hotspots" set up in Greece and Italy, FRA Opinion – 3/2019, February 2019 [hereinafter: *FRA Opinion 2019*], 25 ff.

4 FRA Opinion 2019 (fn. 3), 7 ff. On 6 November 2019, the head of FRA has described the EU hotspot approach as implemented in Greece as "the single most worrying fundamental rights issue that we are confronting anywhere in the European Union", see: https://euobserver.com/migration/146541.

5 FRA Opinion 2019 (fn. 3), 7 ff., 21: "without comprehensively looking at all fundamental rights risks arising from the operation of the hotspots".

6 See II.3.

7 On accountability see in particular: *Bovens/Schillemans/Goodin*, Public Accountability, in: Bovens et al. (eds.), The Oxford Handbook of Public Accountability, Oxford 2014, 1, 9; *Curtin*, Executive Power of the European Union. Law, Practices, and the Living Constitution, Oxford 2009, 246 ff. For an assessment of a complaint to the European Ombudsman as accountability mechanism in the context of EU hotspots see: *Tsourdi*, Holding the European Asylum Support Office Accountable for its role in Asylum Decision-Making: Mission Impossible?, German Law Journal 21 (2020), 506. From the perspective of accountability, the chapter is concerned with "judicial accountability", cf. *Carrera et al.*, The Peculiar Nature of EU Home Affairs Agencies in Migration Control: Beyond Accountability versus Autonomy?, European Journal of Migration and Law 15 (2013), 337, 339: "here accountability becomes an absolute requirement [...] precisely to have access to effective remedies and claim rights envisaged in the EU Charter of Fundamental Rights."

a Court for fundamental rights violations occurring in EU hotspots, and in which procedure?[8]

Finding an answer to this question is crucial for three reasons. First, it contributes to *addressing the systemic deficiencies* in the EU hotspot administration.[9] The informality and flexibility of the regulatory framework combined with the sheer number of actors operating in those centres leads to responsibility-shifting between the European Commission, the host Member State and local authorities.[10] Hence, defining who is responsible contributes to enforcing EU law. Second, finding an answer to the question of who is responsible contributes to the understanding of the *Common European Asylum System*. EU hotspots have become quite a permanent component of that system and provide the paradigm example for increased vertical administrative cooperation.[11] Third, clarifying who is responsible contributes to the understanding of the *integrated European administration* more generally.[12] The challenge of determining the responsible actor is not specific to the administration of the Common European Asylum System, but rather arises wherever the Union and its Member States, or the Member States amongst themselves, cooperate on the administrative level.[13]

And yet, the question of who is responsible for fundamental rights violations occurring in EU hotspots has so far not been clarified. This seems

---

8 Given the limits in terms of space, the chapter cannot fully answer the question, but sets the ground for further doctrinal analysis, see III.4.

9 See II.3.

10 See *Carrera et al.*, European Journal of Migration and Law 15 (2013) (fn. 7), 337, 353 ff.; *Ziebritzki/Nestler*, MPIL Research Paper Series (fn. 1), 8 ff. with further references.

11 See II.1. and II.2.

12 The administrative cooperation between national authorities and EU bodies is referred to here as *integrated European administration*, or short: *European administration*. See *Schmidt-Aßmann*, Einleitung: Der Europäische Verwaltungsverbund und die Rolle des Europäischen Verwaltungsrechts, in: Schmidt-Aßmann/Schöndorf-Haubold (eds.), Der Europäische Verwaltungsverbund, Tübingen 2005, 1, 2; *Hofmann/Türk*, The Development of Integrated Administration in the EU and its Consequences, European Law Journal 13 (2007) 253, 254.

13 Cf. *Türk*, Judicial review of integrated administration in the EU, in: Hofmann/Türk (eds.), Legal Challenges in EU Administrative Law: Towards an Integrated Administration, Cheltenham 2009, 218; *Della Cananea*, The European Union's Mixed Administrative Proceedings, Law and Contemporary Problems 68 (2004), 187, 198 ff., 216 formulates the requirement of "better understanding the way in which public authorities act within the European legal order"; *Eliantonio*, Judicial Review in an Integrated Administration: the Case of "Composite Procedures", Review of European Administrative Law 7 (2015), 65.

due to a lack of knowledge on how the EU hotspot administration actually works on the one hand, and a lack of doctrinal analysis of that particular administrative structure on the other hand.[14] This chapter seeks to address both.[15] With a view to the gaps of knowledge on the practical implementation of the administrative cooperation,[16] the chapter relies, in addition to the partly publicly available regulatory framework, on documents requested via the Transparency Regulation,[17] on interviews conducted with administrative staff of EU agencies,[18] on the author's own experience,[19] as well as on work on the administrative involvement of EASO in EU hotspots.[20] With a view to the doctrinal question, the study mainly relies on work concerning the right to an effective remedy in the context of an integrated European administration,[21] as well as concerning the potential of EU public liability law for holding the Union liable, in particular for

---

14 The lack of litigation is further explained by the insufficient legal aid capacity in the EU hotspots, FRA Opinion 2019 (fn. 3), 4.

15 While remaining cursory with regard to the doctrinal analysis, see III.4.

16 Cf. *Carrera et al.*, European Journal of Migration and Law 15 (2013) (fn. 7), 353 ff. noting that "there is often a simple lack of information".

17 For the purpose of this chapter, a request for access to documents under Regulation (EC) No. 1049/2001 of May 2001 regarding public access to European Parliament, Council and Commission documents [hereinafter: *Transparency Regulation*] has been submitted to Frontex, EASO and the European Commission. The request to Frontex has been successful only insofar as access has been granted to the documents concerning the European Regional Task Force. Access to the relevant Operational Plans including the Handbooks and the Annexes was denied by Frontex with reference to Art. 4 para. 1 (a) first indent Transparency Regulation. EASO has continuously informed that more time is required to answer the request. The European Commission has not replied to the request. All relevant documents are on file with the author.

18 For the purpose of this study, an interview, focusing on the administrative cooperation in the EU hotspots, has been conducted with a senior staff member of EASO working in Greece on 13 December 2019 [hereinafter: *EASO staff interview*]. The transcript is on file with the author.

19 The author worked as legal advisor and coordinator for the NGO Equal Rights Beyond Borders during 2018, providing legal services to asylum seekers staying in the EU hotspots in Chios. She is co-founder and currently board member of that NGO.

20 *Tsourdi*, Bottom-Up Salvation? From Practical Cooperation Towards Joint Implementation Through the European Asylum Support Office, European Papers 1 (2017), 997 and *Tsourdi*, German Law Journal 21 (2020) (fn. 7), 506.

21 In particular: *Türk*, in: Hofmann/Türk (eds.) (fn. 13), 218; *Hofmann*, Rechtsschutz und Haftung im Europäischen Verwaltungsverbund, in: Schmidt-Aßmann/Schöndorf-Haubold (eds.), Der Europäische Verwaltungsverbund. Formen und Verfahren der Verwaltungszusammenarbeit in der EU, Tübingen 2005, 353;

the conduct of the European Commission, of Frontex,[22] or of the European Asylum Support Office (EASO),[23] and concerning liability of the Union for non-formally binding administrative conduct.[24]

To be sure, a comprehensive answer to the question of who is responsible would include analysing the responsibility of the host Member State, of the participating Member States and of the Union.[25] This chapter however focuses on the question of the *Union*'s responsibility. The reason lies in the structure of the EU hotspot administration itself: The distinctive characteristic of EU hotspots, in comparison to other asylum processing centres at EU external borders,[26] is the close administrative cooperation between Union and host Member State. As the EU hotspot approach shifts formal decision-making power to the host Member State,[27] so far, only the host Member State has been considered responsible for human rights vio-

---

Schmidt-Aßmann, Kohärenz und Konsistenz des Verwaltungsrechtsschutzes. Herausforderungen angesichts vernetzter Verwaltungen und Rechtsordnungen, Tübingen 2015.

22 In particular: *Fink*, Frontex and Human Rights. Responsibility in 'Multi-Actor Situations' under the ECHR and EU Public Liability Law, Oxford 2018; *Fink*, EU liability for contributions to Member States' breaches of EU law, Common Market Law Review 56 (2019), 1227, stating at 1231 that "the *potential of the action for damages* in *addressing the challenges* of accountability in the *EU's integrated administration* has received very limited attention" (emphasis added); *Fink*, The Action for Damages as a Fundamental Rights Remedy: Holding Frontex Liable, German Law Journal 21 (2020), 532.

23 *Carrera et al.*, European Journal of Migration and Law 15 (2013) (fn. 7), 345 already note the possibility of liability based on EASO conduct, however without further assessment. Also *Fink*, Common Market Law Review 56 (2019) (fn. 22), 1228 notes that liability could arise based on the administrative conduct of EASO.

24 In particular: *Rademacher*, Realakte im Rechtsschutzsystem der Europäischen Union, Tübingen 2014; *Rademacher*, Factual Administrative Conduct and Judicial Review in EU Law, European Review of Public Law 30 (2018), 399; *Xanthoulis*, Administrative factual conduct: Legal effects and judicial control in EU law, Review of European Administrative Law 12 (2019), 39.

25 The question whether the host Member State or the participating Member States could be considered responsible under EU public liability law – either in addition or instead of the Union – hence falls outside the scope of this study.

26 Such as e.g. the asylum processing centres at the Eastern EU external border. See on those: *Voynov/Franková et al.*, Pushed Back at the Door: Denial of Access to Asylum in Eastern EU Member States, Report, Hungarian Helsinki Committee, 2017.

27 See II.1. and II.2.

lations occurring in EU hotspots, namely under the ECHR.[28] The considerable involvement of EU agencies and the European Commission in the EU hotspot administration however suggests examining whether the Union bears judicial responsibility. Further, a comprehensive analysis would include an assessment of the responsibility of the Union as such, as well as of its agencies under international law[29] and under EU law.[30] As this chapter is concerned with finding a means for enforcing the rule of EU law, it is however limited to assessing the Union's responsibility under EU law.

Hence, the chapter firstly sets out the integrated EU hotspot administration (II). Secondly, it explains why EU public liability law[31] has a particular potential for holding the Union or its agencies liable (III). The chapter thus sets the ground for further doctrinal analysis.

---

28 See II.3. Regardless of whether a violation of the ECHR is found in the individual case, the case law unequivocally considers *Greece*, as the host Member State, responsible under the ECHR.

29 The responsibility of the Union for human rights violations in EU hotspots under international law has been analysed by *Casolari*, The EU's Hotspot Approach to Managing the Migration Crisis: A Blind Spot for International Responsibility?, in: The Italian Yearbook of International Law Vol. XXV, Leiden 2015, 109. Cf. *Hoffmeister*, Litigating Against the European Union and Its Member States – Who Responds under the ILC's Draft Articles on International Responsibility of International Organizations?, European Journal of International Law 21 (2010), 723. The responsibility of Frontex under international law has been analysed by *Mungianu*, Frontex and Non-Refoulement, Cambridge 2016. Cf. *Orator*, Völkerrechtspersönlichkeit von EU-Agenturen?, Zeitschrift für öffentliches Recht 72 (2017), 271.

30 Cf. *Fink*, Frontex and Human Rights (fn. 22), who assesses the responsibility of the Member States seconding staff to Frontex teams under the ECHR as well as under EU public liability law. This chapter addresses the question in the context of EU hotspots. Fink explicitly *excludes* that particular case from her study, see fn. 122.

31 EU public liability law is understood here as encompassing the law on non-contractual liability of the Union (cf. Art. 340 para. 2 TFEU) on the one hand, and on non-contractual liability of the Member States (cf. CJEU, Joined Cases C-6/90 and C-9/90, ECLI:EU:C:1991:428, Frankovich, judgement of 19 Nov 1991 and following case law) on the other hand. For the purpose of this chapter, only the former is of relevance. See for that definition *Aalto*, Public Liability in EU Law. Brasserie, Bergaderm and Beyond, Oxford 2011, 12 ff., 197 ff., passim.

II. The integrated EU hotspot administration

The EU hotspot approach, introduced as an emergency crisis response, has become quite a permanent component of the Common European Asylum System (II.1.). The administration of those centres provides the paradigm example of vertical cooperation in the integrated European asylum administration, with Union actors and national authorities closely cooperating on several levels (II.2.). The EU hotspot administration can be characterised as systemically deficient due to the dire reception conditions as well as due to the procedure, designed in accordance with the aim of deportation to Turkey (II.3.).

1. The regulatory framework

Even though the EU hotspot approach has been perpetuated to a certain extent, its regulatory framework is still characterised by informality and complexity (1.a). While the function of the EU hotspots is conceived as flexible in the sense that it can be adapted to different political aims (1.b), the stable characteristic of the EU hotspot approach is the mode of operation of those centres, namely the close administrative cooperation between Union actors and national authorities (1.c).

a) Perpetuation of a crisis mechanism – the informal and complex legal nature

Almost four years after the so-called refugee crisis, it has become a commonplace that the legal construction of the Common European Asylum System remains to be improved.[32] Nevertheless, the envisaged fundamental reform is still uncertain. While struggling with regard to legislative reforms, the Union has proven to be much more efficient with regard to so-called immediate action in the aftermath of the crisis.[33] The latter is often based on the technique of effectively bringing about change in the EU le-

---

32 See only *Costello/Mouzourakis*, The Common European Asylum System. Where did it all go wrong?, in: Fletcher/Herlin-Karnell/Matera (eds.), The European Union as an Area of Freedom, Security and Justice, London 2017, 263; *Thym*, The "Refugee Crisis" as a Challenge of Legal Design and Institutional Legitimacy, Common Market Law Review 53 (2016), 1545.

33 Cf. European Commission, Communication from the Commission to the European Parliament, the Council, the European Economic and Social Committee

gal system without formally amending EU legislation, but simply by adopting certain policies. This technique can be described as "*ad hoc* soft regulation". It generally leads to a high degree of informality, entailing a complex legal nature, and thus a lack of legal certainty.[34] Several of those crisis mechanisms, have, somehow silently, become quite permanent components of the Common European Asylum System.[35]

The EU hotspot approach provides an illustrative example of such a perpetuated crisis policy.[36] The approach was introduced in 2015 by the European Commission as part of the European Agenda on Migration.[37] It was conceived as a cornerstone of the EU's reaction to the crisis of the Com-

and the Committee of the Regions. A European Agenda on Migration, 13 May 2015, COM (2015) 240 final [hereinafter: *EAM*]. The EAM differentiates between immediate action and structural reform – while the former has mainly been implemented, the latter has mainly not been implemented so far. Four years after the deficiencies of the legal construction of the Common European Asylum System became visible, neither the Dublin III Regulation nor any other secondary law instrument of the Common European Asylum System has been reformed. The only exception is the Frontex Regulation.

34 Cf. *Kleine*, Informal Governance in the European Union, Journal of European Public Policy 21 (2014), 203.

35 Cf. for the example of resettlement: *Ziebritzki*, The objective of resettlement in an EU constitutional perspective, in: Leboeuf/Foblets (eds.), Humanitarian Admission to Europe. The Law Between Promises and Constraints, Baden-Baden/Oxford 2020, 285 ff.

36 Cf. European Court of Auditors, Audit Preview: EU Migration management: Hotspots and beyond (January 2019), available at: https://www.eca.europa.eu/en/Pages/DocItem.aspx?did=49078 [hereinafter referred to as *ECA Report Preview*], at 8 noting that "the hotspot approach […] has evolved into a *long-term instrument* and the key element in the support to Greece and Italy" (emphasis added).

37 European Commission, EAM (fn. 33), 6 ff. As the Council requested a more detailed presentation of the EU hotspot approach, the Commission, together with the relevant EU agencies as well as Italy and Greece, developed the non-public "Explanatory Note on the 'Hotspot' Approach", available at: http://www.statewatch.org/news/2015/jul/eu-com-hotsposts.pdf [hereinafter referred to as: *COM, EU Hotspot Explanatory Note*]. A few months later, the Commission published a shortened version of the "Explanatory note" as Annex to the Communication from the Commission to the European Parliament, the European Council and the Council. Managing the refugee crisis: immediate operational, budgetary and legal measures under the European Agenda on Migration, 29 September 2015, COM (2015) 490 final, Annex 2, available at: https://ec.europa.eu/transparency/regdoc/rep/1/2015/EN/1-2015-490-EN-F2-1-ANNEX-1.PDF.

mon European Asylum System.[38] Initially, the approach was explicitly understood as a temporally limited mechanism to be implemented only during an emergency situation.[39] However, the EU hotspots have by now been operating for almost four years. Neither EU nor national actors have expressed their intention to discontinue the implementation of the approach. Nevertheless, the EU hotspots are still framed as a crisis mechanism. The regulatory framework of EU hotspots is hence still characterised by informality and complexity.

Namely, the pertinent framework still consists in a *fragmented patchwork of EU and national soft law and legislation.*[40] The EU hotspot approach itself can be qualified as EU soft law.[41] The approach was introduced in a non-formally binding form, but has never been legally irrelevant: Quite to the contrary, it reshaped the application of existing law, and, where this was not sufficient, required and shaped new law.[42] The implementation of the EU hotspot approach confirms that the technique of *ad hoc* soft regulation leads to a lack of legal certainty.[43] The Frontex Regulation consolidates the EU hotspot approach, however, without limiting its temporal scope of application. Notably, the Frontex Regulation defines that "a 'hotspot area' means an area in which the host Member State, the Commission, relevant Union agencies and participating Member States cooperate, with the aim of managing an existing or potential disproportionate migratory challenge characterised by a significant increase in the number of migrants arriving

38 Cf. FRA Opinion 2019 (fn. 3) at 15 noting that "the EU hotspot approach is a building block of the EU response to significant numbers of refugees and migrants arriving at external borders".

39 Cf. European Commission, EU Hotspot Explanatory Note (fn. 37) 3: "In principle, an external border section should be considered to be a 'Hotspot' for *the limited period of time* during which the *emergency or crisis* situation subsists and during which the support of the 'Hotspot' approach is necessary." (emphasis added).

40 *Tsourdi*, German Law Journal 21 (2020) (fn. 7), 516 ff. however understands the role of EASO in asylum decision-making in Greece as being "currently regulated exclusively by national administrative law".

41 EU soft law is understood here as "rules [...] which, in principle, have no legally binding force but which nevertheless may have practical effects", following the definition of *Snyder*, The Effectiveness of European Community Law: Institutions, Processes, Tools and Techniques, The Modern Law Review 56 (1993), 19, 32. Cf. *Schwarze*, Soft Law im Recht der Europäischen Union, Europarecht 46 (2011), 3, 6 ff.; *Terpan*, Soft Law in the European Union – The Changing Nature of EU law 21 (2015) European Law Journal 68, 70.

42 *Casolari*, in: The Italian Yearbook of International Law Vol. XXV (fn. 29), 117; *Ziebritzki/Nestler*, MPIL Research Paper Series (fn. 1), 7.

43 *Ziebritzki/Nestler*, MPIL Research Paper Series (fn. 1), 53.

at the external borders."[44] The regulatory framework is further defined by national law. Initially, the EU hotspots were set up in a legal vacuum.[45] In April 2016 however, the Greek asylum system was reformed fundamentally,[46] transposing the Asylum Procedures Directive[47] and the Reception Conditions Directive[48] in a manner tailor-made to the implementation of the EU hotspot approach.[49] The October 2019 reform of the Greek asylum law provides for further restrictive measures with regard to EU hotspots, and consolidates the legal basis for the administrative support by EASO.[50] Furthermore, the EU asylum acquis is of relevance to the regulatory frame-

44 Art. 2 para. 23 Regulation (EU) 2019/1896 of the European Parliament and of the Council of 13 November 2019 on the European Border and Coast Guard and repealing Regulations (EU) No. 1052/2013 and (EU) 2016/1624 [hereinafter: *Frontex Regulation*]. The legal definition of a "hotspot" was introduced with Regulation (EU) 2016/1624, which confirms the function of the EU hotspot approach as law-shaping.

45 *Konstantinou/Georgopoulou/Drakopoulou*, AIDA Country Report: Greece, 2016, Update March 2019, available at: https://www.asylumineurope.org/reports/country/greece, 23.

46 Law No. 4375 of 2016 on the organisation and operation of the Asylum Service, the Appeals Authority, the Reception and Identification Service, the establishment of the General Secretariat for Reception, the transposition into Greek legislation of the provisions of Directive 2013/32/EC, 3 April 2016 [hereinafter: *Greek Asylum Law 4375/2016*], unofficial English translation available at: https://www.refworld.org/docid/573ad4cb4.html. See on the several reforms with a view to the administrative involvement of EASO: *Tsourdi*, German Law Journal 21 (2020) (fn. 7), 516 ff., 520.

47 Directive 2013/32/EU of the European Parliament and of the Council of 26 June 2013 on common procedures for granting and withdrawing international protection [hereinafter: *Asylum Procedures Directive*].

48 Directive 2013/33/EU of the European Parliament and of the Council of 26 June 2013 laying down standards for the reception of applicants for international protection [hereinafter: *Reception Conditions Directive*].

49 EU hotspots are since then defined as "Reception and Identification Centres" (RIC), and the procedure is conducted in the form of a "fast-track border procedure", cf. Art. 19, 60 para. 4 Greek Asylum Law 4375/2016.

50 Law 4346/2019, "The International Protection Act" of 1 November 2019 [hereinafter: *Greek Reform IP Act*], available at: https://www.hellenicparliament.gr/UserFiles/bcc26661-143b-4f2d-8916-0e0e66ba4c50/dietnis-prostasia-pap-aposp.pdf. See on the reform: *Mouzourakis* (ECRE) and Refugee Support Aegean (RSA), All but last resort: The last reform of detention of asylum seekers in Greece, eumigrationlawblog (18 November 2019); *Tsourdi*, German Law Journal 21 (2020) (fn. 7), 516 ff., 520.

work of EU hotpots.[51] The legal basis for the administrative support by the EU agencies is provided for in the respective founding Regulations, in particular the Frontex Regulation and the EASO Regulation.[52] The Frontex Regulation foresees a particular form of administrative support designed for the EU hotspot administration.[53] Finally, EU soft law regulates the procedure and the administrative cooperation in the EU hotspots in more detail. The EU hotspot procedure is laid down in the regularly updated "Standard Operating Procedures" (SOP–Hotspots–GR).[54] The details of the cooperation between EU agencies and national authorities of the host Member State Greece are laid down in the relevant Operating Plans, namely, the Frontex Operating Plan relevant to the Joint Operation "Poseidon" (Frontex–OP–Poseidon)[55] and the "EASO Operating Plan to Greece" (EASO–OP).[56] Concerning the coordination and monitoring level, the cooperation is further specified in the "Terms of cooperation for European Union Regional Task Forces" (ToC–EURTF) and the "Rules of procedure of the

---

51 Concerning the procedure, in addition to the mentioned transposed Directives, notably Regulation (EU) No. 604/2013 of the European Parliament and of the Council of 26 June 2013 establishing the criteria and mechanisms for determining the Member State responsible for examining an application for international protection lodged in one of the Member States by a third-country national or a stateless person [hereinafter: *Dublin III Regulation*].

52 Regulation (EU) No. 439/2010 of the European Parliament and of the Council of 19 May 2010 establishing a European Asylum Support Office [hereinafter: *EASO Regulation*].

53 Namely, the Migration Management Support Teams (MMST), cf. Art. 2 para. 19, Art. 40 Frontex Regulation, see II.2.b).

54 Standard Operating Procedures for the implementation of the Border asylum procedures in the context of the EU Turkey Statement 18/03/2016, version of June 2019 available at: https://fragdenstaat.de/anfrage/standard-operating-procedures-for-the-implementation-of-the-border-asylum-procedures/425864/anhang/SOPS_border_en_jointEASO_August16_190624redacted.pdf.

55 Cf. Frontex, Frontex Evaluation Report, JO Poseidon 2018, Operational Response Division, Field Department Unit, Warsaw 11/06/2019, available at: https://frontex.europa.eu/about-frontex/key-documents/?category=frontex-evaluation-reports [hereinafter: *Frontex Report JO Poseidon 2018*]. The relevant Frontex Operational Plans are not available to the author, see fn. 17.

56 EASO, 2020 Operational & Technical Assistance Plan, agreed by EASO and Greece, Valleta Harbour and Athens, 20 December 2019, applicable from 1 January to 31 December 2020; 2019 Operating Plan, agreed by EASO and Greece, Valletta Harbour and Athens, 19 December 2018 [hereinafter: EASO OP 2019], both available at: https://easo.europa.eu/archive-of-operations. Hereinafter, reference is made to the latter.

European Union Regional Task Force for migration management support to Greece" (RoP–EURTF–GR).[57]

b) From relocation to return – the flexible function and the repercussions on the procedure

The regulatory framework explicitly conceives the function of EU hotspots as flexible.[58] The Frontex Regulation formulates the objective of the administrative cooperation, namely "the management of a migratory challenge", so broadly that it can be adapted to almost any policy aim.[59] As the hotspot procedure is not defined in EU legislation, the design of the procedure follows from the function of the centres and is then laid down in EU soft law.

Initially, when established in 2015, EU hotspots were conceived as platforms for the implementation of the Relocation Program.[60] With the entry into force of the EU–Turkey Statement in March 2016, however, the function of the EU hotspots in Greece was changed fundamentally.[61] As the EU–Turkey Statement serves the objective to "end irregular migration from Turkey to the EU", the return policy aims at the swift deportation of those applicants who entered the EU irregularly via the Greek Aegean islands.[62] Accordingly, the EU hotspots have been transformed into return centres which entailed a complete overhaul of the EU hotspot procedure.[63] The design of the procedure mainly relies on the application of so-called protection elsewhere clauses. Those clauses allow for the rejection of a

57 Cf. Terms of cooperation for European Union Regional Task Forces, Ref. Ares (2018) 1622597 – 23/03/2018; Rules of procedure of the European Union Regional Task Force for migration management support to Greece as endorsed on 4 October 2018. Neither document is publicly available, both are on file with the author, see fn. 17.

58 EASO–OP 2019, 5.

59 Art. 2 para. 23 Frontex Regulation.

60 The Relocation Programme was established by Council Decision (EU) 2015/1523 of 14 September 2015 and Council Decision (EU) 2015/1601 of 22 September 2015 resp. establishing provisional measures in the area of international protection for the benefit of Italy and of Greece. The Programme expired in September 2017.

61 Cf. ECA Report Preview, p. 6 referring to approximately 34,000 relocations as of 31 October 2018.

62 EU–Turkey Statement (fn. 2).

63 *Ziebritzki/Nestler*, MPIL Research Paper Series (fn. 1), 7.

claim as inadmissible if a third country, such as Turkey, can be considered as a "safe third country" or a "first country of asylum" for the concerned applicant.[64] The details of the administrative process depend on the country of origin of the concerned applicant.[65] In addition their freedom of movement is restricted to the respective island.[66]

c) *Administrative cooperation – the mode of administration as distinctive characteristic*

The *distinctive characteristic* of an EU hotspot is the mode of its administration. Namely, an EU hotspot is "an area in which the host Member State, the Commission, relevant Union agencies and participating Member States *cooperate*".[67] Accordingly, the few provisions in EU secondary law, national law, and EU soft law, which concern EU hotspots, are mainly concerned with regulating the administrative cooperation.[68] It should be kept

---

64 The "safe third country" resp. the "first country of asylum concept" is provided for in Art. 38 resp. 35 Asylum Procedures Directive, and transposed into Art. 55 resp. 56 Greek Asylum Law 4375/2016. The following focuses on the practically more relevant safe third country concept.

65 Those different administrative processes are laid down in the SOP–Hotspots–GR. For applicants originating from Syria or so-called high recognition rate countries, a preliminary inadmissibility procedure ensures the systematic application of the protection elsewhere clauses. For applicants originating from so-called low recognition rate countries, the substance of the claim is examined. For applicants originating from so-called high recognition rate countries, a so-called merged procedure is foreseen, including both the assessment of the admissibility and of the eligibility of the claim.

66 Art. 14 Greek Asylum Law 4375/2016. Even though this so-called geographical restriction allows the concerned persons to move around on the respective island, it *de facto* amounts to a residence obligation with regard to the respective EU hotspot refugee camp, cf. Equal Rights Beyond Borders, Report 12/19, The Lived Reality of Deterrence Measures: Inhumane Camps at Europe's External Border, available at: https://www.equal-rights.org/post/vial-report [hereinafter: *Equal Rights, Vial Report*], 22 ff.

67 Art. 2 para. 23 Frontex Regulation (emphasis added).

68 Accordingly, the few EU secondary law provisions consolidating the EU hotspot approach establish rules for the administrative cooperation between Union and national actors, Art. 2 para. 23, Art. 40, passim Frontex Regulation. The administrative cooperation is further regulated by EU soft law and national law. The Greek asylum law 4375/2016 explicitly provides that the Asylum Service shall "cooperate" with EASO, that EASO may be entrusted with handling specific procedures, and that EU agencies may provide assistance with regard to reception and

in mind that in practice, the EU hotspot administration is characterised by an even greater multitude of actors: Several EU agencies, including not only EASO and Frontex, but also Europol and Eurojust, and numerous national authorities operate alongside international organisations and private actors.[69] However, given the definition of the EU hotspot approach and due to the scope of this chapter, the following is limited to the cooperation between Union and national actors, more specifically to the most relevant of those, namely: the European Commission, and the EU agencies Frontex and EASO on the Union level, and the Greek First Reception and Identification Service, the Hellenic Police and the Greek Asylum Service on the level of the host Member State.

2. *Vertical administrative cooperation*

To begin with, it is useful to have a short look at the structure of the integrated European asylum administration more generally (2.a). Against this background, the EU hotspot administration, namely administrative cooperation on the operational level (2.b) and on the coordination and monitoring level (2.c), can be set out.

a) *Integrated European asylum administration and the role of the Union*

The Common European Asylum System can be described as a regional protection system consisting of the largely harmonised European asylum law on the one hand and an increasingly integrated European asylum administration on the other hand.[70] The European asylum law[71] is, in principle, implemented by national authorities, which cooperate among each

---

identification procedures as well as, in particular, with the implementation of the border procedures, Art. 1 para. 2 (f), Art. 2 para. 7, Art. 11 para. 10, Art. 14 para. 6, Art. 39 para. 3 (b), and in particular: Art. 60 para. 4 (b) Law 4375/2016.

69 For an overview see FRA Opinion 2019 (fn. 3), 19; Equal Rights, Vial Report (fn. 66), 10 ff.

70 *Tsourdi*, German Law Journal 21 (2020) (fn. 7), 508 ff. speaks of the "gradual emergence of an 'integrated European administration' in the asylum area", and at 520 describes the current situation as "*de facto* administrative integration".

71 The notion "European asylum law" is understood here as encompassing the EU asylum acquis, the relevant international refugee law, and the largely harmonised national asylum law of the Member States.

other (horizontal administrative cooperation).[72] At the same time, EU agencies and the European Commission are increasingly involved in the implementation of the European asylum law (vertical administrative cooperation).[73] As national authorities and Union bodies are unified in their task to implement the EU asylum law, and to this end closely cooperate, it seems appropriate to refer to a composite or integrated *European asylum administration.*[74] While the Dublin system represents the paradigmatic example for advanced horizontal administrative cooperation, the EU hotspot approach represents the paradigmatic example, and to a certain extent the testing ground, for advanced vertical administrative cooperation.[75]

With a view to analysing the EU hotspot administration, it is useful to recall two aspects defining the role of the Union in the European asylum administration more generally. *First*, its role is characterised by a tension between limited administrative competences[76] and the increasing practical relevance of Union actors. The limited competences seem to be due to the traditional understanding that asylum derives from national sovereignty.[77] Even though the latter has been, at least partly, overcome with the estab-

72 Art. 291 para. 1 TFEU. See on horizontal administrative cooperation within the Common European Asylum System: *Bast*, Transnationale Verwaltung des europäischen Migrationsraums: Zur horizontalen Öffnung der EU-Mitgliedstaaten, Der Staat 46 (2007), 1; *Costello*, Administrative Governance and the Europeanisation of Asylum and Immigration Policy, in Hofmann/Türk (eds.), EU Administrative Governance, Cheltenham 2006, 287.

73 See on vertical administrative cooperation insofar as EASO is concerned: *Tsourdi*, German Law Journal 21 (2020) (fn. 7), 506.

74 See fn. 12, fn. 70.

75 Cf. *Tsourdi*, Hotspots and EU Agencies: Towards an integrated European administration?, eumigrationlawblog (26 January 2017). Frontex is understood here as part of the European asylum administration insofar as the agency is involved in the implementation of EU asylum law.

76 Cf. Art. 78 para. 2 TFEU. See in particular Art. 78 para. 2 (d) TFEU which does not confer upon the Union the administrative competence to issue individual asylum decisions: *Hailbronner/Thym*, Legal Framework for EU Asylum Policy, in: Hailbronner/Thym (eds.), EU Immigration and Asylum Law. A Commentary, 2nd edition, Munich 2016, 1023, para. 27.

77 *Morgenstern*, The Right of Asylum, British Yearbook of International Law 26 (1949), 327; *Goodwin-Gil/McAdam*, The Refugee in International Law, 3rd edition, Oxford 2007, 357: "From the point of view of international law, therefore, the grant of protection to its territory derives from the State's sovereign competence, a statement of the obvious."; *Kirchhof*, Staatliche Souveränität als Bedingung des Asylrechts, in: Jochum/Fritzemeyer/Kau (eds.), Grenzüberschreitendes Recht – Crossing frontiers. Festschrift für Kay Hailbronner, Heidelberg 2013, 105.

lishment of the Common European Asylum System,[78] the repercussions of the traditional understanding are still visible in the limited administrative competences. Nevertheless, in particular in the aftermath of the crisis of the Common European Asylum System, Union actors have become increasingly important for the implementation of EU law: vertical administrative cooperation is indeed crucial for the functioning of the Common European Asylum System. Agencification remains the most important development in this regard.[79] A less noted development is the increasingly important role of the Commission for the European asylum administration. It is worth noting that the tension between limited competences and increased practical relevance seems to provide an explanation for the tendency of EU agencies to systematically overstep their competences until the relevant EU secondary law extends the agency's competences.[80] Finally, the practical relevance of Union actors for the functioning of the EU hotspot administration should be taken into account when considering the legal consequences of a potential action for damages against the Union.[81]

Second, the Union's role in the European asylum administration differs between its involvement in composite administrative procedures[82] on the one hand, and the enactment of EU soft law[83] and supervisory relation-

78 Cf. *Groenendijk*, Introduction: Migration and Law in Europe, in: Guild/Minderhoud (eds.), The First Decade of EU Migration and Asylum Law (2012) who at 10 explains the "surprisingly quick Europeanisation of migration law" with the "transfer of sovereignty"; *Guild*, The Europeanisation of Europe's Asylum Policy, International Journal of Refugee Law 18 (2006), 630; *Bast*, Ursprünge der Europäisierung des Migrationsrechts, in: Jochum et al. (eds.) (fn. 77), 3.

79 See on agencification in particular: *Chamon*, EU Agencies. Legal and Political Limits to the Transformation of the EU Administration, Oxford 2016; *Rijpma*, Hybrid Agencification in the Area of Freedom, Security and Justice and its inherent tension: The case of Frontex, in: *Busuioc/Groenleer/Trondal* (eds.), The Agency Phenomenon in the European Union: Emergence, Institutionalisation and Everyday Decision-Making, Manchester 2012, 84.

80 See II.2.b), in particular fn. 104, fn. 121. In the same vein, the national law is adapted *Tsourdi*, German Law Journal 21 (2020) (fn. 7) 516 ff., 520.

81 As the situation would practically be even more difficult without EU agencies, it is doubtful whether withdrawal of Union actors would constitute an effective remedy.

82 Composite administrative procedures are understood here in line with the definition in the ReNEUAl Draft Rules Art I-4(3) as an "administrative procedure where EU authorities and the authorities of a member state or different member states have distinct functions which are inter-dependent".

83 Note that insofar as EU agencies are concerned, the extensive soft law powers can be understood as circumventing the objections resulting from a strict interpretation of the Meroni doctrine, cf. *Chamon*, EU Agencies (fn. 79), 348 ff.

ships[84] on the other hand. When EU actors and national actors cooperate in *composite procedures,* usually, one actor is entrusted with taking the administrative decision ("decision-issuing actor"), whilst the other provides support ("supporting actor").[85] In the context of the European asylum administration, it is the Member State who bears responsibility for individual decision-making. This is precisely due to the limited administrative competences of the Union, which accordingly usually has the supporting role.[86] The support is usually provided by EU agencies. Administrative support is often referred to as "preparatory act"[87] and can either consist in the provision of a legal opinion on the interpretation of EU law ("interpretative support"), or in the provision of information ("informational support").[88] Even though preparatory support is the rule in the European integrated administration more generally, Frontex also provides support with regard to executing a national decision ("executive support").[89]

With a view to the determination of responsibility, it is important to note from the outset that the line between issuing decisions and support is sometimes not that easy to draw, in particular when the support is preparatory: This is well illustrated e.g. by EASO conducting interviews and drafting legal opinions, which are usually followed by the national administration.[90] Further, it is important to note from the outset that administrative support as such can violate the fundamental rights of individuals: This is well illustrated e.g. by Frontex using force towards individuals when exe-

---

84 See on supervisory obligations, however limited to those of the Commission: *Cassese*, European Administrative Proceedings, Law and Contemporary Problems 86 (2004), 21 ff.

85 Cf. *Fink*, Frontex and Human Rights (fn. 22), 255; *Rademacher*, Realakte (fn. 24), 274 ff. Similarly *Della Cananea*, Law and Contemporary Problems 68 (2004) (fn. 13), 199 ff.; *Eliantonio*, Review of European Administrative Law 7 (2015) (fn. 13), 72 ff.

86 Cf. *Fink*, Common Market Law Review 56 (2019) (fn. 22), 1230.

87 Cf. *Bastos*, Derivate Illegality in European Composite Administrative Procedures, Common Market Law Review 55 (2018) 101, passim. For the purpose of this chapter, the general term "administrative support" is preferred.

88 Cf. *Fink*, Frontex and Human Rights (fn. 22), 255; *Rademacher*, Realakte (fn.24), 274 ff.; *Shirvani*, Haftungsprobleme im Europäischen Verwaltungsverbund, Europarecht 46 (2011), 619. Both interpretative and informational support can either relate to an individual case or can be generalised – from this perspective, EU soft law appears as generalised interpretative support.

89 See e.g. Art. 48 Frontex Regulation on the competences of the agency in the area of return.

90 See II.2.b).

cuting a national deportation decision.[91] While the Union's administrative competences are limited concerning formal decision-making *vis-à-vis* the individual in the context of the Common European Asylum System, the Commission has general and quite broad competences in the realm of the enactment of EU soft law and supervisory tasks. Those broader competences are mainly due to the role of the Commission as guardian of the Treaties. With a view to the agencies however, the limited administrative competences of the Union become relevant again. It seems that this is the reason for the design of the supervisory obligations of EU agencies in a manner which could, at least for the purpose of this chapter, be described as similar to "a "voice or exit" mechanism".[92] The EU agency usually, on a first level, bears monitoring obligations i.e. obligations to work towards administrative cooperation in compliance with EU law.[93] However, as the agency does not have the competence to force the Member State to comply with EU law, it is sometimes, on a second level, obliged to withdraw from the administrative cooperation altogether: that option is well illustrated by the obligation of Frontex to withdraw from an operation if fundamental rights violations are of a serious nature or likely to persist.[94]

b) *Cooperation on the operational level in the EU hotspot administration – EASO and Frontex*

Against this background, the structure of the EU hotspot administration becomes clear. To begin with, the cooperation on the operational level mainly consists in *composite procedures*.[95]

In line with the above, the formal responsibility for the implementation of the EU hotspot approach on the operational level lies with the national authorities of the host Member State – both concerning decisions on asy-

91 Cf. Art. 2 Nr. 18, 19, 29, Art 39, 40, 52 in conjunction with Art. 82 para. 8 Frontex Regulation regulating the "use of force, including the carrying and use of service weapons, ammunition and equipment" by members of the respective Frontex support teams.

92 Cf. *Hirschmann*, Exit, Voice and Loyalty. Reponses to Decline in Firms, Organizations and States, Cambridge 1970. Hirschmann however means a different mechanism.

93 Cf. II.2.b).

94 Art. 46 para. 4 EASO Regulation.

95 Cf. fn. 82. *Tsourdi*, German Law Journal 21 (2020) (fn. 7), 509, 513 ff., defines the involvement of EASO as "joint implementation", relying on a different categorisation, but in substance referring to composite procedures as defined here.

lum claims and deportation orders, and concerning reception conditions.[96] EU agencies provide extensive preparatory respectively executive support to the host Member State in both regards.[97] Indeed, about half of the administrative staff operating in EU hotspots is provided by Frontex and EASO.[98]

EASO deploys *asylum support teams* which provide comprehensive preparatory support in the context of the asylum procedure as well as concerning reception conditions.[99] In addition, EASO seconds staff to the Greek Asylum Service.[100] The procedure-related cooperation includes processing applications for international protection.[101] EASO team members conduct vulnerability assessments, as well as admissibility and eligibility interviews, and draft according legal opinions recommending the rejection

---

96 The Greek Asylum Service, subordinate to the Ministry of Migration, is responsible for the asylum procedures Art. 1 Greek asylum law 4375/2016. The Greek First Reception and Identification Service, an authority subordinate to the Hellenic Ministry of Migration Policy, bears the overall responsibility for the EU hotspot facilities, Art. 8 para. 2 Greek asylum law 4375/2016. However, RIS does not provide most of the services itself, but relies on several other actors, see: Equal Rights, Vial Report (fn. 66).

97 Cf. FRA Opinion 2019 (fn. 3), 19: EU agencies are "significantly involved in the day-to-day administration".

98 In 2019, the procedure-related support to the EU hotspots *inter alia* consisted in the deployment of about 100 case workers, 10 flow managers, 30 seconded administrative staff, and about 90 interpreters, see EASO-OP 2019, 12 ff. The reception-related support to the EU hotspots *inter alia* consists in the deployment of about 30 seconded reception assistants, 20 experts for specific purposes, and 10 interpreters, see EASO-OP 2019, 12 ff, 18 ff.

99 EASO-OP 2019, 6; Art. 13 EASO Regulation. It should be noted that the legal basis, namely Art. 13 EASO Regulation, allows for the deployment of such teams only for "a limited time", while EASO teams provide extensive operational support to Greece since 2011 continuously. See II.1.a).

100 EASO-OP 2019, 13 ff. The legal basis of the secondment is not entirely clear, as Art. 13 EASO Regulation seems to conclusively regulate the support to Member States under particular pressure, and is limited to the deployment of asylum support teams. In practice, the seconded staff is "embedded" into the Greek asylum service in the sense that EASO only defines certain "deliverables" which are then implemented under the instruction of the national authority, cf. EASO staff interview (fn. 18). In any case, since examining the responsibility of Greece is not the purpose of this article, the EASO staff seconded to national authorities is not further analysed.

101 EASO-OP 2019, 12 ff.

or the acceptance of the asylum claim in the individual case.[102] Based on those opinions, the national authority takes a decision.[103] The extent of the procedure-related support provided by EASO exceeds the competences of the agency, since Art. 2 para. 6 EASO Regulation excludes any powers in relation to decisions by Member States' asylum authorities on individual asylum claims.[104] The reception-related cooperation *inter alia* includes operational support with regard to the management of first reception procedures and advice concerning the administrative management more generally.[105]

The EASO asylum support team consists of EASO national experts (seconded staff),[106] so-called EASO interim staff (contracted staff)[107] as well as the agency's own staff (statutory staff).[108] The latter are usually entrusted with coordination tasks.[109] All members of the asylum support team are instructed by EASO and are fully integrated into the agency's decision-mak-

---

102 SOP-Hotspots-GR, 25. As specified explicitly, "the task of the EASO case officers during the interview is in the first place […] to *examine the claim* for international protection" and draft a corresponding legal opinion (emphasis added).

103 While the Greek Asylum Service is not legally obliged to follow that legal opinion, this is usually the case. Cf. EASO staff interview (fn. 18); *Tsourdi*, German Law Journal 21 (2020) (fn. 7), 512, 517 with further references.

104 Art. 2 para. 6 EASO Regulation. The legal basis in national law cannot replace the requirement of an EU legal basis. While the European Ombudsman has confirmed genuine concerns about the extent of the involvement of EASO teams in assessing asylum applications in the Greek hotspots, the pertinent inquiry has been closed, see European Ombudsman, Decision in case 735/2017/MDC on the European Asylum Support Office's (EASO) involvement in the decision-making process concerning admissibility of applications for international protection submitted in the Greek Hotspots, in particular shortcomings in admissibility interviews, available at: https://www.ombudsman.europa.eu/en/case/en/49987. Cf. *Tsourdi*, German Law Journal 21 (2020) (fn. 7), 522, 528 ff.

105 EASO-OP 2019, 18 ff.

106 EASO national experts are officers of the asylum authorities of the Member States who are employed on secondment to the agency, see: Art. 15, 16, 38 para. 4 EASO Regulation. Those national experts retain their position as officers of their home State during the deployment. This is relevant with regard to the legal responsibility of the home Member State, which is not in the focus here.

107 EASO interim staff is contracted on a temporary basis in order to ensure a stable number of staff despite the fluctuating support provided by the Member States, cf. EASO staff interview (fn. 18).

108 EASO-OP 2019; SOP-Hotspots-GR; cf. EASO staff interview (fn. 18).

109 EASO-OP 2019; SOP-Hotspots-GR; cf. EASO staff interview (fn. 18).

ing structure during their deployment.[110] The members of the asylum support teams, in case of concerns including related to fundamental rights issues, report to the EASO team leader, the EASO local coordinator, or the Union contact point.[111] In case of a violation of the code of conduct, the members of the asylum support team shall inform the EASO executive director.[112] Responsibility for monitoring the correct implementation of the Operating Plan, including fundamental rights compliance, lies with the EASO Union contact point who in turn reports to the agency on all aspects of the deployment.[113]

Frontex deploys *migration management support teams* (MMST) which provide comprehensive preparatory support with regard to first identification procedures as well as executive support with regard to deportations to Turkey.[114] The MMST consist of national officers who are deployed from the border guards of other Member States (seconded staff), and may also

---

110 Art. 23 EASO Regulation. The provisions of the OP-GR and the SOP-Hotspots-GR neither mention any obligations of the members of the asylum support team towards the host Member State nor towards their home Member State.

111 Each asylum support team is coordinated by a so-called local coordinator (EASO statutory staff). Those members of the asylum support team who are in charge of processing asylum claims report to a team leader who is in charge of supervising the quality, and have the possibility to contact the "EASO helpdesk" in case of doubts as to the legal opinion. EASO-OP 2019; SOP-Hotspots-GR; cf. EASO staff interview (fn. 18).

112 EASO-OP 2019, 9. The Executive Director in turn reports to the Management Board, consisting of one member of each Member State and two members of the European Commission, Art. 25 EASO Regulation.

113 Art. 20 EASO Regulation does not mention explicitly the obligation of the Union contact point to monitor the compliance with fundamental rights. This becomes clear however from the interpretation of Art. 20 EASO Regulation in light of recital 31 EASO Regulation, Art. 51 ChFR.

114 Art. 2 Nr. 19, Art. 40 Frontex Regulation. Cf. Frontex Report JO Poseidon 2018 (Fn. 55) which further mentions search and rescue operations – those are however not considered as part of the EU hotspot administration. Based on the publicly available information, the legal basis for the deployment of the Frontex teams cannot be identified with certainty. However, as Art. 2 Nr. 19, Art. 40 Frontex Regulation is tailor-made to the provision of administrative support to EU hotspots, it can be assumed that Frontex indeed deploys MMST to the EU hotspots. This is confirmed by the parallelism of the competences of MMST under Art. 40 Frontex Regulation and the actual support provided by Frontex to the EU hotspot administration according to Frontex Report JO Poseidon 2018 (Fn. 55). This is further confirmed by the RoP-EURTF-GR which refer explicitly to Art. 18 of Regulation 2016/1624, the predecessor to the current Frontex Regulation, which is the provision on MMST.

include own staff of the agency (statutory staff).[115] The members of the MMST are instructed by the host Member State in accordance with the operational plan, and shall, in principle, only perform their tasks in the presence of an officer of the host Member State.[116] The host Member State shall however take into account the agency's views.[117] In case of the involvement of large vessels, the decision-making power *de facto* lies with the home Member State.[118] The responsibility for monitoring the correct implementation of the Operational Plan, including with regard to fundamental rights issues, lies with the *coordinating officer*, who in turn reports to the Frontex executive director.[119] The executive director shall evaluate the activities of the MMST, and shall suspend or terminate the deployment if he or she considers that violations of fundamental rights are of serious nature or likely to persist.[120] The distinct feature of MMST in comparison to other kinds of support teams is that those consist of members of different EU agencies such as, in addition to Frontex, EASO or Europol.[121] Further, and more importantly, the coordination and monitoring structure of MMST differs. – Namely, coordination and monitoring lies with the European

115 Art. 2 para. 19 Frontex Regulation defines: "migration management support teams" to mean "teams of experts which provide technical and operational reinforcement to Member States, including at hotspot areas, composed of operational staff, experts from the European Asylum Support Office (EASO) and Europol and, where relevant, experts from the European Union Agency for Fundamental Rights (FRA), other Union bodies, offices and agencies and Member States."

116 Art. 43 para. 1, para. 3, Art. 82 para. 4 Frontex Regulation.

117 Art. 43 para. 2 Frontex Regulation.

118 *Fink*, Frontex and Human Rights (fn. 22), 58 ff., 71 has shown this with regard to Joint Operations.

119 Art. 44 para. 3 Frontex Regulation.

120 Art. 46 Frontex Regulation.

121 Art. 2 para. 19 Frontex Regulation. Even though the current EASO Regulation does not explicitly foresee MMST, the EU agency teams are currently deployed either as MMST or as what can be described as "*de facto* MMST". This is confirmed by the ToC-EURTF, cf. EASO staff interview (fn. 18). The deployment of a "*de facto* MSST" is possible under the current EASO Regulation as the mandate of the asylum support teams is flexible. Finally, it is indeed the Commission who monitors and coordinates the EU hotspot administration. Indeed, EASO itself differentiates between different kinds of operational support, one of which is dedicated explicitly to the "hotspot approach", see *Tsourdi*, German Law Journal 21 (2020) (fn. 7), 513.

Commission – which is of particular relevance with a view to the question of responsibility.[122]

c) *Cooperation on the coordination and monitoring level in the EU hotspot administration – European Commission and EURTF*

Administrative cooperation on the coordination and monitoring level mainly consists in the enactment of EU soft law and supervisory relationships. In line with the above, the Union plays a central role on this level.[123]

With a view to supervisory relationships, it is crucial that the responsibility for coordinating and monitoring the implementation of the EU hotspot approach lies with the European Commission. The EU agencies and the host Member State provide support to the Commission in this regard. According to Art. 40 para. 3 Frontex Regulation, "the *Commission* shall [...] be responsible for the *coordination* of the activities of the migration management support teams".[124] The mandate to coordinate includes monitoring in the sense of ensuring compliance of the activities of the MMST with fundamental rights.[125] Indeed, the Commission has since 2015 effectively assumed the responsibility to coordinate and monitor the implementation of the EU hotspot approach and the return policy under the EU–Turkey Statement.[126]

---

122 This is exactly the reason why *Fink*, Frontex and Human Rights (fn. 22), 35 excludes the case of MMST of the scope of her study.

123 See II.2.a).

124 Art. 40 para. 3 Frontex Regulation. The Commission's responsibility to coordinate the EU agency support is clearly reflected in the OP EASO-GR, in the ToC-EURTF and in the RoP-EURTF.

125 Art. 40 para. 3 Frontex Regulation, read in light of recital 55 which provides: "In the hotspot areas the different agencies and Member States should operate within their respective mandates and powers. *The Commission*, in cooperation with the other relevant agencies, *should ensure the compliance of activities in the hotspot areas with the relevant Union acquis, including the Common European Asylum System and fundamental rights*." (emphasis added).

126 Initially, this competence seems not to have been exercised exclusively within the framework of the EURTF: In March 2016, on the day of the publication of the EU–Turkey Statement, the European Council stated that "the Commission will coordinate and organise together with the Member States and Agencies the necessary support structures to implement [the Statement] effectively." On the same day, the Commission appointed an "EU coordinator to organise the operational implementation [of the EU–Turkey Statement] in Greece", i.e. the policy of return from the EU hotspots, see European Commission, Press Release 18

Currently, the coordination of the implementation of the EU hotspot approach takes place within the framework of the EU Regional Task Force (*EURTF*).[127] In addition, representatives of the Commission are permanently present in some of the EU hotspots.[128] The EURTF is an administrative structure which consists of regular meetings of representatives of the Commission chairing the meetings, of the EU agencies operating in the EU hotpots, and of the relevant national authorities of the host Member State.[129] The EURTF serves as a forum for coordination, including monitoring the compliance with fundamental rights with a particular focus on the rights of vulnerable persons.[130] It was established in an *ad hoc* manner and without reference to a clear legal basis.[131] After criticism by the European Court of Auditors in this regard, the "Terms of cooperation for the European Union Regional Task Force" (ToC-EURTF) and the "Rules of Procedure of the European Union Regional Task Force for migration man-

---

March 2016: President Juncker appoints EU Coordinator to organise operational implementation in Greece, 18 March 2016, available at: https://europa.eu/rapid/press-release_IP-16-942_en.htm. As the only measure of the Statement to be implemented in Greece is the return policy, coordinating the implementation of the return policy in the EU hotspots was the main responsibility of the EU coordinator. The Commission has since March 2016 provided regular reports on the implementation of the EU–Turkey Statement, available at: https://ec.europa.eu/home-affairs/what-we-do/policies/european-agenda-migration/proposal-implementation-package_en. The Commission has stated, in a procedure before the European Ombudsman, that "developments on the ground are being closely monitored", and that the monitoring reports constitute "a human rights assessment" made in the context of the implementation of the EU–Turkey Statement, see European Ombudsman, Decision of the European Ombudsman in the joint inquiry into complaints 506-509-674-784-927-1381/2016/MHZ against the European Commission concerning a human rights impact assessment in the context of the EU–Turkey Agreement, available at: https://www.ombudsman.europa.eu/en/decision/en/75160.

127 Cf. ToC-EURTF; EURTF-RoP; European Commission, Commission Staff Working Document, Best practices on the implementation of the hotspot approach, SWD (2017) 372 final (15 November 2017), available at: https://ec.europa.eu/home-affairs/sites/homeaffairs/files/what-we-do/policies/european-agenda-migration/20171114_commission_staff_working_document_en.pdf, p 2. EURTFs have been set up in Piraeus and Catania respectively.

128 Cf. EASO staff interview (fn. 18); confirmed by practical knowledge of the author, cf. fn. 19.

129 ToC-EURTF; RoP-EURTF-GR; EASO staff interview (fn. 18).

130 Fundamental rights issues are regularly discussed in the EURTF. Cf. ToC-EURTF; EASO staff interview (fn. 18); FRA Opinion 2019 (fn. 3) 19.

131 Established in 2016 within the Frontex Liaison Office in Piraeus, acoording to ToC-EURTF.

agement support to Greece" (RoP-EURTF-GR) have been adopted, but not been made publicly available.[132] The ToC-EURTF explicitly refer to the responsibility of the Commission under Art. 40 para. 3 Frontex Regulation, to which the mandate of the EURTF indeed corresponds.[133] The decision-making structure suggests that the Commission has the last word: Even though the work within the EURTF is described as being "based on consensus", it is the Commission which is in charge of ensuring that the EURTF participants work together.[134] Hence, the mandate and organisational structure of the EURTF suggest that it is an *administrative structure within the European Commission*.[135]

3. *The systemic deficiencies in the EU hotspot administration*

The EU hotspot approach inherently leads to a risk of fundamental rights violations. Without disregarding the severity of each single fundamental rights violation, this chapter focuses on two issues, namely: the risk of refoulement due to a deportation to a non-safe third country (3.a),[136] and the risk of inhuman or degrading treatment due to inadequate reception con-

---

132 FRA Opinion 2019 (fn. 3) 19, note 37 and 38; ToC-EURTF; EURTF-RoP adopted by each EURTF respectively.

133 ToC-EURTF.

134 RoP-EURTF.

135 FRA Opinion 2019 (fn. 3) 19; EASO-OP 2019, 10. The EURTF has been described as a "shared office", as a "coordination body", or as an "institutionalised" cooperation structure, cf. EASO staff interview (fn. 18), cf. an informal paper published by the European Day for Border Guards, available at: https://bit.ly/2QeNtsR, describing that "the hotspot approach is being implemented by the EURTF" and that "with the hotspot approach, this co-operation [referring to the EURTF] became institutionalised and enhanced."

136 The non-refoulement principle prohibits removal or expulsion to a state where there is a serious risk of inhuman or degrading treatment, as follows from Art. 3 ECHR respectively Art. 4 ChFR, and as explicitly enshrined in Art. 19 para. 2 ChFR ("human rights non-refoulement principle"). The non-refoulement principle further prohibits removal or expulsion to a state where there is a serious risk of persecution in the sense of the Geneva Convention on Refugees 1951 including the 1967 Protocol [hereinafter, the Geneva Convention], as follows from Art. 33 para. 1 Geneva Convention, and as explicitly enshrined in Art. 18 ChFR ("refugee rights non-refoulement principle"). The non-refoulement principle in both forms further prohibits removal or expulsion to a state where there is a serious risk that the destination state would violate the non-refoulement principle in either form ("chain refoulement").

ditions, in particular in case of vulnerable persons (3.b).[137] Both those issues are widespread or inherent to the design of regulatory framework, and at the same time reach the threshold of being relevant for Art. 2 TEU: Hence, the EU hotspot administration can be described as systemically deficient.[138]

a) *The risk of refoulement due to deportation to a non-safe third country*

The EU hotspot procedure, structurally aiming at deportation to Turkey, gives rise to a risk of a violation of the non-refoulement principle as enshrined in Art. 4, 18, 19 para. 2 ChFR. As mentioned, the return policy of the EU–Turkey Statement is based on the assumption that asylum applications can be rejected as inadmissible by referring the applicant to protection in Turkey as a safe third country.[139] However, Turkey cannot be considered as a safe third country at least in the vast majority of cases: Turkey has ratified the Geneva Convention only insofar as refugees originating from Europe are concerned, and the Turkish protection regime does not meet the requirements of the safe third country concept.[140] Accordingly,

---

137 The Greek Reform IP Act (fn. 50), aiming at a re-introduction of a systematic detention policy, increases the risk of a systemic violation of Art. 6 ChFR.

138 See on the notion of systemic deficiencies *Von Bogdandy*, Systemic Deficiency in the Rule of Law: What it is, what has to be done, what can be done, Common Market Law Review 51 (2014), 59; *Von Bogdandy*, Tyrannei der Werte? Herausforderungen und Grundlagen einer europäischen Dogmatik systemischer Defizite, Zeitschrift für ausländisches öffentliches Recht und Völkerrecht 79 (2019).

139 According to Art. 38 Asylum Procedures Directive, transposed in Art. 56 Greek Asylum Law 4375/2016, a third country can be considered as safe if, simply put, the deportation to the third country does not violate the non-refoulement principle in any of its forms including the risk of chain refoulement in any of its forms, if the third country provides access to refugee status in accordance with the Geneva Convention, and if there is a reasonable connection between the concerned applicant and the third country. In any case, the examination of whether a country can be considered as safe for a certain applicant must take into account the individual circumstances of the case. See on the safe third country concept e.g. *Costello*, Safe Country? Says Who?, International Journal of Refugee Law 28 (2016), 4, 601.

140 *Ulusoy/Battjes*, Situation of Readmitted Migrants and Refugees from Greece to Turkey under the EU–Turkey Statement, VU Migration Law Series (2017). In the same vein, Administrative Court of Munich, preliminary decision of 17 July 2019, cf. *Nestler/Ziebritzki*, Unionsrecht statt 'Deals' in the europäischen Asylpolitik, Neue Zeitschrift für Verwaltungsrecht (2020), 129.

the Greek Asylum Service continuously and in the large majority of cases comes to the conclusion that Turkey cannot be considered as a safe third country.[141] This is the reason why the actual number of returns remains low: Within almost four years, only about 2000 persons have been deported from EU hotspots to Turkey, and not even all of them on the basis of protection elsewhere clauses.[142]

One might then wonder why the issue of whether Turkey is a safe third country is considered as being of systemic relevance, despite the low numbers of deportations. The reason is that, as has been explained above, the very function of the EU hotspots consists in the implementation of the return policy, which is why the EU hotspot procedure is designed in line with the aim of deportation to Turkey.[143] In other words: If a deportation to Turkey not only in the individual case, but structurally amounts to a violation of fundamental rights, this is of systemic relevance, because the risk of deportation affects every person subject to the EU hotspot procedure which would in turn call into question the function of the EU hotspots. An individual complaint invoking a violation of Art. 3 ECHR due to a deportation to Turkey is pending before the ECtHR.[144] Taking into account the requirements which have recently been established by the ECtHR in order for a country to be considered a "safe third country",[145] it does not seem that Turkey does fulfil those standards. The CJEU has so far

141 To be sure, the Greek Council of State in September 2017 found that Turkey could actually be considered as safe third country for two applicants of Syrian nationality. However, as the assessment of whether a third country can be considered as "safe" must take into account the individual circumstances of the concerned applicant, the judgement of the Greek Council of State binds neither administrative authorities nor courts with regard to other cases. The Greek Asylum Service, the Appeals Authority (a quasi-judicial body integrated in the asylum authority) as well as Greek administrative courts hence still in a large proportion of the cases come to the conclusion that Turkey cannot be considered a safe third country. See: *Gkliati*, The Application of the EU–Turkey Agreement: A Critical Analysis of the Decisions of the Greek Appeals Committee, European Journal of Legal Studies 81 (2017), 124.

142 The estimation is based on: UNHCR, Returns from Greece to Turkey (under EU–Turkey statement) as of 31 December 2019, available at: https://data2.unhcr.org/en/documents/details/73295, according to which between April 2016 and 31 December 2019, only 2001 persons, out of which 367 of Syrian nationality, have been returned to Turkey.

143 See II.1.b).

144 ECtHR, *J.B. v Greece*, Appl. No. 54796/16, case communicated on 18 May 2017, available at: http://hudoc.echr.coe.int/eng?i=001-174322.

145 ECtHR, *Ilias and Ahmed v Hungary*, Appl. No. 47287/15, judgment, 21 Nov 2019.

hardly made any pronouncement on the safe third country concept,[146] despite the legal uncertainty[147] and the increasing relevance of the notion.[148] A clarification would however be of particular relevance – not only with regard to the operation of the EU hotspots, but also more generally with regard to the reform of the Common European Asylum System. On the EU secondary law level, the interpretation of Art. 38 Asylum Procedures Directive requires further clarification. In addition, the limits to protection elsewhere clauses on the EU constitutional level have not yet been clarified: While it is undisputed that a return must not violate Art. 4, 19 ChFR, much speaks in favour of higher standards based on Art. 18 ChFR.[149] In any case, assuming that a deportation to Turkey violates Art. 3 ECHR, this would at the same time constitute a violation of the principle of non-refoulement under EU asylum law.[150]

---

146 See however European Court of Justice, C-585/16, ECLI:EU:C:2018:584, judgement, 25 July 2018 – Serin Alheto/Zamestnik-predsedatel na Darzhavna agentsia za bezhantsite; European Court of Justice, C-564/18, ECLI:EU:C:2020:218, judgement, 19 March 2020 – LH/Bevándorlási és Menekültügyi Hivatal.

147 See for the debate in the German context: *Lübbe*, Expertise für die Sachverständigenanhörung zur GEAS-Reform im Deutschen Bundestag, April 2018, available at: https://www.hs-fulda.de/sozial-kulturwissenschaften/studieninteressierte/studiengaenge/intercultural-communication-and-european-studies-ma/nicht-verwendet/lehrende-und-mitarbeiterinnen/person/prof-dr-anna-luebbe-356/contactBox ; *Thym*, Stellungnahme für die Öffentliche Anhörung des Innenausschusses des Deutschen Bundestags am Montag, den 16. April 2018, available at: https://www.jura.uni-konstanz.de/thym/aktuelles/aktuelles/Reform-des-europaeischen-Asylsystems/.

148 Cf. The Michigan Guidelines on Protection Elsewhere, Michigan Journal of International Law 28 (2007), 208; *Foster*, Protection Elsewhere: The Legal Implications of Requiring Refugees to Seek Protection in Another State, Michigan Journal of International Law 28 (2007), 223; *Costello*, The Asylum Procedures Directive and the Proliferation of Safe Country Practices: Deterrence, Deflection and the Dismantling of International Protection?, European Journal of Migration and Law 7 (2005), 35. See further: *Moreno-Lax*, The Legality of the 'Safe Third Country' Notion Contested: Insights from the Law of Treaties, in: Goodwin-Gill/Wecke (eds.), Migration and Refugee Protection in the 21st Century: Legal Aspects – The Hague Academy of International Law Centre for Research, 2015.

149 See *Lübbe*, Expertise für die Sachverständigenanhörung zur GEAS-Reform (fn. 147).

150 Cf. Art. 4, 19 para. 2 ChFR.

b) The risk of inhuman or degrading treatment due to inadequate reception conditions

The living conditions in the EU hotspots structurally give rise to a risk of inhuman or degrading treatment as prohibited by Art. 4 ChFR, in particular in case of vulnerable persons.[151] The living conditions in the EU hotspots are not adequate for human beings, as has been consistently documented during the past four years by bodies of the UN, the Council of Europe and the EU, by Greek national bodies, and by NGOs.[152] Taking into account that the ECtHR under Art. 3 ECHR places increased demands upon States in the case of vulnerable persons,[153] the risk of a violation of

151 The notion of "vulnerability" is referred to here in the sense of Art. 21 Reception Conditions Directive, as transposed into Art. 14 para. 8 Greek Asylum Law 4375/2016. For the administrative interpretation of the vulnerability categories see: SOP Hotspots-GR, 5 ff., 11.

152 To name but a few of those reports: OHCHR, UN Special Rapporteur on the human rights of migrants concludes his follow up country visit to Greece, available at: https://www.ohchr.org/EN/NewsEvents/Pages/DisplayNews.aspx?NewsID=19976&LangID=E; Council of Europe, Report to the Greek Government on the visit to Greece carried out by the European Committee for the Prevention of Torture and Inhuman or Degrading Treatment or Punishment (CPT) from 10 to 19 April 2018, 19 February 2019, CPT/Inf (2019) 4; FRA Opinion 2019 (fn. 3); Médecins Sans Frontières, A disastrous policy: vulnerable people trapped on the Greek islands pay the price of inhumane policies of the EU–Turkey deal, available at: https://www.doctorswithoutborders.ca/article/disastrous-policy-vulnerable-people-trapped-greek-islands-pay-price-inhumane-policies-eu; Danish Refugee Council, Fundamental Rights and the EU Hotspot Approach, October 2017, available at: https://drc.ngo/media/4051855/fundamental-rights_web.pdf; Greek Ombudsman, Andreas Pottakis, Special Report. Migration flows and refugee protection. Administrative challenges and human rights issues, April 2017, available at: https://www.synigoros.gr/?i=human-rights.en.recentinterventions.434107.

153 To be sure, Art. 60 para. 4 Greek asylum law provides that vulnerable persons should be exempted from the EU hotspot procedure and transferred to the Greek mainland instead. However, due to the high number of applications on the hand, and understaffing of the EU hotspot administration, vulnerable persons are in a considerable number of cases not identified or transferred to the mainland with a few weeks or months delay, cf. FRA Opinion 2019 (fn. 3) 6, 11; Equal Rights, Vial Report (fn. 66) 25 ff. Further, the inadequate reception conditions in the EU hotspots make people prone to *becoming* vulnerable, cf. FRA Report (fn. 3), 6, 29.

Art. 3 ECHR is indeed significantly higher in those cases.[154] Recently, the ECtHR has granted several interim measures concerning cases of vulnerable persons invoking a violation of Art. 3 ECHR due to the living conditions in the EU hotspots, and has obliged Greece to provide adequate conditions to the concerned applicants.[155] Taking into account the criteria established by the ECtHR,[156] it seems that the reception conditions amount to inhuman or degrading treatment at least for vulnerable persons. An assessment on the basis of the case law of the CJEU leads to the same conclusion.[157]

III. The potential of EU public liability law

As explained, the close involvement of EU agencies and the European Commission in the EU hotspot administration suggests to examine whether the Union is responsible for administrative misconduct. As a matter of course, every violation of an individual right raises the question of who is responsible. However, this question becomes particularly acute where fundamental rights are at stake – and even more so, where this occurs in a systemic manner. Responsibility is understood here as judicial responsibility for administrative misconduct (III.1.). The focus lies on the action for damages against the Union or its agencies (III.2.). The particular potential of EU public liability law for the integration of responsibility in the context of the European asylum administration is due to its several functions (III.3.). In order to assess whether the Union or its agencies are actually liable for fundamental rights violations occurring in EU hotspots, the critical legal questions require further doctrinal analysis (III.4.).

---

154 ECtHR, *M.S.S. v Belgium and Greece*, Appl. No. 30696/09, judgement, 21 January 2011; ECtHR, *Tarakhel v Switzerland*, Appl. No. 29217/12, judgement, 4 November 2014.

155 See for a list of recent interim measures granted by the ECtHR: https://www.equal-rights.org/greece.

156 ECtHR, *M.S.S. v Belgium and Greece*, Appl. No. 30696/09, judgement, 21 January 2011; ECtHR, *Tarakhel v Switzerland*, Appl. No. 29217/12, judgement, 4 November 2014.

157 Cf. European Court of Justice, C-411-10, ECLI:EU:C:2011:865, judgement, 21 December 2011 – N.S. et al.,; European Court of Justice, C-163/17, ECLI:EU:C:2019:218, judgement, 19 March 2019 – Jawo.

1. *The question of judicial responsibility for administrative misconduct*

When speaking of responsibility in the context of refugee law, what first comes to mind is the responsibility to provide protection – more specifically, refugee status in the global context, or international protection status in the context of the EU.[158] When referring to responsibility in the context of the Common European Asylum System, the dimension of the European asylum administration must however not be ignored.[159] Administrative conduct necessarily implies the question of who is responsible in the case that rights of the concerned persons are violated.[160] The right to an effective remedy, enshrined in Art. 47 ChFR as an expression of the rule of law, prescribes that the entity in the name of whom the unlawful administrative conduct was performed, is held responsible.[161] Responsibility in this sense hence means, at least *inter alia*, judicial accountability for the violation of rights, in particular fundamental rights. Usually, the question of who is to be held responsible is quite simple to answer. Where several administrative actors are involved, such as in the integrated European administration, the issue however becomes more complicated.[162]

158 Art. 78 para. 1 TFEU, Art. 2 (a) Qualification Directive.

159 See fn. 12, fn. 74.

160 Cf. *Weiler*, The Transformation of Europe, The Yale Law Journal 100 (1991), 2403, 2417 ff. explaining that the supremacy of the then Community law was only acceptable because the then Community was bound by fundamental rights. The same reasoning applies with regard to the European administration – with the difference that this is now explicitly prescribed, Art. 51, 47 ChFR.

161 Cf. European Court of Justice, 294/83, ECLI:EU:C:1986:166, judgement, 23 April 1986, para 23 – Les Verts/Parliament: "the [then] European Economic Community is a Community based on the rule of law, inasmuch as neither its Member States nor its institutions can avoid a review of the question whether the measures adopted by them are in conformity with the basic constitutional charter, the Treaty. In particular, [...] the Treaty established a complete system of legal remedies and procedures designed to permit the Court of Justice to review the legality of measures adopted by the institutions. Natural and legal persons are thus protected [...]. Where the Community institutions are responsible for the administrative implementation of such measures, natural or legal persons may bring a direct action before the Court [...]."

162 See *Fink*, Common Market Law Review 56 (2019) (fn. 22); *Shirvani*, Europarecht 46 (2011) (fn. 88); *Hofmann*, in: Schmidt-Aßmann/Schöndorf-Haubold (eds.) (fn. 21).

2. The action for damages against the Union or its agencies

Art. 340 para. 2 TFEU provides that "in the case of non-contractual liability, the Union shall, in accordance with the general principles common to the laws of the Member States, make good any damage caused by its institutions or by its servants in the performance of their duties." Art. 41 para. 3 ChFR grants the fundamental right to have the Union make good any damages under the same conditions.[163] The criteria established by the CJEU for the Union's liability under Art. 340 para. 2 TFEU (2.a) also apply with a view to the respective agencies' responsibility, even though the latter might be based on a different legal basis (2.b).

a) The criteria for non-contractual liability of the Union

According to the CJEU's jurisprudence, non-contractual liability of the Union under Art. 340 para. 2 TFEU arises if unlawful conduct of a Union body qualifying as a sufficiently serious breach of a rule conferring rights on individuals has caused damage.[164] Liability of the Union hence requires two main elements, namely, firstly, unlawful conduct of the Union which, secondly, causes damage.[165] The former condition is qualified insofar as the unlawful conduct must consist in a sufficiently serious breach of a rule conferring rights on individuals.[166]

---

163 See on Art. 41 para. 3 ChFR: *Magiera*, GRCh Art. 41 Recht auf eine gute Verwaltung, in: Meyer/Hölscheidt (eds.), 5th edition, Baden-Baden 2019.

164 European Court of Justice, C-4/69, ECLI:EU:C:1971:40, judgement, 28 April 1971, para. 10 – Lütticke: "By virtue of the second paragraph of article 215 and the general principles to which this provision refers, the liability of the community presupposes the existence of a set of circumstances comprising actual damage, a causal link between the damage claimed and the conduct alleged against the institution, and the illegality of such conduct." Cf. *Gutman*, The Evolution of the Action for Damages Against the European Union and its Place in the System of Judicial Protection, Common Market Law Review 48 (2011), 695.

165 *Fink*, Common Market Law Review 56 (2019) (fn. 22), 1232 ff. defines three conditions: unlawfulness of the conduct, damage, and a causal relationship between those.

166 It does not matter whether the rule is enshrined in primary or secondary law, cf. *Fink*, Common Market Law Review 56 (2019) (fn. 22), 1233. See on the requirements regarding the qualification of the condition of unlawfulness: European Court of Justice, C-352/98 P, ECLI:EU:C:2000:361, judgement, 4 July 2000, para. 42 – Bergaderm; European Court of Jusitce, C-282/05 P, ECLI:EU:C:2007:226, judgement, 19 April 2007, para. 47 – Holcim (Deutschland)/COM. Those judge-

b) The legal basis in case of involvement of EU agencies

The CJEU has clarified that Art. 340 para. 2 TFEU regulates the liability of the Union for the conduct not only of its institutions, but also of its agencies.[167] As Art. 97 para. 4, Art. 98 Frontex Regulation respectively Art. 45 para. 3 EASO Regulation provide for non-contractual liability of the agencies,[168] one might, at first sight, consider those as leges speciales to Art. 340 para. 2 TFEU. However, the liability of an agency under secondary law cannot exclude the liability of the Union under primary law.[169] Rather,

---

ments refer to European Court of Justice, C-46 ad 48/93, ECLI:EU:C:1996:79, judgement, 5 March 1996 – Brasserie du Pecheur/Factortame, and thereby partly overcome Euopean Court of Justice, C-5/71, ECLI:EU:C:1971:116, judgement, 2 December 1971 – Zuckerfabrik Schöppenstedt. See on that development: *Aalto*, Public Liability in EU Law. Brasserie, Bergaderm and Beyond (fn. 31); *Craig*, in: Craig (ed.), EU Administrative Law, 3rd edition, Oxford 2018, 738, 741 ff.

167 European Court of Justice, T-411/06, ECLI:EU:T:2008:419, judgement, 8 October 2008, para. 37 – Sogelma/EAR: "The general principle to be elicited from that judgment is that any act of a Community body intended to produce legal effects *vis-à-vis* third parties must be open to judicial review. It is true that the CJEU in its judgement on the case *Les Verts* (fn. 161) para. 24, refers only to Community institutions and the EAR is not one of the institutions listed in Article 7 EC. Nonetheless, the situation of Community bodies endowed with the power to take measures intended to produce legal effects *vis-à-vis* third parties is similar to the situation on the basis of that judgment, and hence: "*it cannot be acceptable, in a community based on the rule of law, that such acts escape judicial review.*" (emphasis added). Cf. *Rademacher*, Realakte (fn. 24), 244 ff.; *Chamon*, EU Agencies (fn. 79), 355 ff. relying on European Court of Justice, 18/60, ECLI:EU:C:1962:26, judgement, 12 July 1962 – L Worms/High Authority of the European Coal and Steel Community, and transferring that argument to EU agencies.

168 Both provisions replicate Art. 340 para. 2 TFEU with the only difference that instead of the Union, now "*the Agency* shall, in accordance with the general principles make good damages caused by its departments or by its staff in the performance of their duties" (emphasis added). As the respective definitions of "staff" include seconded staff, while statutory staff is referred to as the agency's "own staff" throughout the respective Regulations, the provisions are to be interpreted as including seconded staff, cf. Art. 38 para. 3 and 4 EASO Regulation and Frontex Regulation, passim.

169 Otherwise, the Union could exclude its liability under primary law through the creation of further bodies by EU secondary law. This becomes clear already from the fact that Art. 340 para. 3 TFEU explicitly provides for the liability of the European Central Bank instead of the Union, but that there is no such provision replacing the liability of the Union with that of EU agencies, cf. *Carrera et al.*, European Journal of Migration and Law 15 (2013) (fn. 7), 337, 352; *Ruffert*, in: Calliess/Ruffert, EUV/AEUV. Kommentar, 5th edition, München 2016, Art. 340

both the agency is liable under its founding Regulation, and the Union is liable, in a second degree, under Art. 340 para. 2 TFEU.[170] Further, one might wonder about the relation of civil liability as regulated by Art. 42 Frontex Regulation respectively Art. 21 EASO Regulation to Art. 340 para. 2 TFEU. The systematic context as well as the history of those provisions however shows that those provisions do not form part of EU public liability law.[171] Given that Art. 340 para. 2 TFEU, Art. 41 para. 3 ChFR and the respective provisions in the agency's Regulations are to be interpreted in parallel,[172] the following refers to Art. 340 para. 2 TFEU only.

3. The potential of EU public liability law for the integration of responsibility

The particular potential of EU public liability law for the integration of responsibility for administrative misconduct is due to its legal protection function on the subjective (3.a) and the objective level (3.b) while at the same time allocating responsibility among several involved actors (3.c).[173]

AEUV, para. 8. See however: *Gellermann*, in: Streinz, EUV/AEUV, Art. 340 AEUV, para. 12, München 2018; *Craig*, in: Craig (ed.) (fn. 166), 736 ff. Another approach, which is mainly applied in the context of the action for annulment, is to attribute the conduct of the agency to the Commission, in order to avoid legal protection gaps, see European Court of Justice, T-123/00, ECLI:EU:T:2002:307, judgement, 10 December 2002 – Thomae GmbH/Commission; cf. *Chamon*, EU Agencies (fn. 79), 331 ff.

170 *Berg*, in: Schwarze/Becker/Hatje/Schoo, EU-Kommentar, 4th edition, Baden-Baden 2019, Art. 340 para. 1. The second degree liability of the Union becomes relevant e.g. in the case that the agency lacks the resources to make good the damage, cf. *Augsberg*, in: von der Groeben/Schwarze/Hatje (eds.), Europäisches Unionsrecht, 7th edition, Baden-Baden 2015, Art. 340, para. 19.

171 *Fink*, Frontex and Human Rights (fn. 22), 183 ff.; *Augsberg*, in: von der Groeben/Schwarze/Hatje (fn.170), Art. 340, para 15. And even if one considered those provisions as forming part of EU public liability law, they are to be interpreted as either shifting the liability for conduct of seconded staff from the home Member State to the host Member State or as establishing liability of the host Member State in addition to the liability of the home Member State. It seems that the provisions are to be read as: "the *host Member State* [and not the sending MS] shall be liable in accordance with its national law" (emphasis added).

172 *Augsberg*, in: von der Groeben/Schwarze/Hatje (fn. 170) Art. 340, para 19, 59.

173 The question of whether EU public liability law qualifies as a fundamental rights remedy is not addressed here. See on that question in particular: *Fink*, German Law Journal 21 (2020) (fn. 22); *Ward*, Damages under the EU Charter of Fundamental Rights, ERA Forum 12 (2012), 589; *Półtorak*, Action for Damages in the Case of Infringement of Fundamental Rights by the European Union, in: Ba-

a) *The subjective legal protection function of EU public liability law – granting the right to an effective remedy*

As the Union is based on the rule of law, and as the CJEU has the task to ensure that EU law is observed, the EU legal protection system must comply with Art. 47 ChFR.[174] In the case of administrative conduct by a Union actor, the question arises which action grants the right to an effective remedy. Traditionally, the *action for annulment* as laid down in Art. 263 TFEU has been considered the main action providing legal protection in the EU legal system. However, the potential of Art. 263 TFEU is obviously limited due to its restricted admissibility criteria, *inter alia* requiring a formally binding administrative conduct as basis for such an action.[175] This is well illustrated by the case of EU hotspots: It is quite clear that an action for annulment against the Union based on its involvement in the EU hotspot administration would be difficult, or not even possible, already because the Union acts in a non-formally binding manner.[176]

Further, the *preliminary reference* under Art. 267 TFEU grants access to justice in compliance with Art. 47 ChFR. However, the potential of Art. 267 TFEU for the purpose of providing effective legal protection is limited as well, mainly due to the fact that the individual does not have the possibility to force a national court to refer a question to the CJEU.[177] Again, this is well illustrated by a case originating in the EU hotspots, namely the refusal of the Greek Council of State to refer a question on the interpretation of the safe third country concept to the CJEU.[178]

---

gińska (eds.), Damages for violations of human rights: a comparative study of domestic legal systems, 2016.

174 *Rademacher*, Realakte (fn. 24), 152 ff. shows that Art. 47 ChFR sets the standard. See also *Barents*, EU Procedural Law and Effective Legal Protection, Common Market Law Review 51 (2014), 1437, 1442; *Hofmann*, in: Schmidt-Aßmann/Schöndorf-Haubold (eds.) (fn. 21), 280 ff.; *Chamon*, EU Agencies (fn. 79), 327.

175 *Rademacher*, Realakte (fn. 24), 3 ff.; *Fink*, Common Market Law Review 56 (2019) (fn. 22), 1231. See on the origins of the action for annulment: European Court of Justice, 25/62, ECLI:EU:C:1963:17, judgement, 15 July 1963 – Plaumann/Commission.

176 While *Fink*, German Law Journal 21 (2020) (fn. 22), 533 and *Lisi/Eliantonio*, The Gaps in Judicial Accountability of EASO in the Processing of Asylum Requests in Hotspots, European Papers 4 (2019), 589 come to the same conclusion, *Tsourdi*, German Law Journal 21 (2020) (fn. 7), 525 argues in favour of the admissibility of an action for annulment based on EASO's conduct.

177 Cf. *Fink*, Common Market Law Review 56 (2019) (fn. 22), 1231.

178 Cf. *Bünger/Nestler*, From first reception centers to pre-removal facilities – Supreme Administrative court of Greece decides that Turkey is a safe third coun-

Against this background, the *action for damages* under Art. 340 para. 2 TFEU has become *the main action* ensuring the fundamental right to an effective remedy in the case of administrative conduct by Union actors.[179] And indeed, in the context of EU hotspots, the action for damages appears as "the only action available" to an individual who wants to exercise his or her right to an effective remedy against the Union.[180] The importance of the action for damages is, firstly, due to the fact that its admissibility has become *independent* of the admissibility of an action for annulment.[181] It is worth noting here that the CJEU's dismissal of the action for annulment against the EU–Turkey Statement as inadmissible with the argument that the Union was not involved in the conclusion of the statement, is not relevant in this context.[182] Quite apart from the fact that the admissibility of an action for damages is in any case independent from that of an action for annulment,[183] the question of whether the Union has concluded the EU–Turkey Statement is simply irrelevant to the question of whether the

try, JuWiss Blog (13 December 2017). Even though the interpretation of Art. 38 Asylum Procedures Directive can hardly be considered as "acte clair", the Commission did not initiate an infringement procedure against Greece. Cases such as European Court of Justice, C-416/17, ECLI:EU:C:2018:811, judgement, 4 October 2018 – Commission/France, however show that the Commission does sometimes make use of the infringement procedure in case a Member State breaches its obligation to refer a preliminary question to the CJEU under Art. 267 para. 3 TFEU.

179 *Rademacher*, Realakte (fn. 24) 5, passim; *Fink*, Common Market Law Review 56 (2019) (fn. 22), 1231. At first sight, one might argue that Art. 340 para. 2 TFEU is not suitable to fulfil the legal protection function because it is "merely" an action for damages. However, EU public liability law has been developed by the CJEU to an extent that its legal consequences go beyond the financial compensation of damages, cf. *Rademacher*, Realakte (fn. 24) 2, 294 ff.

180 *Fink*, Common Market Law Review 56 (2019) (fn. 22), 1231: "Hence, the action for damages is often *the only action available* to a private party to challenge EU contributions to Member State breaches of EU law." (emphasis added).

181 Cf. European Court of Justice, ECLI:EU:T:2006:292, T-193/04, judgement, 4 October 2006, para 97 – Tillack; European Court of Justice, ECLI:EU:C:2016:701, Joined Cases C-8/15 P to C-10/15 P, judgement, 20 September 2016, para 55 – Ledra Advertising.

182 European Court of Justice, ECLI:EU:T:2017:128, T-192/16, T-193/16 and T-257, orders, 28 February 2017, para 71 – NF, NG and NM/European Council: "the EU–Turkey statement [....] cannot be regarded as a measure adopted by the European Council, or, moreover, by any other institution, body, office or agency of the European Union". The appeal was rejected by the European Court of Justice as inadmissible: European Court of Justice, C-208/17 P to C-210/17 P, ECLI:EU:C:2018:705, order, 12 September 2018.

183 See fn. 181.

Union is liable based on its administrative involvement in the implementation of the Statement in the EU hotspots. Secondly, and mainly, the importance of the action for damages is due to the fact that *non-formally binding administrative conduct* can serve as basis for a claim under Art. 340 para. 2 TFEU. Traditionally, only formally binding administrative decisions were considered as requiring legal protection, meaning that the decision-issuing actor was considered as exclusively responsible. However, taking into account the increasing relevance of other forms of administrative conduct, the CJEU has developed the action for damages as providing an effective remedy also against non-formally binding administrative conduct: In principle, any conduct by a Union actor may incur liability.[184]

b) *The objective legal protection function of EU public liability law – addressing systemic deficiencies by enforcing EU law from below*

While the question of how to enforce EU law is a general one, finding an answer becomes particularly acute in the context of the Common European Asylum System.[185] It seems that, among the approaches ensuring the enforcement of EU law, one can distinguish between top-down procedures, initiated by the Commission as guardian of the treaties,[186] and bottom-up procedures, initiated by individuals.[187] In the context of the latter, the preliminary reference procedure, as the standard mechanism for the enforcement of fundamental freedoms, might first come to mind. But in

---

184 Cf. *Fink*, Common Market Law Review 56 (2019) (fn. 22) at 1233 "consequently, no type of conduct is excluded as a potential source of liability. Liability may arise for acts or omissions, be it of legislative, administrative, judicial, or factual nature. Therefore, also conduct that does not consist in any formal legal act is capable of triggering liability if unlawful."; *Türk*, Judicial Review in EU Law, Cheltenham 2009, 241; *Van der Woude*, Liability for Administrative Acts under Article 251(2) EC, in: Heukels/McDonnell (eds.), The Action for Damages in Community Law, The Hague 1977, 119 et seq.; *Rademacher*, Realakte (fn. 24), 264 ff, passim.

185 Cf. the case law cited in fn. 157; Art. 3 para. 2 Dublin III Regulation.

186 Cf. *Von Bogdandy/Ioannidis*, Das systemische Defizit. Merkmale, Instrumente und Probleme am Beispiel der Rechtsstaatlichkeit und des neuen Rechtsstaatlichkeitsaufsichtsverfahrens, Zeitschrift für ausländisches öffentliches Recht und Völkerrecht 74 (2014). 283, 290.

187 Cf. *Von Bogdandy et al.*, Ein Rettungsschirm für europäische Grundrechte. Grundlagen einer unionsrechtlichen *Solange*-Doktrin gegenüber Mitgliedstaaten, Zeitschrift für ausländisches öffentliches Recht und Völkerrecht 72 (2012), 45.

addition, the procedures in which individuals claim their rights directly before the CJEU can also be considered as forming part of the bottom-up enforcement of EU law. Indeed, those procedures seem to represent the standard mechanism in competition or state aid law. The enforcement of EU law from below is a traditional instrument for the effective enforcement of EU law.[188] In other words, the EU legal protection system does not only serve to guarantee subjective legal protection, but at the same time has an objective legal protection function.[189] This applies to EU public liability law in particular.[190] To be sure, the mechanism of ensuring the rule of EU law via subjective legal protection originates in the context of the enforcement of fundamental freedoms in the internal market. However, the same mechanism works effectively in the context of the enforcement of fundamental rights in the Area of Freedom, Security and Justice. The reason is that the mechanism works as soon as EU law grants individual rights. And this is increasingly the case in the Area of Freedom, Security and Justice.[191] The Charter of Fundamental Rights is the most important development in this regard. In addition, EU secondary law, in particular in

---

188 Cf. *Weiler*, The Yale Law Journal (fn. 160), 2412: "Effectively, individuals [...] became the principal 'guardians' of the legal integrity of Community law within Europe."; *Classen*, Der Einzelne als Instrument zur Durchsetzung des Gemeinschaftsrechts? Zum Problem der subjektiv-öffentlichen Rechte kraft Gemeinschaftsrecht, Verwaltungsarchiv (1997), 645.

189 See on the complementarity of both functions of legal review: *Bastos*, Derivate Illegality in European Composite Administrative Procedures, Common Market Law Review 55 (2018), 10: "Both are vital in upholding the rule of law in the domain of public administration" referring to *Kadelbach*, Allgemeines Verwaltungsrecht unter europäischem Einfluss (1999), 379 ff. See on the ensuing challenges for the design of the procedural law of the CJEU: *Barents*, EU Procedural Law and Effective Legal Protection, Common Market Law Review 51 (2014), 1445 ff.

190 Cf. *Lock*, Is Private Enforcement of EU Law Through State Liability a Myth? An Assessment 20 Years After Frankovich, Common Market Law Review 49 (2012), 1675; *Ward*, Damages under the EU Charter of Fundamental Rights, ERA Forum 12 (2012); *Von Bogdandy et al.*, A European Response to Domestic Constitutional Crisis: Advancing the Reverse-Solange Doctrine, in: Von Bogdandy/Sonnevend (eds.), Constitutional Crisis in the European Constitutional Area, Oxford 2015, 516 considering EU public liability law as one of the instruments ensuring that "the law is observed" and thereby ensuring the legitimacy of the Union.

191 Cf. *Mitsilegas*, The Limits of Mutual Trust in Europe's Area of Freedom, Security and Justice: From Automatic Inter-State Cooperation to the Slow Emergence of the Individual, Yearbook of European Law 31 (2012), 319.

the Common European Asylum System, increasingly grants rights to individuals.[192]

And indeed, a closer look confirms that EU public liability law is the only available mechanism to enforce the respect of EU law in EU hotspots. To begin with, any procedure depending on the Commission's initiative seems unsuitable to enforce EU law from the outset, due to the Commission's involvement in the EU hotspot administration.[193] And in any case, an infringement procedure would not be suitable to address the deficient application of EU law by Union bodies, as it is by its very nature limited to addressing the Member States. Where the Commission is involved in the administration, there is simply no independent institution which could in an ex officio procedure enforce the respect for the EU acquis in a top-down manner.[194] The respect for EU law must hence be enforced in a bottom-up procedure. The preliminary reference procedure is of little use, already because an action for damages against the Union cannot be brought before national courts.[195] Hence, what remains are the procedures granting the individual direct access to the CJEU. And as has been shown above, among

---

192 The rise of individual rights in the Dublin system provides an example of how ensuring the right to an effective remedy at the same time strengthens the rule of EU law in the context of horizontal administrative cooperation, cf. in particular the development from European Court of Justice, ECLI:EU:C:2013:813, C-394/12, judgement, 10 December 2013, para 48 ff., para 56 – Abdullahi, denying the existence of individual rights under the Dublin II Regulation to the acknowledgement of individual rights under the Dublin III Regulation with European Court of Justice, ECLI:EU:C:2016:409, C-63/15, judgement, 7 June 2016, para 51 – Ghezelbash; European Court of Justice, ECLI:EU:C:2016:410, C-155/15, judgement, 7 June 2016 – Karim; CJEU, ECLI:EU:C:2017:587, C-670/16, judgement, 27 July 2017 – Mengesteab; European Court of Justice, ECLI:EU:C:2017:805, C-201/16, judgement, 25 October 2017 – Shiri. This chapter is concerned with the parallel question in the context of vertical administrative cooperation.

193 In fact, the Commission has, despite its competences to do so and despite the systemic deficiencies in the EU hotspot procedure, not initiated an infringement procedure.

194 Cf. *Weiler*, The Yale Law Journal (fn. 160), 2420 stating that "the procedure is political in nature; the Commission (*appropriately*) may have *nonlegal* reasons *not* to initiate a prosecution" (emphasis added). However, where the Commission is itself closely involved in the administration, it seems questionable whether the Commission's refrainment from initiating an infringement procedure for nonlegal reasons can be "appropriate".

195 Cf. id. at. who describes the preliminary procedure as remedying the weaknesses of the infringement procedure, however noting at 2421 that the success of the system depends on the collaboration between national courts and the European

those procedures, only the action for damages provides legal protection against non-formally binding administrative conduct by Union bodies.

c) *The allocation function of EU public liability law – holding the Union and the Member States responsible*

Finally, the potential of EU public liability law for the integration of responsibility is due to its allocation function. EU public liability law is suitable to allocate responsibility between the Union and the Member States in cases where both are involved in the conduct which eventually causes the damage. Indeed, the CJEU has addressed the allocation of responsibility within the integrated European administration mainly in the context of Art. 340 para. 2 TFEU.[196] The reason is that EU public liability law, at least in principle, allows to hold the Union and the Member States jointly liable.[197] To be sure, EU public liability law still has important practical weaknesses with regard to its allocation function: Since the competence for assessing the Member States' responsibility lies with national courts, while the competence for assessing the Union's responsibility lies with the CJEU, there is a risk that each court waits for the other to decide which can lead to extreme delays in the procedures.[198] And yet, the fact that liability of the Union does not per se exclude liability of the Member States as such speaks in favour of assessing the question of the Union's responsibility under EU public liability law.

Court of Justice. The example here shows that where there is a lack of collaboration, e.g. because the national courts do not refer, the preliminary procedure comes to its limits.

196 *Fink*, Common Market Law Review 56 (2019) (fn. 22), passim.

197 The question of the liability of the Member States falls outside the scope of this study, see fn. 25.

198 *Fink*, Common Market Law Review 56 (2019) (fn. 22), 1261 ff. explains the central issue: As the respective actions cannot be brought before a single court, the individual must choose whether to bring action against either the EU before the CJEU, or against the Member State before national courts, or both in parallel. In case of the latter choice, both the CJEU and the national courts might stay the proceedings until the respective other court has decided, which leads to a situation in which neither court decides. Cf. on this vicious circle e.g. CJEU, ECLI:EU:C:1967:31, Joined Cases 5, 7, and 13 to 22/66, judgement, 14 July 1967 – Kampffmeyer, see id. at. note 162 for more case law examples. As a consequence, even though joint liability might be possible from a doctrinal perspective, it is practically difficult to actually hold both the EU and the Member State liable to an extent risking the effectiveness of the remedy.

4. Holding the Union liable?

It has been shown that EU public liability law is, in principle, particularly suitable to hold the Union or its agencies liable for fundamental rights violations occurring in the EU hotspots. Now, the next step would obviously be to unfold that potential. In other words, the argument suggests analysing the integrated EU hotspot administration in light of EU public liability law, in order to assess whether the Union or its agencies could actually be held liable for fundamental rights violations in EU hotspots. Given the scope of this chapter, the necessary comprehensive doctrinal analysis can however not be undertaken here. It must hence suffice to note that the analysis must begin with determining the administrative conduct on the basis of which liability might potentially arise.

Then, three critical legal questions must be addressed in detail – namely, the question of attribution in the context of seconded EU agency staff, the question of causation in the context of non-formally binding administrative conduct, and the question of a sufficiently serious breach of a rule conferring rights upon individuals in the context of supervisory obligations.[199] Those questions arise in the context of the integrated European administration more generally, and have recently been analysed with a view to Frontex operations.[200] The chapter has on the one hand shown that such doctrinal analysis is required with a view to the particularities of the EU hotspot administration, and on the other hand has established the basis for such an analysis by setting out the structure of the integrated EU hotspot administration.

IV. EU law limits to externalisation

The current EU asylum policy relies, not fully, but to an important extent, on the approach to externalise the challenge of dealing with enhanced forced migration. The challenge is often externalised to third States or, where this is not feasible, to Member States geographically located at the EU external border. This raises fundamental challenges to accountability

---

199 See on those questions *inter alia* the works cited in fn. 21 to fn. 24.

200 In particular: *Fink*, Frontex and Human Rights (fn. 22); *Fink*, Common Market Law Review 56 (2019) (fn. 22); *Fink*, German Law Journal 21 (2020) (fn. 22).

in general, and to the right to an effective remedy in particular.[201] EU hotspots can be described as a paradigm example in this regard. As externalisation has an "out of sight, out of mind" effect, it seems possible to forget about daily fundamental rights violations in refugee camps at the EU's external borders. EU public liability law, however, calls into question whether mere externalisation is sufficient to exclude judicial responsibility of the Union. The potential of EU public liability in this regard yet remains to be unfolded.

201 Cf. *Costello/Mann*, Border Justice: Migration and Accountability for Human Rights Violations, German Law Journal German Law Journal 21 (2020), 311 ff.

Regulation 2019/1896 on the European Border and Coast Guard (Frontex): The Supranational Administration of the External Borders?

David Fernandez-Rojo[*]

I. Introduction

On 6 October 2016, the European Border and Coast Guard (EBCG), the successor of the European Agency for the Management of Operational Cooperation at the External Borders of the Member States of the European Union (Frontex), was officially established. On the day of its inauguration, the European Commissioner for Migration, Home Affairs and Citizenship, Dimitris Avramopoulos, indicated that the Agency was a historic milestone in the management of the external borders of the European Union (EU) as it meant the creation of "a fully-fledged European Border and Coast Guard system, turning into reality the principles of shared responsibility and solidarity among the Member States and the Union".[1]

Regulation (EU) No. 2016/1624 and the recently adopted Regulation (EU) No. 2019/1896 represent the third and fourth legislative revision of Frontex' mandate and functions since the Agency was established by Regulation (EC) No. 2007/2004. Previously, Regulation (EC) No. 863/2007 introduced the rapid intervention teams and Regulation (EU) No. 1168/2011 strengthened the Agency's tasks and the protection of fundamental rights. In May 2015, the European Commission deemed the design of a European system of border guards with greater operational tasks as necessary.[2] The adoption of Regulation (EU) No. 2016/1624 was extraordinarily fast[3] since it did not take a year between its proposal by the Commission on 15 De-

---

* PhD in EU Law (University of Deusto, 2018) and assistant professor at the University of Deusto.

1 Council of the EU, Securing Europe's external borders: Launch of the European Border and Coast Guard Agency, Press release 555/16, 6 October 2016.

2 European Commission, A European Agenda on Migration, COM (2015) 240 final, 13 May 2015, 20.

3 Given the urgency in adopting the proposal of the EBCG, and despite its importance, the European Commission did not carry out an impact assessment.

cember 2015 and its publication in the Official Journal on 16 September 2016.

Moreover, less than two years after the adoption of Regulation 2016/1624, the president of the European Commission announced in his speech on the 2018 State of the Union made on 12 September, the Commission's intention to "to further strengthen the European Border and Coast Guard to better protect our external borders with an additional 10,000 European border guards by 2020".[4] On the same day, the Commission put forwards an updated version of the recently adopted EBCG.[5] Again, in record time, Regulation 2019/1896 was published in the Official Journal of the EU on 14 November 2019.[6] Regulation (EU) No. 2019/1896 was in fact one of the very last texts voted at the European Parliament under the 2014–2019 mandate.[7] In particular, on 17 April 2019, the Parliament adopted the proposal put forward by the European Commission to further strengthen the EBCG with a standing corps of 10,000 border guards with executive powers by 2027.[8]

This chapter centres on analysing the reinforced operational mandate of the EBCG *vis-à-vis* the Member States in comparison to its predecessor, Frontex. Specifically, it assesses to what extent Regulations 2016/1624 and 2019/1896 on the EBCG operationally transform Frontex, as the very name of the Agency seems now to suggest, into a fully fledged Border and Coast Guard Agency that Europeanises the administration of the external borders. From an examination of the initiatives and studies that were undertaken with the objective of evaluating the feasibility of designing a European Corps of Border Guards, as well as from an analysis of the new operational tasks conferred on the EBCG, the chapter concludes that Regulations (EU) No. 2016/1624 and 2019/1896 are far from establishing an abso-

---

4 European Commission, State of the Union 2018 – the Hour of European Sovereignty, https://ec.europa.eu/commission/sites/beta-political/files/soteu2018-speech_en_0.pdf, 12 September 2018.

5 European Commission, Proposal for a Regulation of the European Parliament and of the Council on the European Border and Coast Guard, COM(2018) 631 final, 12. September 2018.

6 Regulation (EU) 2019/1896 of the European Parliament and of the Council of 13 November 2019 on the European Border and Coast Guard and repealing Regulations (EU) No. 1052/2013 and (EU) 2016/1624, OJ L-295, 14 November 2019.

7 European Parliament legislative resolution of 17 April 2019 on the proposal for a regulation of the European Parliament and of the Council on the European Border and Coast Guard, P8_TA (2019)0415.

8 Proposal for a Regulation of the European Parliament and of the Council on the European Border and Coast Guard, COM/2018/631 final, 12 September 2018.

lute integration and supranational administration of border management at the European level. Rather, the new operational functions delegated to the EBCG focus on supervising the effective functioning of border management and assisting the national authorities that are subject to an extraordinary migratory pressure. Additionally, the preeminent role that the Member States continue to play in the EBCG's administrative governance ensures their effective and daily control in the Agency's recently reinforced operational mandate.

II. The creation of a European Border and Coast Guard Agency as a constant in the EU political and legislative agenda

The need for a shared responsibility and a common European approach to border management was firstly addressed in a European Parliament Resolution of 3 April 1998 on the implications of the enlargement of the EU for cooperation in the field of Justice and Home Affairs (JHA). This Resolution stated that a "European border control force should be introduced to control future external borders which draws on the national experience of border control forces for implementation at Community level [...]".[9] While the EU enlargement influenced the debate at the European level surrounding the cooperation between Member States in the management of their external borders, the incorporation of the Schengen acquis into the framework of the EU was the key factor for the integration of border management. Precisely, in October 1999, the Tampere Programme stressed that the integration of the Schengen acquis into the Union required an enhanced cooperation and mutual technical assistance between the Member States and the candidate countries to effectively control the European external borders.[10] This section examines the various studies and communications published with the aim of assessing the feasibility of developing a truly European Border Guard and which, directly or indirectly, have influenced Regulations 2016/1624 and 2019/1896.

---

9 Resolution of 3 April 1998 on the implications of enlargement of the European Union for cooperation in the field of justice and home affairs, OJ C-138, 04 May 1998, A4-0107/98, para 19.

10 *Monar*, The Project of a European Border Guard: Origins, Models and Prospects in the Context of the EU's Integrated External Border Management, in: Caparini/Otwin (eds.), Borders and Security Governance: Managing Borders in a Globalised World, Münster 2006, 193, 195.

1. Institutional models for the management of the European external borders

In November 2001, the European Commission announced the adoption of a coherent strategy to guarantee a high standard of external border controls. The Communication called for the creation of a permanent technical cooperation support facility in charge of information gathering and dissemination, coordination of operational cooperation, and the administration of the European migration systems (i.e. Schengen Information System, Eurodac and European Visa Identification System).[11]

Subsequently, in December 2001, the European Council of Laeken considered that a better management of the European external borders would "help in the fight against terrorism, illegal immigration networks and the traffic in human beings". In order to achieve these objectives, the European Council asked the Council and the European Commission "to work out arrangements for cooperation between services responsible for external border control and to examine the conditions in which a mechanism or common services to control external borders could be created".[12]

The European Commission followed the mandate of the European Council of Laeken and financially contributed (through the Odysseus Programme) to a feasibility study led by Italy (with the participation of Belgium, France, Germany, Italy and Spain) regarding the establishment of a European Border Police.[13] On 30 May 2002, the study was made public and two organisational models, "unitary" and "network", were identified according to the degree of integration and supranationality desired to be conferred on the EU in the management of the external borders.

The unitary model would centralise all the executive competences of border control at the European level. This model was organisationally described as the most efficient, since it would eliminate any kind of duplicity or lack of coordination between the several national authorities responsible for border surveillance. However, it would also be the most difficult of models to implement, since not only would the Member States be highly hesitant to delegate such powers, which are directly linked to their nation-

11 European Commission, Communication on a Common Policy on Illegal Immigration, COM (2001) 672 final, 15 November 2001, 19.

12 Presidency Conclusions – Laeken, 14 and 15 December 2001, doc. SN 300/1/01 REV 1, para 42.

13 Feasibility Study for the Setting-up of a European Border Police, Final Report, Roma, 2002, http://www.statewatch.org/news/2005/may/eba-feasibility-study.pdf, 29; see: House of Lords (European Union Committee), Proposals for a European Border Guard, 29th Report of Session 2002–2003, 01 June 2003, 10–11.

al sovereignty, but because it would also require all the national border authorities to merge.[14]

On the other hand, the network model would imply the development of a European Border Corps that would coordinate and assist the national authorities in charge of the external borders. This model would have a more flexible structure, easily adaptable to a context as volatile as the external borders, and the Member States would receive it more positively. Yet, a European Border Corps would not guarantee border coordination at the European level as uniform and effective as the one offered by the unitary model.[15]

The Italian study finally recommended an intermediate and predominantly intergovernmental model, which would consist of "a modified network structure with a centralised body with coordination functions" and "articulated in a series of 'knots', each of them related to specific and sector requirements/objectives, organised as operational Centres with a little nucleus of support and assisted by a certain number of consultants/experts".[16]

Following the mandate of the European Council of Laeken and having consulted the feasibility study led by Italy, the Commission published a communication in May 2002 entitled "towards integrated management of the external borders of the Member States of the European Union".[17] The main challenge that the European Commission identified in the management of the European external borders consisted in the lack of effective operational coordination between the national authorities, preventing the achievement of a uniform level of security in the borders. The Commission considered it essential to design an operational common cooperation and coordination body, which in the short term, would consist of an External Borders Practitioners Common Unit, and in the medium term, a European Corps of Border Guards[18].

The External Borders Practitioners Common Unit would have an intergovernmental nature and would be integrated into the structures of the Council. On the contrary, the European Corps of Border Guards would be an independent supranational organisation in charge of developing first surveillance and control missions at the external borders, and would com-

---

14 Feasibility Study for the Setting-up of a European Border Police, 29.

15 Feasibility Study for the Setting-up of a European Border Police, 30.

16 Feasibility Study for the Setting-up of a European Border Police, 30.

17 European Commission, Communication Towards Integrated Management of the External Borders of the Member States of the European Union, COM (2002) 233 final, 7 May 2002.

18 COM (2002) 233 final, 24.

mission its own border guards at a later stage. The European Commission acknowledged that the design of the European Corps of Border Guards would require revising the Treaties and overcoming a major constitutional challenge such as "conferring the prerogatives of public authority on staff of the European Corps who do not have the nationality of the Member State where they are deployed".[19] Furthermore, two other practical issues would need to be settled: the recruitment, statutory, and disciplinary conditions of the border guards placed at the disposal of the European Corps by the Member States, and the allocation of its own equipment.[20]

Finally, in June 2002, the Council decided to introduce the External Borders Practitioners Common Unit, integrated by the heads of the border control services of the Member States.[21] The Council requested the Member States to initiate joint operations at the external borders and pilot projects, establish a network of Member States' migration liaison officers, prepare a common risk analysis model, and design a common core curriculum for border guard training. The EU political leaders in the Seville European Council welcomed the Council's plan and recommended its immediate implementation.[22] The Member States followed the Seville European Council's mandate and developed joint operations and pilot projects on the external borders, as well as creating *ad hoc* centres.

Hence, the Council abandoned the idea of developing a European Corps of Border Guards, since at the time it was not supported by most of the Member States, thus opting instead for an approach with a strong intergovernmental character – the External Borders Practitioners Common Unit. The Member States considered the operational and financial support of the EU, through the Common Unit, sufficient to ensure a coherent and consistent management of the external borders and to improve the effective implementation of EU law. The Common Unit's mandate was limited to increasing the operational coordination between the national authorities, remaining exclusively competent to manage and monitor their external borders.

---

19 COM (2002) 233 final, 21.
20 COM (2002) 233 final, 21.
21 Council, Plan for the management of the external borders of the Member States of the European Union, doc. 10019/02, 14 June 2002.
22 Council, Presidency Conclusions, Seville European Council, 21–22 June 2002, 22 June 2002, para 32.

2. *Negotiating the establishment of Frontex*

Over the course of a year, the External Borders Practitioners Common Unit had a very limited impact on the efficient management of the EU's borders. The failure of the Common Unit was largely due to its inadequate preparation and planning, as well as an insufficient operational cooperation and legal basis that prevented the Common Unit from developing common operations.[23] Meanwhile, the Member States also failed to fully comply with their obligations towards the Common Unit, which ended up being highly politicised and mainly "promoting individual Member States' pet projects".[24] Ultimately, the realisation of a uniform and effective European border management depended on the operational powers conferred on the Common Unit and the commitment of the Member States to further communitarise this area.

The Common Unit needed to be reviewed with the aim of delegating the operational tasks to a "new permanent Community structure able to exercise this day-to-day management and coordination tasks and to respond in time to emergency situations".[25] Therefore, in a report to the Council by the Greek Presidency, it was considered necessary to design a new institutional structure to promote effective operational cooperation in the management of external borders.[26] In November 2003, following the

---

23 Council, Report on the implementation of programmes, *ad hoc* centres, pilot projects and joint operations, doc. 10058/1/03, 11 June 2003 and Council, Progress Report for the Implementation of the Plan for the management of external borders of the Member States of the European Union and the comprehensive plan for combating illegal immigration, doc. 7504/03, 17 March 2003.

24 *Neal*, Securitization and risk at the EU border: The origins of FRONTEX, Journal of Common Market Studies 47 (2009), 333, 342.

25 European Commission, "Communication in view of the European Council of Thessaloniki on the Development of a Common Policy on Illegal Immigration, Smuggling and Trafficking of Human Beings, External Borders and the Return of Illegal Residents", COM (2003) 323 final, 03 June 2003, 8.

26 COM (2003) 323 final, 6–8.

Thessaloniki European Council,[27] the European Commission proposed the creation of Frontex.[28]

The negotiations for establishing Frontex lasted less than a year, since the Agency was proposed on 20 November 2003 and adopted on 26 October 2004.[29] Two factors rushed these negotiations: 1) the imminent EU enlargement (expected by May 2004); 2) the completion on 1 January 2005 of the five-year transitional period, after which external border matters would be governed by the co-decision procedure, which would imply that the European Parliament would actively be involved, rather than merely consulted, in the legislative process.[30]

While the European Council welcomed the creation of Frontex in 2005, it stressed that the European Commission should assess the establishment of a European system of border guards.[31] In 2010, the Stockholm Programme also invited the Commission to initiate "a debate on the long-term development of FRONTEX [that] should include (...) the feasibility of the creation of a European system of border guards".[32] The Treaty of Lisbon invigorated this debate, leaving a wide margin of appreciation regard-

27 Thessaloniki European Council 19 and 20 June 2003, doc. 11638/03, 01 October 2003, 4. Previously, the European Commission presented a Feasibility study on the control of the European Union's maritime borders, see: Council, Feasibility study on the control of the European Union's maritime borders – Final Report, doc. 11490/1/03 REV 1, 19 September 2003.

28 European Commission, Proposal for a Council Regulation establishing a European Agency for the Management of Operational Co-operation at the External Borders, COM (2003) 687 final/2, 20 November 2003.

29 Council Regulation (EC) No. 2007/2004 of 26 October 2004 establishing a European Agency for the Management of Operational Cooperation at the External Borders of the Member States of the European Union, OJ L-349, 25 November 2004, 1–11.

30 *Leonard*, The creation of FRONTEX and the politics of institutionalisation in the EU external borders policy, Journal of Contemporary European Research 5 (2009), 371, 380. In this respect, the CJEU examined the implementation competences held by the Council after the transitional period of five years, see: European Court of Justice, C-133/06, ECLI:EU:C:2008:257, judgement, 6 May 2008 – European Parliament v. Council of the European Union and European Court of Justice, C-257/01, ECLI:EU:C:2005:25, judgement, 18 January 2005 – Commission of the European Communities v. Council of the European Union.

31 European Council, The Hague Programme: Strengthening Freedom, Security and Justice in the European Union, OJ C-53, 03 March 2005, 6.

32 European Council, The Stockholm Programme – An open and secure Europe serving and protecting the citizens, 04 May 2010, 56; The 2015 external evaluation of FRONTEX also signalled that any future revision of the mandate of the agency should address the feasibility of creating a European Border Guard System; see:

ing the model to be implemented to manage the European external borders. Art. 77 Treaty on Functioning of the EU (TFEU) openly states that an integrated system of external borders should be progressively established.

In June 2013, the European Commission ordered a study from Unisys in order to examine the feasibility of introducing a European System of Border Guards. The study, published on 16 June 2014, put forward a model, divided into three subsequent phases, to gradually achieve an integrated management of the European external borders. On the one hand, the model sought to accommodate the position of Frontex, the European Commission, and a large number of members of the European Parliament[33] that advocated for a greater delegation of powers to the EU. On the other hand, the Member States prioritised a more moderate integration of border management matters.[34]

According to the study conducted by Unisys, the first phase (until 2020) for the development of a European System of Border Guards should consist in deepening and developing Frontex' powers and structure to the fullest. The Agency should continue to support the work of national authorities without being delegated new competences. The second phase, however, could encompass a transferral of executive powers to Frontex but only in the so-called hotspots (geographical areas subject to a disproportionate migratory pressure). That is, while the daily management of the borders would continue to be the responsibility of the Member States, the hotspots' operations would be the exclusive function of the Agency, which would act through its own border guards and equipment[35]. As early as 2030 (phase three), the Unisys study envisaged a EU decentralised Agency

---

Ramboll and Eurasylum, External Evaluation of the Agency under Art. 33 of the FRONTEX Regulation, 2015, 101.

33 The European Parliament has been favourable on strengthening Frontex' powers and mandate; see: European Parliament, Resolution on the mid-term review of the Stockholm Programme, 2013/2024(INI), 02 April 2014, para 80; European Parliament, Resolution on the situation in the Mediterranean and the need for a holistic EU approach to migration, 2015/2095(INI), 12 April 2016, paras 70–72; European Parliament, Resolution on the Special Report of the European Ombudsman in own-initiative inquiry OI/5/2012/BEH-MHZ concerning FRONTEX, 2014/2215(INI), 02 December 2015.

34 Unisys, Study on the feasibility of the creation of a European System of Border Guards to control the external borders of the Union, 16 June 2014, 21; See: Council, Report of the Conference "The Feasibility of a European System of Border Guards: A practitioner's perspective" organised by FRONTEX and ERA, doc. 5496/14, 27 January 2014.

35 COM (2015) 240 final, 7.

that would be completely centralised and in charge of the supranational management of the European external borders. Due to the executive and decision-making powers of this new "EU federal Agency", a reform of the current Treaties and the internal legislation of some Member States is deemed necessary by the Unisys study.

Although the recently adopted Regulations 2016/1624 and 2019/1896 misleadingly refer to a "European Border and Coast Guard",[36] this "new FRONTEX" is not a fully fledged European Border Corps.[37] However, Regulations 2016/1624 and 2019/1896 have not created a federal Agency with centralised and enforcement powers in the management and surveillance of the European borders. The EBCG, despite its new fancy name, will continue to operate in a decentralised border management system. As Carrera and Den Hertog highlighted, the EBCG could be better defined as a FRONTEX+[38] or, according to De Bruycker a mere legal fiction, made up of the sum of the new Agency and the national authorities that remain in charge of the management of the external borders.[39]

The EBCG has not been conferred exclusive and executive powers in the management of the external borders, as was proposed by Unisys in its third and final phase of Frontex' development. The EBCG could be better situated between the first and second phases of the Unisys model, since the technical and operational tasks originally conferred to Frontex have been significantly broadened, yet the Member States continue to conduct executive and coercive activities at their external borders. In this regard, Art. 5 Regulation 2016/1624 and Art. 7 Regulation 2019/1896 state that the Member States are primary responsible for the management of their section of the external borders, and the EBCG's mandate is limited to supporting the application of EU border management measures by strengthening, evaluating, and coordinating the actions of the national competent authorities.

---

36 *Carrera/Den Hertog*, A European Border and Coast Guard: What's in a Name?, CEPS Paper in Liberty and Security in Europe 88 (2016), 1, 1–22.

37 *Acosta Sánchez*, La nueva Guardia Europea de Fronteras y Costas una necesaria evolución de FRONTEX, Boletín Instituto Español de Estudios Estratégicos 4 (2016), 466, 466–482; *Santos Vara*, La transformación de FRONTEX en la Agencia Europea de la Guardia de Fronteras y Costas: ¿hacia una centralización en la gestión de las fronteras?, Revista de Derecho Comunitario Europeo 59 (2018), 143, 143–186.

38 *Carrera/Den Hertog*, CEPS Paper in Liberty and Security in Europe 88 (2016) (fn. 36), 1, 1–22.

39 *De Bruycker*, The European border and coast guard: a new model built on an old logic, European Papers 1(2) (2016), 559, 559–569.

III. The novel supervisory and operational tasks of the European Border and Coast Guard Agency

Frontex was created in 2004 with the aim of operationally coordinating and supporting national authorities in the management of their external borders. Since then, Frontex has assisted the Member States through the development of risk analysis, training programmes, joint operations, rapid border interventions, return operations and signing agreements with third countries. These tasks initially delegated to Frontex were progressively expanded first with the adoption of Regulations 863/2007 and 1168/2011, as well as more recently in May 2015, with the European Agenda on Migration that designed the hotspot approach, a reinforced multilateral cooperation to assist those national authorities subject to an exceptional migratory pressure.[40]

Regulation 863/2007 introduced the rapid intervention teams and a Central Record of Available Technical Equipment (CRATE). As a result, a Member State, upon request, could temporarily use the resources that the other Member States voluntarily put at its disposal. This equipment (aircrafts, vessels, helicopters, mobile radar units and other special technical equipment) was intended to be used on a bilateral basis between Member States. Subsequently, Regulation 1168/2011 reinforced the operational capacity of Frontex and its autonomy. Frontex was allowed to acquire or lease technical equipment. Yet in reality, the resources of Frontex consisted mainly of equipment owned by the Member States. Regulation 1168/2011 created the European Border Guard Teams. Frontex acquired competent border guards seconded by the Member State as national experts. For a period of up to six months, Frontex was competent to decide where and for how long the seconded guest officers were going to be deployed.

In May 2015, the European Agenda on Migration designed the hotspot approach. The hotspots are defined as geographical areas subject to sudden, specific, and exceptional mixed migratory flows that the competent national border and asylum systems are unable to effectively process.[41] Frontex was called to play a threefold operational role at the hotspots; a registration and screening role – by assisting the concerned Member State in fingerprinting and determining the identity and nationality of the arriving migrants; a debriefing role – by contributing to the national illegal mi-

40 Explanatory note on the "Hotspot" approach, 15 June 2015, http://www.statewatch.org/news/2015/jul/eucom-hotsposts.pdf.

41 Explanatory note on the "Hotspot" approach, 3.

grant smuggling and trafficking investigations; and lastly, a return role – by coordinating with the competent national authorities regarding the removal of those migrants that do not qualify for asylum or international protection. All of these tasks were expressly stated in Art. 18 para. 4 Regulation 2016/1624 and now in Art. 40 Regulation 2019/1896, which regulate the deployment of migration management support teams in the hotspots.[42]

Whereas Frontex had not fully explored the tasks and every operational possibility that Regulations 863/2007 and 1168/2011 or the novel hotspot approach offered, on 15 December 2015 the European Commission proposed the creation of the EBCG.[43] The Commission stressed that "the sheer scale of the mixed migratory flows which have crossed the external borders of the European Union and the consequent secondary movements, demonstrated that existing structures at Union and Member State level are inadequate to address the challenges arising from such a large influx".[44] The Commission considered that the control of the European external borders and the maintenance of security within the Schengen Area required, in accordance with the principles of solidarity and responsibility, the progressive development of an integrated system of management of the external borders.

Regulations 2016/1624 and 2019/1896 aim to develop a EU integrated management of the external borders by addressing both the existing deficiencies at the national level and responding effectively to exceptional and sudden migratory flows. To achieve these ambitious objectives, Regulations 2016/1624 and 2019/1896 indicate that the EBCG shall have the fol-

---

42 For an analysis in depth of the hotspot approach see *Casolari*, The EU's Hotspot Approach to Managing the Migration Crisis: A Blind Spot for International Responsibility?, The Italian Yearbook of International Law 25 (2015), 109, 109–134; *Fernandez-Rojo*, Los hotspots: expansión de las tareas operativas y cooperación multilateral de las agencias europeas Frontex, Easo y Europol, Revista de Derecho Comunitario Europeo 61 (2018), 1013, 1013–1056; *Neville/Sy/Rigon*, On the frontline: the hotspot approach to managing migration, Study for the LIBE Committee, PE 556.942, May 2016, 33–40.

43 See: External Evaluation of the Agency under Art. 33 of the FRONTEX Regulation Final report 28 July 2015; FRONTEX Management Board Decision No. 40/2015 adopting recommendations of the Management Board following the evaluation of FRONTEX (Art. 33) 20 October 2015.

44 Proposal for a Regulation of the European Parliament and of the Council on the European Border and Coast Guard and repealing Regulation (EC) No. 2007/2004, Regulation (EC) No. 863/2007 and Council Decision 2005/267/EC, COM (2015) 671 final, 15 December 2015, 2.

lowing operational tasks *vis-à-vis* the Member States: 1) monitor the effective management of the external borders; 2) provide reinforced technical and operational assistance to Member States through joint operations and rapid border interventions and; 3) ensure the practical implementation of EU border management measures in situations requiring urgent action at the external borders. This section centres on comparatively analysing the new operational powers conferred on the new EBCG when supporting the Members States through Regulations 2016/1624 and 2019/1896.

1. The EBCG's supervisory role

Art. 3 para. 2 Regulation 2016/1624 conferred a monitoring role on the EBCG in order to guarantee a common strategy for the management of the European external borders. While Frontex also conducted supervisory activities to a certain extent, the EBCG may now deploy its own liaison officers in the Member States with the aim of fostering cooperation and dialogue between the Agency and the competent national authorities (Art. 12 para. 3 Regulation 2016/1624). The EBCG liaison officers, who are deployed on the basis of a risk analysis carried out by the Agency, should regularly inform the Agency's Executive Director about the situation at the external borders and assess the capacity of the concerned Member State to effectively manage its borders (Art. 12 para. 3 (h) Regulation 2016/1624).

According to the EBCG Management Board Decision 14/2017, the Executive Director of the Agency is in charge of appointing the members of the temporary staff of the EBCG to be deployed as Liaison Officers. The EBCG's Liaison Officers are namely responsible for: 1) acting as an interface and facilitating the cooperation between the EBCG and all Member States' authorities; 2) supporting the collection of information and best practices; 3) monitoring the measures taken by the Member State at its border sections to which a high impact level has been attributed; 4) contributing to promoting the application of the Union acquis; 5) reporting regularly to the Executive Director on the situation at the external borders, on the capacity of the Member States concerned to deal effectively with the situation at the external borders, and on the execution of return and pre-return activities; and 6) monitoring and reporting on the measures taken by the Member States with regard to a situation requiring urgent action at the external borders.[45] These responsibilities have been further detailed in Art. 31 para 3 Regulation 2019/1896.

The information that the liaison officers gather contributes and facilitates the preparation of the EBCG's vulnerability assessments. At least once every three years, the Agency shall monitor and assess the availability of the technical equipment, systems, capabilities, resources, infrastructure, and adequately skilled and trained staff of Member States for border control (Art. 32 para. 2 Regulation 2019/1896). In turn, Member States are required to collaborate with the EBCG in elaborating the vulnerability assessment.

Pursuant Art. 32 para. 1 Regulation 2019/1896, the Agency shall, by decision of the Management Board based on a proposal of the Executive Director, establish a common vulnerability assessment methodology. This methodology consists of a baseline assessment, a simulation exercise, a simulation assessment, and the recommendations issued by the EBCG.[46] During the baseline assessment, the Agency is in charge of checking for vulnerabilities and analysing the data gathered. Subsequently, the Agency's Executive Director may decide to conduct a simulation exercise for selected Member States and a stress test of the competent national authorities' preparedness to specific threats and challenges at the external borders, which may lead to additional recommendations on measures for the Member States.[47] Finally, the Member States are informed of the results of their vulnerability assessments and the EBCG's Executive Director may recommend that the concerned Member State adopt, within a certain period of time, certain measures.

The recommendatory powers conferred on the EBCG are reflected in Art. 32 para. 10 Regulation 2019/1896, which signals that if the recommended measures are not implemented in a timely fashion and in an appropriate manner by the concerned Member State, the EBCG's Executive Director shall refer the matter to the Management Board and inform the

---

45 FRONTEX, Management Board Decision 14/2017 on the deployment of FRONTEX Liaison Officers to Member States, 13 June 2017.

46 FRONTEX, What is Vulnerability Assessment?, 16 October 2017, http://bit.ly/2zsPmsr.

47 European Commission, Report on the operationalisation of the European Border and Coast Guard, COM (2017) 42 final, 25 January 2017, 6; European Commission, Report on the operationalisation of the European Border and Coast Guard, COM (2017) 201 final, 02 March 2017, 7; *Ferraro/De Capitani*, The new European Border and Coast Guard: yet another "half way" EU reform?, ERA Forum 17 (2016), 385, 385–398.

European Commission. The Management Board shall then make a decision, based on the original proposal of the Executive Director, describing the necessary measures to be taken by the Member State and the time limit within which such measures shall be implemented. Importantly, Art. 32 para. 10 Regulation 2019/1896 explicitly declares that the decision of the Management Board is binding on the Member State.

Regulations 2016/1624 and 2019/1896 clearly reinforce the incipient monitoring and supervisory capacity of Frontex. Currently, the EBCG's Management Board is mandated to adopt, by two-thirds majority of the members with a right to vote, binding measures, if the actions or omissions of a concerned Member State may compromise the Schengen Area.[48] It remains to be seen as to the position of the national authorities within the EBCG's Management Board and whether they will adopt measures that effectively ensure that a concerned Member State tackles the vulnerabilities identified in its external borders.

Although the EBCG started to undertake vulnerability assessments a few months after Regulation 2016/1624 entered into force, the presence of liaison officers in Member States had a slow start. It was not until June 2017 that the EBCG's Management Board approved the rules that defined the role and tasks of the Liaison Officers. The European Commission urged the Agency to "step up and accelerate the work towards the deployment of liaison officers", since in September 2017, the Memorandum of Understanding with the Member States, which set out the modalities of deployment, was not adopted and the selection procedures for the recruitment of the Liaison Officers were not yet launched.[49] During 2017, the EBCG smoothly delivered baseline vulnerability assessments and issued recommendations to the Member States with concrete measures, addressing the identified vulnerabilities.[50] In this regard, the competent national authorities were required to improve their processes of data collection, with the aim of efficiently providing complete data on their border management capacities.[51]

While it is still early to assess to what extent Regulation 2019/1896 improves the functioning of the vulnerability assessment and the swift deployment of liaison officers, a novel mechanism of impact levels to exter-

48 European Commission, Fifth Report on the operationalisation of the European Border and Coast Guard, COM (2017) 467 final, 06 September 2017, 7.

49 COM (2017) 467 final, 12.

50 COM (2017) 467 final, 7–8.

51 European Commission, Fourth Report on the operationalization of the European Border and Coast Guard, COM (2017) 325 final, 13 June 2017, 10.

nal border sections has been designed. Arts. 34 and 35 Regulation 2019/1896 state that the EBCG, in agreement with the Member State concerned, may declare three different impact levels and reactions with the aim of swiftly addressing at a given border section a crisis situation. Firstly, when the EBCG declares a low impact level, the competent national authorities shall "organise regular control [...] and ensure that sufficient personnel and resources are being kept available for that border section" (Art. 35 para. 1 (a)). Secondly, if a medium impact level is established, the concerned Member State shall "ensure that appropriate control measures are being taken at that border section" (Art. 35 para. 1 (b)). Thirdly, where a high impact level is declared the national authorities are encouraged to request operational assistance from the EBCG (Art. 35 para. 1 (c)).

In addition, the EBCG may temporarily determine at a given border section a critical impact level, which shall be communicated to the European Commission. Under this scenario, the EBCG's Executive Director will recommend the Member State concerned to request the EBCG's operational assistance through the initiation of a joint operation or a rapid border intervention (Art. 41 para. 1 Regulation 2019/1896). While the obligations for the national border authorities under the low, medium and high impact levels are quite vague, under the critical scenario the Member State concerned shall respond, providing justifications for its decision, to the recommendation of the Executive Director within six working days (Art. 41 para. 2). According to Art. 42 Regulation 2019/1896, should the Member State ignore the EBCG Executive Director's recommendation, the Council, on the basis of a proposal from the European Commission, may adopt a decision by means of an implementing act, identifying measures to mitigate those risks and requiring the Member State concerned to cooperate with the Agency in the implementation of those measures.

2. *The EBCG's expanded operational tasks*

The EBCG continues to provide operational assistance to the Member States, as did Frontex, through the coordination of joint operations and rapid border interventions and through the deployment of teams on the ground (Art. 37 Regulation 2019/1896). For the first time, Regulation 2016/1624 regulated the technical and operational capacity of the EBCG in the hotspots, where the national authorities face a sudden and disproportionate migratory pressure according to the 2015 Migration Agenda.[52] In particular, pursuant to Art. 18 para. 2 Regulation 2016/1624, "the executive director, in coordination with other relevant Union agencies, shall assess a Member State's request for reinforcement and the assessment of its needs for the purpose of defining a comprehensive reinforcement package consisting of various activities coordinated by the relevant Union agencies to be agreed upon by the Member State concerned".

In this regard, Art. 40 para. 1 Regulation 2019/1896 now details that in the hotspot areas migration management support teams, composed of experts from the relevant Union Agencies, will be deployed upon request of a Member State subject to large inward mixed migratory flows. The EBCG's teams deployed in the hotspots are in charge of reinforcing the technical and operational assistance by "screening of third-country nationals arriving at the external borders, including the identification, registration, and debriefing [...] and, where requested by the Member State, the fingerprinting [...]" (Art. 40 para. 4 Regulation 2019/1896). Notwithstanding that the hotspot approach has been incorporated in Regulation 2016/1624 and 2019/1896, which in turn reveals that the approach constitutes a EU long term measure to tackle extraordinary migratory pressures, there is to date no specific legal framework clarifying the functioning, powers and responsibility of the EBCG in the hotspots.

Not only are the operational activities of the EBCG reinforced in regard to the hotspots designed for those Member States subject to an extraordinary and exceptional migratory flow, but also in regard to third countries. The EBCG shall facilitate, in line with Frontex' previous practice, technical and operational cooperation between the Member States and third countries. The EBCG is now competent to sign work agreements, which shall respect EU Law, fundamental rights, and the principle of non-refoulement, with the authorities of third countries in charge of border management (Art. 73 para. 1 Regulation 2019/1896)[53]. In addition, the EBCG may

52 COM (2015) 240 final, 6.

53 These agreements signed by FRONTEX were widely criticised by the doctrine given its lack of transparency, difficult control and potential violation of fundamental rights; See: *Fink*, Frontex Working Arrangements: Legitimacy and Human Rights Concerns Regarding "Technical Relationships", Merkourios-Utrecht Journal of International and European Law 28 (2012), 20, 20; *García Andrade*, EU External Competences in the Field of Migration: How to Act Externally When Thinking Internally, Common Market Law Review 55 (2018), 157, 157; *Santos Vara*, The External Activities of AFSJ Agencies: The Weakness of Democratic and Judicial Controls, European Foreign Affairs Review 20 (2015), 115, 118.

deploy experts from its own staff as liaison officers in third countries (Art. 77 Regulation 2019/1896), as well as to establish antenna offices on the territory of a third country in order to facilitate and improve the coordination of the Agency's operational activities (Art. 60 Regulation 2019/1896). Nonetheless, the main novelty introduced by Regulation 2019/1896 concerns those circumstances that require greater technical and operational assistance, in which the Agency, prior to the adoption of a status agreement, may deploy "border management teams from the standing corps to a third country where the members of the teams will exercise executive powers" (Art. 73 para. 3). That is, on the basis of an operational plan agreed between the Agency and the third country concerned, the EBCG "may coordinate operational cooperation between Member States and third countries and provide technical and operational assistance to third countries in the context of European integrated border management" (Art. 74 para. 1).[54]

Furthermore, with the objective of reducing the dependence of the EBCG on the Member States' technical equipment, Art. 38 Regulation 2016/1624 stipulated that the Agency may acquire its own technical equipment to be deployed during joint operations, pilot projects, rapid border interventions and return operations. The European Commission's reports on the operationalisation of the EBCG stressed that the Agency was especially interested in acquiring small and medium-size assets (e.g. aerial surveillance services or mobile offices). In particular, the European Commission allocated EUR 40 million to the EBCG from 2017 to 2020 in order to acquire its own equipment.[55] In this regard, Art. 63 para. 4 Regulation 2019/1896 points out that where the EBCG acquires or co-owns equipment such as aircrafts, helicopters, service vehicles or vessels, the Agency shall agree with a Member State the registration of the equipment as being on government service.

Both Regulation 2016/1624 and 2019/1896 aim to provide the EBCG with technical and human resources that are immediately and flexibly available to be deployed, with the goal of filling in the operational gaps that continuously afflicted Frontex. However, Regulation 1168/2011 amending Frontex had already attempted, with little success, to increase

54 These new external functions of the EBCG raise important questions in regard to the delimitation of responsibility among the actors involved and the respect for fundamental rights; See: *Rijpma*, External Migration and Asylum Management: Accountability for Executive Action Outside EU Territory, European Papers 2 (2017), 571.

55 COM (2017) 467 final, 4.

the operational autonomy of the Agency. Nevertheless, regarding the acquisition of equipment, not only did Frontex lack the operational and technical capabilities to manage its own aircrafts, vessels, and patrol vehicles, but since the lines of responsibility were not clearly spelled out, the Member States were also unwilling to register ships or aircraft purchased and operated by the Agency.[56] It is true that the European Commission now has a strong budgetary commitment to ensure that the EBCG acquires or leases technical resources, but the Agency still lacks the necessary structures and expertise to effectively manage its own equipment. Regulations 2016/1624 and 2019/1896 do not design a clear framework for the EBCG's responsibility, and it remains highly questionable whether the Member States will authorise the registration of equipment that is beyond their control.

Lastly, a key operational power introduced by Regulation 2016/1624 was the establishment of a Rapid Reaction Equipment Pool, consisting of technical equipment to be deployed in rapid border interventions within ten working days from the date that the Operational Plan is agreed upon by the Executive Director and the host Member State. The EBCG may contribute to the Rapid Reaction Equipment Pool with its own resources and the Member States could no longer shirk their responsibilities by alleging that they are faced with an exceptional situation substantially affecting the discharge of national tasks (Art. 39 para. 7 Regulation 2016/1624).

In accordance with Art. 20 para. 5 Regulation 2016/1624, the competent national authorities shall make available a minimum of 1,500 border guards to the EBCG for their immediate deployment in joint operations and/or rapid border interventions. As was the case with Frontex, the EBCG may contribute to the European Border and Coast Guard Teams (EBCGT) with border guards or other relevant staff seconded by the Member States for a maximum period of twelve months or more, but not less than three months (Art. 20 para. 11 Regulation 2016/1624). The EBCG is in charge of selecting the Seconded Members of Teams in accordance with the Agency's operational requirements. The selected members shall be included in the EBCGT pool, deployed by the Agency, and shall undertake their duties with the interests of the EBCG in mind.[57]

---

56 House of Lords (European Union Committee), FRONTEX: the EU external borders agency, 9th Report of Session 2007–2008, 05 March 2008, 52.

57 FRONTEX, Management Board Decision 27/2017 laying down rules on the secondment of national experts with the tasks and powers of the Members of the Teams to FRONTEX, 27 September 2017.

While the establishment of a Rapid Reaction Pool of 1,500 was a positive measure for emergency situations at the external borders, Regulation 2016/1624 did not manage to overcome the insufficient pooling of Member States' border guards for concrete locations and concrete periods in regular joint operations.[58] For this reason, Regulation 2019/1896 centres on designing a permanent, fully trained and operational Standing Corps of 5,000 Border Guards by 2021 and 10,000 by 2027 based on the distribution key set out in Annex I to Regulation 2019/1896.

Pursuant to Art. 54 para. 1 Regulation 2019/1896, the Standing Corps is composed of four categories of border guards: 1) operational staff members of the Agency (Art. 55), 2) operational staff seconded from Member States to the Agency for a long-term deployment (Art. 56), 3) operational staff from Member States ready to be provided to the Agency for a short-term deployment (Art. 57) and 4) operational staff from the Member States ready to be deployed for the purpose of rapid border interventions (Art. 58). The EBCG's operational staff members is a new category of staff designed by Regulation 2019/1896 in order to ensure the effective management of the external borders. Regarding the other three categories of border guards, the Member States are obliged to second to the Agency operational staff with the aim of ensuring at all times the availability of border guards to be deployed.

However, the main novelty is not so much the establishment of the Standing Corps, but rather the fact that the Standing Corps deployed as team members (category 1) are conferred executive powers (Art. 54 para. 3 Regulation 2019/1896) such as verifying the identity and nationality of persons, authorising or refusing of entry upon border check, stamping of travel documents, issuing or refusing of visas, patrolling or, registering fingerprints (Art. 55 para. 5 Regulation 2019/1896). Importantly, Art. 82 para. 2 Regulation 2019/1896 states that the performance of executive powers by the EBCG's operational staff members shall be subject to the authorisation of the Member State that is hosting the operation.

As the Meijers Committee and the European Council on Refugees and Exiles rightly noted, conferring executive powers on the EBCG's operational staff members may breach the primary law provisions that regard the Member States as ultimately responsible for their own internal security

58 COM (2018) 631 final, 4.

and external border management.[59] While the European Commission considers that Art. 77 para. 2 (d) TFEU provides the legal basis to bestow upon the EBCG's staff members executive tasks if they are clearly defined to match the objective of the establishment of an integrated management system for external borders,[60] Art. 77 para. 2 (d) TFEU shall also be read in light of Arts. 72 and 73 TFEU.

Art. 72 TFEU states that the competences that the EU enjoys in the AFSJ "shall not affect the exercise of the responsibilities incumbent upon Member States with regard to the maintenance of law and order and the safeguarding of internal security". In other words, the EU cannot replace the Member States' prerogatives of coercion and "EU agencies are therefore limited to supporting actions of national authorities, except (and only) to the extent that the Treaty confers express powers to act on such agencies".[61] Relatedly, Art. 4 para. 2 TEU provides that "the Union [...] shall respect their essential State functions, including ensuring the territorial integrity of the State, maintaining law and order and safeguarding national security. In particular, national security remains the sole responsibility of each Member State".

Furthermore, Art. 73 TFEU indicates that "it shall be open to Member States to organise between themselves and under their responsibility such forms of cooperation and coordination as they deem appropriate between the competent departments of their administrations responsible for safeguarding national security". As Mungianu clearly explains "insofar as the EU limits itself to the role of coordinator without any law enforcement power, and insofar as the Member States are free to engage in a form of cooperation among themselves. Art. 73 TFEU has been respected".[62] Hence, while competences are shared between the EU and the Member States in the AFSJ (Art. 4 para. 2 (j) TFEU), Arts. 72 and 73 TFEU limit the powers conferred on the Union in matters directly linked to Member States' national sovereignty (Art. 2 para. 6 TFEU).

---

59 Meijers Committee, CM1817 Comments on the draft for a new Regulation on a European Border and Coast Guard, (COM (2018) 631 final) and the amended proposal for a Regulation on a European Union Asylum Agency (COM (2018) 633 final), 27 November 2018, 4 and European Council on Refugees and Exiles, Comments on the Commission Proposal for a Regulation on the European Border and Coast Guard (COM (2018) 631 Final), November 2018, 9.

60 COM (2018) 631 Final, 7.

61 *Peers*, EU Justice and Home Affairs Law: EU Criminal Law, Policing, and Civil Law, Volume II, London 2016, 27.

62 *Mungianu*, Frontex: Towards a common policy on external border control, European Journal of Migration and Law 15 (2013), 359, 371.

3. *The EBCG's operational power to "intervene"*

The new EBCG's capacity to intervene led to considerable rejection by the Member States during the negotiations of Regulation 2016/1624.[63] Art. 3 para. 2 Regulation 2016/1624 stated that "the Agency shall, by decision of the management board based on a proposal of the executive director, establish a technical and operational strategy for European integrated border management". Currently, Art. 8 para. 2 Regulation 2019/1896 specifies that "the multiannual strategic policy for the European integrated border management shall set out how the challenges in the area of border management and returns are to be addressed in a coherent, integrated and systematic manner [...]".

That is, the national authorities in charge of border management shall conform to the strategy adopted by the EBCG (Art. 3 para. 3 Regulation 2016/1624 and 8 para. 6 Regulation 2019/1896). Member States shall abstain from conducting "any activity which could jeopardise the functioning of the Agency or the attainment of its objectives" (Art. 8 para. 2 Regulation 2016/1624 and Art. 7 para. 5 Regulation 2019/1896). To this end, the EBCG is authorised to supervise the effective functioning of the national external borders, undertake vulnerability assessments, monitor whether a Member State is qualified to effectively implement the applicable EU legislation, and detect deficiencies in the management of the national borders.

The EBCG is thus conferred a supervisory and intervention role, which allows the Agency to adopt quasi-binding measures for the Member States and to directly intervene in the territory of the Member State if such mea-

---

63 Art. 18 para. 1 of the original European Commission proposal stated that "the Commission, after consulting the Agency, may adopt a decision by means of an implementing act, identifying the measures to be implemented by the Agency and requiring the Member State concerned to cooperate with the Agency in the implementation of those measures". Given the rejection that this provision aroused among the Member States, it was decided that the Council, instead of the Commission, shall be responsible for adopting implementing acts. Regarding the rejection of some Member States see: *Avramidis*, EU Border Force Plan Faces Resistance from Governments, Reuters, 13 December 2015, http://reut.rs/1jWwau1; *De La Baume*, Countries Balk at EU Border Force Proposal, Politico, 15 December 2015, http://politi.co/1mmOyhj; see also, *Rijpma*, The proposal for a European Border and Coast Guard: evolution or revolution in external border management?, Study for the European Commission (LIBE committee) (2016), 18; *Rosenfeldt*, Establishing the European Border and Coast Guard: all-new or FRONTEX reloaded?, EU Law Analysis, 16 October 2016, http://eulawanalysis.blogspot.com.es/2016/10/establishing-european-border-and-coast.html.

sures are not effectively implemented (Art. 18 Regulation 2016/1624 and 42 Regulation 2019/1896). In the event that a Member State neither adopts the measures recommended in its vulnerability assessment, nor requests/takes necessary actions in the face of disproportionate and sudden migratory pressure, the EBCG shall ensure a unified, rapid, and effective EU response so as not to jeopardise the functioning of the Schengen Area. In this situation and according to Art. 42 para. 1 Regulation 2019/1896, "the Council, on the basis of a proposal from the Commission, may adopt without delay a decision by means of an implementing act to identify measures to mitigate those risks to be implemented by the Agency and requiring the Member State concerned to cooperate with the Agency in the implementation of those measures".

Since the Council decision is adopted, the EBCG's Executive Director shall, within two working days, draft an operational plan and submit it to the Member State concerned (Art. 42 para. 4 Regulation 2019/1896). Once the operational plan is submitted, the Agency's Director and the Member State concerned shall agree on concrete actions to be adopted, including the deployment of the necessary operational staff from the European Border and Coast Guard standing corps, for the practical execution of the measures identified in the Council's decision.

Art. 42 para. 8 Regulation 2019/1896 requires the Member State concerned to comply with the Council decision by cooperating with the EBCG and taking the necessary actions to facilitate the implementation of the Council's decision and the Agency's operational plan. However, these obligations are tempered when Art. 42 para. 10 Regulation 2019/1896 indicates that the European Commission may authorise the reestablishment of border controls in the Schengen Area, provided that the concerned Member State neither executes the decision adopted by the Council, nor agrees with the EBCG's Operational Plan within 30 days. Ultimately, the Member State concerned subject to the EBCG's "intervention" shall expressly consent and agree with the Agency in regard to the operational support that will be provided in its external borders as to ensure the functioning of the Schengen Area (Art. 42 para. 5 Regulation 2019/1896).

IV. The EBCG's Internal Administrative Structure: Balancing the Agency's Reinforced Supervisory and Operational Tasks

This section studies the EBCG's administrative organisation, constituting an important determinant of the degree of influence that the Member States exert in the increasing operational, supervisory, and implementation powers conferred on this EU decentralised Agency. In other words, the EBCG's operational role is expanding, and thereby, the administration of border management is further Europeanised. However, through the election and supervision of the Executive Director, and through the majority presence of national representatives at the Management Board of the EBCG, Member States continue to effectively steer and control its reinforced operational tasks.

1. *The EBCG's Intergovernmental Management Board*

The Management Board is the EBCG's strategic planning body. The Management Board is in charge of a wide range of key managerial and overseeing activities,[64] which mainly include appointing and exercising disciplinary control over the Agency's Executive Director and annually adopting the general budget, the Work Programme, and the Activity Report. The EBCG's Management Board is composed of twenty-six Member States' representatives that are signatories of the Schengen acquis and two representatives of the European Commission, all with a right to vote.[65] These members shall be appointed for an extendable period of four years on the basis of their degree of high-level relevant experience and expertise in the field of operational cooperation on border management and their relevant managerial, administrative and budgetary skills.

The predominant intergovernmental character of the EBCG's Management Board aims to offset the increasing administrative integration at the EU level of nationally sensitive matters, like border management.[66] Put differently, the European Parliament does not have any representative in the EBCG's Management Board, and the European Commission participation is in a clear minority with only two representatives. Member States have thus secured control over the strategic decisions that are made at the core of the Agency.

Furthermore, the EBCG's Management Board makes current decisions regarding business matters with voting rights by the absolute majority of its members with a right to vote (Art. 105 para. 1 Regulation 2019/1896), and by two-thirds majority for the appointment and dismissal of the Ex-

64 See: Art. 100 Regulation 2019/1896.

65 Frontex' Management Board Membership, http://frontex.europa.eu/about-frontex/organisation/management-board/.

66 *Pi Llorens*, El nuevo mapa de las agencias europeas del Espacio de Libertad, Seguridad y Justicia, Revista de Derecho Comunitario Europeo 56 (2017), 77, 106.

ecutive Director, the designation of the chairperson of the Management Board, and the adoption of the annual budget and the Work Programme.[67] Importantly, Regulation 2019/1896 also provides stricter majority rules in regard to the EBCG's novel operational and supervisory tasks. Art. 100 para. 2 cl. d Regulation 2019/1896 signals that decisions on conducting the vulnerability assessment and monitoring the implementation of the recommendations on the basis of the results of the vulnerability assessments shall be adopted by a two-thirds majority. Similarly, Art. 100 para. 2 (c) states that a majority of two thirds of the members with a right to vote in the Management Board are in charge of adopting decisions on establishing antenna offices or prolonging the duration of their operation.

Previously, Regulation 2016/1624 designing the EBCG also provided stricter majority rules in regard to the novel operational tasks designed, and especially, when deploying EBCGT in the territory of the Member States. Art. 20 para. 4 Regulation 2016/1624 detailed that the Management Board shall decide, by a three-quarter majority, on the profiles and the minimum number of border guards to be made available during rapid border interventions. Additionally, Art. 62 para. 1 (c) and cl. h Regulation 2016/1624 pointed out that any decisions on the EBCG to conduct vulnerability assessments, and the profiles and minimum number of border guards to be made available for the rapid reaction pool of the EBCGT, required respectively within the Management Board a two-thirds and three-quarters majority.

The higher voting thresholds set within the Management Board both with the former Regulation 2016/1624 and the current Regulation 2019/1896 in regard to the reinforced operational and supervisory powers conferred on the EBCG ensure that the Member States have a significant say and control over the Agency. While the competent national authorities have agreed to make national resources and personnel available to the EBCG and to assist the Agency in very sensitive and sovereign matters, the Member States monopolise and steer the strategic operational and monitoring decisions of the EBCG within the Management Board.

67 See: Art. 100 para. 2 Regulation 2019/1896.

2. The EBCG's executive director

The executive directors have a leading position in the governance, management, and day-to-day administration of the EU decentralised agencies[68]. They are in charge of managing the agencies' finances and personnel, effectively implementing the agencies' tasks and acting as their legal representatives. Among many other functions,[69] the EBCG's director must be completely independent and prepare and implement the multiannual programming draft, annual work programmes, the consolidated annual report, and strategic decisions adopted by the Management Board. The Management Board appoints the executive director on the basis of a shortlist drawn up by the European Commission, following an open and transparent selection procedure.[70]

The European Parliament assumes a relevant role in the appointment of the EBCG's executive director since the Management Board is obliged to take into account the Parliament's views.[71] According to Art. 107 para. 2 Regulation 2019/1896, before the EBCG's executive director is appointed, the candidates proposed shall be invited to make a statement before the European Parliament and answer questions put forth by its members. Following such a statement, the Parliament shall adopt an opinion setting out its views and may indicate a preferred candidate. The EBCG's Management Board shall take these views into account when appointing the executive director. In the case that the Management Board decides to appoint a candidate other than the candidate whom the Parliament indicated, the Management Board must inform the Parliament and the Council in writing as to how the Parliament's opinion was taken into account.

Due to the significant responsibilities bestowed upon the EBCG's executive director, the European Institutions and the Member States aim to in-

---

68 *Busuioc/Groenleer*, Wielders of supranational power? The administrative behaviour of the heads of European Union agencies, in: Busuioc/Groenleer/Trondal (eds.), The Agency Phenomenon in the European Union: Emergence, Institutionalisation and Everyday Decision-Making, Manchester: Manchester University Press 2012, 128, 128–150.

69 Art. 106 para. 4 Regulation (EU) No. 2019/1896.

70 Art. 107 Regulation (EU) No. 2019/1896.

71 See: *Carrera/Hernanz/Parkin*, The "Lisbonisation" of the European Parliament: Assessing Progress, Shortcomings and Challenges for Democratic Accountability in the Area of Freedom, Security and Justice, Centre for European Policy Studies Liberty and Security in Europe Paper 58, (2013), 1, 1–44; *Trauner*, The European Parliament and agency control in the Area of Freedom, Security and Justice, West European Politics 35 (2012), 784, 784–802.

fluence her or his appointment. Notwithstanding that the EU Institutions increasingly participate in the appointment process by proposing and being consulted, the Management Board, a predominantly intergovernmental body, makes the final decision and tightly oversees the executive director (Art. 107 para. 4 Regulation 2019/1896).

Consequently, the main limitation to the EBCG's reinforced operational and supervisory role comes from the Member States. While it is true that the EBCG operationally assists the Member States in matters closely linked to their national sovereignty prerogatives, the competent national authorities that vote at the Management Boards tightly control its recently reinforced operational, implementation and supervisory functions. Member States' reluctance to fully abandon their well-established bilateral practices, share information, and operationally cooperate with the EBCG in core national sovereign matters like border management is especially reflected in its Management Board and appointment of the executive director.

V. *Conclusion*

In the aftermath of the "refugee crisis", the transformation of Frontex into the EBCG, as well as the need to promote a shared management of the European external borders emerged as a top political priority for both the EU and the Member States. At the time, the establishment of Frontex was also influenced by conjunctural aspects such as the future expansion of the European Community to the East, the growing migratory pressure on the southern coasts and the terrorist threats after the attacks of 11 September 2001. Currently, Regulations 2016/1624 and 2019/1896 introduce the new EBCG as a guarantor of an integrated management of the European borders. In the European Commission's own words, "by setting new standards and imbuing a European culture within border guards, the European Border and Coast Guard will also become a blueprint on how EU border management should be implemented".[72]

Both Regulations 2016/1624 and 2019/1896 clearly strengthen the EBCG's autonomy since the Agency will depend to a much lesser extent on the specific operational secondments and support of the Member States. The EBCG should finally have its own equipment and operational personnel for its immediate deployment in joint and rapid operations.

72 COM (2018) 631 Final, 2.

However, the most controversial, significant and novel operational powers included in Regulations 2016/1624 and 2019/1896 consist of introducing the Agency's capacity to "intervene" and granting executive powers to the Agency's staff members respectively.

Regulation 2016/1624, in order to avoid endangering the functioning of the Schengen Area, entitled the EBCG to intervene if a Member State decides not to implement the measures recommended by the executive director to tackle the weaknesses detected at its external borders, or if the Member State does not request operational assistance in the face of disproportionate and sudden migratory pressure at its borders. However, it is debatable to what extent the Agency is able to impose the application of certain measures to a Member State that is opposed to them. Regulation 2016/1624, and now Regulation 2019/1896, do not provide much clarity in this respect, which is a common feature of those European legislative instruments in charge of regulating highly sensitive competences that require the support of national authorities.

Regulation 2019/1896 confers executive powers on the EBCG's standing corps deployed as team members. The Member State hosting an operation may empower the Agency to verify the identity and nationality of the arriving migrants, authorise or refuse entry upon border check, stamp travel documents, issue or refuse visas, patrol or register fingerprints. While these executive powers may ensure a more effective, integrated and supranational administration of the European external borders, these activities also entail a significant – and difficult to control – degree of discretion that excessively stretches the Treaty provisions establishing the Member States as ultimately responsible for their own internal security and external border management. In this regard, aware of the impact that the EBCG's expanded operational activities may have in the fundamental rights of the individuals, Regulation 2016/1624 introduced and now Regulation 2019/1896 details the functioning of the individual complaint mechanism, which allows any person who is directly affected by the tasks that the EBCG conducts on the ground to lodge a complaint (Art. 111 Regulation 2019/1896).[73]

Although it is true that currently the EBCG assists the Member States more independently in matters closely linked to their national sovereignty prerogatives, the competent national authorities that vote at the Manage-

73 See: *Carrera/Stefan*, Complaint Mechanisms in Border Management and Expulsion Operations in Europe: Effective Remedies for Victims of Human Rights Violations?, Centre for European Policy Studies, (2018); *Fernandez-Rojo*, Reglamento 2016/1624: de FRONTEX a la Guardia Europea de Fronteras y Costas, Revista General de Derecho Europeo 41 (2017), 223, 223–251.

ment Board will continue to tightly control the Agency's recently reinforced operational and supervisory functions. Only two representatives of the European Commission have voting rights in the EBCG's Management Board and the presence of the European Parliament is non-existent. The Member States have thus ensured control of the strategic operational powers and the daily management of the Agency.

Consequently, despite the fact that the name of the EBCG may lead to misunderstanding and even the European Commission constantly refers to the Agency as a true European system of guarding borders and coasts, Regulations 2016/1624 and 2019/1896 do not create a European Corps of Border Guards with full and exclusive competences in border management. Nevertheless, Regulations 2016/1624 and 2019/1896 do reveal how difficult it still is to strike a balance between designing an effective, integrated strategy for the management of the European external borders and the Member States' resistance to conferring operational powers directly linked to their core national sovereignty. It is still early to conclude whether we are only facing another revision of Frontex' initial mandate as a reaction to an unprecedented migratory pressure or, on the contrary, Regulations 2016/1624 and 2019/1896 constitute the definitive step that will facilitate in the future the establishment of a European Corps of Border Guards with full executive, implementation and decision-making powers in the management of the European external borders.

The Financial Dimension of EU External Policies on Migration

Carmine Conte[*] *and Valentina Savazzi*[**]

I. Introduction: international migration cooperation

International policies on migration have often been considered an exception to the global trend towards international institutionalisation and rule-making, because of the coexistence of different and conflicting interests between countries of origin, transit and destination.[1] However, in recent years, international migration cooperation has increasingly grown and seen the creation of a plethora of institutions, norms, and instruments to foster coordination on migration management and governance,[2] which has been described by some scholars as a "substance without architecture".[3] Against this context, countries of destination started to promote the use of "partnerships", which gradually replaced the traditional resort to unilateral measures and limited bilateral agreements. Partnerships have been presented as effective, inclusive, and horizontal tools leading to "win-win-win" solutions benefiting all parties involved: countries of origin, of transit and of destination, as well as migrants.[4] They ensure the achievement of common goals in the best interest of all parties by fostering equal

---

* PhD in EU Equality Law (Middlesex University of London, 2018) and legal policy analyst at the Migration Policy Group in Brussels.

** Expert in migration and consultant at Ernst&Young.

1 *Kunz/Lavenex*, Partnerships in international migration governance: the missing link?, SNIS Working Paper, 2017.

2 *Lavenex/Panizzon*, Multilayered Migration Governance: The Partnership Approach in the EU and Beyond, Draft paper prepared for the UNRISD Conference "Regional Governance of Migration and Socio-Political Rights: Institutions, Actors and Processes", Geneva 2013.

3 *Aleinikoff*, International Legal Norms and Migration: a Report, in: Aleinikoff/ Chetail (eds.), Migration and International Legal Norms, Cambridge 2003.

4 *Lavenex/Panizzon*, Multilayered Migration Governance: The Partnership Approach in the EU and Beyond, Draft paper prepared for the UNRISD Conference "Regional Governance of Migration and Socio-Political Rights: Institutions, Actors and Processes", Geneva 2013, 1–31.

ownership, transparent dialogue and participation.[5] By contrast, some authors argue that partnerships perpetuate the domination of the South by the North without realising an equal transformation of their relations.[6] Recently, the European Union (EU) promoted the use of partnerships in its external policy dimension by adopting the Partnership and Association Agreements with Eastern European Countries, the Euro-Mediterranean Partnership to the South and the Mobility Partnerships.[7]

At international level, current political developments also exhibit the willingness of UN Member States to better coordinate policies and practices on refugees and asylum. On 19 September 2016, for the first time, Heads of State and Government discussed within the UN General Assembly how to respond to the growing global phenomenon of large movements of refugees and migrants. As a result, 193 UN Member States adopted the New York Declaration for Refugees and Migrants and recognised the need for a comprehensive approach to human mobility and enhanced cooperation at the global level.[8] As part of the New York Declaration, the negotiations on the adoption of two global compacts on refugees and migration started among the UN Member States.[9]

On 17 December 2018, the United Nations General Assembly adopted the Global Compact on Refugees (GCR), which sets out a framework for more equitable responsibility-sharing to find solutions to refugee situations.[10] International cooperation is finally acknowledged as a fundamental instrument to address migration policies. Paragraph 35 points out the importance of fostering cooperation in the areas of development and humanitarian actions:

> "… humanitarian and development actors will work together from the outset of a refugee situation and in protracted situations. They will de-

---

5 *Abrahamsen*, The Power of Partnership in Global Governance, Third World Quarterly 25 (2004), 1453, 1453–1467.

6 *Abrahamsen*, Third World Quarterly 25 (2004) (fn. 5), 1453, 1453–1467.

7 *Kunz/Lavenex*, Partnerships in international migration governance: the missing link?, SNIS Working Paper, 2017.

8 United Nations General Assembly, New York Declaration for Refugees and Migrants, Resolution adopted by the General Assembly on 19 September 2016, Seventy-first session, Agenda items 13 and 117, New York 2016.

9 European Council on Refugees and Exiles, Global Means Global: Europe and the Global Compact on Refugees. ECRE's Recommendations for Implementation of the GCR in and by Europe, Policy Note 15, Brussels 2018.

10 United Nations, Report of the United Nations High Commissioner for Refugees, Part II Global Compact on Refugees, General Assembly Official Records, Seventy-third Session, Supplement No. 12., New York 2018.

velop means to ensure the effective complementarity of their interventions to support host countries and, where appropriate, countries of origin, including in those countries that lack the institutional capacities to address the needs of refugees. Support by bilateral and multilateral development and financial actors for the direct benefit of host communities and refugees will be additional and undertaken in partnership, respecting the primacy of national ownership and leadership, and in a manner that does not negatively impact or reduce support for broader development objectives in the concerned country".

The GCR shows that the allocation of adequate funding represents a key priority for achieving the objectives of the Compact and emphasises the need to provide additional development resources to enable host countries and communities to respond both to immediate humanitarian needs and to longer-term development needs.[11]

To the same extent, the Global Compact on Migration (GCM) also expresses the collective commitment to improve cooperation on international migration in the light of the inherently transnational nature of the phenomenon.[12] To do so, it requires international, regional and bilateral cooperation and dialogue. Paragraph 39 (b) of the CGM calls for:

"…increasing international and regional cooperation to accelerate the implementation of the 2030 Agenda for Sustainable Development in geographical areas from which irregular migration systematically originates owing to consistent impacts of poverty, unemployment, climate change and disasters, inequality, corruption and poor governance, among other structural factors, through appropriate cooperation frameworks, innovative partnerships and the involvement of all relevant stakeholders, while upholding national ownership and shared responsibility".

To this end, deployment of dedicated funding and financial resources is also a fundamental goal of the GCM that underlines the importance of promoting multi-donor approaches and multi-year funding cycle. This will strengthen collaboration between humanitarian and development actors and develop long-term responses and outcomes that ensure respect for the rights of affected individuals.

---

11 *Cortinovis*, Contribuiting to Global Responsibility-Sharing for Refugees: The Role of EU External Funding, Policy Option Brief, ReSOMA, Brussels 2019.

12 United Nations, Global Compact for Safe, Orderly and Regular Migration, Resolution adopted by the General Assembly on 19 December 2018, New York 2018.

Now, an overview of the external dimension of EU migration policies will be given and the main EU instruments to cooperate with third countries will be critically examined in order to assess how financial measures are allocated by the EU to implement refugee and asylum policies.

II. External dimension of EU migration policy

Since the late 1990s, the EU has started to develop the so-called "external dimension" of cooperation on immigration and asylum and to manage migration through cooperation with countries of origin or transit. To do so, the EU attempted to externalise traditional tools of migration control and focused on the prevention of the causes of migration and refugee flows, by means of development assistance and foreign policy instruments. The approach adopted by the EU in migration cooperation with third countries will have a significant impact on crucial areas such as migration flows, migrants' rights protection, humanitarian aid and international relations.[13]

The current political debate is characterised by EU Member States' diverging positions and priorities as regards the internal dimension of migration policy and the reform of the Common European Asylum System (CEAS). However, convergence among Member States and EU institutions appears to be based on the need to strengthen the EU's external migration policy, which implies a close cooperation with countries of origin and transit. It may be said that the EU external dimension of migration is marked by the interplay of a "preventive" approach aiming to address the long-term drivers of migration and a "control-oriented" one that emphasises the goal of enhancing control and security.[14] The negotiations of the UN Global Compacts on Refugees and Migration confirmed unity and cooperation among the Member States in the development of the EU's external migration policy, in particular with regard to the objectives of addressing the drivers of irregular migration, enhancing cooperation on returns, combatting trafficking and smuggling, fostering border management and reducing irregular migration.[15] The most relevant EU financial instruments covering the main aspects of migration will now be illustrated.

---

13 *Boswell*, The External Dimension of EU Immigration and Asylum Policy, International Affairs 79 (2003), 619, 619–638.

14 *Cortinovis/Conte*, Migration-related Conditionality in EU External Funding", ReSOMA Discussion Brief, July 2018, Brussels 2018.

15 *Gatti*, Too Much Unity in the European Union's External Migration Policy, EU Immigration and Asylum Law and Policy, 20 July 2018.

1. *The main EU instruments of external migration policy*

The EU external dimension of migration is widely embodied by the 2005 Global Approach to Migration and Mobility (GAMM), which sets out how policy dialogue and cooperation with non-EU countries must be conducted on clearly defined priorities and embedded in the EU's overall external action, including development cooperation.[16] The GAMM was first adopted in 2005 under the name GAM and was upgraded to its current form in 2012. Implemented through different political and legal instruments, capacity building programmes and projects or operational support, it prioritises four objectives revolving around legal migration, the prevention of irregular migration, migration and development, internal protection and asylum.[17] One of the underlying principles of GAMM is to "establish a comprehensive framework to manage migration and mobility with partner countries in a coherent and mutually beneficial way".[18] GAMM underlines that adequate funding, geographical and thematic financial instruments are required for external cooperation. In this regard, from 2004 to 2013, more than one billion Euros was committed to assisting southern Mediterranean and Sub-Saharan African countries.[19] Yet some authors pointed out the existing gap between the comprehensive narrative proposed by the GAMM and the narrow and conditionality-focused policies deriving from

---

See also the EU statement during the GCM 4th round of negotiation on 15 May 2018, available at https://refugeesmigrants.un.org/sites/default/files/eu_proposal_on_international_cooperation.pdf.

16 European Commission, Global Approach to Migration, Migration and Home Affairs, 2019a. Available at https://ec.europa.eu/home-affairs/what-we-do/policies/international-affairs/global-approach-to-migration.

17 European Commission, Global Approach to Migration, Migration and Home Affairs, 2019. Available at https://ec.europa.eu/home-affairs/what-we-do/policies/international-affairs/global-approach-to-migration.

18 European Commission, Global Approach to Migration, Migration and Home Affairs, 2019. Available at https://ec.europa.eu/home-affairs/what-we-do/policies/international-affairs/global-approach-to-migration.

19 European Commission, Global Approach to Migration, Migration and Home Affairs, 2019. Available at https://ec.europa.eu/home-affairs/what-we-do/policies/international-affairs/global-approach-to-migration.

it, among which the EU Mobility Partnerships and regional migration dialogues.[20]

Among the frameworks created under the GAMM, it is worth highlighting the Mobility Partnerships (MP) and the Common Agendas for Migration and Mobility (CAMM),[21] which both define "a political framework for comprehensive, enhanced and tailor-made dialogue and cooperation with partner countries".[22] As of 2018, the budget foreseen for the second phase of the MP is EUR 12.5 million for the duration of 36 months. These instruments appear to be characterised by a conditionality approach leading to the prioritisation of EU Member States' objectives over the interests of the partner countries[23] and the GAMM existing bias towards the curb of irregular migration.[24] These partnerships may be the result of the EU strategy to enhance its own bargaining power in order to secure the cooperation of third countries by using package deals.[25]

Another crucial instrument to understand the external dimension of migration is the EU Agenda on Migration developed in 2015, which stresses the importance of developing cooperation as a way to tackle the root causes of migration and ensures a strenuous effort to combat migrant smuggling and human trafficking. Under the new Agenda, the EU combined internal and external policy goals, with a view to creating a "comprehensive approach" to migration management. In particular, under the 2015 Agenda on Migration, the New Mobility Partnership Framework (or "migration compacts") was formalised in a Commission Communication of June 2016

20 *Carrera/Hernández i Sagrera*, Mobility Partnership: Partnerships for Policy Coherence and Migration Workers' Human Rights in the EU, in: Kunz/Lavenez/Panizzon (eds.), Multilayered Migration Governance. The Promise of Partnership, London 2011, 97–115.

21 Seven MP have been signed so far with Cape Verde, the Republic of Moldova, Georgia, Armenia, Morocco, Azerbaijan and Tunisia, while 2 CAMM with Ethiopia and Nigeria.

22 European Commission, Global Approach to Migration, Migration and Home Affairs, 2019. Available at https://ec.europa.eu/home-affairs/what-we-do/policies/international-affairs/global-approach-to-migration.

23 *Lavenex/Stucky*, "Partnering" for Migration in EU External Relations, in: Kunz/Lavenez/Panizzon (eds.), Multilayered Migration Governance: The Promise of Partnership, London 2008.

24 *Koenig*, The EU's External Migration Policy. Towards Win-Win Partnership, Policy Paper 190, Jaques Delors Institute, 6 April 2017,.

25 *Lavenex/Panizzon*, Multilayered Migration Governance: The Partnership Approach in the EU and Beyond, Draft paper prepared for the UNRISD Conference "Regional Governance of Migration and Socio-Political Rights: Institutions, Actors and Processes", Geneva 2013.

and endorsed by the European Council in June 2018. The "migration compacts" put broad emphasis on the concept of conditionality by suggesting the use of positive incentives and sanctions according to the partner country's willingness to cooperate or not on migration management, return and readmission.[26] The Council stressed that "cooperation on re-admissions and returns are the key test of the Partnership".[27] Development aid and trade are instead used by the EU as leverage and incentives for obtaining the cooperation of third countries. The EU thus agreed on tailoring "compacts" with several third countries to manage migration flows in a systematic and effective way, including: Ethiopia, Niger, Nigeria, Senegal, Eritrea, Somalia, Sudan, Ghana, Ivory Coast, Algeria, Morocco, Tunisia, Afghanistan, Bangladesh and Pakistan.[28] The first two frameworks with Jordan and Lebanon were established in 2016.

In early May 2018, the Commission launched its first proposal for the next Multiannual Financial Framework 2021–2027 (MFF) to be negotiated by EU institutions.[29] The proposal includes a 26% increase in investment for EU external actions and aims to reshape the EU budget of the external dimension. To do so, it gathers twelve existing financial instruments under a comprehensive neighbourhood, development and international cooperation framework.[30] The main mechanisms and principles underlying the funding instruments adopted to operationalise the EU external migration policy are analysed below. It will show the extent to which the development policy instruments are now integrated into EU migration policy.

---

26 *Koenig*, The EU's External Migration Policy. Towards Win-Win Partnership, Policy Paper 190, Jaques Delors Institute, 6 April 2017.

27 European Council, European Council Conclusions of 28 June 2016, Brussels 2016. Available at https://www.consilium.europa.eu/media/21645/28-euco-conclusions.pdf.

28 *Castillejo*, The EU Migration Partnership Framework: Time for a Rethink? Discussion Paper 28/2017, German Development Institute, Bonn 2017.

29 European Commission, A Modern Budget for a Union that Protects, Empowers and Defends: The Multiannual Financial Framework for 2021–2027, SWD (2018) 171 final, Brussels 2018.

30 *Cortinovis/Conte*, Migration-related Conditionality in EU External Funding", ReSOMA Discussion Brief, July 2018, Brussels 2018.

2. *The conditionality approach of EU external funding policies: a controversial strategy?*

In general terms, conditionality is defined as "an incentive instrument in the relationship between two actors, in which one actor aims at changing the behaviour of the other by setting up conditions for the relationship and by manipulating its cost-benefit calculation by using (positive and negative) material incentives".[31] Conditionality can be either *ex-ante* (the potential benefit is used as a lever to obtain a desired behaviour) or *ex post* (conditions are set during the course of an ongoing contractual relationship), negative or positive. The concept of positive conditionality is based on a "more-for-more" approach, which entails the provision of benefits contingent on the fulfilment of certain conditions, while negative conditionality implies the suspension or termination of benefit if some conditions are not met by the recipient.[32] This theoretical distinction is likely to be less marked in practice, where the "carrot and stick" approach may be used simultaneously.[33]

The conditionality model is widely used in EU external policy. To give an example, the Commission's Communication on the New Partnership Framework pointed out that all areas of EU external action may be instrumental to increase cooperation with partner countries. The conditionality approach as regards the external dimension of migration is clearly illustrated in the Communication: "... for each partner country, the development of a mix of positive and negative incentives, the use of which should be governed by a clear understanding that the overall relationship between the EU and that country will be guided in particular by the ability and willingness of the country to cooperate on migration management".[34]

The resort to conditionality with third countries in the context of development aid was put forward for the first time in the late 1990s by the Aus-

---

31 *Koch*, A Typology of Political Conditionality Beyond Aid: Conceptual Horizons Based on Lessons from the European Union, World Development 75 (2015), 97, 99.

32 *Cortinovis/Conte*, Migration-related Conditionality in EU External Funding", ReSOMA Discussion Brief, July 2018, Brussels 2018.

33 *Koch*, A Typology of Political Conditionality Beyond Aid: Conceptual Horizons Based on Lessons from the European Union, World Development 75 (2015), 97, 97–108.

34 European Commission, Communication from the Commission to the European Parliament, the European Council, the Council and the European Investment Bank on establishing a new Partnership Framework with third countries under the European Agenda on Migration, COM (2016) 385 final, Strasbourg 2016.

trian Presidency of the EU. It was proposed to subordinate the allocation of funds for development to cooperation on re-admission and to establish sanctions for countries unwilling to cooperate. This approach was initially rejected, but it remerged on several occasions, especially at times of increasing migratory pressure on European countries.[35] This idea was relaunched in 2002 during the Seville European Council, when Spain and the UK proposed to make development aid dependant on the efforts by third countries to combat irregular migration. A negative conditionality mechanism has been included in the Seville Conclusions which sets outs that "inadequate cooperation by a country could hamper the establishment of closer relations between that country and the Union".[36] The "more for more" model of conditionality has instead been reiterated after 2015 in order to link policy objectives of border control and readmission with other areas of cooperation and therefore reward third countries willing to support the EU migration agenda.[37] Among the EU institutions, however, the European Parliament opposes a blanket idea of conditionality, stressing the importance of an EU development cooperation that remains unconditional and aims to fight against poverty. Also, in the European Commission, officials working in development and external relations have generally criticised the subordination of development objectives to actions aiming at containing migration fluxes.[38]

A critical position was adopted by non-governmental organisations (NGOs) which issued a joint NGO statement in 2016 underlying the risks of migration compacts or frameworks that divert crucial resources for financing development cooperation and alleviating poverty to merely curb migration. The statement calls for the elimination of any conditionality-based approach on migration control indicators and underlines that "aid is for the benefit of people in need and should not be used as a leverage for migration control".[39] Already in 2004, ECRE argued that the prioritisation of measures to combat irregular migration was leading to a lack of coher-

35 *Cortinovis/Conte*, Migration-related Conditionality in EU External Funding", ReSOMA Discussion Brief, July 2018, Brussels 2018.

36 *Cortinovis/Conte*, Migration-related Conditionality in EU External Funding, ReSOMA Discussion Brief, July 2018, Brussels 2018.

37 *Cortinovis/Conte*, Migration-related Conditionality in EU External Funding", ReSOMA Discussion Brief, July 2018, Brussels 2018.

38 *Boswell*, International Affairs 79 (2003) (fn. 13), 619, 619–638.

39 Plan International, Joint Statement: NGOs Strongly Condemn New EU Policies to Contain Migration. Available at https://plan-international.org/joint-statement-ngos-strongly-condemn-new-eu-policies-contain-migration.

ence between the external dimension of EU migration policy and its development and human rights policy objectives.[40]

A series of measures introduced at EU level to deal with the 2015 "migration crisis" illustrate the increasing trend of integrating development policy instruments into migration policy, with a particular focus on the root causes of migration. The European Commission has recently outlined that the EU follows a comprehensive approach to the development–migration nexus, as it recognises that they are related processes.[41] The interconnection between the external dimension of migration and development is explicitly underlined in the Global Approach to Migration (GAMM), the European Agenda on Migration and the proposed migration compacts. The European Commission, in the 2016 Communication establishing a new Partnership Framework with third countries under the European Agenda on Migration, pointed out that development cooperation is the main leverage to ensure that third countries commit themselves to implementing concrete measures in the domain of migration, especially in terms of return and readmission.[42] According to the Communication, EU development policy must integrate core incentives to reward those countries that fulfil their obligations in terms of re-admission of their nationals, cooperation to stem irregular migration or host people fleeing.[43] "Development and neighbourhood policy tools should reinforce local capacity-building, including for border control, asylum, counter-smuggling and reintegration efforts. All actors – Member States, EU institutions and key third countries – need to work together in partnership to bring order into

---

40 European Council on Refugees and Exiles, Broken Promises, Forgotten Principles: an ECRE Evaluation of the Development of EU Minimum Standard for Refugee Protection, Tampere 1999 – Brussels 2004, Brussels 2004.

41 European Commission, Migration and Asylum, International Cooperation and Development, Building Partnerships for Change in Developing Countries, 2019. Available at https://ec.europa.eu/europeaid/sectors/migration-and-asylum/migration-and-asylum_en.

42 European Commission, Communication from the Commission to the European Parliament, the European Council, the Council and the European Investment Bank on establishing a new Partnership Framework with third countries under the European Agenda on Migration, COM (2016) 385 final, Strasbourg 2016.

43 European Commission, Communication from the Commission to the European Parliament, the European Council, the Council and the European Investment Bank on establishing a new Partnership Framework with third countries under the European Agenda on Migration, COM (2016) 385 final, Strasbourg 2016.

migratory flows".[44] As emphasised by the European Parliament, "the development–migration nexus has evolved from the traditional treaty-based development policy approach, with its requirement of ensuring that all EU policies contribute to development objectives, to a more complex configuration".[45]

NGOs and researchers raise several concerns regarding the possibility of instrumentalising development aid to fulfil purposes related to migration management. Development aid that is conditional on the willingness of third countries to cooperate on migration issues can jeopardise the fundamental objectives of reducing poverty and enhance economic growth.[46] For instance, in the case of the EU Emergency Trust Fund for Africa (EUTF) created in 2015 within the Valletta Action Plan, the excessive focus on the short-term interests of the EU (such as the control of migration flows) risks undermining the long-term development goals for the African partners.[47]

III. The financial aspects of the EU external dimension of migration

The financial dimension of the EU external policies on migration will now be explored and it will be shown how funds are allocated under the main EU instruments such as the EU–Turkey deal, the EUTF and the new Multiannual Financial Framework (MFF).

---

44 European Commission, Communication from the Commission to the European Parliament, the European Council, the Council and the European Investment Bank on establishing a new Partnership Framework with third countries under the European Agenda on Migration, COM (2016) 385 final, Strasbourg 2016.

45 *Latek*, Growing Impact of EU Migration Policy on Development Cooperation, Briefing, European Parliamentary Research Service, European Parliament, Brussels 2017.

46 European Parliament, Growing impact of EU migration policy on development cooperation, Briefing, November 2017. Available at http://www.europarl.europa.eu/RegData/etudes/BRIE/2017/614577/EPRS_BRI(2017)614577_EN.pdf.

47 European Council of Refugees and Exiles, Trust Fund for Africa: Focus on Short-Term EU Policies Jeopardizes Long-Term Development Goals of African Partner, ECRE news, Brussels 2017.

1. The EU–Turkey Deal

On March 2016, the European Council and Turkey reached an agreement to manage the flow of irregular migrants via Turkey to Europe. The EU–Turkey deal showed an unprecedented degree of cooperation between the EU and an external partner to stop migratory flows. According to the EU–Turkey Statement,[48] all new irregular migrants and asylum seekers arriving from Turkey to the Greek islands and whose applications for asylum are inadmissible would be returned to Turkey. In addition, for every Syrian being returned to Turkey from the Greek islands, another Syrian would be resettled to the EU (1:1 mechanism). The agreement mainly aimed at preventing departure from Turkey which would benefit from the EU decision to lift the visa requirements for Turkish citizens and allocate significant financial resources for the Facility for Refugees in Turkey (an initial budget of EUR 3 billion for the period 2016–2017, followed by a second tranche of EUR 3 billion).[49] Recently, the European Commission has communicated the adoption of a new set of measures as part of the second funding instalment to ensure continued support to refugees and host communities in Turkey.[50] The stated overarching goal of the EU Facility for Refugees in Turkey is to provide long-term support and development assistance. However, the EU Facility is considered highly controversial by numerous stakeholders and civil society organisations which underline the containment approach underpinning it.[51] On the other side, this financial arrangement was hailed as a success by the European Commission and its Member States as it represents a joint coordination mechanism that promptly mobilises resources under the EU budget and additional contributions from the European countries.

---

48 European Council, EU–Turkey Statement, Press release of 18 March 2016, Brussels 2016. Available at https://www.consilium.europa.eu/en/press/press-releases/2016/03/18/eu-turkey-statement/.

49 European Parliament, EU–Turkey Statement & Action Plan, Legislative Train, 2019. Available at https://www.europarl.europa.eu/legislative-train/theme-foreign-affairs-afet/file-eu-turkey-statement-action-plan.

50 European Commission, The European Commission has approved a new assistance package worth EUR 400 million, for the education of Syrian refugees in Turkey. Available at https://ec.europa.eu/commission/news/eu-facility-refugees-turkey-2018-jul-25_en.

51 *Cortinovis*, Contributing to Global Responsibility-Sharing for Refugees: The Role of EU External Funding, Policy Option Brief, ReSOMA, Brussels 2019.

2. The EU Emergency Trust Fund for Africa

The creation and implementation of similar "crisis" instruments, associated with the urgency to deal with refugee displacement, often creates a complex trade-off between the need to dispose of flexible tools to respond to situations of emergency and the importance of complying with principles of transparency and democratic accountability.[52] The same issues affect the EUTF, because despite the description of most projects as accessible, "they lack transparency on adoption and implementation".[53] This tool, introduced in 2015 is the main financial instrument that the EU has developed to respond to challenges related to migration with African countries. It is described as an innovative and flexible emergency mechanism which serves the goals of the Valletta Action plan. The EUTF has been designed to "support the most fragile and affected African countries" and address "the root causes of destabilisation, displacement and irregular migration, by promoting economic and equal opportunities, security and development".[54] Despite these goals, there is an increasing concern among stakeholders that the EUTF may be used as a political instrument establishing short-term measures for migration containment, rather than as a tool to effectively implement development projects.[55] As in the case of Libya, it is believed to indirectly contribute to migrants' inhumane treatment and human rights violation.[56] It may be argued that the overarching aim of this instrument is not in line with the primary objective of EU development cooperation as formulated in the Lisbon Treaty, which is characterised by the goal to alleviate and eradicate poverty.

The decision to promote external cooperation with certain beneficiaries under the EUTF seems to be based on the opportunity to target countries of origin, transit and destination of migrants. This initiative represents a

52 *Den Hertog*, Money Talks: Mapping the Funding for EU External Migration Policy, CEPS Paper in Liberty and Security in Europe, Brussels 2016.

53 European Council of Refugees and Exiles, Trust Fund for Africa: Focus on Short-Term EU Policies Jeopardizes Long-Term Development Goals of African Partner, ECRE news, Brussels 2017.

54 European Parliament, Emergency Trust Fund for Africa, Legislative Train, 2019. Available at https://www.europarl.europa.eu/legislative-train/api/stages/report/current/theme/europe-as-a-stronger-global-actor/file/emergency-trust-fund-for-africa.

55 *De Guerry/Stocchiero*, CONCORD EUTF Task Force, Partnership or Conditionality. Monitoring the Migration Compacts and EU Trust Fund for Africa, 2018.

56 *De Guerry/Stocchiero*, CONCORD EUTF Task Force, Partnership or Conditionality. Monitoring the Migration Compacts and EU Trust Fund for Africa, 2018.

further sign of the migration-related focus of the EU external action that risks overlooking the policy objectives of development and humanitarian aid.[57] This approach is also visible in the cases of Libya, Niger and Ethiopia, which are not only legitimate recipients of development and humanitarian support, but also major transit countries for migrants coming to Europe, to whom respectively EUR 281 million,[58] EUR 253 million and EUR 278 million are allocated by the EUTF.[59] According to Oxfam's findings, "22% of the EUTF for Africa budget is allocated to migration management, 13.5% to security, peacebuilding and P-CVE, 63% to development cooperation and 1.5% to research and monitoring".[60]

As of August 2019, "resources currently allocated to the EU Trust Fund for Africa amount to EUR 4.6 billion including more than EUR 4.0 billion from the European Development Fund (EDF) and EU financial instruments including DCI, ENI, HOME and ECHO funding".[61] More in detail, 209 programmes have been approved for a total amount of EUR 4.0 billion: Sahel and Lake Chad are allocated 1.9532 billion, Horn of Africa 1.4061 billion and North of Africa 647.7 million.[62]

The financial framework delineated by the EUTF seem to be widely dedicated to manage and reduce migratory flows towards Europe at the expense of fundamental development priorities.

3. The new MFF 2021–2027: budget, instruments and significance

The next Multiannual Financial Framework 2021–2027 (MFF) is still undefined in terms of its overall architecture and the amount of financial re-

57 *De Guerry/Stocchiero*, CONCORD EUTF Task Force, Partnership or Conditionality. Monitoring the Migration Compacts and EU Trust Fund for Africa, 2018.

58 It is worth noting that the total budget allocated for Libya is spent on border management.

59 European Commission, EUTF. Available at https://ec.europa.eu/trustfundforafrica/index.

60 *Kervyn/Shilhav*, Oxfam International, An Emergency for Whom? The EU Emergency Trust Fund for Africa – Migratory Routes and Development Aid in Africa, Oxford 2017.

61 European Commission, State of Play and Financial resources. Available at https://ec.europa.eu/trustfundforafrica/content/trust-fund-financials_en.

62 European Commission, State of Play and Financial resources. Available at https://ec.europa.eu/trustfundforafrica/content/trust-fund-financials_en.

sources involved.[63] The ongoing negotiations at EU level show some persisting disagreements among Member States, especially on key topics related to migration and asylum: the volume of financial instruments provided for migration-related objectives, the geographical areas that should receive the most significant influx of money and under whose competence funds will be allocated.[64]

Overall, compared to the current MFF, the amount of money proposed marks an increase for the period 2021–2027: it should in fact rise from EUR 1.087 billion to EUR 1.279 billion (commitment appropriations).[65] As regards the structure, the number of headings grows from five to seven, while the correspondence between the old and new headings is still the same despite differences in the names. The 2021–2027 MFF proposal aims at simplifying the structure of the EU budget and aligning it more closely to the political priorities. To do so, it entails the creation of a simpler and more flexible budget, which avoids using multiple programmes and instruments.[66]

The European Commission has to address future challenges while considering the lessons learned in the allocation of funds and the creation of instruments to manage migration issues. In fact, in the current 2014–2020 budget, both internal and external funding proved to be inadequate in responding to the increasing pressure that migration has posed to Europe. EU external policies on migration has so far led to "ad-hoc solutions, reshuffling of funds and the exhaustive use of margins and other flexibility instruments".[67] The Commission now proposes to mainstream migration throughout several financial instruments, both internally and externally, in order to balance EU Member States' desires to prioritise migration and en-

63 Further information about the overall organisation of the MFF are available at https://ec.europa.eu/commission/future-europe/eu-budget-future_en.

64 European Council of Refugees and Exiles, Outspending on Migration? ECRE's Analysis and Recommendations on Funding for Migration Outside the EU to Inform the Negotiations of the Next EU Multi-Annual Financial Framework 2021–2027, Policy Note #18, Brussels 2019.

65 The increased funds should, however, consider the possible withdrawal of the United Kingdom from the EU, which would lead to an MFF for a Union of 27 countries, rather than 28. The comparison should equally not overlook the inclusion of the European Development Fund for the first time in the new MFF.

66 *Dobreva*, Multiannual Financial Framework 2021–2027: Commission Proposal. Initial Comparison with the Current MFF, European Parliamentary Research Service, European Parliament, Brussels 2018.

67 *Knoll/Vernon*, Migration and the Next EU Long-Term Budget: Key Choices for External Action, ECDMP, Discussion Paper No. 250, 2019, 1.

sure complementarity among different measures. The diverging interests of Member States related to the EU external dimension of migration indisputably represent an important factor influencing the ongoing MFF negotiations.

New external funding instruments still emphasise migration containment and prevention and may generate negative implications on individuals in need of international protection by preventing them from accessing the EU territory. According to ECRE, "unless re-framed by introducing safeguards, [the next MFF] also risks "undermining the EU's own objectives and credibility as an external actor as set out in the Lisbon Treaty and the Global Strategy and may hinder the effectiveness of EU development assistance".[68]

a) The current MFF 2014–2020: structure and funds

Before analysing the new Commission's proposal for the next MFF, the main features and the overall structure of the funding mechanisms underpinning the current MFF 2014–2020 should be examined. The budget related to the external dimension of migration can be found under two sections: "Security and Citizenship" (Heading III) and "Global Europe" (Heading IV).

Under the first heading which includes *inter alia* justice and home affairs, border protection, immigration and asylum policy, two funds are relevant for the scope of this analysis, namely the "Asylum, Migration and Integration Fund" (AMIF, EUR 3.137 billion) and the "Internal Security Fund" (ISF, EUR 3.8 billion).

According to the Commission, AMIF "will promote the efficient management of migration flows and the implementation, strengthening and development of a common Union approach to asylum and immigration".[69] It will contribute in particular to strengthening and reforming the Common European Asylum System (CEAS), supporting legal migration and the integration of non-EU nationals, improving the management of

---

68 European Council of Refugees and Exiles, The Price of Rights: Asylum and EU External Funding. ECRE's Preliminary Analysis of the European Commission's Proposal for the EU Multi-Annual Financial Framework 2021–2027: External Funding, Policy Note #12, Brussels 2018.

69 European Commission, Asylum, Migration and Integration Fund (AMIF), 2019. Available at https://ec.europa.eu/home-affairs/financing/fundings/migration-asylum-borders/asylum-migration-integration-fund_en.

return and combatting irregular migration and promoting solidarity among EU Member States, especially among those mostly affected by migration flows.[70] Most of the funding under AMIF is channelled through a shared management system (around 88%), whereby Member States are entrusted by the Commission to implement programmes at national level. The remaining amount (approximately 12%) is instead implemented by means of direct management mechanisms, meaning that the Commission directly manages the budget of projects carried out by its departments.

As concerns the ISF, which is subdivided into the components ISF Borders and Visa and ISF Police, its goal is to promote a high level of security in the EU, which translates into the implementation of the Internal Security Strategy, law enforcement cooperation and the management of the external borders of the EU.[71] In addition to the heading "Global Europe", which covers all EU external actions including development assistance or humanitarian aid (with the exception of the European Development Fund), there are several financial instruments that are dedicated to migration-related policies. Among them, it is worth citing the Development Cooperation Instrument (EUR 19.6 million), the European Instrument for Democracy and Human Rights (EUR 1.3 million), the Neighbourhood Instrument (EUR 15.4 million) and the funds for Humanitarian Aid (EUR 147.94 million). The main developments under the new proposed MFF budget for external action will now briefly examined.

4. *The new MFF Commission proposal: one step forward, two steps back?*

In the 2018 Commission proposal for the next MFF 2021–2027, funds for migration are foreseen under three main headings: Migration and Border

---

70 More in detail, "concrete actions to be funded through this instrument can include a wide range of initiatives, such as the improvement of accommodation and reception services for asylum seekers, information measures and campaigns in non-EU countries on legal migration channels, education and language training for non-EU nationals, assistance to vulnerable persons belonging to the target groups of AMIF, information exchange and cooperation between EU States and training for staff on relevant topics of AMIF". See European Commission, Asylum, Migration and Integration Fund (AMIF), 2019. Available at https://ec.europa.eu/home-affairs/financing/fundings/migration-asylum-borders/asylum-migration-integration-fund_en.

71 European Commission, Asylum, Migration and Integration Fund (AMIF), 2019. Available at https://ec.europa.eu/home-affairs/financing/fundings/migration-asylum-borders/asylum-migration-integration-fund_en.

Management (Heading IV), Security and Defence (Heading V), both administered by the Directorate-General for Migration and Home Affairs (DG HOME) and Neighbourhood and the world (Heading VI), under the competence of the Directorate-General for Neighbourhood and Enlargement Negotiation (DG NEAR), the Directorate-General for International Cooperation and Development (DG DEVCO) and the European External Action Service (EEAS). Against this framework, newly proposed instruments would be the Asylum Migration Fund and an Integrated Border Management Fund (IV), the Internal Security Fund (V) and the Neighbourhood, Development and International Cooperation Instrument (VI).[72]

An initial assessment of these instruments shows a significant increase in the financial resources devoted to migration, border management and security and an extension of the scope of the EU external action in some funds administered by DG Home. However, since programmes related to migration are mainstreamed in numerous budget lines, it results challenging to determine the precise allocation of financial resources to migration in the next MFF. Budget spent in the context of migration will mainly depend on the scope and level of the overall funding.

One of the crucial challenges will be striking a balance between the short-term actions and the long-term strategies of the external dimension of migration. The strong focus on flexibility indicates a crisis-driven approach for the next MFF and largely reflects the positions of some Member States. It can also undermine the predictability in migration-related spending and the possibility of supporting long-term actions in developing countries. Flexibility may also raise concerns around governance and control over the use of resources.[73] Preserving the focus on sustainable development and the long-term dimension of the external action will be essential to achieve humanitarian goals. By contrast, "mixing geopolitics, which is short-term, day-to-day politics, with development cooperation, which is a generational process"[74] may undermine the effectiveness of EU external policies. In other words, there is a risk that the EU development cooperation agenda can be used as an instrument to address migration's policy priorities. Moreover, a higher degree of flexibility in the allocation of funds could lead to an uncoordinated approach among different actors that does

72 *Knoll/Vernon*, Migration and the Next EU Long-Term Budget: Key Choices for External Action, ECDMP, Discussion Paper No. 250, 2019.

73 *Knoll/Vernon*, Migration and the Next EU Long-Term Budget: Key Choices for External Action, ECDMP, Discussion Paper No. 250, 2019.

74 *Knoll/Vernon*, Migration and the Next EU Long-Term Budget: Key Choices for External Action, ECDMP, Discussion Paper No. 250, 2019, 20.

not allow for complementarity and coherence among measures. As ECRE points out, the increasing flexibility envisaged in the funding allocation is of the utmost importance when there is a political need to react swiftly and promptly to new priorities; on the other hand, it "should not mean a reduction in transparency and oversight. Nor should it mean allocation of funding according to priorities set in Brussels or EU capitals rather than at the country level".[75]

a) Assessing the allocation of financial resources under the MFF

To give some details in terms of the financial resources included in the Commission's proposal for the next MFF, EUR 34.9 billion are envisaged under Heading IV Migration and Border Management, almost the triple of the MFF 2014–2020 budget amounting to EUR 13 billion.[76] The new Asylum and Migration Fund (AMF) which aims at providing a comprehensive approach to migration management would receive EUR 10.4 billion, compared to only EUR 3.1 billion in the current MFF. Each Member State would be allocated a fixed sum of EUR 5 million and an additional amount which varies on the basis of the different migration pressures experienced by the Member States. The Fund will cover the needs in the fields of asylum (30%), legal migration and integration (30%) and irregular migration and return (40%). By reducing the emphasis on asylum and integration, some experts argue that this uneven allocation of funds represents a way to encourage return decisions.[77] This conclusion can also be drawn from the fact that there are no compulsory requirements or minimum allocations imposed on Member States for the distribution of funds among the three different priority areas. The lack of common criteria translates into the possibility for Member States to allocate the EUR 5 million according to their own needs and agenda, *de facto* prioritising some areas of "concern" over others. By contrast, according to the Commission's proposal

---

75 European Council of Refugees and Exiles, The Price of Rights: Asylum and EU External Funding. ECRE's Preliminary Analysis of the European Commission's Proposal for the EU Multi-Annual Financial Framework 2021–2027: External Funding, Policy Note #12, Brussels 2018.

76 European Commission, EU Budget: Commission Proposes Major Funding Increase for Stronger Borders and Migration, Press Release, 12 June 2018, Brussels 2018. Available at http://europa.eu/rapid/press-release_IP-18-4106_en.htm.

77 *Westerby*, The Way Forward. A Reflection Paper on the New Proposals for EU Funds on Asylum, Migration and Integration 2021–2027, UNHCR, ECRE, 2018.

"shared management should be the prime vehicle for implementation of the Fund, as it will ensure a level playing field, avoid the mismatch between needs and competition for funding".[78]

In addition, as a result of the increased importance given to the external dimension of migration and cooperation with non-EU countries in the last few years under the AMF, third countries could also become direct beneficiaries of the National Programmes of Member States. For instance, they can receive funds and incentives to counter irregular migration or to accept and integrate returnees. Experts underline that the participation of third countries in the AMF may pose several legal and ethical issues and produce negative implications on the fundamental rights of migrants affected by these actions.[79] According to ECRE, the diversion of a considerable amount of funds outside the EU may contribute to a "substandard asylum system and poor integration services".[80] Support given to third countries under the AMF should only be limited and linked to the internal dimension of the CEAS.[81]

In order to support Member States in managing the EU's common external borders, specific funds are allocated for the new Integrated Border Management Fund (IBMF) covering border management, visas and custom control equipment. This instrument also seeks to foster cooperation between third countries and the relevant Union agencies, such as the European Border and Coast Guard Agency (EBCGA). In particular, EUR 9.3 billion (EUR 3.8 billion for the Internal Security Fund, Borders and Visa between 2014 and 2020) would be provided to financially support border management and visas. The aim is to assist the most affected Member

78 European Commission, Communication from the Commission to the European Parliament, the European Council, the Council, the European Economic and Social Committee and the Committee of the Regions. A Modern Budget for a Union that Protects, Empowers and Defends the Multiannual Financial Framework for 2021–2027, SWD (2018) 171, Brussels 2018.

79 European Council of Refugees and Exiles, Outspending on Migration? ECRE's Analysis and Recommendations on Funding for Migration Outside the EU to Inform the Negotiations of the Next EU Multi-Annual Financial Framework 2021–2027, Policy Note #18, Brussels 2019.

80 European Council of Refugees and Exiles, Outspending on Migration? ECRE's Analysis and Recommendations on Funding for Migration Outside the EU to Inform the Negotiations of the Next EU Multi-Annual Financial Framework 2021–2027, Policy Note #18, Brussels 2019.

81 European Council of Refugees and Exiles, Outspending on Migration? ECRE's Analysis and Recommendations on Funding for Migration Outside the EU to Inform the Negotiations of the Next EU Multi-Annual Financial Framework 2021–2027, Policy Note #18, Brussels 2019, 3.

States and provide them with sufficient capacity to address migration challenges.[82] Target measures are foreseen to enhance cooperation with third countries on border surveillance and border management capabilities in areas of interest to the Union's migration policy and security objectives. This instrument will also build synergies with other funding programmes, such as the Internal Security Fund, Police (ISF) supporting police and judicial cooperation on terrorism and radicalisation, organised crime and cybercrime. The financial support would be doubled to EUR 2.5 billion in this area (EUR 1.18 under the current ISF).[83] In addition, the Commission proposed to allocate EUR 12 billion to reinforce the European Border and Coast Guard Agency FRONTEX and EU–Lisa. This proposal highlights the importance for the EU to promote international engagement and cooperation with third countries on return and migration management. The overall allocation of resources (IBMF, combined with funds for FRONTEX and EU–Lisa) aiming at strengthening the management of external borders would amount to a total of EUR 21.3 billion.[84] The goal of ensuring better border management therefore emerges as one of the main EU priorities as the increase in funding is highly significant in this sector.[85]

NGOs point out that, without the imposition of a maximum allocation requirement for external funding under the AMF and IBMF, there is a risk that Justice and Home Affairs (JHA) funds will be excessively redirected outside of Europe at the expense of the EU objective to develop common asylum systems and integrated border management capacities.[86] JHA funding should mainly foster the development of the Common European Asylum System (CEAS) and a coherent EU migration policy which ensures

---

82 European Parliament, legislative train 07.2019 1, New boost for jobs, growth and investment, MFF – IMBF, the instrument for financial support for border management and visas, and the instrument for financial support for customs control equipment, available at: http://www.europarl.europa.eu/legislative-train/theme-new-boost-for-jobs-growth-and-investment/file-mff-integrated-border-management-fund-(ibmf)-and-related-financial-instrument.

83 *Knoll/ Vernon*, Migration and the Next EU Long-Term Budget: Key Choices for External Action, ECDMP, Discussion Paper No. 250, 2019.

84 *Knoll/Vernon*, Migration and the Next EU Long-Term Budget: Key Choices for External Action, ECDMP, Discussion Paper No. 250, 2019.

85 *Knoll/Vernon*, Migration and the Next EU Long-Term Budget: Key Choices for External Action, ECDMP, Discussion Paper No. 250, 2019, 4.

86 European Council of Refugees and Exiles, Outspending on Migration? ECRE's Analysis and Recommendations on Funding for Migration Outside the EU to Inform the Negotiations of the Next EU Multi-Annual Financial Framework 2021-202, Policy Note #18, Brussels 2019.

the respect for the fundamental rights of migrants. UNHCR underlines that "DG Home-funded actions outside of the EU must however remain limited, complementary and inherently linked to the internal dimension of asylum and migration policies, such as access to the EU and protection within it".[87] JHA funds should therefore support resettlement programmes and legal pathways to Europe.

According to the Commission's proposal, the external dimension of migration would be covered under both national programmes (60% of resources) and the thematic facility (40%). The envisaged structure would provide flexibility and facilitate the deployment of financial resources in urgent cases under the three funding instruments of AMF, IBMF and ISF.[88]

Lastly, under Heading 6 "Neighbourhood and the World" of the proposed MFF, the Neighbourhood, Development and International Cooperation Instrument (NDICI) would have a budget of EUR 89.2 billion, the biggest financial share of the EU external dimension. NDICI represents a fundamental instrument to eradicate poverty, promote sustainable development and enhance peace and stability. However, it also addresses migration issues.[89] The cross-cutting priorities of NDICI will be covered through horizontal spending targets and, in the case of migration, a target of 10% (which roughly corresponds to EUR 8.9 billion) is established to tackle the root causes of irregular migration and forced displacement and to support migration management and governance.[90] The NDICI also adopts a flexible structure by means of the "rapid-response pillar" (EUR 4 billion) designed to swiftly mobilise short-term assistance and react in a timely manner to migration-related challenges.[91] The emerging challenges and priori-

87 UNHCR Regional Representation for EU Affairs, UNHCR's comments on the EU proposal for a regulation establishing the asylum and migration fund (2021–2027), 2019, 11.

88 *Knoll/Vernon*, Migration and the Next EU Long-Term Budget: Key Choices for External Action, ECDMP, Discussion Paper No. 250, 2019, 4.

89 European Commission, EU Budget for the Future. The Neighbourhood, Development and International Cooperation Instrument (NDICI), Brussels 2018. Available at https://ec.europa.eu/commission/sites/beta-political/files/budget-may2018-neighbourhood-development-cooperation_en.pdf.

90 European Commission, EU Budget for the Future. The Neighbourhood, Development and International Cooperation Instrument (NDICI), Brussels 2018. Available at https://ec.europa.eu/commission/sites/beta-political/files/budget-may2018-neighbourhood-development-cooperation_en.pdf.

91 *Knoll/Vernon*, Migration and the Next EU Long-Term Budget: Key Choices for External Action, ECDMP, Discussion Paper No. 250, 2019.

ties cushion (EUR 10.2 billion) similarly allows migratory pressure to be addressed along with new crises and challenges in the EU Neighbourhood region. Moreover, migration policy objectives are enshrined under both the "geographical pillar" and the "thematic pillar" composing the NDICI. The NDICI's structure and scope reflect the EU's priority of tackling migration, even "despite the fact that the link between migration, mobility and development is complex and that the suggestion of more development would lead to less migration or mobility remains contested".[92] Against this background, it appears difficult to quantify the exact amount of funds that will be devoted to migration. ECRE suggests that this funding instrument could dedicate around EUR 23.1 billion to migration, compared to approximately EUR 8.6 billion in the current MFF.[93]

Migration-related spending is strongly envisaged in the proposal for a new Instrument for Pre-Accession Assistance (IPA III), which is part of the set of instruments of the EU external action aiming at preparing and supporting candidate and potential candidate countries to join the EU. Some initiatives put in place related to migration were the establishment of the EUTF (EUR 3.7 billion) or the allocation of funds for the Syrian crisis (EUR 3.7 billion in humanitarian aid). It has been noted that "despite the absence of a clear reference to migration in the thematic list of priorities in the IPA II Regulation, IPA II funds have already been mobilised for that priority, giving an example of EU reactiveness".[94]

The concept of conditionality and incentives strongly resonate in the proposal for the next MFF. As far as migration is concerned, an interest-driven approach seems to underpin development assistance objectives in order to obtain third countries' cooperation and accomplish migration interests of the EU.[95] A "performance-based" or "more-for-more" approach, as conceptualised in the NDICI, embodies the principle that funds can be

---

92 European Council of Refugees and Exiles, Outspending on Migration? ECRE's Analysis and Recommendations on Funding for Migration Outside the EU to Inform the Negotiations of the Next EU Multi-Annual Financial Framework 2021–2027, Policy Note #18, Brussels 2019, 2.

93 European Council of Refugees and Exiles, The Price of Rights: Asylum and EU External Funding. ECRE's Preliminary Analysis of the European Commission's Proposal for the EU Multi-Annual Financial Framework 2021–2027: External Funding, Policy Note #12, Brussels 2018.

94 *Lilyanova/ Svášek*, Instrument for Pre-accession Assistance (IPA III), EU Legislation in Progress 2021–2027 MFF, Briefing, European Parliamentary Research Service, European Parliament.

95 *Knoll/Vernon*, Migration and the Next EU Long-Term Budget: Key Choices for External Action, ECDMP, Discussion Paper No. 250, 2019.

only allocated on the basis of progresses made towards migration cooperation.[96]

IV. Conclusive remarks

It has been shown that, despite different external policy strategies, Member States seem to converge on key EU migration priorities: reduction of irregular migration, the fight against human smuggling and trafficking, prevention of casualties in the Mediterranean Sea and eradication of the root causes of migration. To this end, the EU external dimension of migration policies is characterised by an increasing allocation of financial resources towards migration management, border control and security under the proposed MFF, the EUTF and the various "migration compacts". In the context of the EUTF for Africa, a meagre 3% of the budget devoted to migration management (EUR 400 million) aims at creating safe and regular routes.[97]

The packages and tailoring compacts adopted by the EU with third-country nationals to manage migration flows provide for both "winners" and "losers". Third countries may benefit from the partnership with the EU and the possibility of obtaining important benefits: acceleration of the accession process to the EU, financial and technical assistance, cooperation in the field of security (especially in transit and origin countries) and reputational gain stemming from "institutionalised relations" with the EU.[98] However, these partnerships can negatively affect third countries because of the financial losses related both to reduced remittances and local revenues generated by illicit activities.[99] At the same time, the EU and its Member States will have to consider not only the impact of the financial resources to fulfil the objectives of migration management, but also possible reputational costs for engaging with third-country stakeholders and the

---

96 European Commission, Proposal for a regulation of the European Parliament and of the Council establishing the Neighbourhood, Development and International Cooperation Instrument. COM (2018) 460 final" Brussels 2018, 37.

97 *Kervyn/Shilhav*, Oxfam International, An Emergency for Whom? The EU Emergency Trust Fund for Africa – Migratory Routes and Development Aid in Africa, Oxford 2017.

98 *Koenig*, The EU's External Migration Policy. Towards Win-Win Partnership, Policy Paper 190, Jaques Delors Institute, 6 April 2017.

99 *Koenig*, The EU's External Migration Policy. Towards Win-Win Partnership, Policy Paper 190, Jaques Delors Institute, 6 April 2017.

leverage that external actors may acquire over the EU in the context of a rebalanced partnership.[100] The security-driven approach and the emphasis on containment may provoke a situation whereby migrants remain stranded in transit countries during their migratory route without fully enjoying protection and having the respect of their human rights secured. The creation of safe and legal pathways under these partnerships has not translated yet into tangible and impactful commitments by the EU and its Member States, as required by the Global Compact for Migration.[101]

Koenig argues that the current "win-win" model which characterises EU external relations with third countries should be replaced by a "win-win-win" approach, whereby the migrant population can also sit at the negotiation table and enjoy tangible benefits.[102] Several cases of partnerships (Mali, Libya and Turkey) clearly illustrate how migrants' needs and rights are often neglected or even *de facto* violated. A human rights impact assessment is, in most of the cases, absent in the design and implementation of external partnerships.[103] Prioritising the human costs of the EU external dimension of migration policy is crucial not only from a rights protection perspective, but also in terms of the EU's credibility at the international level.[104] The EU's strong interest in curbing irregular migration, especially from 2015, combined with the flexibility of its instruments to achieve this goal seem to outweigh traditional development cooperation and risks undermining humanitarian protection and migrants' human rights. Development cooperation should instead be "based on values, partnership with third countries, respecting the principles of sustainable development and the primary aim of poverty eradication".[105]

---

100 *Koenig*, The EU's External Migration Policy. Towards Win-Win Partnership, Policy Paper 190, Jaques Delors Institute, 6 April 2017.

101 Global Compact for Migration, Global Compact for Safe, Orderly and Regular Migration, Final Draft, 11 July 2018.

102 *Koenig*, The EU's External Migration Policy. Towards Win-Win Partnership, Policy Paper 190, Jaques Delors Institute, 6 April 2017.

103 *Koenig*, The EU's External Migration Policy. Towards Win-Win Partnership, Policy Paper 190, Jaques Delors Institute, 6 April 2017.

104 *Koenig*, The EU's External Migration Policy. Towards Win-Win Partnership, Policy Paper 190, Jaques Delors Institute, 6 April 2017.

105 Concord, Assessing the Flow of External Migration Funding – CONCORD's Position, Newsroom, 2 July 2018. Available at https://concordeurope.org/blog/2018/07/02/migration-funding-ep-hearing/.

Notes on Contributors

Claudia Candelmo has a PhD in International Order and Human Rights (Sapienza, University of Rome, 2017). She was visiting fellow at the European University Institute in 2018 and is currently post-doctoral research fellow in European Union Law at the Department of Political Science of LUISS University.

Carmine Conte is an expert in EU law, particularly in anti-discrimination, migration and asylum. He works as legal policy analyst at the Migration Policy Group in Brussels. He also contributes to the European network of legal experts in gender equality and non-discrimination. Carmine has a PhD in EU Equality Law (Middlesex University of London, 2018).

Francisco Javier Donaire Villa is Associate Professor of Constitutional Law at the University Carlos III of Madrid. His research dealt with Immigration, Schengen, Fundamental Rights and other issues of Constitutional and EU Law, with 80 scientific publications. He was former visiting researcher at the Institut d'Études Européens ULB (Brussels, Belgium), and at Sant'Anna Scuola Universitaria Superiore (Pisa, Italy).

Arolda Elbasani is visiting scholar at the NYU, academic supervisor for a project on new statehood at Kosovo Foundation for Open Society and senior analyst for the Wikistrat Consulting Network. She has a PhD in EU Conditionality and Democratisation (European University Institute, 2008).

Leonard Amaru Feil is a research assistant at the Chair of Public Law, Public International and European Law (Prof. Dr. Jörn Axel Kämmerer) at Bucerius Law School, Hamburg. He was also active in refugee counselling at the Refugee Law Clinic, Hamburg.

Francesco Luigi Gatta is a research fellow at the Université Catholique de Louvain and member of the Equipe Droits Européens et Migrations (EDEM). He holds a PhD in EU Law (Universities of Padua and Innsbruck) and has been visiting fellow at the European University Institute (EUI) and visiting researcher at the Université de Strasbourg.

Chad Heimrich is a legal trainee at the District Court in Kassel (Germany). He holds an LLM in International Human Rights Law (Queen Mary University, London). His LLM dissertation dealt with the limits imposed by EU law on international agreements concluded by the Member States using the example of the EU–Turkey Statement.

Markus Kotzur is professor of Public Law, European and International Public Law at the Universität Hamburg (UHH). Since 2012 he is also deputy director of the Institute of International Affairs and since 2015 vice dean for academic affairs of the UHH. Since 2011 he is the head of the European and European Legal Studies programme at the Europa-Kolleg Hamburg as well as co-editor of the journal Archiv des Völkerrechts.

Annalisa Morticelli has a PhD in EU Human Rights Protection of Irregular Migrants (Universität Hamburg, 2020). She is also external lecturer at the Universität Hamburg and external researcher at the LUMSA University.

David Moya is professor of Constitutional and Migration Law at the University of Barcelona. He has been working as expert and external consultant for the European Commission, the European Parliament and REA as well as for the Spanish Government and as Special Counsellor for the Government of Catalonia on migration-related issues. He is currently the IP with Sonia Parella of two research projects on forced marriages. At present, he is director of the Observatory of Public Law at the University of Barcelona, and is an acting member of the executive board of the Research Centre for Migration Studies, at the Autonomous University of Barcelona.

Claudia Pretto is a lecturer on Migration Law at the Faculty of Social Affairs at the University of LUMSA as well as researcher and senior legal consultant on human rights, migration and refugee law, and antidiscrimination law. She holds a PhD in Comparative Law (University of Bari Aldo Moro, 2011).

Andrea Romano holds a PhD in Comparative Constitutional Law (Sapienza, University of Rome, 2014) and has been awarded various postdoctoral fellowships in Italy (Sapienza, University of Rome, 2014), Switzerland (University of Fribourg, 2016) and Spain (Institut d'Estudis Autònomics, 2016). The core of his research interests relies on EU Migration and Asylum Law. He focused his PhD thesis on those areas as well as several publications dealing with – inter alia – the ECJ's jurisprudence on the return directive, the concept of vulnerability in EU asylum law and resettlement programmes.

David Fernandez Rojo is researcher and assistant professor at the University of Deusto. He is also key researcher in the Jean Monnet Network European Union–Asia Pacific Dialogue and coordinator of the Jean Monnet Network EU Law Enforcement. He holds a PhD in EU Law with a full PhD scholarship from the Basque Government.

Senada Šelo Šabić works as senior scientific associate at the Institute for Development and International Relations in Zagreb. She holds a PhD in Political Science (European University Institute, 2003) and has two Master's degrees in International Relations (University of Zagreb) and in Peace Studies (University of Notre Dame).

Valentina Savazzi is an expert in migration, asylum and integration. She is currently employed at Ernst&Young to support the Italian Ministry of the Interior in managing the Asylum, Migration and Integration Fund. Savazzi holds an MA in International Cooperation & Development (Catholic University of the Sacred Heart in 2018).

Ülkü Sezgi Sözen is a PhD candidate and lecturer at the Universität Hamburg and works as a research assistant and coordinator at the Albrecht Mendelssohn Bartholdy Graduate School of Law. She holds an LLM in European and European Legal Studies (Europa-Kolleg Hamburg).

Catharina Ziebritzki is a PhD candidate and research fellow at the Max Planck Institute for Comparative Public Law and International Law in Heidelberg.